Corporate Respon...

D0264085

Corporate Responsibility

A textbook on Business Ethics,
Governance, Environment:
Roles and Responsibilities

Tom Cannon

Donation

LIBRARY

ACC. NO. | DEPT.
36045472

CLASS NO.
658.408 CAN

UNIVERSITY OF CHESTER
WARRINGTON CAMPUS

PITMAN
PUBLISHING

London · Hong Kong · Johannesburg · Melbourne · Singapore · Washington DC

To all those colleagues, friends and students who constantly renew one's faith in a better future and confound the sceptics and, of course, Fran who had the vision and the faith, and Charlie, Richard and Philip, my brothers-in-law.

PITMAN PUBLISHING
128 Long Acre, London WC2E 9AN
Tel: +44 (0)171 447 2000
Fax: +44 (0)171 240 5771

A Division of Pearson Professional Limited

First published in Great Britain 1994

© Longman Group UK Limited 1994

British Library Cataloguing in Publication Data
A CIP catalogue record for this book can be obtained from the British Library.

ISBN 0 273 60270 5

All rights reserved; no part of this publication may be reproduced, stored
in a retrieval system, or transmitted in any form or by any means, electronic,
mechanical, photocopying, recording, or otherwise without either the prior
written permission of the Publishers or a licence permitting restricted copying
in the United Kingdom issued by the Copyright Licensing Agency Ltd,
90 Tottenham Court Road, London W1P 9HE. This book may not be lent,
resold, hired out or otherwise disposed of by way of trade in any form
of binding or cover other than that in which it is published, without the
prior consent of the Publishers.

10 9 8 7 6 5 4 3

Printed and bound in Great Britain by Bell and Bain Ltd, Glasgow

The Publishers' policy is to use paper manufactured from sustainable forests.

CONTENTS

Part Two GOVERNANCE AND COMPLIANCE

Part Three THE ENVIRONMENT

Part Four THE ECONOMICALLY AND SOCIALLY DISADVANTAGED

Part Five ISSUES AND CONCLUSIONS

PREFACE

Corporate responsibility is a vital issue in contemporary debate. Much of its currency comes from the scale and influence of the modern corporation. Some ventures are larger than many nation states. Their influence extends across the globe. Their actions can determine the prosperity of communities and the health of environments. The world's ten largest industrial corporations employed three million people in 1991. Their gross sales were over eight hundred billion dollars. They have power and authority, and demand the right to pursue their interests, generate wealth, innovate and change. With great power comes great responsibility. This book attempts to explore some of these responsibilities and the ways they are evolving in the current economic, political and social climate.

There is a determined effort to place the current discussion of corporate responsibility in a wider context. In part, this is inevitable given the range of issues which touch on any examination of corporate responsibility. These include ethics, corporate governance, economics, law, science, technological change, management goals and practices, the environment and social justice. Corporate behaviour raises questions in each of these areas. Each of these topics is examined in the book. There is a systematic attempt to link the practical dilemmas facing executives and their enterprises with a larger body of debate and discussion. This reflects an assumption which permeates the text. That is, that awareness and knowledge of the wider debate is a vital aid to managers facing immediate challenges.

The unity of the topics is emphasised throughout. It is argued that ethics, governance, responsibility to the natural or built environment and justice are facets of the same issue. Here, they are drawn together and related to the notion of the corporate social contract. It is argued that organisations operate with societies on the basis of an implicit or explicit contract which imposes creation duties and responsibilities. These extend far beyond the economic functions attributed by writers like Friedman. These obligations change over time as the state takes on more or less roles and activities or delegates these to other members of society.

This book has drawn on a wide range of sources of ideas and inspiration. Every effort has been made to trace the holders of copyright material and seek their permission to use their material. If any have inadvertently been overlooked, I hope they will accept my apologies.

Any book as wide ranging as this depends on the support of many people. Numerous colleagues have played a part, especially Dr. Nigel Roome, Sir Kenneth Alexander and Professor Brian Moores. A special thanks is due to the many students at Stirling, Manchester and elsewhere who have challenged ideas, commented and stimulated my thinking. Much of the agenda for corporate responsibility has been shaped by those business people who have shown the courage and commitment to look beyond the next horizon. Many of these are acknowledged in the dedication but I am particularly grateful to those executives who I have worked with in Scottish Business in the Community, the Moss Side and Hulme Business Support Group, Cariocca Enterprises and a host of enterprise agencies. My publishers have played a vital part in helping me to develop my ideas and put them together. Simon Lake, Jennifer Mair, Keith Stanley and Liz Rawlings are members of a great team. My wife Fran had the original idea for this book and helped me to shape and develop my thoughts. Robin and Rowan played a special part in formulating my ideas. To these and all those who have helped – many thanks. Naturally, the final responsibility for the book in its final form lies solely with the author.

CHAPTER 1

Ethics and responsibilities: the emerging agenda

Few issues in business excite more interest today than the emerging topic of corporate responsibility. In North America, Europe and Asia, in particular, the responsibilities of corporations to their communities are under intense scrutiny. In part, this reflects growing awareness of the impact of their actions on the environment and the disadvantaged. Elsewhere, the discussion reflects widespread recognition of the changing relationship between companies and communities. New technologies, developments in markets and new ideas are providing insights into the influence of corporate actions and their potential impact on issues which extend far beyond the conventional remit of firms and their managers. The rolling back of the state creates new opportunities and imposes new responsibilities on firms. Corporate leaders are seeking ways to express and define their role in these changing circumstances. The same shifts place increased responsibilities on firms, entrepreneurs and managers. The freedom to act is not the licence to abuse. Many of the shifts in political attitudes toward corporate behaviour reflect abuse by specific business leaders. This was true when Rowntree exposed mistreatment of employees by employers. It recurred when the Teapot Dome scandal highlighted abuse of political power. It was highlighted with the Great Crash when the misuse of Stock Market rules emerged. It was seen when Maxwell exploited trustee compliance and executive freedom. Competent corporate leaders recognise the link between rights and responsibilities. J. S. Mill commented in the last century that 'There is no natural connection between strong impulses and weak conscience.'[1]

Discussion of the role and responsibility of the corporate entity in society is not new. The comment in the Bible that it is 'easier for a camel to pass through the eye of a needle than a rich man to pass through the gates of heaven' touches on the problems of wedding morality and wealth accumulation. Chaucer presented his own special view on the issue in the thirteenth century. In *The Pardoner's Tale*, the gullible are relieved of their wealth on the promise;

> *Now goode men, god foryive you your trespas,*
> *and ware you fro the sinne of avarice:*
> *Myn holy pardon may you alle warice–*
> *So that ye offre nobles or sterlinges*
>   Chaucer: *The Pardoner's Tale*[2]

It was, however, the industrial revolution which brought the issue of corporate responsibility into sharp focus. In part, this was a reflection of the power of the new industrial processes to reshape age-old relationships. Feudal, clan, tribe or family based systems of authority and responsibility were dismantled. Simultaneously, the new techniques and technologies gave 'corporations' vast power and wealth and created the first billionaires. The landscape could be reshaped. Cities built.

> Ephriam Tellwright could remember the time when this part of it was a country lane, flanked by meadows and market gardens. Now it was a street of houses up to and beyond Bleakridge, where the Tellwrights lived.
>
> Bennett, A.: *Anna of the Five Towns*[3]

The power of the machine over man raised major issues of responsibility and morality. The wealth which was accumulated by the new industrial classes gave added emphasis to the debate. It enhanced their power while standing in sharp contrast to the difficulties of the new, industrial proletariat.

> One day I walked with one of these middle-class gentlemen into Manchester. I spoke to him about the disgraceful unhealthy slums and drew his attention to the disgusting condition of that part of the town in which the factory workers lived. I declared that I had never seen so badly built a town in my life. He listened patiently and at the corner of the street at which we parted company, he remarked: 'And yet there is a great deal of money made here, Good morning, Sir!'
>
> Engels, F.: *The Condition of the English Working Class*[4]

The impression is sometimes given that the industrial revolution marks a sharp break with the systems, structures and concerns of the past. This was not the case. Chandler[5] points out that the 'Managerial Revolution' occurred relatively late and showed itself in a number of ways. The family, relationship or trust basis for allocating roles in the firm persisted through the nineteenth century. Notions of professionalism, ie that qualification or skill should dominate appointment criteria came to dominate only in this century. This broke the link between ownership and control. It undermined the paternalism which characterised many of the great business empires of the nineteenth century. Lord Leverhulme saw Port Sunlight as a personal charge and responsibility. Sir Michael Angus, Chief Executive of Unilever in the late 1980s, probably views it as a peripheral asset or even a liability. Versions of nineteenth century paternalism do survive but often through enterprises which have survived since the last century or as part of a more open and highly personalised way of undertaking or promoting business.

Breaking the bond between entrepreneurs and their workforce often coincided with a process of severing links with a community. This 'local' connection was once a key feature in the character and identity of the enterprise. The Pugh family in Philadelphia, the Rockefellers in Cleveland and Ford in Detroit took their interest in the community far beyond the confines of the firm. It encompassed their church, the community, the arts and education. Lever Bros in the North West of England, Imperial Group in Nottingham and Bristol, Rowntree in York symbolised the bond between a firm and a locality. Growth, relocation and acquisition have eroded this relationship. The Rockefellers soon set up their corporate base in NYC. If Unilever has a corporate core it probably lies on Blackfriars Bridge near the City of London. External acquisition can play a part in this process. The acquisition of Imperial by Hanson symbolised changes which went far beyond share ownership. Nestlé took over Rowntree, in spite of efforts to assert a local dimension in the defence. Investment policies look more closely at goodwill in finance houses and the City than goodwill in the community[6]. Unilever's decision to shift production of frozen foods out of the North West of England took little account of 30 years of past production or high local unemployment. The contrast between this and Lord Leverhulme's attempts to redevelop the Western Isles through an exercise in corporate philanthropy is striking.

Examples of paternalism or philanthropy persist. Coca-Cola is a major force in Atlanta – the 1996 Olympics in Atlanta has been dubbed the Coca-Cola Olympics because of the extent of the firm's support. Cadbury has a high proportion of its operations concentrated in Birmingham. Bourneville remains a powerful symbol of affirmative action. Sir Adrian Cadbury's involvement in industry education partnerships and his work for PRO-NED on the reform of corporate governance highlight his personal commitment to a wider role for corporate leaders. The mission statements of firms like United Biscuits and the Co-Operative Bank contain a clear commitment to their communities.

> Good relations means good business. The equation is as simple as that. Therefore today's most important task is encouraging the good relations that will create good business in the future.
>
> Whitbread and Co.: *The Whitbread Way*

In specific communities, such as Moss Side and Hulme in Manchester (England), organisations like the Business Support Group seek to:

> Assist in the economic and social regeneration of Moss Side and Hulme and its immediately surrounding areas of Manchester.
>
> Moss Side and Hulme Business Support Group: *Mission Statement*

It is, however, hard for many firms to sustain this in increasingly international and competitive markets. The two sides of this are vividly illustrated in the recent history of Pilkingtons (UK). The threat of acquisition by BTR in the mid 1980s saw the entire community in St Helens (England) rally to the support of the firm. Marches and other public displays of backing stood alongside more conventional bulwarks against a hostile acquisition. Commentators gave much of the credit for victory to the community defenders of the Firm. Despite that, the next few years saw a major redeployment of the firm's operations away from St Helens. The Europeanisation of its operations prompted the firm to shift its corporate headquarters from the North West of England. The film *Roger and Me* vividly illustrates the changing relationship between Flint, Michigan, the home town of General Motors after the firm laid off 30,000 workers, closed plants and moved production to Mexico.

Corporate responsibility as an area of study and management action is evolving in response to these changes and the demands of managers for guidance and students for insight and understanding. The subject is being shaped by business, government, academia and the wider society.

The approach, however, to corporate responsibility adopted in the text focuses on five broad areas:

1   The social, economic, ethical and moral responsibilities of firms and managers.
2   Compliance with legal and voluntary requirements for business and professional practice.
3   The corporation and the environment.
4   The challenges posed by the needs of the economically and socially disadvantaged.
5   Management of the corporate responsibility activities of businesses.

There is a strong orientation towards an interdisciplinary approach which highlights both the challenges posed to industry and the opportunities created. The attempt to wed insight and sympathy to action and response has characterised attempts to tackle the issue of corporate or entrepreneurial responsibility through the post-industrial revolution era.

REFERENCES

1. Mill, S. J. *On Liberty*, London, Penguin edition (1984).
2. Chaucer, G. *The Pardoner's Tale* (c. 1380).
3. Bennett, A. *Anna of the Five Towns* (c. 1900).
4. Engels, F. *The Condition of the English Working Class* (1848).
5. Chandler, jun., A. D. *Strategy and Structure: Chapters in the History of the American Industrial Enterprise*, Cambridge, MIT Press (1962).
6. McMahon, T. F. 'Models of the Relationship of the Firm to Society', Journal of Business Ethics, vol. 5 no. 3, June (1986) pp. 181–91.

PART 1

Business ethics: context, content and debate

CHAPTER 2

An historical perspective

The Industrial Revolution introduced – and continues to introduce – fundamental changes in the relations between individuals and groups in communities. The combination of large-scale migration: from the country to the town, from one workplace to another and changing social values almost inevitably changes the nature of social relations within and between communities.

> Britain saw the gestation of such a process between the 1740s and the 1780s. Here came a break with a tradition of economic life, and a pace of change, which had lasted centuries and which, in certain essential characteristics, had been universal across all countries of the globe up to that time.
>
> Mathias, P.: *The First Industrial Nation*[1]

The shift from the land was a mixture of 'push' and 'pull'. Landowners found ways to use new technologies or to exploit certain crops to improve their profits while reducing their costs. The enclosure movement had gathered pace since the end of the Middle Ages. The attempts by monarchs such as Henry VIII and Elizabeth I to slow down the enclosure of common land had failed in the sixteenth century. Despite a series of 'Acts of Parliament' during their reigns, the amount of land enclosed grew steadily from the middle of the fifteenth century until the years 1540–55. It only stopped when the wool market went into decline.

DARK SATANIC MILLS

The process of 'enclosure' returned with a vengeance during the eighteenth century. This time endorsed by parliament. Between 1760 and 1815 seven million acres of land were covered by parliamentary enclose awards. Locals seldom won the lion's share of their newly enclosed common land.

> The appropriation to their exclusive use of practically the whole of the common waste by the legal owners meant that the curtain which separated the growing army of labourers from utter proletarianisation was torn down.
>
> Chambers, J. D. and Mingay, G. E.: (1966)[2]

Thompson[3] points out that:

> Those petty rights of the villagers, such as gleaning, access to fuel and the tethering of stock in the lanes or on the stubble, which are irrelevant to the historian of economic growth, might be of critical importance to the subsistence of the poor.

Greater concentration of land ownership combined with different crops, new systems of husbandry to reduce the need for labour on the land. Oliver Goldsmith evokes this change in his poem, *The Deserted Village*:

> *Sweet smiling village, loveliest of the lawn,*
> *Thy sports are fled, and all thy charms withdrawn;*
> *Amidst thy bowers the tyrants hand is seen,*
> *And desolation saddens all thy green:*
> *One only master grasps the whole domain*

Britain's cities grew rapidly during the nineteenth century.

Table 2.1 Urbanisation in Britain

City	1801	1851	1901
	(000's)	(000's)	(000's)
Birmingham	71	265	760
Bradford	13	104	284
Bristol	61	137	329
Cardiff	2	18	164
Glasgow	77	375	762
London	1,117	2,685	6,586
Manchester	75	338	645

The growth of cities like Birmingham, Bradford, Cardiff and Manchester was only a part of a process which changed Britain from a country of villages and small towns to a nation of cities and town dwellers. In the middle of the nineteenth century, almost one in five of the population lived in towns with populations of over 5,000. By the end of the century, it was over half (Table 2.1). Many of the new city dwellers were, inevitably, newcomers to the cities. Migration broke the link between the individual and the community. The semi-feudal links between the landowner and his tenants or workers was lost. In the cities, the mixture of labour mobility, shifts in ownership pattern and population pressure reduced the sense of 'responsibility' for others which was seen to characterise older, rural communities.

This change in attitudes was increased by the values which shaped early Victorian capitalism. The notion that saving, thrift, sobriety and self-restraint offered all the chance to better themselves was widely promulgated by writers like Samuel Smiles.[4] Those who failed to better themselves had only themselves to blame. 'The idleness and depravity of the working class' explained their privations to at least one correspondent to the Board of Agriculture in 1816.

Where natural movements of labour did not occur, force could be used. The infamous 'Highland Clearances' saw entire communities driven from their homes in the cause of 'improvement' by their ancient overlords.[5] Across Britain, the lines of mutual support and loyalty were broken.

> *Better not to dwell under lairds*
> *who will not suffer their tenantry,*
> *who will take gold from a crab's claw*
> *rather than from a good man*

In contrast to the local deprivation described by this Scot, throughout the century, Britain's wealth grew rapidly overtaking its European rivals in the early part of the century and rivalled only by Germany at the close of the 1890s (Figure 2.1).

The change was even more dramatic in the per capita GNP (gross national product). This more than doubled in Britain and Germany during the century. There were, however, increases in the disparities between groups. Deane[6] points out that 'in industries like transport, textiles and iron manufacture output per worker increased beyond all previous experience, though wages per employee rose quite modestly'. During good times, the effects of redistribution of wealth, power and responsibility were mitigated by lower prices but unemployment, recession or illness meant that many workers and their families were worse off than previously. This was especially true in those communities in which old trades and skills were replaced by new technologies.

The wealth of the owners, the scale of their enterprises aroused suspicion about their power, their motives and their methods. The concentration of power could threaten the state and established ways of allocating resources by placing 'new fetters on the poor, and . . . new powers to the rich'.[7] This raised questions about the values which shaped their behaviour and the ethic under which their ventures operated.

There was a powerful demand from among the business community for freedom from interference.

> Our rulers will best promote the improvement of the nation by strictly confining themselves to their own legitimate duties, by leaving capital to find its own most lucrative course, commodities their fair price, industry and intelligence their natural reward, idleness and folly their natural punishment.
>
> Macauley, Lord, 1830, quoted in Langer, W. (1968)[8]

But others suspected that the new corporations would threaten freedom.

'We are today in more danger from organised money than ever we were from slavery.'[9] The ventures – it was claimed – had 'no conscience' and sought only their further aggrandisement of their owners. The debate on the underlying values is well described in the social comment and literature of the day.[10] As the impact of industrialisation on the natural and built environment increased, this

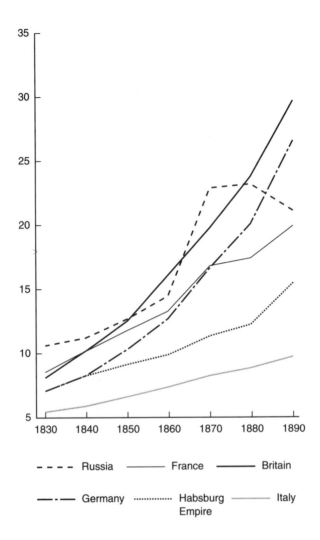

Fig. 2.1 GNP of European powers in billions US$ at 1960 prices
Source: Kennedy[11]

became a new source of concern and comment. The conditions around the factories and in the cities aroused the anger of some and the deep concern of others.[12]

The new, industrial, working classes faced an array of problems. Traditional supports from ancient rights or the community had been eliminated. In good times, the new wealth and higher wages produced improved conditions. In bad times, traditional systems collapsed, poverty grew and landlords like the Duke of Sutherland responded by forcibly transporting tenants to maximise his revenues from his Scottish estates.[13] The government was loath to intervene in a process which was endorsed by its most powerful citizens and had transformed Britain into the most powerful nation in the world. The state's role and its interpretation of its responsibilities had been affected by these developments.

Monarchs like Henry VIII and Elizabeth I had legislated to defend traditional rights especially against enclosures. In the eighteenth and nineteenth centuries, the thrust of government policy had changed. Widespread acceptance of the need for 'improvement' prompted governments to back those seeking to replace crofters with sheep or common pasture with managed farms. The great landed families were to the fore in this process. Even in communities where 'clan' or other loyalties persisted there were few practical inhibitions against change and disruption. The first Duke of Sutherland enjoyed an annual income of £300,000 but felt few inhibitions about evicting large numbers of his 'loyal' tenants, and ignoring their rights, continued to generate wealth at an unheard of rate.[14] Intervention might undermine this process. Between 1760 and 1850 the main preoccupation of legislators in this area was to sweep away 'the mass of government rules and restrictions on economic activity'.[15]

This view was legitimised by the writings of Adam Smith[16] and Spencer.[17] Smith emphasised the importance of keeping restrictions of trade, movement and intervention to a minimum so that every man 'is left perfectly free to pursue his own interest in his own way, and to bring both his industry and capital into competition with those of any other man'. The state's role was confined to defence, prevention of oppression or injustice and certain public works. Spencer went further and argued that 'England's' superiority was founded on this policy of leaving people 'to manage their own affairs'. This contrasted with the 'comparative helplessness of the paternally governed nations of Europe'. For over 150 years – from 1700 to 1850 – public expenditure as a proportion of GNP hardly changed except at times of war. Behind this apparent consistency between prevalent theory and administrative action widespread changes were taking place. Humanitarian legislation in Britain was passed in 1788 to protect chimney sweeps from exploitation; in 1802 to control the conditions of work for pauper children; in 1803 to protect emigrants; in 1833 the Factory Acts; in 1842 to regulate conditions in the mines; in 1847 to establish the Poor Law Board and in 1848 to create the Public Health Act. Much of this legislation grew directly from the concerns of those observers who sought to require or persuade the new entrepreneurs and their firms to adopt a more responsible attitude to the needs of their workers and the communities in which they operated.

Writers like Carlyle[18] and Arnold[19] recognised the dilemmas faced by their society. Carlyle recognised that 'accumulated manufacturing, commercial, economic skill' lay at the core of British power. This was not the greatness of the admired ancient Greeks 'to whom beauty was everything' but a potential source of 'tyranny' capable of 'crushing human bone and flesh'. Arnold's solution was to educate into the new leaders 'a moral thoughtfulness' which would set them on the road to good acts.

VICTORIAN PHILANTHROPY

The pressures for a more sympathetic response to the needs of those who failed to prosper from the industrial revolution can be seen in the early years of the century. Even before Victoria came to the throne *The Times* commented after Peterloo that:

> The two great divisions of society there, are – the masters, who have reduced the rate of wages; and the workmen, who complain of their masters for having done so. Turn the subject as we please, 'to this complexion it must come at last'.

In Britain, Robert Owen, Lord Shaftsbury, Lord Ashley and John Stuart Mill stood alongside Francis Place, William Lovett and others in calling for a more sympathetic and responsible approach to the needs of the disadvantaged. The growth of Methodism at the end of the eighteenth century prepared the ground for those who saw 'the contrast between equality before God and inequality before man . . . [as a basis for criticism] of the social and political order'.[20] Gradgrind's preoccupation with 'facts',[21] Merdle who 'nobody knew . . . had ever done any good to any one'[22] and Dombey's desire for impersonal relations 'a mere matter of bargain and sale'[23] became objects of scorn and criticism. Mill presented the case for greater intervention 'to show that the admitted functions of government embrace a much wider field than can easily be included within the ring fence of any restrictive definition'.[24] However, the defence of property rights played a central role in their world view and ethic.

The individual, entrepreneurial or corporate response took many forms. Chadwick[25] examined conditions in the cities in his report 'The Sanitary Conditions of the Labouring Classes'. William Booth founded the Salvation Army in 1878 to tackle the problems of the dispossessed in the cities. Industrialists met to form such bodies as the Newcastle or Manchester Literary and Philosophical Societies. These sought to address issues of concern. Many went on to play important roles in establishing the English civic universities in Manchester, Liverpool, Newcastle and Birmingham. Booth and Rowntree studied the conditions under which people lived – the former in London, the latter York. Issues as diverse as parliamentary reform, education, health and the scientific development were seen as means to express one's sense of responsibility to the wider community.

THE NONCONFORMIST CHALLENGE IN BRITAIN

Religion played a central role in shaping attitudes and actions in Victorian, Britain. The Christianity practised varied between the Catholicism of the Irish migrant or the High Church Anglicanism of Newman and the determined Quakerism of Gladstone or the Congregationalism of Richard Pilkington. It was, however, the Nonconformist wing of religion especially the Quakers which played an especially important role in shaping the values of the new, entrepreneurial groups. Great brewing families such as the Whitbreads and the Trumans had religion in common with the Lloyds and Darbys in iron making and merchanting, the Barclays and Lloyds in Banking, the Cadburys and Rowntrees in confectionery, the Pilkingtons in glass making and many of the cotton families and tobacco families such as Wills and Players. Their religion introduced several key features to their world view. They were, for example, members of an 'out group' which had been persecuted until fairly recently. Entrepreneurship was one of the few means of social mobility open to them.

> Their training and ideals of character led them to seek an outlet in trade and commerce; indeed their civil disabilities forced them to do so if they wished to become 'successful'.
>
> Briggs, A. (1959)[26]

Many, however, remembered their roots and kept strong links with the wider community encompassed by their church. They were less likely to enjoy the ignorance and indifference of their aristocratic compatriots.

> with their glens emptied and their land under sheep, the lairds had time and money to spend on the Society's [The Society of True Highlanders] theatricals. They held grand balls. . . . They revived the Ancient Caledonian Hunt.
>
> Prebble, J. (1969)[27] *The Highland Clearance*

The softening role of the church should not be exaggerated. John D. Rockefeller had no apparent difficulty reconciling active membership of the Baptist church with a ruthless determination to build the most powerful Trust in North America – Standard Oil.

Their religion introduced two further dimensions to their approach to wealth and industry. First, it gave a strong sense of community. In part, this derived from the chapel or communal meeting place. It was, also, a function of a tradition of community support for co-religionists. Second, their religion emphasised the responsibilities associated with wealth and success. Many of these responsibilities were personal: prudence, thrift, enterprise and abstinence. Mathias[28] points out 'the urgent warnings . . . to remember the parables of the talents' in many of their writings. The same sentiments are epitomised by Mr Bulstrode in Eliot's *Middlemarch*. His 'profitable investments in trades where the power of the prince of this world showed its most active devices, became sanctified by a right application of the profits in the hands of God's servant'.[29]

This application took many forms. In Britain there was support for the Anti-Corn Law League. Although the promise of lower food prices after repeal was not realised – the League demonstrated the power of the new middle classes. This group gave only limited support to Chartism and other movements which offered a clearer threat to the status quo.

> The trade movements were powerful across Europe especially in Holland. The Zollverein in Germany adopted this approach from the 1830s. Even Austria dropped protectionism after Metternich as a response to the demands of the new middle classes to gain access to the Zollverein.[30]

Parliamentary reforms, especially the widening of the franchise, was a recurrent theme of radical action throughout the century in Britain. Direct intervention was used in the attempt to eradicate the worst abuses in the factories, mines and homes. The dominant approach, however, of the Nonconformists and Utilitarians was to create opportunities for self-employment or to advocate changes in behaviour. Sunday schools, subscription libraries, mechanics' institutes, the Society for the Diffusion of Useful Knowledge, the new civic universities and the engineering 'institutions' won support. The opinion that it was 'preordained . . . [that the poor] should be ignorant' eventually gave way to the view that education was needed to 'fit' children for business. This approach to education – encompassed by the 1870 Education Act – was intimately linked with notions of self-improvement.

> [Education] remained a mere 'schooling', starved of liberal or even vocational developments'.[31]

Social or corporate responsibility meant showing the poor the error of their ways or providing golden rules for self-improvement. Drink, indolence, immorality and violence were used to explain the 'ignorant, debauched and brutal' nature of the labouring classes. Employers like the Wedgewoods penalised workers found 'conveying ale or liquor into the manufactory in working hours'. Others moved outside the factory.

> In the largest silk mills at Macclesfield, righteous employers prided themselves upon dismissing girls who made a single 'false step'.
>
> Thompson, E. P. (1986)[32]

Where making an example did not work, Sunday Schools could be instructed to 'tame the ferocity of their unsubdued passions'. Drink was seen to play an especially important role in the 'debauched' nature of the poor. The temperance movement was sponsored by many who saw social improvement and abstinence as inseparable.

The notion that in self-improvement lay the key to success was at the heart of the dominant Victorian approach to entrepreneurial responsibility. Samuel Smiles presented the four main virtues of the 'new' man as thrift, character, self-help and duty. His 'philosophy of self-help' was communicated through sermons, lectures, books, pamphlets and tracts. Free will involved choices because:

> *Nobody adulterates our food.*
> *Nobody fills us with bad drink*
> *Nobody supplies us with foul water*
> *Nobody spreads fever in blind alleys and unswept lanes*

Smiles, S. (1861)[33]

Self Help by Smiles sold almost 150,000 copies in the 30 years after its publication. Its strength lay in giving voice to the least threatening and most comforting approach to social responsibility open to the leaders of the new, industrial society. Threat and fear were never far from their considerations. The mob was a powerful force in eighteenth-century England. It was replaced in the nineteenth century by a number of movements for political, economic and social reform. Some seemed to threaten the power and position of the established order and their new allies in industry and commerce. For much of the century fear of revolution was widespread. In the early part of the century, it grew from memories of the French Revolution and Napoleon. Later, the new demonology included radicals, socialists, communists, syndicalists and anarchists. 'Even a man as remote as Henry James sensed "a sinister anarchic underworld heaving in its pain, its power and its hate." '[34] Among the entrepreneurial classes, leaders emerged who sought to incorporate part of this thinking into new ways of organising labour and building communities. Their form of corporate responsibility meant finding a new form of incorporation. In North America the Social Gospel movement won converts in Tom L. Johnson, the millionaire traction magnate and Samuel M. Jones an oilman.[35] The work of Taylor stimulated ideas of 'scientific management'.[36] In Europe progressive movements stimulated the enthusiasm of industrialists like Whitworth, Milnes, Bauwens and Bessy.

The writings of the Utilitarians; notably Bentham and Mill, were especially important in shaping the philosophical and ethical climate for industrialisation. The notion of the greatest happiness for the greatest number might justify the suffering of 'the few'. Donaldson[37] illustrates the continuing power of this perspective in his discussion of the newspaper headline dealing with unemployment in the 1980s 'Shock Treatment for the Economy May Have Hurt, But It Has Worked'. He raises the question – 'Hurt whom?' and 'Worked for whom?'

ROBERT OWEN

The life and career of Robert Owen symbolised many of the strands of nineteenth-century thinking about the impact of the Industrial Revolution and the socially responsible ways to adapt to its consequences. His early career was that of the successful industrialist. He started his working life as a draper's assistant. In 1789 he started in business in Manchester. His initial capital was £100 borrowed from his brother. His business thrived so that he could buy out his partners in 1809 for £84,000 *in cash*. Ten years after starting his enterprise he moved to New Lanark. He soon set about creating a new type of industrial community. This was one in which co-operation and mutual support was the norm. He introduced a range of welfare support including public health and education while banning drink and advocating temperance. He outlawed child labour and penal conditions. He achieved this seeming Utopia while still making a good profit. This success stimulated widespread interest. Visitors came from across Britain to wonder at this novel form of commercial undertaking. Others attempted to emulate this success but the key turning point came with Owen's effort to replicate the New Lanark achievement in the New World. The New Harmony experiment failed. This forced him to return to Britain and rethink his ideas.

The essential components did not shift markedly. There was a belief that man's 'character' is 'formed for him'[38] by his environment. Their vices of 'theft', 'idleness', 'drunkenness', 'deception', and 'zealous systematic opposition to their employers'[39] resulted from the conditions under which they worked and lived. Change the conditions and their behaviour would change. Alongside this was the notion that surpluses could be earned but their main role was to improve the conditions of the workers. In his 'villages of co-operation' a new, prosperous industrial class could be created. He was, however, not interested – at least initially – in changing the established order. His dedication to 'reason' and 'improvement' hardly wavered throughout the vicissitudes of his later life. He saw the achievements of the physical sciences, the manufacturing improvements as a model for the social and economic sciences. The drift into millenarianism which marked the period after 1820 reflected this notion that the application of 'rational principles' to economic and social systems would produce the millennium.

Owen and his supporters faced three problems in developing this new form of responsible corporation. First, there were shortages of capital. The pages of their newspapers and journals were full of proposals for subscription based funds. The recurrent theme was that small donations by large numbers might fill their 'equity gap'. The results were disappointing. They remained dependant on the occasional large gift from a rich supporter. Second, the artisan supporters of Owen lacked the education and trading skills to develop the viable ventures needed to sustain the movement. Spectacular initiatives such as the Labour Exchange or Bazaar in Gray's Inn Road eventually failed because the naive but inexperienced gentlemen and the pragmatic but untutored artisans failed to establish a balance between commerce and welfare. Music, uplifting talks and festivals satisfied the ambition for enlightenment but blocked the passageways and prevented trade. The special currency – labour notes – freed the producers from the constraints of the official capital markets but no one else would accept them. Third, the link between wealth creation, capital accumulation and wealth distribution was never fully appreciated. The new technologies of the day required capital for development. The markets were volatile. This called for the use of capital to see the new ventures through difficult times. Eventually, it was this 'distance' from the established system which undermined the new co-operatives. Owen and many of his followers responded by looking to either larger unions of workers, notably 'The Grand National Moral Union of the Productive Classes of the United Kingdom' and the 'National Association for the Protection of Labour', or producer or trade co-operatives.

Some of the elements of Robert Owen's ideas recur in the history of corporate responsibility. The creation of Port Sunlight or the Bourneville development in Birmingham reflected the same belief that workers who were treated well would respond well.

> In 1879, George Cadbury and his brother Richard . . . moved their works from the centre of industrial Birmingham to what was then an entirely rural area, four miles from the city. The removal gave George Cadbury an opportunity to put into practice ideas he had long in mind, the result of his contact with working men as a teacher in Early Morning Adult School, with which he was connected for over fifty years. He had been led to the conclusion that the root of most social evils lay in the bad housing conditions in which all too many had to live . . . He bought land in the neighbourhood of the factory, and in 1895 began to build Bourneville village . . . he handed over the whole property to a body of Trustees . . . and secured that all profits . . . be devoted to the development of the Bourneville Estate, and to the promotion of housing reform elsewhere.
>
> Bourneville Publication, quoted in Priestley, J. (1987)[40]

Noblesse oblige gave way in some quarters to belief that enlightened self-interest would improve working and social conditions. The attempts to create 'model' communities could be seen from the Western Isles to Bristol. Priestley's description of a visit to Bristol on his 'English Journey' illustrates the continuing strength of view almost one hundred years after the death of Robert Owen.

> Among the best examples of people actuated by this civic pride are the members of the Wills family, who might easily – following the example of most provincial magnates – have taken themselves and their gigantic fortunes out of the city. But they have chosen to remain in Bristol, the city that made their fortune for them, and they have spent enormous sums of money in the place.
>
> Priestley, J. B. (1987)[41]

These entrepreneurs, however, rejected the notion that profits and responsibility were inconsistent. They viewed the well-managed, profitable firm and proper exercise of responsibility as the same thing.

There could be no worse friend to Labour than the benevolent, philanthropic employer who carries on his business in a loose, lax manner . . . his so-called kindness and benevolence and lack of business principles [means] that sooner or later he will be compelled to close.

Leverhulme, Viscount (1918)[42]

This strand of thinking about corporate responsibility developed alongside the notion that workers needed to take action to tackle their own problems. These developments coincided with a growing awareness of the need to take action to protect the environment. Leverhulme in Britain and Ford in North America were already striving to protect the natural environment.[43] There was, as yet, limited awareness of the scale of the problems and the impact of their own factories, the products and their wastes on the natural environment. For every Harrison who observed that during his youth 'in every city of the kingdom, and even in most parts of London, an easy walk would take a man into quiet fields and pure air. We did not live in a pall of smoke and yellow fog',[44] there were far more Kingsleys to argue that 'The Spinning-jenny of the railroad, Cunard's liners and the electrical telegraph, are to me . . . signs that we are . . . in harmony with the universe.'[45]

CO-OPERATION AND ACTION IN BRITAIN

The link between self-help and co-operation emerged early in nineteenth-century Britain. The Co-operative Congress of 1832 in Liverpool saw cutlery, coffee pots, stockings, lace, shawls, shoes, clogs, prints, iron, brass, steel and Japan wares, brought for exchange. Producer co-operatives soon emerged but it was the retailer co-operative which showed the greatest scope for growth, strength and resilience. The Rochdale pioneers created their pioneering institution in 1844. The 28 Rochdale men invested £1 each in a shop where they sold 'wholesome food at reasonable prices'. The success of retail co-operatives was based on a mixture of sound business and a wider social vision. At the turn of the century co-operatives accounted for almost ten per cent of all retailing. There were almost 1,400 societies. Even today, the Co-Operative Retail Society (CRS) and the affiliates of the Co-Operative Wholesale Society (CWS) stand alongside the Tescos and Sainsburys as major forces in UK retailing. Their share of the UK food market stands at about seven per cent and non-foods at two per cent. Their range of activities includes: farming, car dealership, funerals, banking, dairies, travel and insurance. Developments from the tea plantations in India to the Co-Operative Insurance tower in Manchester stand as a testament to the success of self-help and co-operation. The CWS and the CRS have maintained a tradition of community support. It has included backing for producer co-operatives. Most recently, the Co-Operative Bank sponsored the UK's first Chair in corporate responsibility.

PROGRESSIVES IN NORTH AMERICA

The attempt by Robert Owen to re-create the achievements of the New Lanark project in North America illustrates the links that existed between the Old and the New World. People, ideas and programmes moved across the Atlantic in both directions. Entrepreneurs like Francis C. Lowell, builder of the first American power loom, adopted Owen's ideas. In the early part of the nineteenth century, shortages of labour allied to greater freedom of movement prevented the worst abuses of the factory system from emerging in North America. In the later years and in the early part of this century, different economic, political and social conditions meant that the forms of corporate responsibility differed significantly from those seen in Europe.

Education lay at the centre of North American thinking about individual, entrepreneurial and corporate responsibility. It was a vital means to personal advancement. Many of the early entrepreneurs had strong personal links with educational institutions. Samuel Morse, for example, worked out his invention while teaching at New York university. The great private universities of Harvard, Yale, Cornell, Princeton, Duke, Dartmouth and Columbia benefited from links with progressive entrepreneurs and their enterprises. The public universities especially the land grant institutions followed this lead. The hostility to the federal government introduced a culture of private support for public works which persists today. The growth of Duke University from a small, struggling college – Trinity College at Durham, North Carolina – to one of leading US universities was based on donations of over $270 million in the 50 years to 1980. A similar pattern could be seen in a host of US universities (Table 2.2).

The same pattern of support and endowment could be seen in schools, colleges and other fields of education. The wider commitment to education led the states

Table 2.2 Improvement through education

Donor	Beneficiary	Contributions ($ millions)
Carnegie	Carnegie-Mellon University	180
Pew	Universities of Philadelphia and Pennsylvania	120
Mellon	Carnegie-Mellon University	170
Stanford	Stanford University	90
Duke	Duke University	270
Woodruff	Emory	160
Johnson	Cornell	120
Gannett	Howard	60
Lilley	Notre Dame	50
Rockefeller	Universities of Chicago and Columbia	180

Source: Adapted from Nielsen, W. A. (1985)[46]

Table 2.3 The allocation of Duke's bequest

To	Percentage
Duke University	32
Davidson College, N. Carolina	5
Furman University, S. Carolina	5
Johnson C. Smith University, N. Carolina	4
Hospitals in N. and S. Carolina	32
Orphanages in N. and S. Carolina	10
Superannuated Preachers and widows and orphans of preachers from the Conference of the Methodist church of N. Carolina	2
Building rural Methodist churches in N. Carolina	6
Maintaining and operating Methodist churches in NC	4
TOTAL	100

Source: Adapted from Nielsen, W. A. (1985)[47]

to give a high priority to education. Despite the problems of settlement, migration and conflict, the USA had a primary and secondary school system significantly superior to that in Britain by the 1880s.[48]

The scale of their contribution to education did not deter these philanthropists investing elsewhere to improve conditions, attack problems and contribute to social welfare. The range of their interests was considerable. Some, such as the Rockefellers engaged in a form of scientific philanthropy – designed to identify and tackle the causes of social ills. Others, notably Kaiser and Johnson, were preoccupied with health. Housing and social conditions were tackled by the Mellon family trusts. The guidelines given by James Buchanan Duke for the Duke Foundation give some indication of the eclectic interests of these 'Yankee' philanthropists (Table 2.3).

The commitment to enlightenment as a means of social improvement permeates many of the actions of the early, US entrepreneurs. Henry Ford's museum in Greenfield Village illustrates this view of the world. He wanted people to understand the basis of achievement in order that it could be replicated. The full text of his famous 'history is bunk' comment is a call to learn 'how our forefathers harrowed the land'.

> I discovered that historians knew nothing about harrows . . . I though that a history that excluded harrows and all the rest of daily life is bunk.

> Henry Ford, cited in Lacey, R. (1986)[49]

There was, however, little that was Utopian and even less that was socialist in these North American philanthropists. They were dedicated to the profit motive. Ford, Rockefeller and Carnegie were ruthless in their commercial activities. Rockefeller was the most notorious of the 'robber barons' and was once

Table 2.4 The assets of the largest early foundations in 1990

Foundation	Founded	Assets $ million
Carnegie Corporation	1911	700
Rockefeller	1913	1,400
Cleveland	1914	430
Surdna	1917	350
New York Community	1923	500
Duke	1924	700
Kresge	1924	1,100
Charles S. Mott	1926	750
Kellogg	1930	1,675
Alfred P. Sloan	1934	500
Gannett	1935	450
Ford	1936	4,750
James Irvine	1937	420
Houston Endowment	1937	420
Lilley Endowment	1937	1,100

Source: Adapted from Nielsen, W. A. (1985)[50]

described as 'the supreme villain of his age'.[51] Ford was willing to use armed force to break strikes. Duke tried to create a trust to dominate the world tobacco industry. They exploited the tax laws which prevail in the USA. They went on to use their wealth to create charitable foundations which have assets in excess of $75 billion at 1990 prices. The largest foundations established before 1940 can mobilise assets of over $15 billion as illustrated in Table 2.4. The apparent success of this approach continues to have an effect on thinking about Corporate Responsibility across the world.

SOCIAL ACTION IN EUROPE

Across Europe, industrialisation prompted a range of responses from entrepreneurs and managers. The precise pattern reflected the mixture of social attitudes and fiscal incentives which shaped the response in Britain and North America. In much of Scandinavia there was an early commitment to community-based experiments to establish a bond between the individual and the enterprise. There was a strong emphasis on the provision of support facilities for workers. These ranged from medical services which often extended beyond the immediate workforce to the wider community. Firms supported schools and colleges for workers and their families. This tradition of intervention created the climate which allowed the state to develop the most comprehensive array of social welfare support in the world in the middle of this century. A similar pattern could be seen in the Low Countries.[52]

There were several key differences between industrialisation at the heart of Europe and at the periphery. The most evident was the far greater degree of industrialisation. The coal, iron and textile industries of Northern Europe were among the largest in continental Europe. The entrepreneurs came from three types of background. Migrants, like James Cockerill, played an important role especially in the development of the iron industry. Self-made men, like Henri Bury and Francois Dupont, played their part. There was, however, a strong sense of continuity through the involvement of the nobility and representatives of 'old' wealth. The approach to corporate or individual social responsibility generally reflected their route to success. Self-help dominated among the new, entrepreneurs. They were in a small minority. The dominant views were shaped by those with a longer tradition of responsibility. This produced a greater tendency to intervene or accept the involvement of the state in activities like education, welfare and health services. The links between towns like Haarlem – the Manchester of Holland – and radical thinkers in Northern Britain provided a further impetus to a more overt commitment to corporate social responsibility.

This mixture of local response and political action could be seen in the two greatest industrial nations in continental Europe in the nineteenth century; France and Germany. In both, much of the impetus for industrialisation and change came from government action.[53,54] Both 'nations' had a long history of direct intervention. In the late seventeenth century the monarch had provided the loans to set up the indigenous iron and steel industry[55] while at the end of the eighteenth century Hausman and Herzog was the largest firm in France, in part because of monopolies provided to encourage investment and innovation.[56] Under Frederick the Great similar initiatives were started in Prussia which led to the first coke blast-furnaces and built the first steam engines in Germany. There was a determination to challenge Britain's industrial power.

> World history is now dominated by the economic struggle . . . the free expansion of the peoples who live here is restricted by the world dominance of English [our aim is] breaking England's world domination.
>
> Admiral George von Müller, Chief of the Kaiser's Naval Cabinet. Quoted in Massie, R. K. (1991)[57]

This 'partnership' between industry and business established a model that was developed far more extensively in mainland Europe than Britain until the middle of this century.

The evolution of iron production in the Creusot region of France was partly the result of entrepreneurial action but equally the consequence of deliberate state action to support this development. 'Ingenieurs des Mines' played a crucial role in research into mining conditions beside supervising conditions. France had a Ministry of Manufactures almost a century before British governments would consider such a development. The great technical schools of the revolution, Ecole polytechnique, Conservatoire des Arts et Métiers, Ecoles d'Arts et Métiers and the privately funded Ecole Centre des Arts et Manufactures, provided the finest technical education in Europe for most of the century. Private finance for the institutions or scholarships for students were provided by the new, industrial corporations and their proprietors. Conflict existed. There was the continuing debate on the correctness of help. Notions of 'survival of the fittest' were as strong in France as Britain. The emergence of socialist or communist threats to the political and social order provoked resistance to change and encouraged increasing conservatism.[58]

The pattern of economic development in Germany was largely shaped by similar forces. War, political turbulence and social conflict made it hard to build up a consistent picture of corporate, social responsibility. In the period prior to World War I, a pattern of development based on an active and expansionist state and a confident, well-educated middle class was established. Trades unions were small and weak for most of the century. The government's control over key sectors like mining and railways seemed to avoid the worst excesses of exploitation while its investment in education reduced the need for private investment. The success of this model was already threatening British hegemony by the 1870s. The British Education Bill of 1870 was, perhaps, the first recognition of the need to catch up with German success.

> If we leave our work-folk any longer unskilled, notwithstanding their strong sinews and determined energy, they will become overmatched in the competition of the world.
>
> W. E. Foster's speech to Parliament introducing the 1870 Education Bill[59]

In the later years, the nature of the key industries shaped the character of the corporate response to social and economic needs. Two industries dominated: chemicals and electricals. Individual enterprises operated on a far larger scale than in the cotton or iron industries. They required a better-educated, skilled and stable workforce. The mass of artisans which characterised the pool of labour in the first half of the century was inappropriate for the new companies and their leaders. Werner von Siemens was one of the new corporate leaders who shaped this new relationship between the firm and the community. A similar pattern emerged in all the science-based industries; such as around Zeiss in Jena. The approach of the German industrialist is summarised by Borchardt.[60]

> The German employer regarded himself as a patriarch, as the master in his own house in pre-industrial terms, with total responsibility for the whole social organism of his enterprise and generally well beyond it.
>
> Borchardt, K. (1975)[61]

This posed major problems when conflicts occurred. Often they were viewed as 'evidence of disobedience and ingratitude and hence of immorality'.[62] In the century that followed the balance between state intervention and involvement and corporate action swung wildly to reflect the political turbulence in the nation. Despite this, the central commitment to intervention, education and a form of partnership between the state and the enterprise to deliver social goals persisted.

Across Europe the same pressures shaped the response. Industrialisation in some countries was largely state sponsored. This was true in Russia before and after the 1917 revolution. In Austria, Hungary and the area now covered by the Czech Republic and Slovakia, the growth of industry was marked by small-scale enterprise and limited intervention by entrepreneurs in social affairs. Italian individuals like Camillo Cavour made the transition from industry to government. They combined intense nationalism with a wish to tackle the exploitation of female and child labour. The two Italies phenomenon – north and south – meant that economic and social progress in the north was not matched by developments in the south. The scale of many of the new Italian enterprises meant that they lacked the resources for intervention in key aspects of social responsibility, e.g. education and health. This pattern was matched in the less developed Mediterranean countries. The combination of forces which retarded economic growth also tended to weaken progressive social movements.

> Hungarian aristocrats and Russian landowners spent too much time on conspicuous consumption in the cities. Italian entrepreneurs were unwilling to take risks, Spanish society was too rigid, there was social resistance to change and the educational system developed all the wrong qualities for industrial progress.
>
> Pollard, S. (1991)[63]

RESPONSES IN THE THIRTIES

The industrial revolution introduced a new economic order into the world. New sources of wealth and power emerged. The rate and scale of growth in output, population, concentration and power forced individuals, enterprises and communities to re-examine the nature of their operations and their interrelationships. The corporation grew to dominate economic life. The ten largest US industrial firms in 1909 mirrored the new, industrial environment with operations ranging from steel to rubber (Table 2.5). The scale of their operations and their importance to the national economy forced their leaders to play an active role in the wider community.

These ventures needed skilled operatives and managers, their leaders accepted and sought roles in the wider community. They were expected to show leadership. Projects as diverse as Henry Ford's 'Peace Ship' and the Mayo Clinic reflected the ambitions and aspirations of the entrepreneurs and their corporations. Three external threats challenged their power and authority. These were: war, recession and political change. These forces, in combination, posed a particularly powerful

Table 2.5 The ten largest US industrial firms in 1909

Rank	Enterprise
1	US Steel
2	Standard Oil
3	American Tobacco
4	International Harvester
5	Amalgamated Copper
6	Central Leather
7	Pullman
8	Armour & Co
9	American Sugar Refining
10	US Rubber

Source: Kaplan, A. D. H. (1954)[64]

hazard. This was illustrated in the pressure for change following the 'great' recession of the 1870s to 1890s and the revolutions which followed World War I.

The Depression of the 1930s posed a comparable threat to the existing order. The challenge was more severe because the actions of business and businessmen were seen as largely responsible for the problems facing the industrial nations. Hoover, Baldwin, Mussolini were heads of state with strong business connection, while familiar business names like Kellogg were active in international affairs. The collapse of prices on the New York Stock Exchange on Black Thursday symbolised the limitations on the power of the new corporations to stop or even stem the collapse in world markets. Powerful figures like J. P. Morgan tried in vain to halt the decline. By the end of 1929, governments on both sides of the Atlantic were taking action such as McDonald's £42 million public works programme and Hoover's federal construction programme. Individual entrepreneurs like Henry Ford launched initiatives like his surprise wage hike in November but there was a decisive shift towards government as the key agent of change in Britain and the USA. The election of Franklin Delano Roosevelt with his powerful commitment to 'The New Deal' based on government intervention to tackle the social and economic problems which the market and the corporation cannot resolve marked a major change in US thinking. It mirrored developments in the rest of the developed world. This did not, however, mean that entrepreneurs and companies withdrew. The forms and balance of corporate action to satisfy their responsibilities changed.

The work of the Scottish Council for Development and Industry illustrates this change. The Council was created in 1931 by a group of Scottish businessmen following a meeting convened by the Convention of Royal Burghs. They were backed by local authorities, trades unions and 'public spirited Scotsmen and women.'[65] Its aims were:

- to mobilise the resources that existed to support industrial development and job creation in Scotland;
- to supplement government and other remedial action;
- to encourage firms to locate in Scotland;
- to create a climate for growth and prosperity;
- to dispel myths and misinformation about Scotland and its economic prospects.

It used the good offices of leading industrialists like Sir James Lithgow to establish a basis for operations and a series of expert panels. Its successes could be seen in the new industrial estates, new firms and increased links between the public and private sector. It survives today as a mixture of ginger group, think tank and bridge between the public and private sector.

Across Britain, similar initiatives were tried. Some blossomed quickly. Few showed the ability to survive and adapt of the Scottish Council. All demonstrated a desire among some industrialists to contribute to the prosperity of their community. In Priestley's words from the early 1930s these 'employers have acted in good faith, and genuinely prefer to spend their money on their factory and their employees instead of on racing stables and Monte Carlo'.[66] Elsewhere in Europe and North America there were comparable experiments. Some depended on philanthropic employers.

> He [Ford] provided seeds for men to cultivate in their gardens. He purchased sewing machines for the women and had dressmaking classes organised for them. Within a matter of months the village of Inkster was back on its feet again.
>
> Lacey, R. (1986)[67]

Others relied on government incentives. Many were serious attempts to mobilise the resources of an entire community to tackle community-wide problems largely created by economic change.

POST-WAR STATISM

The end of World War II prompted a widespread re-examination of the relationship between industry, the state and the community. Socialist economic planning in Britain, French étatism, even US Marshall Aid and MacArthur's reconstruction programme in Japan were built on specific assumptions about the relationship between industry and the state. This had a marked effect on their respective roles within the community and the role of corporate responsibility. In Britain, the view was widely held that wartime success was based on a national will translated by the state into action. If it could bring success in the war against Hitler why not in the wars against poverty, disadvantage, unemployment and social injustice.

> We must use the qualities of youth as well as the experience of war-time administration

to overhaul our economic, social and educational practice in order to secure for all a reasonable standard of life.[68]

These notions were reinforced by the leadership achieved by Keynes[69] in shaping economic thinking. *The General Theory of Employment, Interest and Money* dominated economic thinking in the aftermath of the war. It indicated that government could manage the economy to achieve stability and near full employment by manipulating fiscal and monetary policy to manage the level of demand. In theory, government could manage increases in demand to boost the economy if it slowed or contracted demand if there was inflation. Industry was a part of this system but capable of being managed through macroeconomic policy to produce definable output.

Selfish greed, the moral legacy of Victorian capitalism, would give way to a Christian community, motivating men to work hard for the good of all.

Barnett, C. (1986)[70]

This would emerge through the work of disinterested planners and far sighted politicians not determined and entrepreneurial industrialists. For most of the forties, fifties and early sixties the results in terms of unemployment and inflation were quite impressive. Declining competitiveness could be seen in Britain's relatively slow rate of growth in annual output but with unemployment low there was a strong sense that Britain *had never had it so good* (Table 2.6).

This image was gradually eroded during the early 1960s as the years of 'stop-go' in economic policy were clearly hurting industry and eroding the UK's international competitiveness.

The UK's share of world trade slipped from the high twenties to the low teens in little more than a decade. The election of the Labour Government in 1964 reflected a belief that more *but better* state direction was needed. In social policy, housing, education, health and employment new aspects were added to traditional interventionist policies. In industry, state planning and restructuring was added to nationalisation as arms of government policy. Agencies like the Industrial Reorganisation Corporation (IRC) reflected the belief that 'the need for more concentration and rationalisation to promote the greater efficiency and

Table 2.6 Average annual rate of growth of output

Country	per cent growth 1948–62
USA	1.6
UK	2.4
Belgium	2.2
France	3.5
Federal Republic of Germany	6.8
Italy	5.6

international competitiveness of British industry . . . is now widely recognised'.[71] The defeat of the Labour government in 1970 ushered in a decade of debate and increasing turbulence. The Conservative government of 1970 abolished the IRC but felt forced to intervene to prevent factory and shipyard closures. The later Labour government created the National Enterprise Board but appointed the first minister with specific responsibility for Small Firms. The 1980s led to a new reappraisal of corporate responsibility.

CONCLUSION

In this chapter the historical background to current thinking about corporate responsibility was explored. The different strands of thought recur in different ways at various times. The conflict between freedom of action for the few and responsibility for the many can be seen in the Middle Ages, during Tudor times, before and after the Industrial Revolution and today. At times, the state has acted to support or attack different positions. The Tudors intervened to protect the peasants from seeing their common land enclosed. At the end of the eighteenth century, the commitment to improvement prompted governments to press for enclosure. The extent of state involvement has varied. In Britain, the 'hands off' approach of government was central to the credo of the early industrialists. In Germany, the state owned the mines and largely built the railways. Many of the arguments presented today for less (or more) government intervention mirror those of the last century. The potential benefits of corporate action to active social and economic goals can be seen in most countries at different times.

Robert Owen showed that production could be efficient and responsible. The ventures created by the Levers and the Cadburys have survived far longer than many of those run by their more 'hard-headed' contemporaries. Their monuments extend beyond the confines of Bourneville and Port Sunlight. Education has been a major beneficiary. In North America, in particular, the greatness of the major universities is inseparable from the contributions of their business sponsors. In the arts and humanities, support and sponsorship by industry has created great centres such as the Metropolitan Museum while providing support for innovation and experimentation. In health and welfare, problems were exposed, innovative solutions endorsed and systems established to tackle them with the backing of corporation dedicated to meeting, in full, their social responsibilities. It has not be smooth or easy. Many of the changes were wrung out of business by workers' groups at enormous cost. Pioneers were often criticised or ridiculed by 'wise men' or the 'hard headed'. Today, a new paradigm seems to be emerging. It is hard to see it being a return to 'Victorian values'. These reflected particular concerns at a moment in time. They were overtaken by events even during Victoria's reign. The success of Germany and the achievements of US industry relegated Britain to a diminishing role in industrial, economic and social issues. The new paradigm will need to reflect a new relationship between the means to generate wealth and the strategies to distribute wealth. It will be founded on an understanding of ethics and values in the contemporary world with a recognition of the limits and risks of executive action. If the past teaches anything about corporate social responsibility, it is that the risks of doing nothing, far outweigh the risks of doing something.

QUESTIONS

1 Draw out the parallels and differences between the ways in which any of the corporate leaders named in the sets below developed their personal business vision

- Henry Ford
- Lord Leverhulme
- Alan Sugar
- Charles Forte

- Richard Branson
- Anita Roddick
- Bill Gates
- George Cadbury

2 Gather information from press and other sources. Use this data to discuss the ethical position adopted by either Pilkingtons (UK) or General Motors (as described in the film *Roger and Me*). Explore the extent to which the firms had any choice in their decisions and outline practical ways in which the effects might be lessened.

3 Describe the ways in which the Enclosures Act of the nineteenth century differed in spirit, aim and values from the Enclosures Acts of the sixteenth century in Britain.

4 Describe the effects of migration and religious diversity on the evolution of corporate social responsibility in Britain or the USA. How did forms of social action reflect the different experiences of nineteenth-century industrialists?

5 Discuss the extent to which 'the new deal' highlighted the failure of laissez-faire capitalism to resolve the problems posed by rapid economic and industrial change.

6 Does the history of The Scottish Council for Development and Industry teach us anything about the long-term impact of contemporary initiatives like Business in the Community?

7 Can 'Victorian values' make a significant contribution to balancing current demands for economic growth and corporate social responsibility?

8 Value driven businesses are easier to manage and are more relevant to current environments than traditional firms. Discuss the implications of this statement for company development.

9 '"Shock treatment" for the economy may have hurt, but it has worked.' Outline the ethical implications of this statement for policy makers on a national and local level.

10 Define or write brief notes on:

(a) The Teapot Dome Scandal
(b) Corporate Responsibility
(c) 'Self-help'
(d) Zollverein
(e) The 'New Deal'

(f) Paternalism
(g) Enclosure
(h) Urbanisation
(i) Owenism
(j) Fordism

REFERENCES

1. Mathias, P. *The First Industrial Nation*, London, Methuen (1983).
2. Chambers, J. D. and Mingay, G. E. *The Agricultural Revolution, 1750–1880* (1966).
3. Thompson, E. P. *The Making of the English Working Class*, Harmondsworth, Penguin (1986).
4. Smiles, S. *Self Help* (1857).
5. Prebble, J. *The Highland Clearances*, Harmondsworth, Penguin (1969).
6. Deane, P. *The First Industrial Revolution*, Cambridge, Cambridge University Press (1969).
7. Rousseau, J. J. *A Discourse on the Origin of Inequality* (1762).
8. Langer, W. *The Rise of Modern Europe: Political and Social Upheaval, 1832–52*, New York, Harper and Row (1968).
9. Beecher, H. W. *Proverbs from a Plymouth Pulpit* (1887).
10. Fielden, J. *The Curse of the Factory System* (1826).
11. Kennedy, P. *The Rise and Fall of Great Powers*, New York, Random House (1988).
12. Gaskell, E. *Mary Barten* (1848).
13. Prebble, J., ibid.
14. Prebble, J., ibid.
15. Deane, P., ibid., p. 203.
16. Smith, A. *The Wealth of Nations*.
17. Spencer, H. *Social Statistics* (1850).
18. Carlyle, T. *On Heroes, Hero-Worship, and the Heroic in History* (1841).
19. Arnold, T. *Christian Life, Its Course, Its Hinderances and Its Helps* (1841).
20. Briggs, A. *The Age of Improvement*, London, Longmans (1959).
21. Dickens, C. *Hard Times* (1854).
22. Dickens, C. *Little Dorrit* (1855–7).
23. Dickens, C. *Dombey and Son* (1847–8).
24. Mill, J. S. *On Liberty* (1859).
25. Chadwick, E. *The Sanitary Conditions of the Labouring Classes* (1832).
26. Briggs, A., ibid.
27. Prebble, J., ibid.
28. Mathias, P. *The First Industrial Nation*, London, Methuen (1983).
29. Eliot, G., *Middlemarch* (1871–2).
30. Pollard, S. *Peaceful Conquest*, Oxford, Oxford University Press (1992).
31. Ensor, R. *England 1870–1914*, Oxford, Oxford University Press (1992).
32. Thompson, E. P., ibid.
33. Smiles, S. *Thrift* (1861).
34. Tuckman, B. *The Proud Tower*, London, Papermac (1980).
35. Miller, W. *A New History of the United States*, London, Paladin (1970).
36. Taylor, F. W. *The Principles of Scientific Management*, New York, Harper and Row (1947).
37. Donaldson, J. *Key issues in Business Ethics*, London, Academic Press (1989).
38. Owen, R. *A New View of Society: Third Essay* (1813).
39. Owen, R., ibid.
40. Priestley, J. B. *An English Journey*, Harmondsworth, Penguin (1987).
41. Priestley, J. B., ibid.
42. Leverhulme, Viscount *The Six Hour Day*, London, Allen and Unwin (1918).
43. Taylor, F. W., ibid.
44. Quoted in Houghton, W. *The Victorian Frame of Mind*, New Haven, Yale University Press (1957).
45. Houghton, W., ibid.
46. Nielsen, W. A. *The Golden Donors*, Weidenfeld and Nicolson (1985).
47. Nielsen, W. A., ibid.
48. Briggs, A., ibid.
49. Lacey, R. *Ford*, London, Pan (1986).
50. Nielsen, W. A., ibid.
51. Tarbell, I. *The History of the Standard Oil Company* (1904).
52. Pollard, S., ibid.

53. Cole, C. W. *Colbert and a Century of French Mercantilism* (2 vols), New York (1939).
54. Ritter, U. P. *Die Rolle des Staates in der Frühstadiender Industrialisierang*, Berlin (1961).
55. Cole, C. W., ibid.
56. Henderson, W. V. *The Industrial Revolution on the Continent; Germany, France and Russia*, Liverpool, Liverpool University Press (1967).
57. Massie, R. K. *Dreadnought*, London, Pimlico (1991).
58. Caron, F. *An Economic History of France*, New York, Wiley (1979).
59. W. E. Forster's speech to Parliament introducing the 1870 Education Bill, 17 February 1870, Hansard, series iii, vol. 199, cols 465–6.
60. Borchardt, K. *The Industrial Revolution in Germany 1700–1914*, in Cipola, C. M. *The Emergence of Industrial Societies*, London, Fontana (1975).
61. Borchardt, K., ibid.
62. Borchardt, K., ibid.
63. Pollard, S., ibid.
64. Kaplan, A. D. H. *Big Enterprise in a Competitive System*, Washington, Government Printing Office (1954).
65. Kirkwood, W. C. *Twenty Five Years*, Scotland (1956).
66. Priestly, J. B., ibid.
67. Lacey, R., ibid.
68. Quoted in Barnett, C. *The Audit of War: The Illusion and Reality of Britain as a Great Nation*, Macmillan (1986).
69. Keynes, J. M. *The General Theory of Employment, Interest and Money*, Cambridge, Cambridge University Press (1936).
70. Barnett, C., ibid.
71. HMSO, Cmnd 2889 (1966).

CHAPTER 3

The role of business in society

Much of the current literature on corporate responsibility takes a simplified view of the role of business in society. It is sometimes implied that the aim of the good business is to make 'you . . . feel good about yourself'.[1] This is as questionable as the notion that the only guiding principle can be that 'it is the business of business to make profits.'[2] Businesses perform a number of roles in society. They change over time. It is, for example, no longer assumed that 'business' will wage war on behalf of the nation in the manner of Drake and Hawkins. The conquest of empire or its administration was an acceptable activity for entrepreneurs like Raffles or companies like the East India Company but is rejected today.

The role of business in society alters but these changes centre on the economic and social role of the firm, its owners and those with a stake in the venture. Unless the enterprise performs its economic functions it will not have the resources to perform other roles nor will it survive long enough to be an agent for any form of change.

> Business corporations exist primarily to produce goods and services that society wants and needs. Achieving this objective is their first and foremost responsibility; if they are unsuccessful in this mission, they cannot reasonably be expected to assume others.
>
> Task Force on Corporate Social Performance (1980)[3]

At the same time, business depends for its survival and long-term prosperity on society providing the resources – people, raw materials, services, infrastructure – which it needs to convert inputs into profitable goods or services. Business relies on society supplying a means of exchange – typically money – to allow it to convert the goods it produces into assets. Without a legal, judiciary and policing system business could not be certain that it was safe to enjoy the rewards of its enterprise. Trade agreements and defence are needed to ensure long-term, stable trading conditions. All these, in turn, depend on all the members of the society supporting the values and norms it endorses.[4,5]

There exists an implicit or explicit contract between business and the community in which it operates. Business is expected to create wealth; supply markets; generate employment; innovate and produce a sufficient surplus to sustain its activities and improve its competitiveness while contributing to the maintenance of the community in which it operates. Society is expected to provide an environment in which business can develop and prosper, allowing investors to earn returns while ensuring that the stakeholders and their dependents can enjoy the benefits of their involvement without fear of arbitrary or unjust action. The interdependence between society and business cannot be understated. Commerce requires the external defence and internal order; the agreed sets of rules and means of enforcing them and the mechanisms for exchange that society provides. When these break down business suffers. The growth of the nation state was inseparable from the emergence of modern industry.[6] The state provided an internal market in which the entrepreneur could trade. The existence of a national currency provided a means of exchange which was easy to move and could convert goods produced into goods purchased. Labour could be recruited and rewarded. Credit enables firms to make investments or accommodate changes in trade conditions.[7] The legal and banking systems allow contracts to be enforced while providing a set of rules to guide behaviour.[8] In 50 BC Cicero observed that 'justice is indispensable for the conduct of business'.[9] International trade could develop because currencies were convertible and trade *agreements sustained.* Industrialisation requires a willingness to invest today *for tomorrow.* This will not occur if tomorrow is unknown or fraught with risk. Social stability provides a framework for planning and investment in the expectation that the fruits of these efforts will be retained. The enterprise, its proprietors and other stakeholders depend on the community in which they operate for their existence and prosperity.

This is not a one way street. Society expects business to make its contribution. The fundamental role of commerce is to provide the means by which the material needs of the community are met.[10] These include the products and services produced by firms. Equally important to the community are the jobs created directly and indirectly. These are underpinned by the wealth created by the enterprise. This might be immediately realised through wages, dividends, taxes or loan repayments or deferred through investments, accumulated profits or loans to others. This notion of investment in the future is central to the modern notion of the contract between business and society. Much of the social infra-structure on which industry depends, roads, schools, hospitals, defence, etc., are long-term commitments. Industry is expected to match this with a long-term investment in its long-term competitiveness through new products and services; more highly skilled workers; more efficient plant and operations and greater effectiveness. It may be true that 'no one ever went bust taking a quick profit' but it is equally true that wealth has to be invested to create the opportunity for any profit. Society grants to business two very special rights to assist in performing its roles and achieving these rights. The first is 'potential immortality', the second is 'limited liability'.

> A state grants to a business corporation the blessings of potentially perpetual life and limited liability to enhance its efficiency as an economic entity.
>
> Relinquist, W. (1978)[11]

The line between the economic and social roles of business cannot easily be drawn. The firm contains within it a social organisation. This can be formal – the hierarchies and relationships defined by the institution – or informal – the relationships that evolve through the attitudes and actions of people. The effectiveness of the enterprise depends on both types of relationship. Carmichael[12] points out that: 'everyone in business wants to feel good, and everyone wants to be part of a successful business'. Tuleja[13] notes that the poor image of American business in the 1970s and 1980s hit recruitment, prompted government to legislate and made criticism of industry in the media proliferate. In the competition for scarce resources, firms with a poor reputation in the wider society will find themselves severely disadvantaged. They will be forced to either produce more profits, pay higher wages or find other ways to counterbalance their image *or change their behaviour*. The recurrent problems of Lonro and the pressures on Hanson illustrate the treadmill facing the firm which seeks to ignore these public pressures. Wealth creation is central to the economic role of business but society determines the extent to which this wealth can be enjoyed and the values systems which surround the enterprise. This view is summarised by the comments of two of the most successful entrepreneurs of their day but in distant continents, in different centuries.

> There is but one right mode of using enormous fortunes – namely, that the possessors from time to time during their own lives should so administer these as to promote the permanent good of the communities from which they were gathered.
>
> Carnegie, A. (1862)[14]

> Business only contributes fully to a society if it is efficient, profitable and socially responsible
>
> Lord Seiff, 1962[15]

It is hard for enterprise to prosper or realise its full potential in an environment which is hostile or indifferent to the needs of industry and commerce. Stacey[16] argues that (in Britain):

> it has contributed to a declining share of world trade, the under-exploitation of inventions, tardy application of industrial reorganisation, reduced enthusiasm for industry, recurring balance of payments crises . . . and, most lamentably of all, a decline of the entrepreneurial spirit.

Barnett[17] links Britain's industrial decline over the last century to a culture and environment which questioned and often denied the value of industry, commerce and related activities:

- in the 1800s, this saw; 'dwelling on imports and exports' as 'undignified and contemptible';
- by the 1860s believed that 'A University . . . is not a place of professional education';

- during the early 1900s accepted that the leading 'technological' universities, Birmingham, Manchester and Liverpool would have only 377 students studying engineering, in contrast to the 17,000 studying in Germany;
- as late as the 1940s, equated industry with 'trade';
- even in the late 1980s and early 1990s could still use management as a pejorative term, consider business as of doubtful value and view industry as an option extra for an advanced economy.

Against this background, industry must compete for scarce human, technological and financial resources to perform its primary role in creating wealth.

THE ECONOMIC ROLE

Organisations have evolved to perform a number of functions or tasks in society. Broadly speaking, these are:

1 *The economic and production tasks*: these include land maintenance and food production, manufacture and distribution of goods and services and all tasks associated with the creation and maintenance of wealth. Farms, mines, manufacturers, distributors, retailers and the myriad of enterprises which make up the business and commercial world perform these and the related economic roles.

2 *The maintenance tasks*: these exist to hold the society together, maintain its stability and ensure its continuation. Most activities which are involved with transmitting and shaping knowledge and culture fall into this category. Education, religion, health and welfare service and some aspects of the media provide the clearest examples of the institutions which undertake these roles.

3 *The adaptive functions*: these provide the means by which the society responds to change. Research, the creative activities, even the means for shaping and managing debate or conflict undertake this. Universities (their research activities), research organisations and the arts are the clearest examples of this form of venture.

4 *The managerial or political tasks*: any society or community requires institutions and systems to identify and implement policy for the group and related agencies to arbitrate and assess conflicting demands or expectations. The society is likely to interact with other communities; institutions are required to manage these relationships. Government, political parties, the law, and the military perform these tasks.

The evolution of society, especially over the last two centuries, has seen increasing specialisation in the performance of these roles in the West. In clan- or family-based society all these roles were integrated. Later, the feudal landlord owned the land through a direct relationship with the monarch. Holding this fief imposed many obligations which included key 'maintenance' tasks. The church in Europe was a major landowner but retained its religious, welfare and educational roles. Sponsorship of the Arts and other sources or adaptation was entirely through the church or feudal nobility. Alongside these, were the governmental, legal and military roles of the feudal lords. The Bishop of Durham was 'the Prince Bishop' responsible for maintaining order in the North of England while Durham Cathedral was 'half church of God, half castle against the Scot'. Parallels could be seen during the Shogunate in Japan, Boyar rule in Russia, the Empires of China and at different times in the history of South America, the Middle East and Africa. These responsibilities diverged; partly, as a result of the need for increasingly specialised knowledge and expertise and partly from fears in some quarters about overlap and concentration of power.

Specialisation has had an especially significant effect on those organisations responsible for the economic functioning of society. This has occurred at two levels. First, they have distanced themselves (or been distanced) from the other tasks in society. This has not occurred to anything like the same extent elsewhere. It is accepted that artists can portray or comment on industry. Bennett, Dickens, Lawrie, Lodge, Shaw and Vidal are among the multitude of others who have felt free to portray, comment and instruct industry in ways that would be seem as a gross intrusion if reversed. Academics feel few reservations about presenting their views on commerce or taking an active role in its work through consultancy, publications and subsidised competition. An attack on academic freedom is perhaps the minimum critique for a reversal of roles. The abuse which followed Sir Hugh Cortazzi's questioning of the appointment procedure for the Vice Chancellor of Sussex in 1991/2 illustrates a common attitude. Although he was a member of that University's Council – its governing body – his comments were 'inaccurate', his acquaintance too 'short lived' to understand 'due process', his 'partiality' clear to any 'impartial reader' thus the University 'cannot thank Sir Hugh'.[18] The principle of put up and shut up reflects the attitude of many universities in Britain to industry. Government and the church seem as determined to protect their right to intervene as to deny industry's right to comment.

This specialisation of purpose is matched with even greater specialisation of activity. The politician, academic, churchman, lawyer, artist, even soldier of yesterday would probably recognise, even understand, the function of their contemporary equivalent. It is hard to believe that Josiah Wedgewood would recognise the financial analyst; Robert Owen appreciate the Organisational Behaviour manager or Henry Cavendish welcome a new product development assistant. The builders of ships, railways or iron bridges and the producers of calico or bicycles would find it equally hard to appreciate a business environment in which the 'products of the year' were Microsoft Windows 3, ConAgra, Healthy Choice Foods and the Panasonic PV-40 Palmcorder.[19] The notion of specialisation affects the way industry has defined its role.

The *profitable* production, distribution and sale of the goods and services is the distinctive function of business in a society.[20] Other institutions will produce, distribute even sell goods. But the notion that they do this in order primarily to make profits distinguishes commerce from other agencies. A university will charge fees for its courses but the development and transmission of knowledge is its goal, not the distribution of a profit to shareholders. A hospital might charge for all or some of its services, but most people would reject the notion that ability to pay should be the criterion for treatment. A charity shop will expect its customers to buy the goods on display, but the buyers will anticipate that any surplus goes to the needy. A commercial enterprise is set up to make money. It will expect to confine its sales to those who can pay. Its investors will expect to be the beneficiaries of any surplus. Much recent debate has centred on the issue of how far business should confine itself to this task.[21]

Friedman,[22] Hayek[23] and others[24] have argued that business should confine itself to its commercial roles. Several reasons are given for this. The most basic is 'specific competence'. Wealth and profit creation is the one area in which the commercial enterprise has a special proficiency. No other types of institutions have demonstrated the same ability to perform these socially necessary tasks. The collapse of the Marxist regimes in Central and Eastern Europe and the early success of many of the privatised enterprises in Britain and elsewhere highlights the inability of the state to compete with private enterprise as a wealth or profit creator. Other public and voluntary bodies seem equally unable to match this distinct talent. This argument suggests that the private sector should concentrate on the activities it performs best. It is, however, possible that the resources generated or the skills shown can be more widely deployed. In effect, the private sector might be better at performing some of the roles currently undertaken by the state or other agencies.

Even if this was true, Friedman would argue that it is still inappropriate for the entrepreneur or firm to undertake these 'social' tasks.

> If businessmen do have a social responsibility other than making maximum profits for their shareholders, how are they to know what it is? Can self selected private individuals decide what the social interest is?
>
> Friedman, M. (1962)[25]

Business has no democratic mandate, historic role or other basis for legitimacy in this area. Any choices made, e.g. to back one type of 'cause' or another, are not sanctioned by any agreed system of legitimacy and end up reflecting the interests, prejudices or aims of current corporate leaders.[26] In the USA, 'vanity' sponsorship of prestige activities like the Metropolitan Opera is cited as a clear example of this phenomenon. The 'gong' hunting of the leaders of British and Commonwealth firms is subject to similar criticism. In response, it is argued that these roles were performed in the past. Little great art and few universities would exist without patrons or endowments. Many of the most significant social developments of the nineteenth century succeeded because of the support of entrepreneurial philanthropists. These ranged from employee pension schemes to free medicare.[27] There are mechanisms to overcome the personal or the 'vanity' problem. Programmes like fixed percentage of profits schemes, shareholder polls or sponsorship committees minimise or eliminate these risks. Sponsorship is like any other policy decision with an ethical dimension.

The challenge to maximise wealth or profits poses a similar dilemma. Does management have the right to decide on moral grounds which products to make or policies to adopt?

> There is only one social responsibility of business – to use its resources and engage in activities designed to increase its profits so long as it stays within the rules of the game, engages in open and free competition, without deception or fraud.
>
> Friedman, M. (1962)[28]

This would be an easier position to defend in a specific market operating under conditions of perfect competition and facing no change. Few significant firms operate under these conditions. The internationalisation of business means that today's corporation will trade in a number of markets. Different 'rules' will apply[29] but there will be feedback between markets. The dilemma facing the profit maximising manager is which rules to apply. They might be the home market rules in California or the local market rules in Bhopal. Often, there are 'enforced' and 'unenforced' rules.[30] Most of the time it is possible to play the game: turning a blind eye to corruption; failing to enforce safety rules or pushing an inappropriate product to maximise profits. When, however, the 'rules' or the choices are exposed the costs are incalculable. The protagonists of profit maximising end up in the similar dilemma as the pleasure maximising Utilitarians, the infinite possibilities and outcomes machine could not be built. In sum, choices will be made using criteria other than profit. These choices will inevitably have a moral dimension.[31]

A variation on this theme, suggests that intervention by business will distort the social agenda. There is a tendency by business to use its wealth to

- support the established or prestigious programme;
- develop those activities which endorse or sustain its position;
- concentrate its investment in certain areas.

Critics of corporate giving to the Arts assert that resources will be concentrated on 'vanity' projects: the New York Metropolitan Opera, Glyndebourne to the disadvantage of more local, more needy areas. The 'stars' get richer but the rest get nothing is the common complaint. There is some evidence for this. The Glyndebourne Festival Society will have over two hundred corporate members; from APV Hall Products to Woodhouse Drake & Carey Ltd, while the NIA Centre for Caribbean Arts in Manchester less than twenty. Many of the leading sponsors have a deliberate policy to support a wide range of activities. This does, however, mean that the larger, more prestigious and costlier sponsorship will take the lion's

Table 3.1 International comparison of recipient sectors

Sector	USA (% of total)	UK (% of total)
Education	43	27
Arts & Culture	12	10
Health	28	23
Community Projects	13	21
Other	4	19
TOTAL	100	100

Source: (US) Fishman, S.: *New Formulas for Philanthropy* and (UK) Norton, M.:
A Guide to Corporate Giving 1989[32]

share of donations. An analysis of the pattern of corporate giving in Britain and the USA suggests that the problems is less severe than suggested (Table 3.1). Community projects, health and education win the bulk of support.

The variation between the USA and the UK reflects the different tax and public sector involvement in the two countries. There remains a persistent concern that executive 'vanity' is a factor in specific allocations. Corporations seeking to avoid this will often establish non-executive committees to determine policy or arrive at a 'bench-mark' strategy against which all requests are measured (Table 3.2).

The notion of 'enlightened self-interest' has shaped much of the debate on corporate giving. The 'enlightenment' matrix can be used to identify the position of companies or specific endowments (Figure 3.1).

This emphasis on self-interest prompts the criticism that firms concentrate their support in areas that meet their immediate or long-term aims[33]. New business will be won under the guise of social responsibility. Affinity cards are used by credit card companies to win new business. It is suggested that the corporate interest lies in recruiting the card holder not helping the charity. A more fundamental critique lies in the overall pattern of giving. The support for 'enterprise' agencies in Britain during the 1980s and 1990s was ostensibly to help tackle unemployment and solve local economic problems. They were, however, vulnerable to the criticism that they supported a specific view of the causes of these problems, i.e. that private or personal enterprise was the only way to tackle growing unemployment.[34] The determined efforts of Business in The

Table 3.2 Bench-mark strategies by firms

Firm	Strategy
Levi Strauss & Co.	Projects must incorporate active employee involvement
Marks & Spencer	Seek matching contributions, ideally from employees
Body Shop	All donations through autonomous Foundation
Shell UK	Concentrate on small donations

Fig. 3.1 The enlightenment matrix

Community in Britain to shift the enterprise agency agenda was an attempt to respond to this criticism.

These concerns were summarised by Leavitt[35] in the notion of the 'encircling business ministry'. His conclusion, that 'business should be business' and stick to 'long-run profit maximisation . . . [as] the one dominant objective in practice as well as theory' mirrors the conclusion drawn by Friedman.[36] It does not,

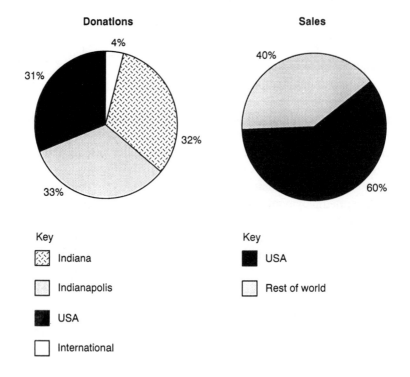

Fig. 3.2 Contrasting donations and sales income for Eli Lilly and Co.

however, resolve the recurrent problem of just where to draw the line. Much marketing expenditure and the bulk of public relations is designed to prepare the ground for the firm successfully to trade. Preoccupation with short-term profits maximisation raises questions about these investments while long-term profits maximisation is hard to calculate especially given the diversity of the intervening variables.

More recently criticism has centred on the failure to fit corporate investment with the business interests or profile of the enterprise. Logan[37] points out that the majority of US multinationals concentrate their activities – consciously or unconsciously – on the home base or original corporate centre. A firm like EXXON generates almost 70 per cent of its earning outside continental USA but makes less than 30 per cent of its charitable donations outside the USA. This pattern can be seen elsewhere, but the pattern seems very exaggerated for US multinationals (Figure 3.2).

This pattern contrasts with the marked shift in donations activities seen at Pilkingtons as the company had internationalised its business (Figure 3.3).

The dominance of the pattern – earn away, spend at home – has produced pressure for intervention by politicians demanding a fairer distribution. Freidman's fear is that this will mean that firms will 'eventually be entrapped by their own overreach . . . [and] the captain of industry [will] . . . ultimately become a mere public flunky'.[38] These are genuine dangers which require constant surveillance. The ultimate test is whether corporate leaders are able to manage these affairs effectively.

Simon[39] suggests that industry and its managers do not have the knowledge, skills or competence to tackle the types of social issues which are the centre of

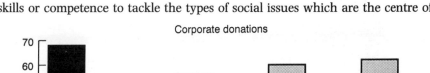

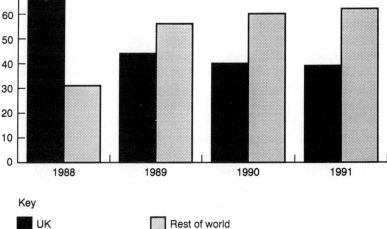

Fig. 3.3 Corporate giving at Pilkington: percentages over time

much corporate, social action. There are – in the words of Bradshaw (President of Atlantic Richfield) – 'many and varied institutions' which have the skills to undertake this work. Companies would satisfy the demands of their shareholders and the needs of the community by paying their taxes and leaving this work to those organisations and people best able to undertake this work. The evidence on this issue is sketchy and inconsistent.[40,41] Other writers[42] have examined the direct cost to firms of intervention in these areas. These costs are then passed on to consumers through higher prices.

The experiences of an especially active firm like The Body Shop illustrate the scope and limitations of corporate intervention. Easterhouse in Strathclyde (Scotland) and Nepal in the Himalayas are just two communities which have seen The Body Shop's involvement in community affairs projects. Easterhouse is a community in north-east Glasgow suffering from severe economic and social problems. The Body Shop are active members of the Easterhouse Partnership; a scheme designed to inject private-sector expertise and finance into this community. The cornerstone of The Body Shop's involvement is the 'Soapworks', soap factory. At one level this is a considerable success. Over three years, it grew to employ almost 100 people. The output increased to almost 5 million bars of soap. There are confident expectations of continued growth and employment stability. Other projects have included support for a range of community activities. Despite this, there are critics. There is the basic questioning of the relevance and appropriateness of the development – 'an inner city soap factory – we had these in the last century'. Alongside this, there are complaints of insensitivity. A factory poster saying 'If I do not work, these words will perish' caused so many complaints in an area of 70 per cent unemployment, that it was withdrawn.

Reservations were expressed about the publicity The Body Shop won for their development. A description of Easterhouse as 'the Third World of the United Kingdom' reinforced the positive features of The Body Shop investment but did little for community self-confidence. The ultimate concern centres on the extent to which projects like this can have a material impact on a community suffering 70 per cent unemployment. Similar concerns are expressed about The Body Shop paper making project in Nepal. This once significant industry had contracted rapidly over the previous decades. The Body Shop development centres on handmade paper for gift items and packing. Soon, it employed 40 people and made profits. It is, however, a tiny development which some suggest is regressive in terms of skills and overdependent on the West.

Despite these criticisms, the private sector seems no less capable than the public sector in its management of this type of project. There is some evidence that the diversity of private sector funding is an advantage.[43] There may be less bureaucracy in these projects. The commitment of key individuals like Anita Roddick makes the scheme more personal and accessible to the communities involved. In some areas of corporate intervention, it seems that the private sector has a distinct competence. Economic development, business and job creation have seen symbiotic links between the public and private sector. Business in The Community in the UK has mobilised corporate expertise on management, production, marketing, finance and a host of other areas. These are not usually available in the public sector. Secondments, sabbaticals, early retirement schemes and finance make these skills available to private and voluntary agencies. The debate about 'competence' fails to acknowledge the convergence in systems, awareness and skills that has occurred over the last decade. There are shortages in certain areas and limitations on application elsewhere but the scope for mutually profitable partnerships is genuine.

> Many respondents in companies, intermediary bodies and community groups stressed that the partnership approach to company investment brought significant benefits to all concerned.
>
> Christie, I. et al: *Profitable Partnerships*[44]

Effective selection of projects, backed by sustained involvement and quality management is as important in managing corporate responsibility activities and individual programmes as it is in any other part of company activity.[45] Clutterbuck proposed a systematic approach which can be converted to a flow chart as in Figure 3.4.

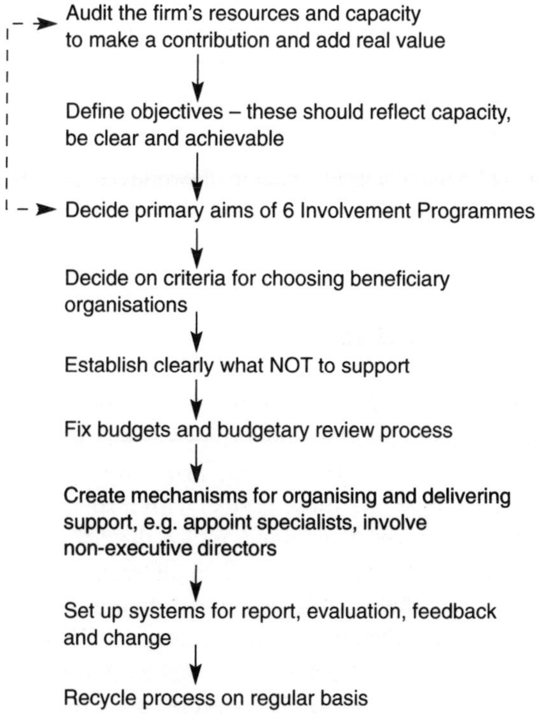

Audit the firm's resources and capacity
to make a contribution and add real value
↓
Define objectives – these should reflect capacity,
be clear and achievable
↓
Decide primary aims of 6 Involvement Programmes
↓
Decide on criteria for choosing beneficiary
organisations
↓
Establish clearly what NOT to support
↓
Fix budgets and budgetary review process
↓
Create mechanisms for organising and delivering
support, e.g. appoint specialists, involve
non-executive directors
↓
Set up systems for report, evaluation, feedback
and change
↓
Recycle process on regular basis

Fig. 3.4 The community involvement choice flow

The private sector, through sole traders; partnerships; limited companies and other forms of enterprise has shown itself to have a distinctive competence in wealth creation. The principles of the division of labour suggest that the search for profits and the creation of wealth will remain the primary concern of corporations and their leaders. Modern society is, however, highly integrated and interdependent. Movement between functions is consistent with functional specialisation and distinctive competence. Ambiguity and change characterise the relations between the community and the corporation.[46] The attempt to eradicate ambiguity by, for example, the state regulating for all moral, social or environmental issues would place an intolerable burden on industry. Self-regulation is likely to be the lowest cost and most effective form of regulation. Imperfect information especially during change poses the same dilemma. The executive is often the first to be aware of an issue or problem. It is cheaper and more profitable for the corporation to make moral judgements or intervene beyond the demands of the current rule system. The alternative is punitive taxes to finance the regulatory and inspection system to monitor and control commerce. The view that 'we pay the government well. It should do its job and leave us alone to do ours'[47] contrasts with the approach of the Confederation of British Industry:

> The law establishes the minimum standard of conduct with which a company must comply if it is to be allowed to exist and trade.[48]

Like all contracts, the arrangement between society and the enterprise has implicit and explicit elements. The cost of attempting to spell out all the 'rules' is so great that it is in the interests of both parties to accept this.[49]

> The expense of confrontation between business and government may be one of the critical reasons for US non-competitiveness in the world economy, but the actual impact of all the laws, all the regulations, and all the bureaucrats on large corporations is surprisingly small.

THE SOCIAL CHALLENGE

Society expects many things of its corporate sector. These include core obligations like wealth and job creation and peripheral responsibilities such as arts sponsorship. Stakeholder analysis is used by some firms to identify and classify these expectations. 'Stakeholders' are those groups with a stake in the firm.

Table 3.3 indicates some of the demands which the different stakeholders place on firms. These will vary over time and in different societies. The primary expectations centre on the wealth or profit function of the enterprise. The ownership group(s) will anticipate a financial return on their investment usually in the form of profit. Failure to achieve this will lead to finance drying up and the value of the enterprise declining. These profits are a reward for the risk taken by investors or derive from their ability to innovate[50] or engage in arbitrage.[51] Employees invest their time and effort for payment. The payments will turn on

Table 3.3 Stakeholders and their expectations

Stakeholder	Expectations	
	Primary	Secondary
Owners	Financial return	Added value
Employees	Pay	Work satisfaction, training
Customers	Supply of goods and services	Quality
Creditors	Credit worthiness	Security
Suppliers	Payment	Long-term relationships
Community	Safety and security	Contribution to community
Government	Compliance	Improved competitiveness

a mixture of their skills and negotiating position. All firms depend on their ability to meet the needs of customers. Survival relies on a capacity to adapt to changing needs and establish a profitable exchange.[52] The firm can be viewed as a conversion process. Inputs such as money, labour, supplies and services are converted into products and services. Credit is needed to facilitate this process. Banks and other suppliers of credit will support those firms which offer them security for their finance. Suppliers require payment for the goods and services provided. The enterprise operates within a society. The community expects firms to offer safety and security within its areas of operation. Typically, this will be endorsed and enforced by the state and its agencies.

The firm undertakes these primary tasks to perform the core functions of wealth and profit creation. Society, however, places other demands on the enterprise. Some relate directly to these economic roles. These include: adding value, training the workforce, securing payment and sustaining long-term relations with suppliers. Beyond this,

> Consumers will continue to demand products that are safe, reliable, and useful, services that are responsive to their changing needs, and advertising that is honest and informative. Communities in affected regions will continue to be concerned about plant relocations and plant closings. The public at large will expect business to help protect the physical environment and the health and safety of all who are exposed to dangerous technologies or dangerous substances. Issues such as corporate power and corporate accountability, corporate ethics and corporate law compliance, corporate activities abroad and corporate disclosure of information will continue to concern more select members of the community.
>
> Task Force on Corporate Social Performance, *Business and Society*

In these and a host of other areas including support for the arts, tackling personal hardship, community relations, sound governance, research and development, the social challenge placed before industry is increasingly clear and well articulated (Figure 3.5).

The formulation and expression of these views ranges from the attempts by

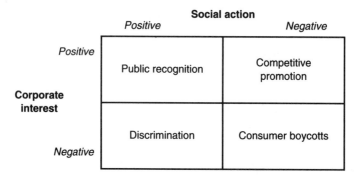

Fig. 3.5 The form of the social challenge

society to reinforce positive corporate action to attacks on behaviour which is seen as unacceptable. In Britain the success of Business in The Community is based, in part, on this pattern of positive reinforcement of positive actions. Business in The Community and its many initiatives grew from industry's concern and determination to address problems. Hector Laing, Alastair Pilkington, Adrian Cadbury and the other founders acted spontaneously to tackle the problems they saw in Britain during the 1980s. Other groups in society endorsed, extended and rewarded their actions. HRH the Prince of Wales, the Prime Ministers of the time and the leaders of the main opposition parties supplied national support. Locally, the same pattern recurred. In a community like central Scotland, the Labour Provost of Stirling collaborated with the local conservative MP to endorse projects like the STirling Enterprise Park (STEP).

This type of fit between the aims of industry and the aspirations of the community are relatively rare. Sometimes, the community has certain goals which industry is reluctant to support. These can be seen in the internal and external operations of the enterprise. The community will then discriminate in favour of certain firms or enterprises or against others. Training emerged during the late 1980s as one such area. There was widespread demand among young people for quality training and development. Those firms which supplied this won the pick of new recruits especially from the universities. Local communities may act in the same way towards companies seeking to locate their operations in an area. Certain industries or firms are welcomed while others are shunned. Japanese companies in the USA suffered from a 'bad neighbour' image. This lead to high costs in plant location and development as local groups were formed to oppose their operations.

Elsewhere, firms use their positive acts as a means of competitive advantage.[53,54] The success of The Body Shop is partly based on this form of competitive promotion. The firm was established by Anita Roddick in 1976 to offer natural care products. These were originally based on the recipes she had found during her work for the United Nations. She insisted that her products were natural, free

Fig. 3.6 Imitation: the sincerest form of flattery?

from animal test and had a minimum impact on the natural environment. In less than 15 years, the group grew to over 500 outlets worldwide. Other retailers and manufacturers were forced to respond to this success (Figure 3.6).

In financial markets, the growth of ethical investments illustrates the same strategy.[55]

There is another side to the positive assertion of corporate interest which has a potentially negative social response. This can occur when industry organises to achieve its economic goals through the political or some other process. Epstein[56] explored this issue in his *The Corporation in American Politics*. He argues that industry is part of 'the highly complex and diversified [power structure]' which is an integral feature of a pluralistic society. Democracy requires competition between interest groups in order to avoid stagnation and ensure change. Corporations play their part in this through four types of competition. These are illustrated in Table 3.4.

Participation by industry is an integral feature of the democratic process. Questions are raised about the nature and scale of this participation. This is especially true of the extent to which industry has access to resources and skill which are not available to other groups.

One response to this concern about 'the level playing field' is the attempt by other groups to use the techniques of persuasion and action traditionally employed by industry. The increased sophistication of public interest groups is a distinct feature of the recent social challenge to industry. Pressure groups have emerged to articulate and address concerns about corporate responsibility.

Table 3.4 Patterns of social and political competition

Intrafirm	Managers in the firm compete for their political or policy interests, e.g., the manager of a conglomerate might want it to cease producing cigarettes and start producing low sugar confectionery.
Interfirm	Corporate leaders back different interest groups, e.g., Barclays Bank might back the Conservatives and the Co-Operative Bank support Labour.
Intra – other interests	Members of government or public agencies might endorse different firms or corporate interests, e.g., some might advocate lead free petrol, others endorse diesel – the outcome will be dissimilar for different firms.
Inter – other interests	Other social groups will compete through their attitude to corporate policies, e.g., one union might advocate single union agreements while others reject them.

Source: Based on Mitnick, B. M.: 'Chasing Elephants among Chickens on a Tilted Field'[57]

Smith[58] classifies these in terms of the degree of political specialisation and the nature of the membership. This approach can be used to map different groups (Figure 3.7).

Pressure groups use a range of approaches to achieve their goals. These include awareness building, communicating information, attempting to change attitudes and direct action. Environmental groups have proved to be very effective at creating awareness of the effects of certain types of corporate action on the environment. Their use of the media to highlight global warming, ozone depletion and the effects of toxic dumping have created widespread public awareness of the issues. Awareness may not be enough to change behaviour by either producers or customers. Information on the way to tackle an issue may be needed. Business in The Community used information on the scope and potential for new business creation to help communities to set up Enterprise agencies. A scheme like Bolton Business Ventures was set up to tackle local unemployment because local businesses and the public sector saw the progress achieved elsewhere. Information

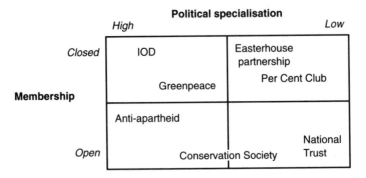

Fig. 3.7 Mapping pressure groups

Source: Based on Wootton, G. (1979)[59]

Table 3.5 Two and a half centuries of boycotts

Time	Event
1750s	New England merchants boycott British goods over Stamp Act
1800s	Britain enforces the Continental Blockade on France
1850s	Chinese boycott Western products in attempt to stop Opium trade
1880	Captain C. C. Boycott provokes the action which gives the phenomenon a name
1900s	Chinese boycott US goods after ban on immigration
1920s	Ghandi calls for boycott of British textiles
1940s	Arab boycott of Israel after creation in 1948
1950s	US boycotts Cuban goods, Montgomery City Line Bus boycott
1960s	Dow Chemicals boycott during Vietnam war, non-returnable bottles boycott
1970s	Sugar and Coffee boycotts, California grapes boycott, Douwe Egberts and Angola Coffee boycott, Nestlé boycott
1980s	South African boycott, *The Sun* newspaper boycott after Hillsboro disaster, Furs boycott, Aerosols with CFCs boycott
1990s	Tuna boycott, *Satanic Verses* boycott

about a project like Cariocca Enterprise will inform members of the African Caribbean community about the scope for self-help. Persuasion may be needed to prompt action by firms or individuals. The criticisms of the high wages for senior managers persuaded many firms in Britain and the USA to reform their procedures for determining salaries.

It is, however, the area of direct action especially initiatives like consumer boycotts that have provoked the most fierce debates. The boycott is an ancient weapon (Table 3.5). Communities have used it to force changes in taxes notably the notorious salt taxes in the eighteenth century. Governments used boycotts to put pressure on foreign rivals or domestic dissidents. It can even be argued that the roots of the American Revolution lay in the boycott of British goods following the Stamp Act of 1765. The boycott of the East India Company's tea was to oppose 'a monster that may be able to destroy every branch of our commerce, drain us of our property, and wantonly to leave us to perish in our thousands'.[60] Ghandi's use of boycotts was an important weapon in the efforts to overthrow English rule in India.

The boycott tactic has changed significantly over the last 30 years. It has shifted from being predominantly linked with political action or endorsed by the state to a more spontaneous, specific and tightly directed action. Boycotts organised as part of labour disputes have declined in significance while consumer boycotts to tackle a problem or change producer behaviour have increased in importance. Pressure groups are more aware of the management issues and problems associated with this tactic while firms are more conscious of the options in managing their response.[61]

STANDARDS AND VALUES

The growing awareness of the impact of business decisions on the wider community, the natural environment and the nature of the society has prompted a re-examination of the standards and values used in business. The rules laid down in the company handbook, the prescriptions of professional societies, even the underlying ethic employed by individuals elsewhere, are seldom adequate guides for executives. In part, this is because the implications of some key decision have consequences that cannot be predicted. Besides this, the interaction between decisions may mean that the 'right' action is neither obvious nor easy to square with other equally moral outcomes.[62]

The predictability issue is perhaps the most widely understood. Firms make decisions about technologies, investments and developments which have consequences which may be impossible to predict.[63] Firms like ICI developed the use of CFCs for use in refrigeration systems, aerosols, etc., with no knowledge of the long-term environmental impact. Other developments in chemicals, biotechnology, etc., may seem beneficial in the predictable future but the long-term consequences cannot be guessed at. The dilemma lies in wedding the need to develop the enterprise and capitalise on new technological opportunities with the imperative to protect the environment or other groups in the community.[64] Today, there is greater awareness of these consequences.[65] This is vividly illustrated in the debate about Alfred P. Sloan's decision not to fit safety glass to Chevrolet Cars in the 1920s. Mintz and Cohen[66] describe this as 'one of the single most important protections ever devised against avoidable automotive death, disfigurement and injury'. Despite this, and regardless of the apparent success of the introduction of safety glass into Cadillacs, Sloan decided that its use 'would have reduced the return on our capital'. This decision reflects Sloan's wider concern at the time to 'INCREASE EARNING POWER through IMPROVED EFFECTIVENESS and REDUCED EXPENSE'.[67] His general letter to the General Motors organisation from which this quotation is taken spells out the GM goals for the future. It deals with a range of issues but never mentions safety.

The challenge of the genuine, ethical dilemma is less well understood. Fred Friendly tackles this in the video *Doing Business, Doing Good*.[68] A firm can face a problem with two outcomes, each of which breaks one moral principle but is justifiable on the same grounds. The case of equality of opportunity versus health and safety illustrates this problem. In the example, the firm has a strict policy of non-discrimination on the grounds of gender and produces a product like batteries. In the product process certain chemicals are used. Research suggests that some of these chemicals can have a harmful effect on the unborn child. The dilemma faces a dilemma. Does it abandon its equal opportunities policy on health and safety grounds or stick with equality of opportunity despite the health risk. Managers will face this type of conundrum with increasing frequency as the implications and interactions of their decisions become more evident.

Perhaps the only way to deal with this type of conundrum is to develop value systems which reflect a willingness to internalise that responsibility, not externalise it.

Two of the most popular and pragmatic guides to implementing corporate responsibility programmes posit different ways to 'developing' or 'maintaining' an ethical position.

Building the Ethical Enterprise

Clutterbuck	*Carmichael and Drummond*
Set a clear example.	Acknowledge the personal dimension to ethical behaviour.
Publish a code of ethics.	Monitor symptoms of personal, ethic-related stress.
Use reward and punishment mechanisms.	Analyse feelings about venture and its activities – link analysis to diagnosis of problems.
Include ethics in recruitment criteria.	Draw up personal and corporate ethics checklist.
Reinforce policies through training and development.	Explain your ground-rules to others.
Provide mechanisms for negotiating concerns.	Set up systems of justice and reinforce these through contract and ethics statements.
Establish openness and transparency into decision processes.	Communicate ethics positions.
Provide feedback.	

Clutterbuck's institutional and control-oriented approach dovetails with the more personalised developmental position adopted by Carmichael.

Much, management thinking acknowledges this responsibility. These issues and the recent debate about the writings of contemporary writers like Hayek[69] and Havel[70] are considered more fully in Chapters 4 and 5. Current notions of enterprise or corporate and managerial freedom, especially in the development of markets, assume that freedom is not licence. Actions by the state or other organisations to liberalise behaviour is part of an implicit contract which assumes a licence to behave responsibly. This form of freedom is implicit in the values of Christianity, Judaism, Islam and most systems of morality. It is not the freedom to act in any way desired but the freedom to make moral choices.[71]

Freedom of action and managerial discretion raise important questions for those involved in the education, training and development of managers. New generations will require an awareness of these issues and the knowledge and competence to tackle decisions arising from options which pose ethical dilemmas. Business Schools have a special responsibility in this area.[72] In part, this is because they have tended to emphasise short termism, instrumentalism and functionalism. These understate the long-term issues and interdependencies which highlight problems of values and standards. Four substantive areas of discussion have emerged. These go to the heart of the activities of entrepreneurs and managers and the work of their organisations. These are:

1   Building systems of corporate ethics and values into the enterprise.
2   Tackling questions of compliance and governance.
3   Meeting the needs of the economically and socially disadvantaged.
4   Satisfying responsibilities to the environment.

These issues can be tackled in several ways. In education, there is a need to explore the individual and corporate strategies which enable firms to acknowledge and meet their responsibilities. In society, opportunities can be created for groups with different experiences, demands and perspectives to gain access to management. This can be through better career opportunities for outgroups, e.g. women, the disabled or minorities and improved lines of communication for those

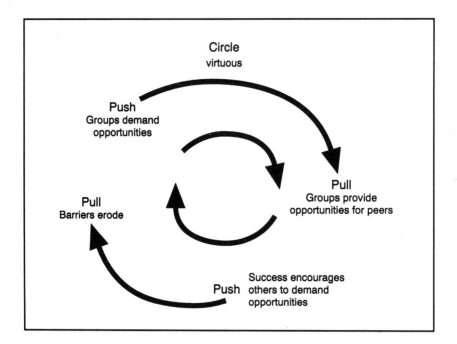

Fig. 3.8 The virtuous circle

with concerns. This push and pull can create a virtuous circle for responsible development (Figure 3.8).

There is an increased coincidence of interest between the call for the individual to behave responsibly, create opportunities and behave morally and the needs of the firm to tap new pools of talent, cope with a changed environment and prosper through freedom. The values and standards that are adopted provide the lubrication for the virtuous circle of opportunity, enterprise and responsibility. Some of the most successful firms are those which acknowledge these responsibilities. The problems of ITT contrast with the success of IBM. The responsible approach of firms like Mercedes Benz highlights the failures of firms like Leyland/Rover. The achievements of The Body Shop emphasise the problems of Tie Rack.

QUESTIONS

1 The maxim that 'no one ever went bust making a quick profit' should be the guiding principle of all corporate leaders – discuss.

2 Describe the dangers and costs to business of the poor image of US or UK industry during the 1980s. Identify the major abuses and put forward ways responsible firms can tackle these – individually or in concert.

3 Outline the economic and social roles of business – identify any potential conflicts and the means by which these might be resolved. Illustrate these from examples drawn from your recent experience or knowledge.

4 'Businessmen have neither the right nor the responsibility to direct corporate resources to serve social goals.' Discuss.

5 Identify the limitations on corporate intervention in tackling the economic and social problems of a deprived inner-city area. Using illustrations indicate ways in which a firm might overcome these limitations.

6 Describe the changing nature of boycotts over the last century. Outline ways in which firms can respond to a consumer pressure group boycott of their products. How might this response change if the criticisms are supported by a major trade intermediary?

7 Is 'business ethics' an oxymoron?

8 Using the ethics, corporate governance or social responsibility statements from at least 5 firms (available directly from firms or published in annual reports) draw out the common features and identify any key omissions.

9 Outline the steps needed to build an ethical stance into the policies and operations of a firm and illustrate, where possible, with material used by a national or local firm.

10 Define:

(a) The economic and product tasks in society.

(b) The concept of 'specific competence' as applied to business.

(c) Social responsibility.

(d) Employee volunteership.

(e) Enlightened self-interest.

(f) Bench-marking.

(g) Stakeholders.

(h) Boycotts.

REFERENCES

1. Carmichael, S. and Drummond, J. *Good Business*, London, Hutchinson (1989).
2. Friedman, M. *Capitalism and Freedom*, Chicago, University of Chicago Press (1962).
3. Task Force on Corporate Social Performance *Report on Business and Society: Strategies for the 1980s*, Washington, US Department of Commerce (1980).
4. Galbraith, J. K. *Economics and the Public Purpose*, Harmondsworth, Penguin Books (1974).
5. Dolan, E. G. *Basic Economics*, New York, Dryden (1991).
6. Jones, E. L. *The European Miracle: Environments, Economics and Geopolitics in the History of Europe and Asia*, Cambridge, Cambridge University Press (1987).
7. Cottrell, P. L. *Industrial Finance 1830–1914: The Finance and Organisation of English Manufacturing Industry*, London, Methuen (1980).
8. Payne, P. L. *The Emergence of the Large Scale Company in Great Britain: 1870–1913*, Economic History Review, 2nd series, xx (1967).
9. Cicero *De Officiis* (50 BC).
10. Shaw, S. and Cannon, T. *The World of Business*, London, Balberry (1991).
11. Rehnquist, W. Dissenting Opinion; US Supreme Court, *1st National Bank of Boston v Belloti* (1978).
12. Carmichael, S. and Drummond, J. ibid., p. 10.
13. Tuleja, T. *Beyond the Bottom Line*, New York, Facts on File Publications (1985).
14. Carnegie, A. *The Gospel of Wealth and Other Timely Essays* (1862).
15. Quoted in James, S. and Parker, R. *A Dictionary of Business Quotations*, London, Routledge (1990).
16. Stacey, N. *Living in an Alibi Society*, London, Rubicon Press (1988).
17. Barnett, C. *The Audit of War: The Illusion and Reality of Britain as a Great Nation*, London, Macmillan (1986).
18. Letter in the *Times Higher Education Supplement*, 10 April (1992).
19. 'New Products of the Year' *Fortune*, 2 December (1990).
20. Kay, J. A. 'Economics and Business' *The Economic Journal*, vol. 101, pp. 57ff.
21. Davis, K. 'The Case for and Against Assumptions of Social Responsibilities' *Academy of Management Journal*, pp. 312–22 (1978).
22. Friedman, M, ibid.
23. Hayek, F. A. 'The Corporation in a Democratic Society: In Whose Interest Ought it and Will it be Run?' in Ansoff, H. I. *Business Strategy*, Harmondsworth, Penguin (1969).
24. Heilbroner, R. L. *In the Name of Profit*, New York, Doubleday (1972).
25. Friedman, M., ibid.
26. Wang, Jia and Coffey, A. 'Board Composition and Corporate Philanthropy' *Journal of Business Ethics*, vol. II, no. 10, October (1992) pp. 771–8.
27. Bradley, I. C. *Enlightened Entrepreneurs*, London, Allen and Unwin (1989).
28. Friedman, M., ibid.
29. Langlois, C. C. and Schlegelmulch, B. B. 'Do Corporate Codes of Ethics Reflect National Character? Evidence From Europe and the US' *Journal of International Business Studies*, 21, Winter, (1990) pp. 519–40.
30. Briloff, R. *The Truth about Corporate Accounting*, New York, Harper and Row (1976).
31. Council on Economic Priorities *Rating America's Corporate Conscience*, Reading, Mass., Addison-Wesley (1987).

32. Chetwood, P. et al. *UK Corporate Giving in the 1990s*, unpublished MBA project (1991).
33. Donaldson, J. and Davis, P. 'Business Ethics? Yes, But What Can it Do for the Bottom Line' *Management Decision* vol. 28, no. 6, pp. 29–33 (1990).
34. Metcalf, H., Pearson, R. and Martin, R. 'Companies' Role in Charitable Job Creation' *Employment Gazette*, 97, September (1989) pp. 478–84.
35. Leavitt, T. 'The Dangers of Social Responsibility' *Harvard Business Review*, September–October (1958).
36. Friedman, M. ibid.
37. Logan, D. *Corporate Giving by US Multinationals*, Washington, Institute for the Foundations (1989).
38. Tuleja, T., ibid.
39. Simon, J. G., Powers, C. W. and Gunnemann, J. P. *The Ethical Investor: Universities and Corporate Responsibility*, New Haven, Yale University Press (1972).
40. Filios, V. P. Review and Analysis of the Empirical Research *Journal of Business Ethics*, Vol. 5, no. 4, August (1986) pp. 291–306.
41. Dickie, R. B. and Rouner, L. S. (ed) *Corporations and the Common Good*, Indiana, University of Notre Dame (1986).
42. Cartwright, D. 'What Price Ethics' *Managerial Auditing Journal*, vol. 5, no. 2 (1990) pp. 28–31.
43. Confederation of British Industry *Initiatives Beyond Charity*, London, CBI (1988).
44. Christie, I., Carley, M. and Fogarty, M. *Profitable Partnerships*, London, Policy Studies Institute (1991).
45. Clutterbuck, D. *Actions Speak Louder*, 2e, London, Kogan Page (1992).
46. Heald, M. *The Social Responsibilities of Business: Company and Community 1900–1960*, New Brunswick, Transaction, 2nd edn (1988).
47. Silk, L. and Vogel, D. *Ethics and Profits: The Crises of Confidence in American Business*, New York, Simon and Schuster (1976).
48. Quoted in Smith, N. C. *Morality and the Market*, London, Routledge (1990).
49. Marks, R. A. G. and Minow, N. *Power and Accountability*, Glasgow, Harper Collins (1991).
50. Schumpeter, J. *Capitalism, Socialism and Democracy*, New York, Harper and Row (1942).
51. Kirzner, I. *Competition and Entrepreneurship*, Chicago, University of Chicago Press (1974).
52. Cannon, T. *Basic Marketing*, London, Cassell (1992).
53. Abratt, R. and Sacks, D. 'The Marketing Challenge: Towards Being Profitable and Socially Responsible' *Journal of Business Ethics*, vol. 7, July (1988) pp. 497–507.
54. Amietta, P. L. 'Valorie gerarchie etiche' *Economics and Management*, vol. 15, July (1990) pp. 45–7.
55. O'Leary, C. 'Environmental Way to a Healthy Return' London, *Daily Telegraph*, 7 November (1992).
56. Epstein, E. M. *The Corporation in American Politics*, Englewood Cliffs., New Jersey, Prentice Hall (1969).
57. Mitnick, B. M. 'Chasing Elephants among Chickens on a Tilted Field', in Post, J. E. *Corporate Social Performance and Policy*, Greenwich, Connecticut, JAI Press (1991).
58. Smith, N. C. *Morality and the Market*, ibid.
59. Wootton, G. *Pressure Politics in Contemporary Britain*, Lexington, Lexington Books (1979).
60. Quoted in Morison, S. E., Commanger, H. S. and Leuchtenburg, W. E. *The Growth of the American Republic*, Oxford, Oxford University Press (1962).
61. Bowie, N. 'New Directions in Corporate Social Responsibility' *Business Horizons*, vol. 34, no. 4, July/August (1991) pp. 56–65.
62. Small, M. 'Ethics in Business and Management: An International Perspective' *Journal of Business Ethics*, vol. 12, no. 4 (1993).
63. de Borchgrave, Rodolphe 'Its Not Easy Being Green' *Journal of European Business*, vol. 4, no. 3, January/February (1993) pp. 48–52.
64. Post, J. E. 'Managing as if the Earth Mattered' *Business Horizons*, vol. 34, no. 4, July/August (1991) pp. 32–8.
65. Vogel, D. 'Business Ethics: New Perspectives on Old Problems' *California Management Review*, vol. 35, no. 4, Summer (1991).
66. Mintz, M. and Cohen, J. 'Crime in the Suites' in Nader, R. (ed.) *The Consumer and Corporate Accountability*, New York, Harcourt Brace Jovanovitch (1973).

67. Sloan, A. P. *My Years with General Motors*, Harmondsworth, Penguin (1986) (his emphasis).
68. *Doing Business, Doing Good* produced by Business in the Community, 227a City Road London EC1V 1LX Tel. 071. 253. 3716.
69. Hayek, *Law, Legislation and Liberty*, London, Routledge (1979).
70. Havel, V. *Living in Truth*, London, Faber and Faber (1987).
71. Kelm, G. 'Management Behaviour and the Social Responsibilities Debate: Goals versus Constraints' *Academy of Management Journal* (1978) pp. 57–68.
72. Etzioni, A. 'Are Business Schools Brainwashing Their MBA' *Business and Society Review*, Summer (1989) p. 18–19.

CHAPTER 4

Key issues in business ethics: innovation, people, technology and markets

Ethical issues pervade business life. Engineering directors who have to decide whether to introduce a new technology face a moral dilemma. They know it might put loyal employees out of work because the new equipment needs less people or their skills are redundant. The trades union officers who want to 'embargo' cheap imports from a poor developing country. They know that this country desperately needs the foreign exchange. They must decide whether to put the needs of their members before those of third world peasants. In the Uruguay Round of GATT negotiations, US demands for licence fees for software products were ranged against the calls for easier access to northern markets for southern agriculture. The marketing policies of firms raise a host of ethical issues. These range from the kinds of images used in advertising – the Benetton 'Aids' advertisement is a vivid illustration – to the types of products offered to the market. In recent years, the stewardship of private and public assets has been at the centre of the policy debate on corporate values. Bribery in Japan, misuse of the funds of Saving and Loans and theft of pensioners' funds at Maxwell are among the issues shaping the public agenda. Views on ways funds are invested and allocated by and for companies has swung between the 'Greed is Good'[1] motto of Gordon Gekko to the ethical investments of the Working Assets Money Fund or the Ecological Building Society. Often the hardest questions centre on the choice between the short, medium and long term. A bank will need to decide whether to call in a loan putting a firm at risk or wait and put the loan at risk.

Firms and managers try to resolve these questions in a host of ways. Traditionally, it was assumed that a general social ethic permeated the society. In the West this was generally seen as a mixture of individualism and Christianity. Smith summarises the first of these with his observation that 'it is not from the benevolence of the butcher, the brewer and the baker, that we expect our dinner, but from their regard to their own best interest'.[2] The Christian tradition was closely linked to the rise of capitalism in the work of Weber. He saw a powerful link between Protestantism and capitalism. The increasingly secular nature of society in the West and the successful industrial development of communities with powerful corporatist or communal traditions has created a more eclectic base for values and morality.[3] The challenges managers face and their awareness of the limitations on their ability to predict or control outcomes has made them increasingly aware of the nature of the ethical challenge facing them.[4]

INNOVATION AND CHANGE

No aspect of business raises more questions of ethic and values than innovation and change. This challenge may occur because of the threat that change poses to individuals and communities. The apparent powerlessness of industry and the community to resist the pressures for change and increasing demand for innovation highlights the difficulty of those trying to *ride the tiger*.

> Firms which are skilful at innovation – the succesful exploitation of new ideas – will secure a competitive advantage in a rapidly changing world market, those which are not will be overtaken.
>
> HMSO (1993)[5]

> The drive for improvement never ends. The best culture, systems and plans do not remain for long. Economic conditions, competitors behaviour, market dynamics, technological advances and the political environment demand changes.
>
> Russell P., Saad, K. N. and Ericksm, T. J. (1991)[6]

Drucker[7] has gone as far as saying that 'innovation' is one of the two basic functions of business. Deane[8] argues that change is the key characteristic of industrial society. The challenge was recognised from the first by Luddites and other machine wreckers who sought to stop the introduction of the new technology. It is seen every day in the firm that seeks to extend the life of a declining product or resist the pressure to use new technologies and novel techniques.

Schumpeter[9] called 'creative destruction' the way innovation and change continually raise questions which affect society, the economy, culture and the environment.

The most common social issues centre on the nature and location of employment. The pressure for change prompts companies to invest in new equipment and plant.[10] It is seldom possible to arrive at an exact fit between the skills available to the current workforce and the skills needed by the new technologies. Sometimes, the process innovations require changes that those affected are reluctant to accept. Sawyer[11] found this in her examination of book selling. Staff saw the use of electronic databases as a form of deskilling. It changed the nature of the job in ways that eliminated much of their satisfaction. They could learn the new skills but it fundamentally changed the nature of the work. Elsewhere, those affected are unable to change. The changed nature of cargo handling on the docks with the advent of containerisation eliminated many jobs while changing the character of the rest of the work. Dockers with long service were seldom able to compete with new entrants with more appropriate skills.

> A growing and efficient economy must somehow solve the problem of shifting people from declining to growing industries, from low productivity to high productivity jobs: it must be able to absorb the consequences of technical change. At a very minimum this involves overcoming complex problems of education, retraining and relocation.
>
> Smith, K. (1986)[12]

Communities can be blighted by this process. The changes in the mining and steel industries in Europe demonstrate this. Production in these sectors was typically concentrated in communities with few alternative sources of employment locally. Closing the mine or steelworks could mean killing the community. The greater the change, the more widespread the effect. This can occur even where the wider 'benefits' are widely recognised. It is being said that 'the peace dividend' won after the changes in Eastern Europe is being won by the prosperous communities of south-east England, southern Germany, Spain and California at the expense of northern England, south-west France, central USA and northern Germany.

The ethical challenge to managers and firms exists on two levels. These are:

● Should we make the change?
● What responsibility do we have to minimise the impact?

Often, the pressure for change leaves the firm or community with no option. There have been attempts to stand against the pressure of new products and processes. Ghandi's attempt to return to handmade cloth did not reverse the demand for the machine-made product. Clinker-built boats were relegated to a small niche in the market after the introduction of glass reinforced plastic boats. Integrated transport planning has hardly slowed the move from rail to road transport. Examples abound of firms that tried to resist technological change. It is hard to identify any which have succeeded. The accumulated evidence is a powerful case against resistance. The threat to the enterprise is often a sufficiently strong argument to end any debate about the necessity of change.

> There is no evolution without change. We need new ideas, new styles of leadership, new attitudes, new perceptions, new structures, new approaches and new values. Above all, new values.
>
> Frye, M.: *Inaugural Address*[13]

But, the social cost of change is seldom paid by the promoters of innovation and novelty. The jobs lost are seldom those held by the advocates nor are the communities destroyed those in which they live. Commerce is a major source of change and has a clear responsibility to address its social consequences. This is especially true when the changes affect the social values which bind communities.

There are several fundamental contradictions in some commonly held propositions. An example is the conflict between:

- Proposition A: that the family is the 'cornerstone' of the community or community care for the elderly or the weak

and

- Proposition B: that in the face of shortages of employment, labour – often heads of families – should *get on their bikes* and seek work, if necessary away from the family.

Similar issues affect most debate on innovation and change. The imperative for change is now linked with the notion that these changes contain, within them, the benefit of increased choice or wider options. Most of these propositions derive from the positivist view of social and economic change and the resulting emphasis on the tangible, measurable and verifiable benefits. There is, however, greater awareness now of the price of change to the community, the economy and the environment. Alongside this, the intangible costs are viewed as increasingly relevant to any debate.

> In sum, the processes which produce economic and business growth without considering the value implications are inevitably unable to recognise the crises and value consequences because the ideologies attached to the techniques forbid it.
>
> Donaldson, J. (1989)[14]

The social challenge to the demand for innovation and change comes from many sources. The most basic is the attempt by a society or community to stand outside the process. Japan, between the middle of the sixteenth century and the Meiji Restoration of the 1860s, was a vivid example. The Khymer Rouge terror in Cambodia was an especially vicious attempt to stop certain forms of innovation. In the Islamic world there is widespread concern about the effects of change on values and social systems which are held very strongly. Havel[15] – with his concern about the automatism of technology and the industrial-consumer society – Suggate[16] through his Christianity, Williams[17] and others[18] share this concern about the social and moral case for innovation and change.

> If all important problems are technical, they are in principle soluble without risk to our sense of ourselves, our moral self perception. The identification of the technical 'can' with the moral 'should' – or the blotting out by the former of questions about the latter – is endemic in our culture. We are largely incapable of asking ourselves what human purpose technology in such areas serves.
>
> Williams, R. (1989)[19]

Those businesses and individuals which seek to advocate and introduce change have a responsibility to these communities and their enterprises to acknowledge and address these concerns. Simple advocacy is unlikely to be sufficient. Danley[20] highlights the weakness of the conventional recourse to Pareto optimality, i.e., that it is *best for all*. He points out that 'it is impossible to make judgements about what is best in situations in which an actual preference will be overridden'. In this case, the desire of the group or the community to stay as they are. The moral basis for continued change and the social gain to the community and its members requires justification. The means to address the dislocative and distributive effects of change are an integral part of the argument.

The economic benefits of innovation and change are commonly presented as the primary justification. The individual, enterprise or community will lose out economically if there is a failure to respond to new opportunities, processes or technologies. Corelli Barnett[21] bases much of *The Audit of War* on the thesis that the attempt to create a New Jerusalem in Britain after the end of World War II was partly an attempt to replace the imperatives of change and innovation with social engineering.

> If Britain after the war was to earn the immense resources required to maintain her cherished traditional place as a great power and at the same time pay for New Jerusalem at home, she had to achieve nothing short of an economic miracle. Such a miracle could only be achieved through the transformation, material and human, of her essentially obsolete industrial society into one capable of triumphing in the world markets of the future. Had all the most powerful groups and institutions in that society been willing to throw themselves behind the process of transformation, it would still have been difficult enough to achieve, given the scale of the inherited problems. But instead of such willingness there existed the massive internal resistance to change which was so manifest in the history of Britain as an industrial society; a resistance that not even the shock of war had proved strong enough to budge more than a little.
>
> Barnett, C. (1986)[22]

Managers in Steel, Shipbuilding, Aerospace and Mining were as resistant to new techniques, novel technologies and innovative products as artisans, riveters and miners (Table 4.1).

The extent of this opposition indicates a society in which the pay-offs from economic change are not seen to be sufficient compensation for the risks. Those corporations striving for the economic and financial gains from change and innovation have a duty to identify and implement change while accepting their responsibility to accommodate the needs of those groups affected by change. At the same time, resistance to those changes which affect the vested interests of management or particular ventures undermines the process of change.

> It must be considered that there is nothing more difficult, more dangerous or more apt to miscarry than an endeavour to introduce new institutions. For he that introduces will make enemies of all those who do well out of the old institutions, and will receive only cool support from those who would do well out of the new ones. This coolness is caused partly by fear of their opponents, who have the old laws on their side, and partly

from the natural scepticism of mankind, who have no faith in new arrangements until they have been confirmed by experience.

Niccolo Machiavelli (1981)[23]

The needs of the natural and built environment are especially difficult to accommodate during change and innovation. The impact of new technologies may be impossible to predict. This sense of powerlessness is not a basis for denying the ethical and corporate implications of innovation. It emphasises the importance of exhaustive attempts to construct 'what if' scenarios. Even these, may not identify the threats. Constant vigilance and openness are critical features of the attempt by firms to meet their obligations in this area.

> The effective regulation of major hazard installations, as an example of business enterprise, necessitates a more open policy of discourse between interested and affected parties and such a move would entail moving the process of risk assessment and management into a more democratic phase.

Smith, D.: Strategic Management and the Business Environment[24]

The ideas included in this statement are limited by the twin constraints on corporate action. These are the problems of forecasting the long-term technological consequences and the concern about wedding public accountability to competitive advantage. Internal systems of accountability may be an integral feature of a responsible treatment of this topic by firms.

Table 4.1 Resistance to change: the real British disease?

Management	Workers	Policy makers
No to	**No** to	**No** to
Mechanical coal loading and other innovations	End of small pits	Training for mining and other engineers
Specialist technical staff	Productivity agreements	Industrial strategy
Process innovations	Proper apprentice training	Investment allowances
Modular and batch production	End of demarcation disputes	Priority for vocational training
Systematic replacement of obsolete equipment	No to 'dilution' of 'skilled' by trained	Redirection of science to industry
Management education	Training centres	Design education
Re-investment	End of 'slack' time	Concentration
Air conditioned, properly lit plants	Rationalisation of unions	Universal primary education until 1880s
Retooling by choice not necessity	End of restrictive practices	Trade strategy
Agreed delivery and quality standards	Qualifications	Large-scale investment in industrial modernisation

Source: Based on Barnett, C. (1986)[25]

EMPLOYMENT

The impact of innovation and change on employment has raised more questions and posed more problems for communities, entrepreneurs and corporations than almost any other aspects of development.[26] The cries of displaced labour echo down the years.

The weaver's comments in the early 1800s:

> if I was working with my family at home, I could give them employment, one to wind bobbins, another to work at the loom and another at the jenny; but if I must go to the factory they will not allow me to take those boys, but I must leave them to the wide world to perish
>
> Committee on the Woollen Trade[27]

has a tragic echo in the pleas today for more work in the same factories and traditional industries. The economic difficulties of the early 1980s in Britain, the USA, mainland Europe and other parts of the developed world forced many firms to assess their approach to corporate responsibility during a period of economic transformation. Traditional industries, especially in manufacturing, contracted while new industries required different skills. The problems were especially acute for those new entrants into the labour force with few skills and older, less well-educated workers. In some communities – notably the inner-cities – public order seemed to be breaking down. The notion that there was an obligation on the part of firms to act to protect the social or economic order from which they gain was widespread. This was, on one level, akin to the philosophical notion of *prudential obligation*. That is to say, it is in the best interests of corporations to tackle these problems.[28]

Many corporate leaders acknowledged the bond between their enterprise and the community in which they operated. In even simpler terms 'business has a massive stake in the nation's cities . . . their balance sheets reflect the cost and value of the assets involved'.[29] This stake was deeply rooted in the links that had evolved between firms, their workers and the communities they served. Some would suggest that there exists a form of contract between the firm and the community.[30] This includes both an obligation on the state to allow the firm to pursue its activities and an obligation on the firm to meet certain responsibilities to the labour force which is an integral part of the economic community. Business in The Community was created in Britain; initially, by industry, to deploy corporate resources to overcome the problems of unemployment. The agenda was soon widened to address other issues and shifted to place 'wealth creation' as the key to 'job creation'. Emphasis on help in starting new businesses was part of a mutually beneficial process of:

New Firms = New Suppliers = Improved Performance = Quality Jobs

This accent on the wider pool of labour accepted the notion that the corporation's responsibilities went beyond its current workforce. This may be an implicit recognition that modern industrial society requires a reserve pool of labour – not currently in work. This group is needed to facilitate transition and change in markets and technology. The assumption is that this reservoir is necessary for successful innovation and change. This places an obligation on the society to meet their needs. As industry is the prime initial beneficiary of successful change, it has a special responsibility to enable this group to perform this role effectively. This will widen the role of the responsible corporation beyond reducing the barriers to entry and re-entry into the workforce. It will include the provision of support, training and resources to ensure those not in work currently have the skills and competencies to facilitate and expedite change.[31]

The results of this type of intervention during the 1980s in Britain were remarkable. A host of firms became involved in Enterprise Agencies, Job Clubs, Business Clubs, Enterprise and Small Business Units in universities, etc. It soon, however, became clear that the results of these activities were very uneven. Some unemployed benefited quickly and well. Others, notably inner-city communities, ethnic minorities, the disabled and women, did badly. Carley[32] noted that inner-city residents in the USA were often excluded from the new jobs created in urban renewal programmes – even those in their immediate environments. Many forms of city centre regeneration – hotels, conference centres, office developments, higher education – provide few opportunities for older, unskilled or semi-skilled workers. Even those open to women tended to be lowly paid, part-time jobs. The European evidence that exists confirms the persistence of this problem.[33] Spencer[34] noted that the unemployment rate among black people was twice that of white. Members of the Asian and African Caribbean communities were heavily represented among the unemployed (Figure 4.1).

Affirmative action to help specific groups shifts the agenda for corporate responsibility much further than the immediate interests in a minimising of the costs of transition or economic change. It implies that firms have a direct interest in social engineering. The argument of *prudential obligation* was used extensively in North America to justify this type of intervention. Prudential obligation meant that it was prudent of business to acknowledge its wider obligations in order to avoid worse and more threatening problems or threats to its survival or prosperity.

The violence in the cities of Detroit, Chicago, Los Angeles, Newark etc., provoked corporate leaders like Henry Ford II to acknowledge that 'equal opportunity policy is more than the elimination of deliberate racial discrimination'. The latter was required by the law; Friedman's *rules* required it. The new agenda went beyond even *prudential obligation* to an attempt to achieve economic equity. In Britain, this approach is gaining wider acceptance through a mixture of enlightened self-interest and a general recognition that the diversity of the community by race, gender and capability should be reflected in the range of economic opportunities. This is often justified in terms of either Locke's[35] *natural rights*[36] or a form of the Utilitarian[37] principle that this will contribute the *greatest good to the greatest number.*[38]

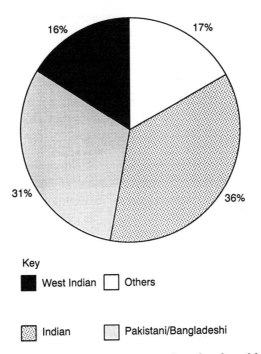

Fig. 4.1 Distribution of unemployment among the minority ethic community
Source: Spencer, L. (1988)[39]

RESTRICTIVE TRADE PRACTICES

Discussion of no area of group or corporate behaviour is more likely to deserve the censure that it generates *more heat than light* than restrictive trade practices. In part, this reflects the pervasive nature of the phenomenon. Restrictive trade practices can be found within the firm, e.g. restrictions on output of quota restrictions by workers.[40] Similar restriction can be found between firm, e.g. a trade body requiring all work of a certain type to go through certain suppliers. It might centre on entry into a trade or sector. The restrictions on membership by unions or professional bodies illustrate this. It is seen in criteria or advancement. In universities, the requirement for a doctorate (any) or publications in refereed articles is employed regardless of relevance to control entry to lectureship or Chairs.[41] On occasion, restrictive practices have been used to control exit from the sector. The guild system occasionally imposed this limitation. The purpose is usually to reduce the effective working of a market, e.g. for labour. Prices (wages) can be controlled and competition restricted. Most ethical codes find it hard to justify this pattern of behaviour. The Utilitarians or Friedmanites see restrictive practices as the few using their power to impose their requirements on the many.

The only purpose for which power can be rightfully exercised over any member of a civilised community, against their will, is to prevent harm to others. His own good, either physical or moral, is not a sufficient warrant.

Mill, J. S. (1865)[42]

In some cases, *the prevention of harm to others* is used as the justification of restrictive trade practices. The restriction of output by working groups is often justified as the attempt by the stronger, more capable members to 'protect' their weaker, less capable or older colleagues. Studies of a wide range of industries identified the creation of standards or norms of output which every member of the work group could achieve.[43] The same justification is not possible for other efforts to reduce or restrict output. These can range from attempts to sustain acceptable 'fare rates', through efforts to level out work flows, even forms of sabotage.

> The group had established a norm of how much output was 'fair', namely 6,000 units, a figure which satisfied management but well below what the men could have produced had fatigue been the only limiting factor. Related to this basic norm were two others: 'one must not be a rate buster', which meant that no member should produce at a rate too high relative to that of others in the group, and 'one must not be a chisler', which meant that one must not produce too little relative to the others.

Handy, C. (1985)[44]

Each of these places the interests of the group before the interests of the enterprise or the community.

Further complications are introduced through two common variations on this phenomenon. The first is management collusion. This can be implicit or explicit. The above comment indicates that the restricted output *satisfied management*. Work by Simon[45] and Cyert and March[46] suggests that 'satisficing' is often a better explanation for management's behaviour than maximising or optimising. In accepting these standards, managers can be accused of acting against their shareholders' interests. This has become part of a wider criticism of 'managerialism'. This occurs when the interests of the executives of the firm can be placed before their responsibilities to the owners and risk takers, i.e. shareholders.[47,48] Typically, this occurs when the protection afforded by diluted, distant or disinterested ownership allows management to abuse their position. In some cases,[49] the executive group use their ability to manipulate corporate resources to further disenfranchise the ownership group. A range of approaches from 'poisoned apple' strategies to 'greenmail' have gained notoriety in the USA as ways to protect entrenched corporate, managerial interests. These might involve the creation of obligations on the firm, including golden parachutes or new debt, to deny potential acquirers the benefits of acquisition.[50] This is hard to justify. These groups lack the legitimacy to impose restrictions on acquisition, other barriers to the free movement of ownership or reduce the rights of shareholders. Only the state has the right to introduce restrictions of the freedom of shareholders to transfer ownership or control. Executives embarking on these policy are, *de facto*, usurping governmental authority without democratic or other forms of legitimacy.[51]

The second variation of the theme of control of output by the group is when this behaviour is endorsed or defended by trades unions, professional bodies or other parties able to restrict entry into the working group. The rights and power of these institutions vary considerable over time and between communities. The 'closed shop' was a major means of 'defending' the position of work groups in Britain until recently. Many of these 'closed shops' have been outlawed in the UK. There remain, however, many comparable situations, e.g. in professional groups, which are still sustained. These restrictions on the free movement of labour can be justified in some cases by an overwhelming public interest. A chartered engineer may be needed to accept that a newly built bridge is safe. Medicine is generally seen as a field in which the free movement of labour contains too many risks to be acceptable. There are, however, some areas in which this notion of public interest is less widely accepted. There are also fields in which the evidence that the public interest is genuinely protected is harder to identify.

In these circumstances, unions and professional bodies act just like any other monopoly supplier. It is in their interest to force up the price of labour while forcing down the amount supplied. This interference in the working of the market cuts 'total economic output as well as redistributing pay from those employees whose monopoly power is low or zero'.[52] These restrictions in the working of the market reduce choice among buyers while eroding the quality and utility of the services supplied. It will always be in the interest of the union or professional body to keep the supply of qualified staff below that needed. Simultaneously, there will be a tendency to adopt approaches to the development of the group which favour its interests rather than the needs of the community. Three common criticisms of powerful unions and professional institutes are:

1   They restrict entry through lengthy training containing much redundancy.
2   They emphasise extensive often redundant learning.
3   They use their power to eliminate competition.

The apprenticeship mode of craft training with its emphasis on serving time rather than practical training is often presented as an abuse of the monopoly power of the crafts. In universities, a similar criticism of the apprentice mode of doctoral study is apt. Much of the time involves tasks which are not central to the doctorate. Training in important areas, e.g. data gathering and secondary analysis can be cursory. The high dropout and failure rates act as an effective restriction on entry. In the professions 'redundancy' in education and training is widespread. This might involve students studying areas they will never use or ignoring the balance of their likely future work. Accountants studying law or economics they will not use or legal training which denies that most solicitors will work in a narrow range of areas. The time and extent of study serves to keep down the number of entrants while reinforcing the power of the institute or professional body. This power can be employed to eliminate competition. The recent attack on 'standard wills' and the attempts to eliminate competition in conveyancing in Britain indicate the determination of professional bodies to defend their interests – if necessary, at the expense of the community. The erosion of these restraints would seem to be an integral feature of any attempt to reduce restrictive trade practices and confine them to areas in which there is:

either

- an identifiable and sustainable overwhelming public interest

or

- a genuine need to protect a disadvantaged group.

MARKETS AND MARKETING

The primary justification of the entrepreneur, firm or corporation lies in their contribution to the economic well being of the community.[53,54] This is intimately linked with the effective working of markets to ensure that goods are allocated and prices charged in ways which create wealth and produce profits. Restrictions of the working of the market through internal restrictions or external impositions reduce the ability of industry to perform its economic function. The concentration of power in the hands of certain enterprises is, perhaps, the most widely accepted internal restriction. Monopoly is the most extreme example of this distortion in the operations of the market.

> Every day in our lives monopoly takes its toll. Stealthily it reaches down into our pockets and takes part of our earnings. For many, what is left must be spread more thinly over the necessities of life; for others, some of the amenities must be sacrificed. . . . Excessive prices constitute one important consequence of monopoly. They appear to be the inevitable result of an economy wherein private control has superseded the forces of the market. . . . Workers are denied opportunity for jobs in the industrial expansion that would have occurred if competitive conditions existed.
>
> Kefauver, E. (1965)[55]

Kefauver's damning criticism summarises many of the key criticisms of excessive concentration. These are:

1   Increased prices.
2   Reduced opportunities because the monopolist will always restrict output to sustain monopoly profits.

to these can be added

3   Restricts innovation as the monopolist has no interest in or need for novelty.
4   Less pressure for quality improvements.
5   Eroding competitiveness which will make the community vulnerable to rivals from more competitive hence more innovative, lower price economic rivals.

The economic difficulties of highly concentrated, heavily protected markets like those in Central and Eastern Europe reinforce the image created by other monopoly or limited competition markets at home and internationally such as India.[56,57,58]

The abuse of market power through monopoly or oligopoly is the 'classic' concern about the way markets and marketing operates.[59] Other critics have concentrated their attention on other aspects of marketing. These include: the abuse of purchaser power; restricting opportunities or stereotyping; the promotion of dangerous products and the introduction of suspect values beside specific abuses in fields like advertising to children.[60] These latter issues reflect a social concern that firms use their economic power to affect the 'maintenance', 'adaptive' or 'political' functions in a society.[61] Some critics, notably Galbraith,[62] link the two propositions. He suggests that industrial concentration; monopoly or oligopoly concentrates power in the hands of relatively few suppliers. They act to defend their interests through further restrictions on competition, advocating certain types of consumption and opposition to regulation.

> Perhaps the most powerful myth about corporations is that they are ultimately held accountable by the marketplace and they therefore must maximise profits to compete for investors. The reality is that their profit maximisation model does not provide an accurate explanation of the way in which large corporations function in our society. Essentially, modern corporations often use their power to reduce risks and transfer costs on to others creating results that were not intended, that are not in the interests of society as a whole, and that have nothing to do with profit.[63]

They can do this because of their ability to exercise market power because of the lack of competition.

The evidence on these issues is mixed. Concentration is a feature of most market economies. The pressures in this direction are many and diverse (Table 4.2). The propensity to concentrate and the apparent strength of the giant corporations must be viewed with some caution. Many markets are still fragmented.

> Farmers, lawyers, cleaners and cobblers, bookstores, musicians and houses of casual pleasure still survive. Here, the market still rules; here consumer sovereignty is still inviolate . . . [but] with increasing size and corporate power the market gives way to planning.
>
> Galbraith, J. K. (1974)[64]

Since this list was published, concentration has increased in several of these

Table 4.2 The tendency to concentrate

Pareto's law	The top 20 per cent account for 80 per cent of an activity
Capital barriers to entry	Those established in a market will find it easier to fund their activities than new entrants
Technological barriers to entry	Existing firms will understand the technologies better than outsiders
Marketing barriers to entry	Previous investments mean that customers are more familiar with and have more confidence in existing firms
Conglomeration	There is a tendency for systems to conglomerate, i.e. similar entities– even in the natural world . . . come together to form larger organisms
Failure	Management failure means that some ventures will cease to exist or be absorbed by others
Market widening	Internationalisation and parallel developments mean that intermarket competition through larger ventures increases in importance
Success	Some ventures will improve their competitiveness, hence their market position at the expense of others
Imperfect information	The knowledge used by some firms to gain market advantage will not be accessed by others
Darwinism	The survival of the fittest

sectors, e.g. lawyers and bookstores. New, far less concentrated markets have emerged or grown in importance such as software production, plastics processing and business services. Equally noticeable are the failures of the giants successfully to defend their position. Firms like IBM and General Motors have signally failed to protect their interests against new or overseas rivals. The concentration ratios – the proportion of the market held by the top three or five – have contracted in some major markets. In the UK automobile industry, the concentration of production in four majors – Leyland, Ford, Rootes and Vauxhall– is now replaced by six majors – Rover (Leyland), Ford, Vauxhall, Peugeot (Rootes), Nissan and Toyota. There are major countervailing forces against concentration (Table 4.3).

The apparent failure of nationalisation and government intervention as strategies to bring the corporate giants under control and make them more sensitive to market needs contrasts sharply with the effectiveness of entrepreneurship, technological change and customer action. Some of the worst abuses of managerial indifference to market and 'owner' needs are seen in public utilities like rail and coal [65] and in the public sector generally. [66] Some of the best illustrations of price competition, growth and customer service occur in markets which saw, until recently, great concentration, e.g. air travel and computers. These successes cannot blind responsible corporations to the imperfections in the economic system identified above. They impose a duty of self-restraint and highlight the dangers to their venture.

Table 4.3 The pressures for competition and fragmentation

Entrepreneurship	Entrepreneurs will spot gaps and exploit market opportunities
Technological change	Large, established firms have a vested interest in existing, potentially obsolete technologies or processes
Limits to management	Increased size makes managing the venture increasingly difficult
Market fragmentation	Greater consumer power and wealth prompts buyers to look for differentiated products
Shift to services	Barriers to entry and exit in services tend to be very low
Customer action	In some sectors, buyers attempt to sustain competition
State intervention	Government may act 'in the public interest' to prevent or break up monopoly
Diseconomies of size	In areas like management, logistics, innovation etc., size produces inefficiencies which undermine the firm's position
Competition	When firms start to make 'monopoly profits' other companies will spot the opportunity and enter the market

The catalogue of products or services which have been introduced into markets despite known or acknowledged dangers is frightening. Each decade sees illustrations of the apparent willingness of firms to put their customers or others at risk; the Pinto in the 1960s, dried baby foods in Africa in the 1970s, Thalidomide in the 1970s and 1980s, IUDs in the 1980s. These were not introduced by small 'cowboy' concerns, even by enterprises desperate for survival, but by large, seemingly successful enterprises. In most cases, concerns were expressed *inside the firm* before the problems emerged in the market. In these cases, internal systems of restraint failed to prevent abuse. Even when 'whistle blowing' occurred, it was often the 'whistle blower' who suffered not those acting irresponsibly.[67,68] The dilemma facing society is whether the costs and benefits of imposing and sustaining an external system of *rules* outweigh the costs and benefits of internal systems of regulation. There is a notion that you cannot 'trust' industry to act ethically therefore it must be closely regulated. This is countered by the argument that these are exceptional cases and *hard cases make bad laws*.

Beside this, only the firm has the knowledge, resources and capacity to regulate its affairs effectively. The hostility to industry prompted by these cases has made business keenly aware of the 'costs' of failure. When even the *Wall Street Journal* asks whether business ethics is an oxymoron, business leaders will get the message. A poor image for business makes it easier for the state to penalise firms through increased taxes, etc., while the standing of executives in the community affects recruitment, retention and job satisfaction. Stipes[69] points out that 'most businessmen depicted in post-1945 serious literature are still characterised as greedy, unethical and immoral (or amoral)'. In *Nice Work*,[70] Lodge gives some flavour of this attitude with the comment by Robyn: 'Oh brave new world, where only the managing directors have jobs'. Surveys in the USA and Europe consistently highlight public concern about the honesty and ethical standards of managers. Even self-interested corporate leaders recognise the dangers to their position in this climate. Self-regulation of the marketing activities of firms is now seen by many corporate leaders as both right and efficient.

> Corporate self regulation . . . will help to limit the arbitrary and oppressive impact of corporate activity.
>
> Simon, J. G. et al. (1972)[71]

Internal systems are being reinforced through sub-committees of Boards often made up largely of independent directors. Perhaps, the most conspicuous failure in these cases lies in the inability of professional institutes or societies to ensure 'ethical' behaviour of their members in firms.

> An allegiance to one's employer should not, as corporations would have us believe, supersede that of an individual to society, or to a higher moral authority.
>
> Nader, R. (1990)[72]

There is a burgeoning debate on the balance between the loyalty of the members of a professional body to their institute or society and their employer when abuses are identified. Intermediaries such as these have an important role in voluntary systems of self-restraint. In the market, they are joined by consumer action groups. This pattern of voluntary action by groups is an integral feature of democratic society.[73] Consumer groups have an important part in the process of monitoring and regulating market behaviour. The value of their contribution relies on a combination of four factors. These are:

1   Recognition of their role by all parties.
2   Freedom and skill to organise.
3   Disclosure of information.
4   Access to media.

In a series of recent cases, corporate leaders have responded quickly – perhaps winning commercial advantage – to concerns raised by consumer groups. 'What is good for an ethical stance, moreover is also in the long run going to be good for the business'.[74] The introduction of the 'dolphin' sticker on tuna cans drove firms persisting with dubious fishing practices out of the market. Innovations like the 'Green Consumer Guide'[75] create new opportunities for competitive advantage through ethical marketing. There is even evidence from market research that consumers take a broad view of ethics, i.e. relating their concerns to wide-ranging views about the firm or its products rather than a narrow – how does it affect me – view. In Table 4.4 some aspects of this are illustrated. Underpinning this pattern of self-regulation and consumer action is the system of legislation, monitoring and enforcement imposed by the state.[76] Ideally this

Table 4.4 Consumer widen the agenda

Consumers' view on business values

Consumers are interested in corporate behaviour even beyond areas that affect them

They do not expect firms to be altruistic but expect to see companies making a contribution to society

Consumers are attracted by companies and products that help them feel good about their values, relieve guilt or make a positive difference on issues of governance or ethics

Consumers take a wide view of the firm's behaviour. They take into account environmental performance and community involvement when making purchase decisions as well as specific product-related issues

Companies can gain a competitive advantage by being seen as innovative in areas like the environment, fair trading, employee welfare, community involvement and ethical marketing

Dragon International, quoted in Mazur, L. (1991)[77]

operates on minimax criteria. These are the minimum of redundancy in processes or bureaucracy and the maximum of responsiveness or action against transgressors.[78] Smith[79] provides an excellent analysis of the debate on the alternatives of condign, compensatory and conditioned power as the alternative approaches to enforcement. There is a case for introducing aspects of the market into this process. The use of private contractors in areas like illegal parking of cars in the UK suggests that although there is scope for using the private sector to enforce legislation in even more complex areas it requires codification of standards and careful monitoring.

The means employed by firms to communicate with, reach and influence markets are the subject of considerable criticism (Table 4.5).

Table 4.5 Marketing practices and social criticisms

Values	Firms undermine the social values of society by promoting consumption rather than restraint and self-interest rather than community needs
Targets	Companies try to reach groups who are unable to exercise proper judgements, e.g. the young
Misrepresentation	Communications distort or misinform, e.g. hearing aid advertisements which wrongly imply that hearing is restored
Exclusion	Some groups are excluded from 'acceptable' images of society, e.g. black or physically disabled
Distortion	Advertisements exploit or encourage exploitation of groups, e.g. women
Danger	Some products, e.g. cigarettes, are dangerous and should not be promoted
Offence	Some forms of marketing offend against wider concerns from pyramid letters to the Benetton Aids advertisement

Together, these raise a series of dilemmas for those interested in the working of markets. In some cases, personal or corporate restraint plays a part in regulating behaviour. Some media will not accept certain types of advertising, e.g. the *Readers Digest* embargo on cigarettes. Elsewhere voluntary codes operate within industries to establish and maintain certain standards.[80] Pressure groups may intervene to criticise particular promotions or patterns of behaviour. Elsewhere, the state imposes requirements or standards. These provide the structure of influence and system of rules within which the firm must operate. The balance of debate lies between those who argue that the market provides sufficient implicit or explicit restraints on abuse or that the community is obliged to protect itself through intervention.[81] Gist[82] argues that as consumers 'we vote by purchasing things we wish to encourage in institutions we wish to encourage. We vote by not buying things we wish to discourage'. This works best in the most free markets. Its fundamental flaw lies in the lack of an effective opposition in many cases. The counter-case suggests that articulate consumers and successful pressure groups require the support of 'an effective opposition', 'policeforce', or 'fire-fighter' to be effective.

CONCLUSION

Business ethics are not a distinct and separate aspect of corporate life. They permeate all aspects of the firm, its operations and links with the community. In his analysis of ethical decision making, Michael Rion[83] identifies a series of questions which face managers as they deal with issues of production, purchasing, corporate affairs personnel, and investment. He identifies six questions which can usefully guide managers trying to identify ethical issues and dilemmas. These are:

Question	Stage
Why is this bothering me?	The warning signs of problems
Who else matters?	Awareness of others
Is it *my* problem?	Recognition of responsibility
What is the *ethical* concern?	Acknowledge implications
What do others think?	Learning
Am I being true to myself?	Recognise the importance of integrity

These questions are relevant to all aspects of the firms' works and the dilemmas faced by all managers.

QUESTIONS

1 Using secondary sources identify the ways in which technological change has affected either a specific industry or named community. List ways in which businesses can help people and communities cope with change.

2 Williams[84] argues that 'The identification of the technical "can" with the moral should or the blotting out of the former with questions about the latter is endemic in our culture.' What are the implications of this statement and how can ethicists help communities and firms to cope with these issues?

3 Different approaches to relocation can affect the ways in which people cope with change. Compare the ways in which patterns of employment and social arrangement will shape the way groups in the US and Europe cope with change.

4 Was the search for a New Jerusalem realistic or appropriate for a Britain emerging from a world war?

5 What can the socially responsible manager learn from Niccolo Machiavelli's comments about the management of change?

6 Discuss the relevance of either (a) Locke's concept of natural rights or (b) the utilitarian principles of the 'greatest good to the greatest number', to the debate on minimising the effects of technological change on job prospects.

7 Is there a moral justification for restrictions on entry to a profession? Analyse this in terms of:
   (a) a situation in which there may be a direct . . . competence or safety reason, e.g. medicine;
   (b) a situation in which there may be no direct . . . competence or safety reason, e.g. teaching business at university.

8 To what extent are the restrictions of membership imposed by a profession like accountancy a legitimate attempt to maintain standards or a systematic effort to restrict trade? Justify your answer in terms of a specific professional body and its codes of practice.

9 'Perhaps the most powerful myth about corporations is that they are ultimately held accountable by the marketplace.' Why is it argued that market accountability is a myth? If this comment is valid, what are the implications for public policy?

10 Define

   (a) Innovation
   (b) Protestant ethic
   (c) Luddites
   (d) The Peace Dividend
   (e) Prudential obligation
   (f) The reserve pool of Labour
   (g) Job clubs
   (h) Fair rates
   (i) Monopoly
   (j) Pareto's Law

REFERENCES

1. Gordon Gekko, a character in the film *Wall Street*, Oliver Stone dir., Twentieth Century Fox (1987).
2. Smith, A. *The Wealth of Nations* (1776).
3. Schein, E. 'The Problem of Moral Education for the Business Manager' *Industrial Management Review*, vol. 8 (1966) pp. 3–14.
4. Malachowski, A. 'Business Ethics 1980–2000: An Interim Forecast' *Managerial Auditing Journal*, vol. 5, no. 2, pp. 22–7.

5. HMSO *Realising the potential*, cmnd 2250, London (1993).
6. Russell, P. and Saad, K. N. and Ericksm, T. J. *Third Generation R & D*, Boston, Harvard Business School Press (1991).
7. James, S. and Parker, R. *A Dictionary of Quotatations*, London, Routledge (1989).
8. Deane, P. *The First Industrial Revolution*, Oxford, Oxford University Press (1968).
9. Schumpeter, J. *Capitalism, Socialism and Democracy*, New York, Harper and Row (1942).
10. Womack, J. P., Jones, D. T. and Roos, D. *The Machine that Changed the World*, New York, Macmillan (1990).
11. Sawyer, L. *The Impact of New Technologies on Female Employment in Retailing*, unpublished PH.D. thesis, University of Stirling (1987).
12. Smith, K. *The British Economic Crisis*, Harmondsworth, Penguin (1986).
13. Frye, M. *Inaugural Address to the Royal Society for the Encouragement of Arts, Manufactures and Commerce*, vol. CXL, December (1991).
14. Donaldson, J. *Key Issues in Business Ethics*, London, Academic Press (1989).
15. Havel, V. *Living in Truth*, London, Faber and Faber (1985).
16. Suggate, A. M. *Personal Responsibility: Hayek and Havel in a Christian Perspective*, unpublished Mimeo (1991).
17. Williams, R. 'The Ethics of SDI', in Bauckham, R. J. and Elford, R. J. (eds) *The Nuclear Weapons Debate: Theological and Ethical Issues*, London, SCM Press (1989).
18. Crowley, B. L. *The Self, the Individual and the Community*, Oxford, Clarendon Press (1987).
19. Williams, R., ibid.
20. Danley, J. R. 'Polestar Refined: Business Ethics and Political Economy' *Journal of Business Ethics*, vol. 10 (1991) pp. 915–33.
21. Barnett, C. *The Audit of War: The Illusion and Reality of Britain as a Great Nation*, London, Macmillan (1986).
22. Barnett, C. ibid.
23. Machiavelli, N. *The Prince*, London, Edition (1981).
24. Smith, D. 'Strategic Management in the Business Environment: What Lies Beyond the Rhetoric of Greening?' *Business Strategy and the Environment*, vol. 1, no. 1, Spring (1992).
25. Based on Barnett, C., ibid.
26. McKendall, M. 'The Tyranny of Change: Organisational Development Revisited' *Journal of Business Ethics*, vol. 12, no. 2, February (1993) pp. 93–104.
27. Committee on the Woollen Trade (1806), quoted in Thompson, E. P. *The Making of the English Working Class*, Harmondsworth, Penguin (1968).
28. Raphael, D. D. *Problems of Political Philosophy*, London, Macmillan (1982).
29. Task Force on Urban and Business Regeneration *Initiatives Beyond Charity*, London, Confederation of British Industry (1988).
30. Plamenatz, J. *Man and Society*, Oxford, Oxford University Press (1963).
31. Aron, R. *18 Lectures on Industrial Society*, London, Weidenfeld and Nicolson (1967).
32. Carley, M. *Housing and Neighbourhood Renewal*, London, Policy Studies Institute (1992).
33. Schorr, L. B. *Within Our Reach: Breaking the Cycle of Disadvantage*, New Jersey, Doubleday (1988).
34. Spencer, L. 'Bridging the Unemployment Gap Between Black and White People in Britain' *Journal of RSA*, March (1988).
35. Locke, J. *Second Treatise of Government* (1821).
36. Hay, R. D., Grey, E. R. and Smith, P. H. *Business and Society: Perspectives on Ethics and Social Responsibility*, Cincinatti, South Western (1989).
37. Mill, J. S. *Principles of Political Economy*, London, Longman (1865).
38. Shaw, W. H. *Business Ethics*, London, Wadsworth (1992).
39. Spencer, L., ibid.
40. Roy, D. 'Quota Restrictions and Goldbricking in a Machine Shop', *American Journal of Sociology*, vol. 57 (1952) pp. 427–42.
41. Sykes, C. J. *Profscam*, New York, St Martin's Press (1990).
42. Mill, J. S., ibid.
43. Sayles, L. R. *The Behaviour of Industrial Work Groups*, New York, Wiley (1958).

44. Handy, C. *Understanding Organisations*, Harmondsworth, Penguin (1985).
45. Simon, H. A. 'A Behavioural Model of Rational Choice' *Quarterly Journal of Economics*, 69 (1955) pp. 00-118.
46. Cyert, R. and March, J. *A Behavioural Theory of the Firm*, Englewood, Cliffs., New Jersey, Prentice Hall (1963).
47. Chandler, A. D. *The Visible Hand: The Managerial Revolution in American Business*, Cambridge, Harvard University Press (1977).
48. Mintzberg, H. 'Who Should Control the Corporation?' *California Management Review*, vol. 23 (1984) pp. 43–55.
49. Epstein, E. J. *Who Owns the Corporation? Management vs Shareholders*, New York, Priority Press (1986).
50. Hanley, K. 'Hostile Takeovers and Methods of Defense: A Stakeholder Analysis' *Journal of Business Education*, vol. 11, no. 12 (1992) p. 895–914.
51. Freedman, R. *Strategic Management: A Stakeholder Approach*, MA., Pitman (1981).
52. Donaldson, J., ibid.
53. Lease, R. H. 'The Nature of the Firm' *Economica*, new series, November (1936) pp. 384–405.
54. Hurst, J. W. *The Legitimacy of the Business Corporation in the Law of the United States 1780-1970*, Charlotsville, University of Virginia Press (1970).
55. Kefauver, E. *In a Few Hands*, Harmondsworth, Penguin (1965).
56. Porter, M. *The Competitive Advantage of Nations*, New York, The Free Press (1991).
57. Aslund, A. *Gorbachev's Struggle for Economic Reform*, New York, Cornell University Press (1989).
58. Deyo, F. C. *The Political Economy of the New Asian Industrialisation*, New York, Cornell University Press (1989).
59. Robinson, J. *The Economics of Imperfect Competition*, Cambridge, Cambridge University Press (1933).
60. Cannon, T. *Advertising: The Economic Implications*, London, Blackie (1976).
61. Katz, D. and Kahn, R. *The Social Psychology of Organisations*, New York, Wiley (1965).
62. Galbraith, J. K. *American Capitalism: The Concept of Countervailing Power*, Harmondsworth, Penguin (1963).
63. Monks, R. A. and Minow, N. *Power and Accountability*, Glasgow, Harper Collins (1991).
64. Galbraith, J. K. *The New Industrial State*, Harmondsworth, Penguin (1974).
65. Hodgson, G. *The Democratic Economy*, Harmondsworth, Penguin (1984).
66. Osborne, D. and Goebler, T. *Reinventing Government*, Harmondsworth, Plume (1993).
67. Callaham, E. and Collins, J. W. 'Employee Attitudes Towards Whistleblowing, Management and Public Policy Implications' *Journal of Business Ethics*, vol. 11, no. 12, December (1992) pp. 937–48.
68. Victor, B. Trevino, L. K. and Shapiro, D. L. 'Peer Reporting of Unethical Behaviour' vol. 12, no. 4 (1993) pp. 253–64.
69. Stipes, E. *The Businessman in American Literature*, Athens, Geo., University of Georgia Press (1982).
70. Lodge, D. *Nice Work*, Harmondsworth, Penguin (1988).
71. Simon, J. G., Powers, C. W. and Gunneman, J. P. *The Ethical Investor: Universities and Corporate Responsibility*, New Haven, Yale University Press (1972).
72. Nader, R. quoted in Smith, N. C. *Morality and the Market*, London, Routledge (1990).
73. De Tocqueville, D. *Democracy in America* (1834).
74. Mazur, L. 'Morality Marketing' *Marketing Business*, no. 3, September (1991) pp. 32–5.
75. Elkington, J. and Hailes, J. *The Green Consumer*, London, Gollancz (1987).
76. Wright, E. 'Liability and Responsibility: 1985 and 1992 EC Directives' *British Food Journal*, vol. 95, no. 1 (1993) pp. 26–32.
77. Mazur, L., ibid.
78. Hemphill, T. A. 'Self-regulating Industry Behaviour' *Journal of Business Education*, vol. 11, no. 12 (1992) pp. 915–20.
79. Smith, N. C., ibid.
80. O'Boyle, E. J. and Dawson, L. E. 'The American Marketing Association Code of Ethics: Instructions for Marketers' *Journal of Business Education*, vol. 11, no. 12, December (1992) pp. 921–30.
81. Clinard, M. B., Yaeger, P. C., Bussette, J., Petrashek, D. and Havies, E. *Illegal Corporate Behaviour*, National Institute of Law Enforcement and Criminal Justice, Washington DC (1979).

82. Gist, R. R. *Marketing and Society: A Conceptual Introduction*, New York, Rinehart and Winston (1971).
83. Rion, M. *The Responsible Manager*, London, Harper Collins (1986).
84. Williams, R., ibid.

CHAPTER 5

Stewardship and finance

STEWARDSHIP

A series of events over the last decade served to place the issue of stewardship at the centre of the policy agenda. Proper stewardship is a responsibility placed explicitly on all those responsible for the goods or funds of others. In effect the board serves as 'a guardian of assets'.[1] It imposes a duty to exercise due diligence, i.e. care, rigour and attention, in the management and disposal of all those assets for which the officer is given responsibility. Many of the cases which hit the headlines illustrated the scope which existed for those managing corporate resources to deploy them for their personal benefit. In Britain Barlow Clowes, Maxwell International, Guinness, the Lloyds Names were among the most blatant cases. These are not new issues. Chaucer's Reeve provides a model.

> Ther koude no man bringe hym in arrerage.
> Ther nas bailiff, ne herde, nor oother hyne,
> That he ne knew his slieghte and his covyne
>
> . . .
>
> He koude bettre than his lord purchace.
> Ful riche he was astored prively,
> His lord wel koude he plesen subtilly
> To yeve and lene him of his owene good
> An have a thank, and yet a cote and hood

Chaucer: Prologue

His cunning (sleighte) and fraud (covyne) or his private wealth (riche) highlights issue which recur more recently in such familiar characters as Uriah Heep. He added a sense of hypocrisy ('umble) while reinforcing an overall image which has echoes today.

> An invitation arrives 'to the inaugural luncheon in the Mayfair Business Luncheon Series . . . the guest speaker will be Ernest Saunders . . . any tips on a) avoiding the fraud squad

Bussman, T.: Zeitgeist[2]

The Challenge

The proliferation of recent cases seems to highlight more widespread collapse of the notion of responsible stewardship which extends from sweetheart deals, which covered every part of the private life of corporate executives from homes to holidays, to remuneration packages, which take little note of either competitive conditions or corporate performance. Elsewhere, the notion of abuse of trust recurred. In the USA, the Savings and Loan scandals threatened the stability of the Bush administration[3] while Fred Wang's pay-offs, James Stewarts's travel and the wage deals of corporate leaders provoked a host of questions from workers, customers and shareholders.[4] The Anglo-Saxon world is not alone. Lockheed and Nomura in Japan, Michelin and Perrier in France and Olivetti in Italy have been affected by intense debates about the stewardship of corporate resources.

Criticism of the present approach to stewardship has come from the reformist left, those within firms and related agencies and the radical right. The reformers argue for a reform of company law allied to a strengthening of the supervisory agencies such as the Securities and Exchange Commission in the USA and the Department of Trade and Industry in Britain. Stakeholders within firms are demanding a clearer say based on better information about policies and rewards. The radical right argue that imperfections in markets allied to external restraints on entry and exit create an environment for abuse.[5] The recommendations of the Social Security Committee of the House of Commons on *The Operation of Pension Funds*[6] provide a clear exposition of the type of argument being put forward for legislative intervention. The work of PRO-NED in the UK illustrates some of the internal reforms of company practice which are deemed necessary by those seeking internal reform. The US, United Shareholders Association[7] is an increasingly powerful voice for those who want to 're-assert that directors of companies are fiduciaries representing the interests of the owners'.[8]

The advocates of legislative action and strengthened statutory agencies highlight the failures of the present voluntary systems of supervision and control. These 'mechanisms to constrain behaviour'[9] operate to control the interest groups while asserting the wider public or community interest in responsible stewardship. This is especially true given the increasing distance between the point of ownership and the point of control. In many British and US firms the genuine 'point of ownership' is the subscriber to a pension scheme or financier of institutional investors. He or she can only exercise ownership power through a long line of trustees, investment advisors, fund managers and corporate officers. At this distance, it is hard for some to see how genuine 'ownership' can be exercised without the support of the state. The 'legitimacy' of state intervention is endorsed by the costs to the Exchequer of the tax relief on pension schemes (Table 5.1). One witness to the Social Security Committee commented that 'the current legal framework does not even provide a safeguard to revenues which might rightly accrue to the Revenue'.[10]

This committee endorses the findings of a series of enquiries into governance, investor rights[11] and the workings of the financial sector[12] that intervention by the state is an integral and increasingly important element in ensuring sound stewardship of corporate assets.

Table 5.1 Occupational pension schemes: cost of tax relief in 1991/2

Relief for	Amounts £ million
Employee contributions	2,200
Employer contributions	3,400
Investment income of funds	7,000
Lump sum payments from unfunded schemes	350
Less tax liable on:	
Pension payments	3,500
Refunds by funds to employers in connection with pensions fund surpluses	400
Total (to nearest £100 million)	9,100

Source: Social Security Committee (1992)[13]

Critics of this approach[14] highlight:

- the high costs of legislative reform and intervention;
- the technical difficulties;
- the scope for voluntary control and internal reform.

Internal and voluntary reform is the key to sound stewardship in the eyes of many of those who acknowledge the problems.[15] They see government action as likely to impose high costs on all – the responsible and the irresponsible – while addressing the wrong problems in a cumbersome way. In the UK, the creation of PRO-NED under the sponsorship of the Bank of England, British Institute of Managers, Confederation of British Industry and others highlighted the needed for internal, self-supervision through non-executive directors.[16] In the USA, the recommendations of the Business Roundtable[17] and in Europe the Fifth Directive and the European Company Statute mirror many of the same concerns while drawing broadly similar conclusions.

They concentrate their attention on establishing internal systems and voluntary codes of practice to ensure that directors – in particular – exercise the duties placed upon them. These duties combine those of an executive with management

Fig. 5.1 Cynicism about enforcement of standards
Source: Alex II – Magnum Force, by Charles Peattie and Russell Taylor.

responsibility and a trustee of assets. This means that directors are expected to act:

- in loyalty and good faith in performing duties
- with skill and care in managing assets

and that as trustees

- they cannot profit from their position of trust.

Their duties are to the firm. This includes an obligation to act within the law. The reform proposals in Britain and Europe have developed along broadly common lines. They emphasise:

Direction	Clearer requirements and tighter controls of top management notably the CEOs
	Better access for shareholders to senior management especially before major resource disposal or acquisition decisions
	Shareholders to use their 'ownership' power where necessary
Representation	More 'shareholder' directors or clearer voice in Board level appointments
	Better organised and more full representation of shareholders including, but not only, institutions
Information	Better information for shareholders
	Identify and communicate local, national and international interests
Monitor and control	More explicit role(s) for independent directors
	More use of 'independent' committees, e.g. audit and remuneration
Investigation	Closer but more strategic scrutiny by government agencies
	Systems of legislative compliance under closer scrutiny
Other	More emphasis on adding value to shareholder assets rather than short-termism

There is widespread acceptance among shareholders of the proposition that excessive pressure for external control and governance can inhibit effective management.[18] There is, however, less acceptance among top management that shareholders have title and that in a system of private enterprise their rights come before those of the paid executives.

> Excessive corporate governance . . . can also chill innovation and risk taking . . . Corporate governance by referendum instead of by board of directors has all the same drawbacks as federal governance by referendum instead of by Congress.
>
> The Business Roundtable[19]

Audit plays a crucial role in sustaining this balance between the needs of managers to *get on with the job* and the rights of shareholders to see *just what job is being done.*[20] The spate of recent frauds allied to the apparent failure of current auditing arrangements to flag the problems has provoked a widespread debate on current arrangements.[21] These events have prompted a large-scale questioning of the assumption that the external auditor's role is to keep shareholders properly informed about the 'true' state of the company finances and the quality of stewardship exercised by directors.[22] In law, this role is far more closely defined and more restricted. Even this more restricted role is influenced by the trading relations that develop between the auditors, accountants and their clients or employers.[23]

> The accountant in industry is in a Catch 22 situation. Either he says nothing and compromises himself, or he puts his livelihood at stake . . . Even if he is proved to be right, he is branded as a trouble maker.
>
> Lindsay, D.[24]

Internal audit committees have grown in importance in part as a means of providing close but non-intrusive scrutiny and partly as a means of ensure proper independent examination through the independent directors.

Chandler[25] has highlighted the importance of the creation of new structures 'to make possible continuing effective mobilisation of resources to meet both changing short term market demands and long term market needs'. The era of managerialism was part of this process but not the final stage. There is every indication that the current stage in the evolution of the market economy will call for the creation of new structures if mangers are to work effectively, opportunities are to be developed, community needs satisfied and ownership rights respected. Failure, for example, to respect the latter's rights will strip industry of a primary source of support and a major element in its legitimacy.

PROFITS AND PAY

The infamous 'fat cats' visit by President Bush to Japan, the dramatic increases in salaries for directors of newly privatised companies in Britain, headings in the *Financial Times* the *Wall Street Journal*, etc., combine to highlight concerns about systems for establishing levels of pay in industry (Figure 5.2).

Lies, Damn Lies and Directors' Salaries

Fig. 5.2 The public challenge
Headline, *Financial Times*, April 29, 1992

The debate on compensation is driven by a number of forces. These include:

- The apparent injustices in the process of determining levels of pay;
- The latitude allowed directors and other institutional or corporate leaders;
- The lack of a clear relationship between organisational performance and pay;
- The proliferation of 'packages' or hidden supplements;
- The weakness of the systems of supervision.

The combination of the factors prompts Crystal[26] first to ask 'Is the system [of top management remuneration] rotten around the core or is it rotten to the core?' and eventually conclude 'I'll take choice B'.

These are not issues confined to the private sector although there is a tendency to focus attention on business leaders. The contrasts in the public sector can be even more stark. It is, for example, possible to identify vice-chancellors whose 'packages' would match or exceed those of industrialists. Often, the contrast between the deals offered to the head of a university and wages of the worst paid

Table 5.2 The vice-chancellor and the porter

	Vice-chancellor	Porter
Salary	Between £80,000 and £100,000+ p.a.	Less than £3.50 per hour
Term	To retirement at 67	One month's notice
Perks	Generous salary-based pension	Occupational pension
	Chauffeur driven car	Uniform
	Travel and entertainment expenses	
	House, often large landed property	
	Full maintenance and service on house	
	Probability of knighthood and other honours	
	Board position with pay on university companies	
	Others as negotiated	
	No public scrutiny of terms and conditions	

Based on large civic university

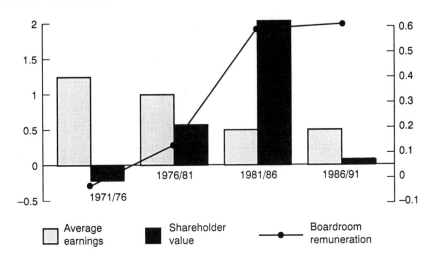

Fig. 5.3 Boardroom remuneration and shareholder value in the UK (per cent changes)
Source: Hay Management Consultants, 1991[27]

staff is far more stark than those seen in industry (Table 5.2). The same comments can be made about senior civil servants and leaders of public agencies.

The public disclosure of senior executive remuneration allied to disappointing performance of many firms in the USA and the UK has placed top managers' salaries at the centre of the debate on corporate governance (Figure 5.3).

The consistent increases in payments to directors while the rate of growth in average earning has tended to decline and shareholder value has fluctuated has provoked criticism of the levels of pay and the means to establish levels. Greater awareness of the salary supplements to senior executives have increased this concern. The conventional mechanisms for setting wages in industry and their assumed justification may not be working in the case of top management (Table 5.3).

Table 5.3 Setting remuneration: forms and justifications

Form	Justification
Simple comparisons	A level is set based on information about rates elsewhere – remuneration seeks equity while it minimises losses to firms paying more
Job analysis	The work is analysed and remuneration is set based on 'comparing like with like'[28] with fairness as the key justification
Negotiated wages	Directly or through a third party is determined through negotiation with the justification based on a contract
Administered systems	An 'external' agency, e.g. government creates a formal procedure under which acceptable levels of remuneration are determined

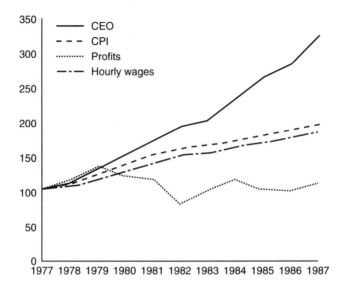

Fig. 5.4 CEO compensation rate compared with inflation wage and profit rates, 1977–1987 (1977=100)[29]
Source: Sibson & Co.

In the USA, concern about the levels of remuneration, the add-ons and sweeteners has provoked demands for better information, external intervention, even the suggestion that top salaries should be based on a government formula, e.g. not more than 22 times that of the lowest paid employee. There is concern in many countries that top management are abusing their positions of trust and using their power to gain private benefit from their role as trustees of corporate resources (Figure 5.4 and Table 5.4).

Information and external scrutiny are seen as vital elements in any attempt

Table 5.4 Leading causes of concern in the top management package

Issue	Concern
Salary	Excessive absolute levels
	Poor or no link with performance
Term	Overlong service contracts or other means of ensuring security at the expense of enterprise
	Golden parachutes or other ways to avoid cost of failure
Perks	Golden hellos and handcuffs or other means of adding to the package
	Undeclared stock options
	Overgenerous allowances for cars, medicare, etc.
	Medical care
	Pre-emptive rights
	Private sweeteners, e.g. cars for other family members, houses, options to buy company property, free holidays, etc.

Table 5.5 Percentage of companies reporting committees

	1992 UK (N=300)	1989 US[1] (N=805)
Audit	54	97
Compensation	74	82
Executive	5	71
Nominating	3	49
Finance	10	27
Pension/benefits	NA	18
Stock options	74[2]	13
Public policy	2	11
Planning	–	7
Contributions	–	3

1. *Source*: Demb, A. and Neubauer, F. (1993)[30]
2. Covered by compensation committee.

to overcome the appearance or reality of abuse. Remuneration committees with a majority of independent directors is accepted increasingly as a key feature of any attempt to establish legitimacy and proper accountability for the current system. Table 5.5 indicates the extent of the committee structure which has developed in US and UK companies to scrutinise performance. These are supported by guidelines which are increasingly explicit. Their legitimacy is sustained by a mixture of contract and conditioned power.

> Corporate managements . . . are constrained to work within a framework of surrounding conceptions which in time impose themselves
>
> Berle, A. E. (1954)[31]

The terms and conditions of a remuneration committee will usually include:

- Establishing the corporate policy on salaries
- Tailoring the individual packages to match the culture, management style and competitive environment
- Making judgements on specific cases taking into account performance
- Reporting to shareholders on its membership and practice.

These are fully spelled out in Appendix C: PRO-NED on page 159. This highlights the role remuneration plays in balancing rights and responsibilities[32] while wedding legitimacy to performance.[33] There is an implicit 'ethical contract' by management to establish and maintain systems which link their role as trustees with their needs as executives (Figure 5.5).

The ethical contract is closely linked to the more traditional, operational contracts between the executive and the other stakeholders in the venture. The legitimacy of the leadership role within the firm is sustained by the interaction

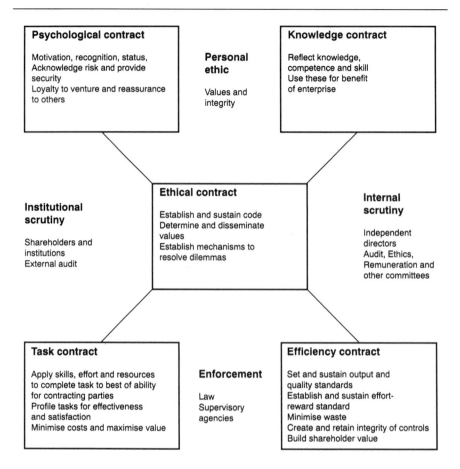

Fig. 5.5 The contracts between directors and other stakeholders
Source: Based on Gowler, D. 1974[34] and Mumford, E. 1972[35]

of these 'relationships.'[36] External legitimacy is sustained and controlled by the developing and constraining roles of the personal ethic of individuals and the internal and external systems of scrutiny, each of which is reinforced by mechanisms for enforcement. Together, these underpin the 'corporate contract' between the employee and the firm.

INVESTMENT AND ALLOCATION

The 'private' ethics of managers which affect their own position provoke some of the most heated outbursts from shareholders and commentators (Figure 5.6). They may, however, have a less wide ranging effect than the criteria employed to make more conventional investment and allocation decisions. The dilemmas faced by managers are genuine and often have massive implications. They can

Fig. 5.6 Images of leadership

result from changes in the political, economic, technological or commercial environment. The choices made can affect entire communities. The issues raised recently by leading industrialists include:

- Do the developments in South Africa justify new investment by IBM?
- Should Unilever close vegetable oils processing plants in Britain to sustain newly acquired but more inefficient plants in the former East Germany?
- Should Bank of America withdraw its finance for Union Carbide over Bhopal, placing the entire enterprise at risk?
- Should a bank, like the Co-Operative Bank, close accounts because it does not approve of the perfectly legal activities of a client?

In each case, management can make decisions which can be justified in terms of most moral codes. Kant's[37] guiding principles of 'good will' and 'universalisability', i.e. *I am willing for anyone faced with the same choice to adopt the same rule*, can be applied to the contradictory outcomes.[38] Hence, the Chairman of Unilever, acting with *good will* could subscribe with equal justice to both proposition A and proposition B.

Proposition A
'Given the circumstances in Central Europe – the traumatic changes and harsh economic circumstances – I feel I should deploy my new investments in vegetable fats processing into Eastern Germany. I believe it is morally right for anyone facing this choice to make the same decision. If we all do it, the economy will pick up and we will earn good returns.'

Proposition B
'Despite the obvious needs in Central Europe my first loyalty is to my current employees and existing markets. The difficulties in Eastern Germany mean

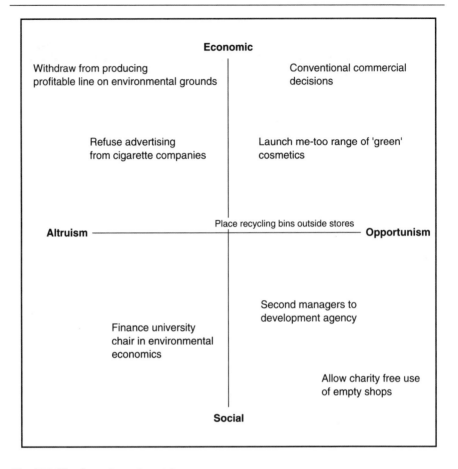

Fig. 5.7 The investment matrix

that government should take the lead and provide any funds needed for investment in this region. If we industrialists persuade governments, they might act.'

Each proposition is reasonable and reflects the type of issue faced by corporate leaders. These and related issues can be analysed in terms of the investment matrix (Figure 5.7).

Investment and allocation decisions are subject to some generally agreed constraints. At the most basic, they should operate within prevailing laws and do no harm to others. The firm or its executives that use a stratagem in order to, say, avoid compliance with laws passed by a properly constituted legal authority know they are engaged in wrong doing. Their economic functions do not give them extra-legal rights. Harming others is rather more difficult. If society's *rules* preclude investment in certain activities, e.g. drug dealing, no corporate rights

Index value of funds

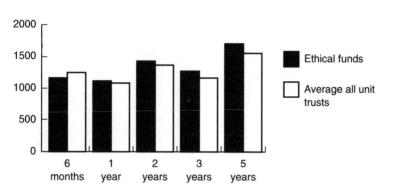

Fig. 5.8 Values of ethical funds versus average of all unit trusts
Source: Which, July 1993. Figure 5.8 shows that ethical funds perform at least as well as unit trusts in general.
The information shows that it is only in the first six months that ethical funds perform worse than the average of
all unit trusts. After that, ethical funds consistently outperform the average of all unit trusts.

have precedence. DeLorean faced this when his drug dealings were exposed. Other
investments can involve decisions which are less clear cut or on which society
has not ruled.[39] Cigarette, defence or investors in particular foreign regimes face
these problems.

The growth of 'ethical investment' has provided an option for those investors
wishing to exercise certain choices to express their wishes (Figure 5.8). Other
investors look to the profile of corporate activities. On this basis they make private
choices about the direction of their expenditure. Some unions, certain public
authorities, several pension funds and many individuals withdrew their money
from firms investing in South Africa or corporations making products which were
unacceptable. Most would accept the Kant's premise that they were acting
'rationally', 'in good faith' and would accept all others applying the same rule.[40]
This notion of choice based on information is taken even further by the decision
of enterprises like the Co-Operative Bank to publicise their investment policies
(Figure 5.9).

In part, this is an attempt to win competitive advantage with certain groups
by highlighting lending policies. The choice and restraint in these terms is
consistent with the notion of a business contract with society. Other firms will
seek to minimise external, state intervention by choosing strategies which
minimise the pressure for intervention. This can be wholly consistent with the
notion that the best long-term interests of the firm lay in the minimum of political
involvement. Avoiding certain investments, choosing others or allocating resources to achieve wider goals can wed Jacoby's Social Environment Model[41] to
Mises's[42] belief in minimum intervention. The former recognises that 'corporate
behaviour responds to political as well as market forces' while the latter highlights
the 'freedom and liberty' implicit in the market economy.

This is the pony

The Watsons bought

Using money they kept
in their bank

Who'd lent their
money

To a company that tests

The cosmetics it makes

On animals.

It happens.
But not at the Co-operative Bank.
Our customers know there are some things we
will never invest in.
Such as companies that test the cosmetics they
make on animals.
Our policy is to lend only to companies
we believe to be as sound ethically as they are
financially.
Of course, we still provide all the normal
services you'd expect from a clearing bank with
assets of £2.5 billion, 5,000 'Link' cash machines
and a full telephone banking service.
The difference is that along with financial
peace of mind our customers receive one other
important benefit.
More peace of mind.

The CO-OPERATIVE BANK

FOR MORE INFORMATION CALL 0145 414 414, OR WRITE TO DEPT IN, THE CO-OPERATIVE BANK PLC, FREEPOST, SKELMERSDALE, LANCS, WN8 6BR.

Fig. 5.9 The Co-Operative Bank's lending policy

THE CHALLENGE TO THE MULTINATIONAL

Rights we take for granted are sometimes trampled abroad. Child labour plagues Central America. . . . In other countries the rights to minimal education, free speech, basic nutrition, and freedom from torture are little more than dreams. **What obligations do multinational corporations have in such contexts?**

Donaldson, T. 1991[43]

It would be easy to add other abuses to Donaldson's catalogue. They might include exploitation of minorities, lack of health and safety legislation. Industry is not only a passive partner. Often, the international firm takes the lead in behaviour which would be unacceptable at home. Some of the most public criticisms are listed in Table 5.6.

The attempt to address these issues faces a series of new questions. They range from questions about the transferability of one moral code to another culture or community, to the claim that firms shift production to exploit loopholes in legislation.

Wages in Mexico and the Caribbean are often only an eighth of southern rates . . . one reason why southern congressmen have led the fight against a North American Free-Trade area.

Economist, 2 May 1992

Table 5.6 The accusations against international business

The role of business

Passive (ignores or complies with)	Active (takes part in)
Attacks on human rights	Breaking external sanctions, e.g. Rhodesia, Libya
Poor nutrition	Boycotts, e.g. Arab boycott of Israel
Child labour	Environmental dumping, e.g. chemicals in Nigeria
Discrimination	Exploiting natural resources, e.g. rain forests
State violence	Blacklists, e.g. trades unionists in Latin America
Lack of education	Exploitation of labour
Corruption	Sale of dangerous products
Militarism	Exploiting customer ignorance, e.g. Nestlé's infant foods
Persecution	Bribery and corruption, e.g. Lockheed
Poor health care	Active discrimination, e.g. against Catholics in Northern Ireland
Abuse of the environment	Dumping Undermining government: ITT in Chile Monopoly or trust building

The injunction that *when in Rome do as the Romans* gains added weight when fear of cultural imperialism stands alongside the constant accusation of economic imperialism laid against the international firm. The extent of the issue has provoked government action such as the US Foreign Corrupt Practices Act as well as efforts to develop codes of international practices between and within firms.[44]

Much of the debate centres on the distinction between two distinct patterns of behaviour:

- the response of firms to 'established practice' in local markets;
- the attempts by firms to introduce behaviour to benefit themselves.

In essence, a distinction is made between the firm that conforms to a local tradition of baksheesh[45] and one that attempts to bribe its way to success despite local injunctions. The Friedmanite reliance on *rules* has limited value as managers are operating within several rule structures.[46] These will include the rules of the 'home' country, those of the 'host' market and any accepted international regulations, e.g. UN Charter of Human Rights.

Even the notion of profit maximisation can have a different meaning to a Japanese and a USA businessperson.[47] This increases the obligation on the individual or the enterprise to establish an internal sustainable, externally justifiable code of ethics and practice. In effect, the 'business contract' is spelt out by the party best able to understand, outline and sustain its terms and conditions. The underlying principle was spelt out by Choicer[48] when he said that the corn merchant arriving at the famine-stricken town is obliged to inform his customers that other merchants are following him. It is a proposition repeated by *Advertising Age* when it points out that 'the absence of sophisticated regulatory mechanisms in the Third World should not be misconstrued as an open invitation to free-wheeling marketing behaviour'.[49] Donaldson[50] tackles the problem of arriving at the contract where the regulator or partner is unable or unwilling to define his or her terms by distinguishing between minimum and maximum rights, duties or terms. The list of 'fundamental international rights' might include:

1 Freedom of physical movement
2 Ownership of property
3 Freedom from torture
4 A fair trial
5 Non-discriminatory treatment
6 Physical security
7 Freedom of speech and association
8 Minimal education
9 Political participation
10 Subsistence

These fundamental rights impose on firms a duty to refrain from behaviour which deprives individuals or communities of their rights. There is, however, not always a duty to take action outside their immediate sphere of operations to assert these rights. Donaldson suggests that international firms always have a duty to avoid depriving individuals or groups of their rights but never have a duty to aid the deprived from winning their rights.

This approach is open to criticism[51] because it fails to draw out the interdependence between the different actions nor does it address all the dilemmas created by local government action. A firm in South Africa can avoid depriving its workers of their right to non-discriminatory treatment by employing blacks on the same terms and conditions as whites. Their continued investment in South Africa might deprive others in South Africa of their rights.[52] Another predicament faces the firm trading against a background of state discrimination to address social problems. In Malaysia, the government expects banks to discriminate in favour of lending to Bumiputra-owned businesses – at the expense of Chinese-owned ventures. Is it acceptable for international banks to support these policies? There are two, readily identifiable, routes forward under these circumstances. First, Hartman[53] suggests that the enterprise ought to go beyond the minimum duties. He calls it 'avoiding helping to deprive people of their rights'. Second, firms might act together to establish standards to impose generally or in specific communities. The Sullivan Principles which were drawn up by US Secretary of Health and Human Services, Louis Sullivan, to grade US companies, are an illustration of this type of action.

In conducting its mainstream business, the international firm influences the economic and social development of a community in a number of ways. It can *contribute* to shaping the goals and aspirations of the nation. The venture might *reinforce* existing aims or processes. Its actions may *frustrate* the country's aspirations. Company policies can *undermine* national goals.[54] Regardless of the form of response, it seems inevitable that the nature of the corporate contract in international business will be subject to increasing scrutiny as firms become more mobile, barriers between markets erode and the globalisation of industry increases.[55]

OTHER PLAYERS, OTHER VALUES?

Cultural, ethnic and social variety is not confined to international markets. Close examination of most mature economies, markets and communities highlights their internal complexity. Economic development has been shaped by migration, interaction between different groups and the actions of outgroups. Nonconformists in Britain, Scottish migrants in North America, the Jewish community across Europe and Calvinists in Germany played a disproportionate role in shape of the industrial revolution in the last century. Their debates about the purpose of commerce – from Smith (the Scot) to Hayek (the Austrian migrant) – continue to mould discussion. Their influence on the discussion on corporate responsibility has, if anything, been even greater. The Welshman, Owen, Cadbury, the Non-conformist and the Scot, Carnegie, symbolise the ability of individuals from outside the establishment to raise new issues and question the values and assumptions of the dominant community. There is a distinct Islamic dimension to business in many communities in the USA and Europe. Changes in today's business environment suggest that new players are entering the economic arena. Their aspirations and values are influencing the debate on corporate responsibility and governance.

Some derive their codes of ethics from outside the Judeo–Christian tradition which dominates European and American business.[56] Shinto in Japan, Hinduism from India and Islam impose different obligations and have different expectations of their believers. Japanese products can be seen on every high street and their factories and offices exist in most communities. Entrepreneurs whose roots lie in Asia and the Middle East are valued members of business communities across Europe and the USA. Their ethical codes are seldom incorporated in discussions of corporate responsibility. It is, however, increasingly important to explore the ways the values of these new players will influence the debate on ethics and responsibilities. The emphasis in Japan on the group, for example, contrasts sharply with the individualism which dominates Anglo-Saxon debate on values and responsibilities. The attention paid to harmony within the group; *Amae*, and with nature; *Shibui*, have few equivalents in European or USA thinking. In Islam, attitudes towards religious observance and social obligation struggle to co-exist with Western materialism. Fate, caste, family and respect play a complex part in shaping the business behaviour of Hindu business.

A more subtle, but, potentially equally important change is being wrought by the new generation of female managers and entrepreneurs. There is some evidence that many have a stronger sense of group or community than their male counterparts.

> Prima facie evidence from studies of female entrepreneurs suggests that their personal goals and value profiles differ significantly from their male counterparts.
>
> Carter, S. and Cannon, T. (1991)[57]

The bimodal[58] nature of female employment allied to perceived internal barriers to advancement[59] may create attitudes and values among women managers which differ from those of their male counterparts.

The conventional business stereotype of ethics and values based on the Judeo – Christian male values are being reshaped. The modern business community is culturally complex, ethnically diverse and not gender based. It reflects increasingly the community in which it operates. The nature of the contract between business and its community is being renegotiated to reflect these changes.

CONCLUSION

Business is showing growing awareness of the challenges it faces in addressing issues of stewardship, employment and investment in an international environment characterised by complex and changing expectations. It acknowledges the impact of its actions and its responsibility to satisfy the economic functions of the firm in an environment of trust. The decision by the community to give industry greater freedom in recent years acknowledges the link between freedom and prosperity. Like all political decisions it is conditional. One of the implicit terms of this contract is that self-regulation delivers the economic benefits while ensuring the community is maintained and developed effectively at a minimum cost. The values of the executives who are responsible for delivering their side of this 'bargain' are shaped by a tradition of debate which gains added momentum from all the new issues and perspectives that are emerging today.

QUESTIONS

1 Identify the sources of legitimacy for a)shareholders, b)senior management. What rights and responsibilities does this form of legitimacy impose on these groups?

2 Analyse the recommendations of the Social Security Committee of the House of Commons Report on The Operation of Pension Funds. How far do these satisfy the concerns which arose following the Maxwell affair?

3 Outline the duties and responsibilities imposed on directors. Indicate the extent to which the recommendations of the Cadbury Report are a sufficient or adequate attempt to ensure that directors meet these obligations.

4 Is there any evidence to support the proposition that excessive corporate governance can 'chill innovation'? Please outline this evidence if it exists and indicate what can be done to achieve a balance between appropriate levels of scrutiny and necessary levels of risk-taking.

5 List the problems faced by accountants in industry who attempt to balance the demands of their profession and their employers. Indicate the role, if any, of the internal audit committee in resolving these problems.

6 Use the Annual Report and Accounts of five plcs to identify the remuneration packages available to their top managers. Indicate the extent to which these meet the reasonable expectations of shareholders for disclosure in the terms discussed by Cadbury.

7 Hayek[60] argues that 'so long as the management has one overriding duty of administrating the resources under their control as trustees for the shareholders and for their benefit, their hands are largely tied; audit will have no arbitrary power to benefit this or that private interest. But once the management of a big enterprise is regarded as not only entitled but even obliged in its decisions whatever is

regarded as the public or social interest, or to support good causes and generally to act for public benefit, it gains indeed an uncontrollable power, a power which could not be left in the hands of private managers, but would inevitably be made the subject of increasing public control.' How would you answer this proposition and present the case for boards acting in the public interest even if it conflicted with the interests of shareholders.

8 Discuss the strengths and weakness of disinvestment as a means of shareholder control and influence on corporate behaviour.

9 Outline the system of setting top management salaries in

    (a) A Plc,
    (b) A large, semi-autonomous public agency, e.g. a university,
    (c) A department of state, i.e. Department for Education.

How far do these meet the requirements of a fair, open and publicly accountable system? Do you believe they need reform? If so put forward your proposals.

10 Define:

    (a) Stewardship
    (b) Disclosure
    (c) Greenmail
    (d) Golden handcuffs
    (e) Conditioned power

    (f) Compensatory power
    (g) Minimax Criteria
    (h) Condign Power
    (i) Due Diligence
    (j) The ethical contract

REFERENCES

1. Demb, A and Neubauer, F. *The Corporate Board*, Oxford, Oxford University Press (1993).
2. Bussman, T. 'Zeitgeist' *Guardian*, 2 May (1992).
3. Pilzer, P. Z. and Deitz, R. *Other People's Money: The Inside Story of the S & L Mess*, New York, Simon & Schuster (1989).
4. Burrough, B. and Helyar, J. *Barbarians at the Gate*, London, Cape (1990).
5. Langbein, J., Schotland, R. and Blanstein, A. *Disinvestment: Is it Legal? Is it Moral? Is it Productive?* National Legal Centre for the Public Interest, Washington DC (1988).
6. Social Security Committee of the House of Commons *The Operation of Pension Funds*, London, HMSO (1992).
7. Talner, L. *The Origins of Shareholder Activism*, Invester Responsibility Research Centre, Washington DC (1983).
8. Dale Hanson, quoted in Business International Limited *New Directions in Corporate Governance*, London, Business International Limited (1991).
9. Plant, R. *Responsibility and Accountability*, Mimeo, University of Southampton (1990).
10. Social Security Committee, ibid.
11. Gower, J. *Review of Investor Protection*, London, HMSO, cmnd 9125 (1984).
12. Wilson, Lord *Review of the Functioning of Financial Institutions*, London, HMSO, cmnd 7937 (1980).
13. Social Security Committee, ibid.
14. PRO-NED *Tenth Annual Review*, London, PRO-NED (1992).
15. Levy, L. *Reforming Board Reform*, HBR, vol. 59, no. 2 (1981) pp. 71–86.
16. PRO-NED, ibid.

17. The Business Roundtable *Corporate Governance and American Competitiveness*, 200 Park Avenue, New York 10166 (1990).
18. Epstein, E. J. *Who Owns the Corporation? Management vs Shareholders*, New York, Priority Press (1986).
19. The Business Roundtable, ibid.
20. Vinten, G. 'Internal Audit After Maxwell and BCCI' *Managerial Auditing Journal*, vol. 7, no. 4 (1992) pp. 3–5.
21. Axline, L. 'The Bottom Line on Ethics' *Journal of Accountancy*, vol. 170, no. 6 (1990) pp. 87–91.
22. Spicer, B. 'Investors, Corporate Social Performance and Information Disclosure: An Empirical Study' *Accounting Review*, January (1978(a)) pp. 94–111.
23. Green, C. N. 'Identification Modes of Professionals', *Academy of Management Journal*, vol. 21, no. 3 (1978) pp. 486–92.
24. Lindsay, D. of the Institute of Chartered Accountants, quoted in Donaldson, J. ibid.
25. Chandler, A. D., jr. *Strategy and Structure: Chapters in the History of the American Industrial Enterprise*, Cambridge, Mass., MIT Press (1962).
26. Crystal, G. S. *In Search of Excess*, New York, W. W. Norton (1991).
27. Hay Management Consultants *Boardroom Review*, London, Hay Group, Spring (1992).
28. Lupton, T. and Bowey, A. *Wages and Salaries*, Harmondsworth, Penguin (1974).
29. Marks, R. and Minow, N. *Power and Accountability*, Harper Collins, Glasgow (1991).
30. Demb, A. and Neubauer, F., ibid.
31. Berle, A. E. *The Twentieth Century Capitalist Revolution*, New York, Harcourt Brace and Company (1954).
32. Gowler, D. 'Values, Contracts and Job Satisfaction' *Personnel Review*, Autumn (1974).
33. Rothe, H. 'Does Higher Pay Bring Higher Productivity', in Fleishman, E. A. (ed.) *Studies in Personnel and Industrial Psychology*, London, Dorsey Press (1961).
34. Gowler, D., ibid.
35. Mumford, E. 'Job Satisfaction; A Method of Analysis' *Personnel Review*, Summer (1972).
36. Allen, R. and Nixon, B. 'Developing a New Approach to Leadership' *Management Education and Development*, vol. 19 (1988) pp. 174–86.
37. Kant, I. *Fundamental Principles of the Metaphysic of Morals* (1785).
38. L'Etang, J. 'A Kantian Approach to Codes of Ethics' *Journal of Business Ethics*, vol. 11, no. 10, October (1992) pp. 737–44.
39. Binyon, M. 'MEPs Seek Total Ban on Tobacco Promotion' *The Times*, 14 March (1990).
40. Purcell, T. V. 'Management and Ethical Investors' *Harvard Business Review*, vol. 57, September (1979) pp. 24–44.
41. Jacoby, N. H. *Corporate Power and Social Responsibility*, New York, Macmillan (1973).
42. von Mises, L. *Human Action: A Treatise on Economics*, London, William Hodge (1949).
43. Donaldson, T. J. 'Rights in the Global Market', in Freeman, R. E. *Business Ethics*, Oxford, Oxford University Press (1991).
44. Mongelluzzo, W. 'Group Forms to Track Software Pirates' *Journal of Commerce*, 10 December (1987).
45. Reardon, K. 'It's the Thought that Counts' *Harvard Business Review*, September–October (1984) pp. 136–41.
46. Mayo, M. A. 'Ethical Problems Encountered by US Small Businesses in International Marketing' *Journal of Small Business Management*, vol. 29, no. 2 (1991) pp. 51–9.
47. Wines, W. A. 'Towards an Understanding of Cross-Cultural Ethics: A Tentative Mode' *Journal of Business Education*, vol. 11, no. 11, November (1992) pp. 831–42.
48. Cicero, *Discourses*.
49. Tuleja, T. *Beyond the Bottom Line*, New York, Facts on File Publications (1985).
50. Donaldson, T. J., ibid.
51. Jackall, R. *Moral Mazes*, Oxford, Oxford University Press (1988).
52. Hartman, E. M. Donaldson on rights and Corporate Obligations, in Freeman, R. E. *Business Ethics*, Oxford, Oxford University Press (1991).
53. Hartman, E. M., ibid.

54. Fayerweather, J. *International Business Strategy and Administration*, Cambridge, Mass., Ballinger (1982).
55. Donaldson, T. Can Multinationals Stage a Universal Morality Play *Business and Society Review*, no. 81, Spring (1992) pp. 51–5.
56. Whipple, T. and Swords, D. 'Business Ethics Judgements: A Cross-Cultural Comparison' *Journal of Business Education*, vol. 11, no. 9, September (1992) pp. 671–9.
57. Carter, S. and Cannon, T. *Women as Entrepreneurs*, London, Academic Press (1991).
58. Hakim, C. *Occupational Segregation*, London, Department of Employment Research Paper, no. 9 (1979).
59. Hymounts, C. 'The Corporate Woman – The Glass Ceiling' *Wall Street Journal*, 25 November (1986).
60. Hayek, F. A. *Law, Legislation and Liberty*, vol. 3, Chicago, University of Chicago Press (1979).

CHAPTER 6

Dilemmas and debates in theory and practice

The issues identified in Chapters 4 and 5 have provoked a discussion on corporate responsibility which is more intense today than any time this century. The debate addresses the ways organisations govern their affairs and the character of the relationship between the enterprise and the community. Corporate leaders in the private sector acknowledge their responsibility to respond to the new climate of scrutiny and expectation.

> Proberty of companies, even those which are household names, is very much under scrutiny nowadays. Stakeholders are rightly concerned about the principles and practices of the companies in which their own livelihoods and reputations – and in the case of institutional investors, considerable sums of other people's money. As a result, good corporate governance will increasingly be seen as the hallmark of successful companies.
>
> Clarke, R. 1991[1]

The attention paid to corporate behaviour comes from a coincidence of several factors. Perhaps the most important is the increased awareness of the need to wed increased freedom to perform the economic functions of the enterprise with a demand for this freedom to be used responsibly.[2] In some cases,[3] this is linked to a demand for greater participation by business in tackling the economic and social problems associated with economic development. Elsewhere, proberty and governance have emerged as issues as the community looks to industry to show moral as well as economic leadership.

> More and more, business leaders find themselves facing problems that require them to choose between actions that are based on existing norms and those that are based on some higher ethical standard. The latter course of action requires bold leadership and moral courage.
>
> Cuilla, J. B. (1991)[4]

The coincidence of these pressures affects the internal workings of the firm. Managers find themselves at the centre of a web of conflicting pressures (Figure 6.1).

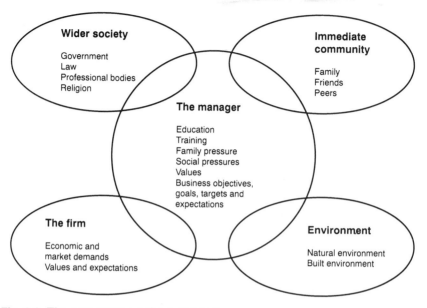

Fig. 6.1 The pressures on the managers

The attitudes and values held by the manager are shaped by a lifetime of experiences. These views continue to be influenced by pressures from within the firm. Company culture is a key factor[5]. This can be explicit as in the case of IBM's commitment to its stakeholders or The Body Shop's environment programmes. Sometimes, the commitments are long established as at Eli Lillee or Rowntree. Elsewhere, they are part of a deliberate programme of change as at the Co-Operative Bank in Britain (see Appendix A, page 126). The values of the firm shape the expectations of managers and their views about 'right' and 'wrong' behaviour in a corporate context. External pressures on the firm influence its character and the way managers think and act. This is seldom a simple relationship of the type 'they're rich and have easy pickings so they can afford a conscience' or 'we cannot afford the luxury of ethics'. A medium-sized firm like Seton's in Oldham, England operating in the highly competitive medicare market will make a major commitment to training or an organisation like the St John's ambulance. At the same time, a bank like Rothschild's might find every excuse to avoid developing its role – 'If we give to charity our clients will think our profits are too high, etc.'. There is some evidence that firms are recognising the benefits to be gained from appreciating the nature of the values which underpin its operation. The value-driven business seems to require less internal supervision and lower costs, may be more flexible and innovative and offers greater satisfaction to employees and better return to its stakeholders. The priorities chosen might reflect the composition of the board[6] or the views of top management about where the priorities lie or to whom they are responsible (Table 6.1). The wider environment affects

Table 6.1 Rank-order of 'to whom accountable'

Item	Average
The company	2.72
Shareholders	3.84
Employees	4.50
The chairman	5.47
Clients/customers	5.78
Myself	5.78
The community	6.41
Other directors	6.53
Government/people	6.75

Note: 1 = high; 9 = low
Source: Demb, A. and Neubauer, F. L.[7]

the values managers adopt and the way executives respond to different demands. The Christian ethic was a powerful and overt influence on managerial behaviour in the last century.[8] Office and work regulations made candid statements of this commitment (Table 6.2).

Table 6.1 shows how a sample of directors allocated their priorities in terms of defining to whom were they responsible. The strongest feeling was that they were responsible to 'the company' while the weakest sentiment was that they were responsible to government or the people. Some features of this type of public commitment to a specific ethic can still be seen today.[9]

The Lambeth partnership established by the Archbishop of Canterbury seeks 'to foster a new partnership between lay and ordained Christians so that the skills of professional people in secular employment can be harnessed properly'. In many Islamic communities there is a clear determination to integrate faith into commercial relationships.[10] This has prompted some countries and groups to look beyond the Western model of business to seek out an Islamic approach to

Table 6.2 Extracts from office and workplace regulations

Explicit	**Godliness,** cleanliness and punctuality are the necessities of a good business
	Daily **prayers** will be held each morning in the main office
	Boys will attend **Sunday School** every week
	Employees should not endanger their children's **morals** by allowing them to associate with people about whom they know little
Implicit	The craving of tobacco, wines or spirits is a weakness and, as such, is forbidden to all of the clerical staff
	The company will not approve, as profit sharers, men who herd themselves in overcrowded boarding houses
	Oaths and profanities are forbidden

industry and commerce. In Japanese firms the link between wider social values and the behaviour of executives is accepted and endorsed.[11] The most obvious ways in which the wider community shapes the attitudes and behaviour of managers is through government action and the legal system. This can take several basic forms:

- *Endorsement*: some forms of behaviour can be singled out for praise or recognition. Presidential awards in the USA, the honours system in Britain are replicated in different ways in most countries. They can be employed to endorse and reinforce certain values.
- *Influence*: the community can take this further by using influence to shape behaviour. In the USA, it is hard for firms discriminating against the economically and socially disadvantaged to win government contracts. In 1992, the UK government made prompt payment to small suppliers a criterion in its requirements for firms tendering for business.
- *Power*: penalties can be deployed against transgressors against the law. Fines, imprisonment, even closure of the enterprise are used to shape behaviour and influence attitudes.

Some of the options for influence open to the state are available to other groups in the community. A customer might refuse to buy from suppliers failing to comply with certain standards. The individual boycotting South African fruit was seeking to influence the attitudes of retailers. The requirement of Motorola (USA) that all its suppliers tried to win Demming quality recognition is a conscious attempt to shape values. Recourse to law is an option which is open to all those affected by the actions and approaches of firms or managers. Professional bodies influence the behaviour of their members through pre-entry training, performance standards or requirements and a variety of sanctions including expulsion. The nature of the institution affects the form of its influence or control over the values of its members.

In Britain a chartered institute like the engineers or the Law Society or British Medical Association is not only a professional grouping, it is also a licence to trade. Other learned societies depend more on influence to shape behaviour. The Chartered Institute of Marketing, for example, uses exhortation where it cannot employ control. Its means of enforcement are limited. There is no general requirement that marketing executives are members of a professional institute. Many businessmen are not in any professional association. They may be members of other groups which strive to influence the way they conduct their affairs. Bodies like the Royal Society for the encouragement of Arts, Manufactures & Commerce, Rotary, Institute of Directors, etc., strive to influence the ways their members conduct their business.

We shall look at ways of developing human capabilities within and outside formal systems of education and training, for work and leisure, for social and private purposes.

We shall try to unpick some of the deep issues of those whose responsibility it is to be wise rather than merely exploitive, when we exist in a global environment.

Thomlinson, J. 1989[12]

The most powerful influences on managers generally lie in the family and the networks of friends and peers who introduce, respond to, encourage or endorse particular codes or patterns of behaviour. Family businesses illustrate this interlinking of the family and the enterprise. It can be seen in a host of situations. Concerns at home about the environment will influence the way managers shape the environment policies of their firms. Attitudes to honesty and codes of conduct learned in the home are powerful factors in determining the ways executives behave at work. Peer group pressure has a tangible and immediate effect on executive action.[13] Colleagues who accept or cover up wrong doing are, in effect, endorsing this type of behaviour. In examining the behaviour of those involved in the Maxwell scandal, the Social Security Committee was very critical of the behaviour of those who ignored concerns and were 'blind' to the spreading problems.

Pontius Pilot would have blushed at the spectacle of so many witnesses washing their hands in public before the Committee of their responsibilities in this affair.

Social Security Committee 1992[14]

The behaviour of managers will often reflect their view of the actions their colleagues and superiors seem to endorse or criticise. Some actions reinforce the

Undermining	Reinforcing
Rewards for quantity over quality	Emphasis on quality
Bottom line pressure for profits at any cost	Clearly formulated ethical standards
Closed door practices and emphasis on secrecy	Fully articulated standards
Punishments for reporting policy violations	Openness
Uncertainty about ethical standards	Frequent and public endorsement of standards
Patterns of deception throughout management	Clear channels of communication on breaches of standards
Emphasis on 'group' loyalty even at expense of others	Standards committees
Group think	Follow through
Reluctance to act where problems identified	Reward and recognition systems which emphasise standards
Social bullying	Prompt non-adversarial remedial action
Fear	

Fig. 6.2 Peer and corporate pressures for and against standards

notion that an ethical code matters while others will undermine this belief (Figure 6.2).[15]

In virtually all the recent scandals in Britain, the USA, Japan, Europe and elsewhere there is clear evidence of widespread knowledge of the misdemeanours[16] at least within the firm – often there is evidence of collusion and complicity.

> Those involved in the bid, both within Guinness and outside, did nothing to redress the balance. They either had their jobs to protect or they were suppliers who wanted to retain company contracts, or were individuals who wanted to play down their role in order to minimise their own potential liability.

> Saunders, J. (1989)[17]

In Guinness, Barlow Clowes, Polly Peck, BCCI, Maxwell, the Saving and Loans, Recruit-Cosmos, Nomura and Nikko the numbers directly involved and the scale of wrong doing makes it clear that many others knew or suspected the wrong doing. Often, even those with a fiduciary responsibility to monitor behaviour failed to act.

CASE STUDY 6.1

The strange case of the DeLorean

In the Prologue to their book on DeLorean,[18] Fallon and Strodes emphasise that 'other men must share the blame for the wreck of the DeLorean dream machine, but so do many of the institutions we rely on to protect us from just this kind of disaster. This is also a story about the failure of government watchdog agencies, the probity of our financial centres, and the credulity and dubious accuracy of our newsgathering organisations. Later, they note that while financial analyst, David Healy: could observe *when people ask my advice about investing in Mr DeLorean's venture, I tell them to put the money in wine, women and song. They get the same return and have more fun.*

Insiders knew, just how true this was, as a confidential internal report was: 'utterly damning of the prototype, Doris 1. The body and chassis structure was weak and needed a steel backbone; front and rear suspensions were unsatisfactory; almost every component fouled its neighbour; there were no sunvisors, ashtray or space for a spare wheel. The door latches and water sealing were poor; the electrical system was incomplete; the rear lamps were only mock-up. DeLorean had produced written results of tests on the air conditioning – but the air conditioning had not been connected on the car and would not even fit.' Soon, a 'personal and confidential' report put on record 'serious doubts about the project' but these were kept from the proper authorities while further, large requests for finance were progressed. Perhaps because 'if the Northern Ireland authorities, who were supposed to be monitoring the project, had even caught a hint of it, they would soon have lost their composure' but might have lost less public money.

CASE STUDY 6.2

The case of Johnson Matthey: the 'appalling', the 'bizarre', the 'incompetent' and the 'mismanaged'[19]

The reluctance to speak in Northern Ireland might be excused as an attempt to avoid doing anything to undermine the slim hopes for new manufacturing jobs in a deprived region. No such explanations hold water in the richest part of Britain – the City of London. Stephen Fay's[20] description of the 'horrors' at Johnson Matthey Bank notes that the Bank of England first showed concern in 1983 but took only limited action. Even when 'an investigator in maritime fraud' warned that Johnson Matthey Bank's largest customer 'was involved in a £3 million fraud claim' there was no action. Other customers seemed to see Johnson Matthey Bank as 'a remarkably easy touch'. There was, however, little useful information passed by the staff of Johnson Matthey Bank to the main regulator – the Bank of England – who were, anyway, 'not used to busting in like the VAT man'.

The 'trusting nature' of the Bank of England's relationships with its client was based in part on assumptions about the integrity of its partners. Fay does, however, note that 'the supervisor (with responsibility for Johnson Matthey Bank) discussed her cases with her colleagues, sharing her gloom about both Continental Illinois and Johnson Matthey Bank. The joke was: which would go first? But she did not share the joke with Brian Quinn' (the senior executive in charge at the Bank of England). The net result was a massive loss to the Bank of England. The failure to inform and the provision of misleading information undermined the reputation of the Bank of England 'for always knowing what was going on' with long-term effects on its reputation. Perhaps the most revealing comment was made by the Chancellor of the Exchequer who observed that 'misreporting, even on the appalling scale that has occurred in this case, does not constitute a fraud. That is a point of law.'

In some cases, the parties involved even failed to appreciate the nature of the problems.

> Some Tokyo press commentators called the deals bribes; others could not understand what the fuss was about. Cheap shares had long been a way of making political contributions in Japan

Tricker, R. (1992)[21]

The cost to the community and the firms involved in these recent failures is almost impossible to estimate especially in situations like the US, Savings and Loans frauds. In Table 6.3 the overall cost of some of the larger, more public British cases is put at over £6 billion at current prices, excluding all the costs of time and the human costs to those affected directly and indirectly.

The judgements made by those who managed or observed these events were central to the direction and success of these firms. This is recognised to an increasing degree by industrial leaders and legislators. The complexity and scale of the modern enterprise makes it hard for the twin strands of traditional control: private scrutiny and market forces, to work. The comments of Lord Shawcross

Table 6.3 The costs of deficiency

Case	Cost ($ millions)
DeLorean Cars	285
Johnson Matthey Bank	250
Guinness	295
Barlow Clowes	250
Polly Peck	740
BCCI	2,750
Maxwell	1,650
Lloyds Names	200
Total	6,220

on the breakdown of traditional networks of control and supervision could be repeated elsewhere.

> Under the old rules, there were rules, unwritten rules, that people adhered to. There used to be an axiom that 'my word is my bond.' No-one operates on that principle today.
>
> Lord Shawcross, quoted in Paxman, J. (1991)[22]

Some of the information is hard to gather on a consistent basis. This is especially true for informal operational information, e.g. the cost of maintenance.

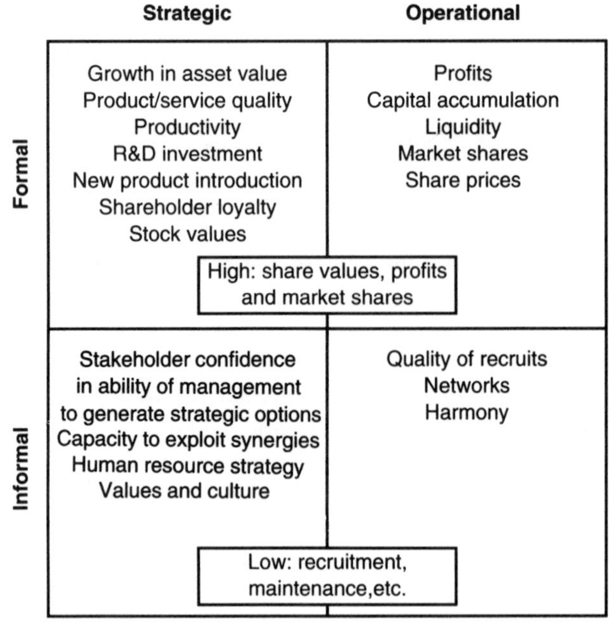

Fig. 6.3 Types of control mechanisms
Adapted from Demb, A. and Neubauer, F.[23]

This measures the cost of maintaining the venture's internal and external standing, e.g. low labour turnover will produce a low maintenance cost. Sometimes indicators will point in different directions (Figure 6.3).

In a perfect market, investors would be aware of the problems and take remedial action or disinvest. Failing this, corporate collapse might follow corruption and inefficiency. Perhaps, more effective, better-managed firms will mobilise their resources to acquire or save the enterprise. There are, however, few perfect markets. Investors are often poorly informed. The sources of information are imperfect and have their own goals.[24] The interlinking of private, institutional and public funds means that the different aims of the parties distorts the market. The politician will frequently worry more about the losses in votes through a 'scandal' than the loss of money through inefficiency. In firms with market capitalisations into the $billions acquisition or the working of other market forces is slow and imperfect. The complex system of corporate control such as that outlined in Figure 6.3 depends on a mixture of good-quality information, clear signals and consistency of interpretation. Unfortunately this combination is all too rare. An effective system of ethics can be a powerful means of resolving conflicts but will turn on the values adopted by managers and the source of their personal or group ethic.

A TWO-LEGGED CREATURE

In a famous passage on the nature and source of human values Locke[25] commented that 'God has not been so sparing to man to make them barely two legged creatures and left it to Aristotle to make them rational . . . He has given them a mind that can reason without being instructed in methods of syllogising'. Lillie[26] adds that 'a similar remark might be made about man's powers of distinguishing right and wrong . . . (the moralist) lives himself in a social environment where certain moral standards . . . are accepted and these standards serve as the data or material'. The study of ethics is the study of these 'standards' and the criteria used to judge which conduct is right or wrong; good or bad. Business ethics does not stand outside this study. It is part of the wider field. Implicit in this study is the notion that 'values, moral and non-moral, can be handled systematically, and that business and industrial practices can be objectives evaluated from a moral (ethical) point of view.'[27] It would be wrong to attempt to summarise this vast field in this book. The roots of the subject are so deep and the evolution of the argument so important that primary sources and their current interpretations call for individual study by the serious student (Table 6.4). The aim, here, is merely to provide a perspective and place current thinking on corporate responsibility into context.

The contrast between the material success of the mixed or free market economy and its main rivals, the command or communistic economy calls for an even closer examination of its underlying values and the ways they are

Table 6.4 Key sources for the study of business ethics

Category	Key Work(s)
Primary sources	Hobbes, T. *The Leviathan*, (1651) Hume, D. *A Treatise Concerning Human Nature*, (1739) Rousseau, J. J. *The Social Contract*, (1762) Smith, A. *The Wealth of Nations*, (1776) Kant, I. *Groundwork to the Metaphysics of Morals*, (1785) Bentham, J. *Introduction to the Principles of Morals and Legislation*, (1789) Paine, T. *The Rights of Man* (1791) Mill, J. S. *Utilitarianism* (1861) Spencer, H. *Essays* (1891) Moore, G. *Principia Ethica* (1903)
'Radicals'	Hayek, F. A. *The Road to Serfdom*, London, Routledge (1944) von Mises, L. *Human Action*, London, William Hodge (1949) Galbraith, J. K. *The New Industrial State*, Harmondsworth, Penguin (1967) Medawar, C. *The Social Audit Consumer Handbook*, London, MacMillan (1978) Friedman, M. and Friedman, R. *Free to Chose*, London, Secker and Warburg (1980)
Modern Commentators	Post, J. E. *Research in Corporate Social Performance and Policy*, Annual Series, London, JAI Press Silk, L. and Vogel, D. *Ethics and Profits*, New York, Simon and Schuster (1976) De George, R. *Business Ethics*, New York, MacMillan (1986) Conference Board *Corporate Ethics*, Washington, Research Report No 900 (1987) Mahony, J. *Business Ethics: Oil and Water?* London, Kings College (1988) Donaldson, J. *Key Issues in Business Ethics*, London, Routledge (1989) Craig Smith, N. *Morality and The Market*, London, Routledge (1990) Freeman, R. E. *Business Ethics*, Oxford, Oxford University Press (1991)

translated into action. Friedman[28] touches on those when he commented that 'history suggests that capitalism is a necessary condition for political freedom. Clearly it is not a sufficient condition.' The achievements are used by some to imply that a form of 'social Darwinism' has occurred. The fittest system has survived. This, in turn, is used to imply a form of moral superiority for the system and its agents.

POSITIVISM

This notion that the observable achievements should provide the basis for comparison, is a feature of the *positivist* approach to thought in the economic and social sciences. Positive economics is 'the study of what "is" in economic theory rather than what ought to be . . . (it) seeks to identify relationships between economic variables, to quantify and measure these relationships, and to make predictions of what will happen if a variable changes'.[29] It contrasts with normative economics which examines 'what "ought to be" . . . normative statements reflect peoples' subjective judgements of what is good or bad and depend on ethical considerations such as "fairness" rather than strict economic rationale'.[30] These two notions; *is* and *ought* are not connected and one cannot pass from one to the other.

> In every system of morality, with which I have hitherto met with, I have always remark'd that the author proceeds for some time in the ordinary way of reasoning . . . or makes observation . . . when all of a sudden I am surpris'd to find, that instead of the usual copulations of proposition, *is* and *is not*, I meet with no proposition that is not connected with an *ought* or *ought not*. This change is imperceptible, but it is, however, of the last consequence. For as this ought or ought not, expresses some new relation or affirmation, 'tis necessary that it should be observ'd and explain'd; and at the same time that a reason should be given for what reasons altogether inconceivable, how this relation can be deducted from others, which are entirely different from it.
>
> Hume, D. (1739)[31]

The literature of business and economics abounds with attempts to pass from *is* or *is not* statements to *ought* or *ought not* statements. Drucker[32] moves easily from descriptions of innovation and the notion that change is or has been the driving force of industrial society to the notion that it ought to be the driving force. Adair[33] slips from descriptions of the role leaders *have* played to assumptions about the role they *ought* to play in shaping industry. Successful industrialists from Ford to Harvey-Jones are especially prone to making the logic lead from *is* to *ought*.

In its more extreme forms, positivism either asserts that moral issues cannot be addressed or should not be addressed when the opportunity exists to substitute observation and prediction. Freed from 'contamination by values'[34] the study or practice of business and economics can deliver a host of benefits to society.

> The capitalist achievement does not typically consist in providing more silk stockings for queens but in bringing them within the reach of factory girls in return for ever decreasing amounts of effort.
>
> Schumpeter, J. (1942)[35]

The fit between science, technology and economic progress sustains this notion that benefits will flow from the growth and development of industry in a capitalist economy. These might be distributed unevenly but this is a small price to pay for the aggregate gains. As Churchill[36] commented 'the inherent sin of capitalism is the unequal sharing of blessings. The inherent virtue of socialism is the equal sharing of miseries.' If these assumptions are true then the returns may justify the price. The positivist will strive to identify and measure these returns. The focus of attention lies in the tools for identification, classification, measurement and calculation. 'Scientific Management' was the attempt to introduce these principles to workplace relations and corporate behaviour. It replaced 'initiative and incentive' with 'science'.[37] The principles of scientific management were:

1   The recording, tabulating and reduction to laws, rules and mathematical formula the knowledge 'which in the past has been in the heads of the workers'.
2   The scientific selection and development of the workman to do the 'most profitable class of work for which his natural abilities fit him'.
3   The 'bringing together' of the knowledge gathered and the workforce in the most efficient way.
4   The 'division of labour' for maximum output.

There is little overt consideration of values, either in the initial assumptions about ownership and control of the workers' 'knowledge' or the allocation of the returns from this bringing together. The measurable improvement in output provided sufficient justification. Later research highlighted the powerful inter-plays between behaviour,[38] technology[39] and other variables[40] but most took as read the positivist perspective. The strength of the approach is reflected in the range and quality of the research and development which has emerged. Its weakness lies in a failure to account for the values which underly its own assumptions and the failure to indicate any underlying purpose beyond growth, development and materialism. Failure to predict the problems associated with the science or the technologies allied to recurrent concern about the nature of the bargain between the community, the contributors and beneficiaries calls for an attempt to address issues of value and ethics.

UTILITARIANISM

The various strands in the evolution of ethics and philosophy have been organised and classified in various ways. The interplay between classical thought and the Judeo–Christian tradition helped to shape the ideas of the *Enlightenment*.[41] In Britain, during the eighteenth century Hobbes, Hume, Locke, Berkeley and others sought to address questions of the sources and nature of moral behaviour in society.[42] Some emphasised subjectivism or intuition while others attempted to derive moral laws from deeper understanding of the nature of man and the social condition. This latter view is closely entwined with the work of continental Europeans like Rousseau and Kant.[43] In the nineteenth century, the growing sense of men's control over their world and the gains from the results of science produced a greater emphasis on morality centred on the results of actions. This notion lies at the core of the thinking of the Utilitarians; Bentham, Mill and others.[44] Their ideas have had a powerful influence on the character of business ethics. This type of thinking is often presented as *teleological*, i.e. rightness or wrongness depends on the consequences of action. It is contrasted with *deontological* theory which emphasises the action itself or its purpose.[45]

The classic distinction is between Kant's emphasis on the importance of 'good will'[46] and J. S. Mill's stress on the measurable outcome of 'the greatest good to the greatest number'.[47] For Kant, a rational man with good will can derive moral laws by asking himself whether the maxim which underlies his behaviour can become 'universal law'. His example of the refusal to repay borrowed money has much relevance to those asserting that it is right for developing countries to refuse to pay debts to bankers. Kant might argue that this type of behaviour is only moral if the debtor – acting with good will – is ready for everyone else in the same or similar circumstances to refuse to repay debts. It would be as valid for the taxpayer in their own country as themselves. This is less of a problem for the Utilitarian. The consequences are what matter. The debtor country can refuse to pay because the cost of payment in human misery is so great that refusal will create the greatest happiness for the greatest number. The cost to the bankers, even the cost to local taxpayers, is swamped by the 'happiness' created by converting these funds to jobs, local medical services, even defence. More immediately, Kant might be willing to counternance the actions of the owners of the firm who emphasised good works at the expense of economic performance. Management time could be deflected from research, innovation and marketing to ensure that employee health services, pensions arrangements or charitable donations were prioritised. Even if the firm failed, the managers were acting morally. The Utilitarian would not take so sanguine a view. The failure of the firm, its inability to perform its long-term economic function or the unhappiness caused by resulting unemployment would condemn the owners regardless of their intentions.

These twin notions of measurement and judgement on the basis of outcomes were very attractive to industrialists in the nineteenth century. Features of it can be found in the work of the modern 'radicals' and libertarians.[48] In its broadest terms, the moral superiority of capitalism is 'proved' by its ability to produce more of the goods, services and benefits which make people happy. The inequalities are a small price to pay for the benefits. At the core of this thinking is the central proposition that 'all people seek to be happy'. This might be empirically verifiable. It may be derived from the ways they act: avoiding things that make them unhappy; seeking things that cause them happiness. Even if people claim to seek other benefits these are a means to the end of gaining pleasure. Faced with a moral dilemma the manager's task is to calculate which action would produce the greatest good to the greatest number. The immediate difficulties occur in calculating these outcomes.

CASE STUDY 6.3

The vegetable fats dilemma

In the late 1980s a major European processor of vegetable fats completed a comprehensive analysis of its production capacity across Europe. It operated twelve plants in six countries. A productivity/market index, i.e. unit costs of production linked to market access, highlighted wide variations in 'productivity'.

Table (a) Productivity index

Country	Plant	Productivity/ market index	Capacity index
UK	Merseyside	55	10
	Humberside	62	10
	Reading	45	11
France	Lyons	70	8
	Amiens	57	9
	Bordeaux	61	9
W. Germany	Cologne	72	8
	Hamburg	69	10
Belgium	Antwerp	59	8
	Rotterdam	35	8
Spain	Barcelona	71	10
Italy	Milan	80	10
	Perugia	41	11
Belgium	Bruxelles	65	9
Norway	Oslo	71	9

The report noted that there was currently just over 40 units of excess capacity using the firm's standardised capacity index measure. This measured the capacity of the plants using standardised measures. Plans were put in train to close the four 'least productive' plants: Merseyside, Reading, Rotterdam and Perugia. New developments in haulage and distribution meant that the firm could continue to service all its market needs from this reduced capacity.

The collapse of the communist regimes in Eastern Europe coincided with these developments. Initially, this seemed to have no significant implications for these aspects of the firm's operations. This changed with the collapse of the Berlin Wall and the subsequent re-unification of Germany. The meeting of the European Board was faced with a request from the CEO of its German operations that the company acquire and take over the operations of the two plants owned and operated by the former German Democratic

Republic (GDR). This would secure their market position. They were in areas of high unemployment. They were, however, grossly inefficient and would require substantial unemployment to reach the minimum standards accepted elsewhere. Expansion into this new market would require ten units of production capacity. This could be supplied from current (pre-closures) capacity of the old East German plants.

Table (b) Productivity index

	Plant	Productivity/ market index	Capacity index
UK	Merseyside	55	10
	Reading	45	11
Holland	Rotterdam	35	8
Italy	Perugia	41	11
former GDR	Dresden	14	4
	Leipzig	11	6

The CEO of the German operations was under considerable political pressure to keep the 'new' plants open. The dilemma facing the firm was whether to proceed with the planned closure and employ the facilities in Dresden and Leipzig or use the existing plants to supply the market. As the Chairman commented 'it is, in effect, making the workers of Merseyside pay with their jobs for the jobs in Germany with no real economic justification'.

The weaknesses of the Utilitarian approach can be seen in the vegetable fats case. It is probably impossible to calculate which option provides the greatest good to the greatest number. The approach often fails to resolve genuine dilemmas. Its inherent flaws have been the source of considerable debate. They range from the failure to resolve the *is, ought* question, i.e. even if it *is* true that people always seek to maximise happiness can we show that this *ought* to be the case.

INTUITION, REASON AND RULES

Some authors would argue that the solution lies in intuition. G. E. Moore,[49] for example, argues that 'we can if think about it hard enough recognise the good things . . . our duty therefore, can only be defined as that action which will cause more good to exist in the universe than any possible alternative.'[50] In the vegetable fats case, the genuine attempt to recognise the good in each problem will result in a decision which will intuitively produce the correct solution. In contractual terms, it means that society expects its partner to think hard and use its intuition to arrive at the policies and actions which do the most good, given the resources at industry's disposal and the demands placed on it. This might be viewed as the 'spirit of the agreement'. These notions of acceptance (of the terms) or approval (of the way the spirit or letter of the agreement is implemented) provide a useful link to the positivism of 'emotive' theory. Values or value statements 'do not only serve to express feeling. They are calculated to arouse feeling, and so to stimulate action.'[51] These twin notions of 'expressing our attitudes' and 'inciting . . . actions' lie at the heart of emotivism. They provide valuable clues to the way the community – directly or through its agents in the enterprise – define the business contract and guide behaviour.

Hare[52] adds considerably to this by using the notion of *rationality* to break down the barriers between the *subjectivist* and *objectivist* arguments and attempt to end the 'spurious' argument between these views.

> *Subjectivism.* In its simplest form, the position held by someone who believed that all moral actions are a matter of personal taste. 'Eating people is wrong', for example, and its contradiction becomes not true or false, but simply expressions of the dietary references of the speaker.

> *Objectivism.* The belief that there are certain moral truths that would remain true whatever anyone or everyone thought or desired. For instance, 'no one should ever deliberately inflict pain on another, simply to take pleasure in his suffering' might be thought of as a plausible example. Even in a world of Sadists, who all rejected it, the contention remains true, just as $5 + 7 = 12$ remains true even if there is no one left to count.

> Flew, R. M. (1982)[53]

Hare distinguished between first order statements which deal with *right* or *wrong* behaviour and second order statements which deal with *good* or *bad*. A good manager is one who has 'the characteristic qualities [whatever they are] which are commendable'. This is turn will depend on the viewpoint of the observer and the characteristics sought. Geach[54] takes this even further by suggesting that *good* is an attributive adjective, i.e. it gets its meaning from its context. For the executive it means that the meaning of good depends not only on the perspective of the observer but the context in which it is used. In terms of the 'business contract', it requires an implicit or explicit flexibility which allows for different requirements and different conditions. The Utilitarian principle remains because 'the demand to universalise our judgements is ingrained in the language of morality'[55] but is confined to a much more limited array of propositions.

The examination of these areas, the underlying rules or 'Golden Rule' is a well established strand of study in political economics or business ethics. Hobbes' golden rule 'Quod tibi fieri non vis, alteri ne feceris' – *don't do to another what you don't want done to you* – is a classic statement of a golden rule. Its various reformulations are underpinned by some assumptions about rights such as Jefferson's rights to *life liberty and the pursuit of happiness*. Nozick[56] identifies three central propositions in the notion of rights or entitlements which shape relationships.

1 The principle of initial acquisition of holding: we own our own bodies and its abilities and we can come to own external objectives.

2 The principle of transfer of holdings: we can trade or give away the things we own.

3 The principle of rectification: we must remedy unjust acts; for example, acts of theft or illegitimate initial acquisition.

Brown, A. (1986)[57]

These rights are held equally by all and cannot be forcibly taken away by any other authority without their agreement. The respect for these rights is the implicit underpinning of all contracts between individuals and between them and the state. They therefore do not need to be restated in every new or reformed contract. Rawls[58] presents this notion of rights at the centre of his critique of Utilitarianism. It is linked with notions of fairness and equity which provide a potentially powerful bridge to theories of market economics. His central rule of fairness is based on the principle of maximin. This is that:

All social primary goods are to be distributed equally unless an unequal distribution is to the advantage of everyone.

Rawls, J. (1971)[59]

The justification of a form of economic order, e.g. the market economy lies in 'the extent to which it improves the position of the least well off'.[60] This is not an act of philanthropy it is an acknowledgement that the actor involved might now, or at some point in the future, be the least well off. This proposition does justify inequal distribution of goods but only under specified circumstances. The entrepreneur can benefit from his risk taking and his talent because his achievements mean that the least well off is better off than if the entrepreneur avoided risk because he would not benefit. This process will ultimately prompt everyone to try as hard as they can to maximise the benefits to themselves under this regime. Even the least able or most in need will gain more than in a system which discourages personal effort and endeavour. For some,[61] the Achilles heel of the approach lies in its failure 'to give a statement of the doctrine of the rule of general laws which will make clear what it implies in particular cases'.

This can be achieved through the notion that there exist a *contract* between the firm and the society. The state will reserve the right to intervene to enforce those aspects of the contract which affect its economic and other functions. The leaders of the enterprise will seek the minimum of external intervention by the state in the workings of the market. It is in the interests of the firm to keep the costs to the enterprise of state intervention to a minimum by internalising the implicit and explicit terms of the contract. It is in the interests of the state to favour those enterprises which keep the costs to the community of intervention to a minimum. A version of the Prisoner's Dilemma illustrates this point.

CASE STUDY 6.4

The prisoner's dilemma revisited

In its traditional formulation, the Prisoner's dilemma presents two individuals with a series of absolute choices. It might be two soldiers, Tom and Dan, manning two strongholds in an attempt to hold up an enemy advance. If they both stay at their post there is a 50:50 chance of both surviving. If they both run away, the enemy will overrun the frontier and the chance of either surviving drops sharply to, say, 1:5. If one runs and the other stays, the chances of the deserter increase substantially to, say 8:1 while that of the defender drop dramatically to 1:10. Acting reasonably but without any information or collusion, both will act selfishly to their perceived best advantage but arrive at a sub-optimal solution.

> Tom reasons: if Dan remains at his post, I shall have a much better chance of surviving if I run than if I stay; but also if Dan runs away I shall have a better chance of surviving than if I stay; so whatever Dan is going to do, I would be well advised to run. Since the situation is symmetrical, Dan's reasoning is exactly similar. So both will run. And yet they would each have had a better chance of survival, that is, of achieving the very end they are, by hypothesis, aiming at, if both had remained at their posts.
>
> Mackie, J.[62]

The dilemma is partly resolved and the chances of an optimal solution is increased if they agree the 'ground-rules' in advance and can observe each other's behaviour. In the case of two economic agents, Alpha and Omega, the opportunity exists to agree the ground-rules in advance. This is the implicit and the explicit contract. Information can easily pass between them. It is in their interest to communicate. In most economic relationships, transactions are repeated in some form. This leads to learning and a progressive reduction in the need for explicit rules and intervention unless one or other parties breaks the *agreement*.

This notion of optimisation from learning or the results of action provides a case for the state and business to adopt specific strategies in their business policies. Dawkins[63] uses an illustration from the work on Game Theory by Maynard Smith.[64,65] This can be adapted for this purpose. There are two types of governments or firms; hawks and doves. Hawks are always determined to get their own way. They will fight hard and unrestrainedly. A state of this kind might force legislation which it deems is necessary on industry or firms might threaten or challenge the state using all means at their disposal. Doves avoid conflict. They might posture but they always retreat. If a hawk fights a hawk they fight to the end. A hawk government and a hawk firm will fight to the end – regardless of consequences. A dove government and a dove firm might posture but both eventually will withdraw. The initial convention of the model requires that it is assumed that there is no way initially to recognise type and there is no memory

Table 6.5 Competition pay-off (the limited case)

Starting with a population of doves	average pay-off
When doves fight no one gets hurt. Winner +50, both lose –10 for wasting time, this results in a total pay-off of 30	+15 (doves)
A hawk, however, emerges in the population With only doves to fight, it scores +50 every fight,	+50 (hawks)
Soon there are less doves and far more hawks When hawks fight, the winner gets +50, but the loser fights so hard that it is seriously injured scoring –100	–25 (hawks)
The last remaining dove loses all its fights	0 (doves)

of past events. 'Now as a purely arbitrary convention we allot contestants points. Say 50 points for a win, 0 for losing, – 100 for being seriously injured and – 10 for wasting time'.

The question is which approach is the most stable, i.e. has the best chance of survival. Dawkins asks which is the most 'evolutionarily stable strategy (ESS)'. The outcomes of particular contest are clear. If the hawk meet the dove it will always win. If doves meet no one gets hurt. When hawks meet one will get seriously injured. A pay-off table can be calculated (Table 6.5).

This pattern will tend to produce 'continuous oscillation in the population'. This is a phenomenon which is familiar to all observers of British economic history over the last fifty years. Hawkish governments of the left and right have met hawking organisations, e.g. firms, trade unions. They have fought for their positions until both are hurt.

There are stable points but even these are sub-optimal for both populations. A variant described by Maynard Smith and Price offers a way out. This introduces a retaliator. The retaliator behaves like a dove at the beginning of the confrontation but if its opponent attacks it retaliates. 'A retaliator is a *condition strategist*'.[66] There is a second form of conditioned strategist – the bully. It behaves like a hawk until attacked, at which point, it acts like a dove. The third form is prober-retaliator. Normally, it acts like a retaliator but sometimes tries a brief escalation of the contest. In computer simulations of these strategies 'only one of them, retaliator, emerges as evolutionarily stable'. In human behaviour learning, information and the ability to predict can affect these outcomes. It is, however, likely that the underlying approach provides a vital clue to the character of corporate ethics within the firm and between business and the community. The retaliator approach – avoid intervention until forced – then act like the hawk *to hawks* is optimal.

The interaction between notions of values and rules in order to achieve optimum behaviour lies at the centre of the analysis of business ethics.[67]

Business ethics is a field to the extent that it deals with a set of interrelated questions to be untangled and addressed within an overarching framework. This framework is not supplied by any ethic theory – Kantian, Utilitarian, or theological – but by the systematic interdependence of the questions, which can be approached from various philosophical or other points of view.

De George, R.[68]

A genuinely useful approach will provide a framework for dealings between the firm and its different stakeholder groups: shareholders, customers, employees and groups in the community such as the state.

CONTRACTS AND MISSIONS

The notion of a business contract akin to the social contract can accommodate these different groups. It can find its expression in different forms but there is a growing pressure and demand to give some formulation to the key principles which guide the firm. Mission statements perform this role in an increasing number of firms. Appendix A at the end of this chapter shows the mission statement of the Co-Operative Bank. Typically, these combine:

● An acknowledgement of the nature of the relationship between the enterprise and its community – basis of the contract;
● A broad vision – the nature of the contract;
● The means of delivery – the terms of the contract;
● A system of review and revision – managing the contract;
● The character of the investment – the price(s).

These features can be seen in the mission statements of firms and the framework under which they are developed.

A firm like Prudential Corporation acknowledges that 'the relationship between any commercial organisation and the community in which it thrives must be one of mutual give and take'. This view is expressed even more sharply by British Rail's affirmation that 'the prosperity of British Rail is closely intertwined with the prosperity of the economy as a whole'. In the USA, Aetna Life and Casualty mirror these sentiments in the proposition that 'tending to the broader needs of society is essential to meeting our economic role'. This can take a more affirmatory role. Citicorp's Public Issues Committee tries to 'strengthen the institution's corporate citizenship in its host communities. Elsewhere, the development of one and two per cent clubs are part of a process of advocating certain roles and responsibilities.

This is, typically, part of a broader vision of the nature of the relationship (contract) between the firm and the community. Lord Laing of United Biscuits expresses this as a recognition that 'the vitality of the society in which your company operates is directly relevant to its business interests'. Lord Seiff of Marks and Spencer expressed this as the notion that 'Business only contributes to society if it is efficient, profitable and socially responsible'. His colleague, Lord Rayner,

Table 6.6 The delivery system

Professional systems	Leadership
Clear and stated policies and priorities	Board-level commitment
Communication with stakeholders	Individual and personal endorsement
Planned programmes	Company-wide involvement
Allocation of resources	Strategic perspective
Win commitment	Give high profile
Ensure proper range of activities	Win stakeholder endorsement and support
Planned review and development	

added the codicil that 'it is not the aim of this company to make more profit than is prudent'. Business in The Community highlights at least three direct benefits:

1 *Direct commercial spin-offs*: e.g. better sources of supply, increased purchasing power.
2 *Good employee relations*: from higher motivation and greater satisfaction.
3 *Favourable public relations*: with the firm's different publics.

The terms of the contract are shaped by a mixture of external demands and internal capacity.[69] Guinness emphasise, however, that it involves a true commitment to deliver not 'just corporate window dressing'. Atlantic Richfield Co. expect to employ 'the best control systems, procedures and processes'. This requires a capacity to deliver, which in turn depends on professionalism and leadership (Table 6.6). 'The opportunity for top management to make strong ethical values part of "the normal way we do things here" has never been greater.'[70]

> Connecticut General Life Assurance has created an external affairs planning system which is fully integrated into the company's business planning process.
>
> Task Force on Corporate Social Performance (1980)[71]

An effective system of management requires the creation of systems to review and revise the value and effectiveness of the operations. Tony Cleaver of IBM called for the system to be as professionally managed as 'any other aspects of the business'. The Business in The Community guidelines emphasise 'evaluation proceedures'. Although Johnson and Johnson make clear that 'our final responsibility is to our stockholders', J. C. Penny highlights evaluation as the means 'to improve constantly'. The price can take several forms. Mission statements can be as explicit as that of National Westminster Bank.

> As a founder member of the One Per Cent Club, NatWest has for some years committed itself to reinvesting a fixed percentage of its pre-tax profits for the benefit of the community. At present this amounts to over £10 million per annum.
>
> National Westminster Bank: *Action for the Community*

Glaxo followed a similar route.

> The Glaxo Companies in the United Kingdom gave a total of £2,621,000 in the year ending 30th June 1989.
>
> Glaxo Group of Companies: *Policy on Charitable and Other Community Contributions*

The nature of the contract(s) between the firm and its stakeholders suggests that transparency is the logical conclusion of any attempt to build business ethics into the system of corporate governance at the level of the firm or the community. This helps all members of the enterprise share the mission[72] while minimizing the negative impressions of the firm.[73]

CONCLUSION

The debate on corporate responsibility is shaped by a range of forces. Some reflect the environment in which firms operate. The shift in the relationship between the firm and the community is partly occasioned by the ideas of those who decried the costs and social implications of the expanded role of the state after World War II. The withdrawal of the state was prompted by a mixture of economic pressures and doubts over its capability. The former was prompted in Britain and North America by a growing realisation of the limits on government power to resolve the economic difficulties facing these societies in the late 1970s. There were those who asserted that the state was not competent to plan a lead role in economic management. This view was part of the assault of ideas which prompted the slow withdrawal. It is, however, a conditional withdrawal. The conditions reflect the grounds on which the retreat took place. There is the expectation that the new relationship will lead to the better performance by industry of the economic function.

Alongside this, are assumptions about the values underpinning the relationship between industry and the community and the ways these are delivered through behaviour. The notion that managers and their enterprises are mere creatures of their owners is both unrealistic in the current environment and begs the question of the behaviour sought by these owners.

> In a free enterprise, private property system, a corporate executive is an employee of the owners of the business. He has direct responsibility to his employers. That responsibility is to conduct the business in accord with their desires, which generally will be to make as much money as possible while conforming to the basic rules of society . . . in so far as his actions raise the price to consumers, he is spending the customer's money. Insofar as his actions lower the wages of some employees, he is spending their money.
>
> Friedman, F. (1971)[74]

The growing body of literature in business ethics and corporate responsibility is part of a long tradition of debate on the relationship between the entrepreneur, the enterprise and the community. It has some overlap with parallel debates, notably medical ethics.[75] There are major differences which make the extension of the links between these fields tenuous and difficult to sustain. Two are especially important. The first is the *voluntary* and *active* nature of the economic and business relationship. Typically, the parties volunteer to engage in the transaction. This often involves two active parties. The notion of the marketing exchange[76] is an especially vivid illustration of this.

> (Marketing) emphasises mutuality of benefit. The exchanges work and persist because it is in the best interests of both parties to continue. Through this, both prosper as needs are satisfied by goods and services which suppliers will continue to supply because they profit and which are bought because customers' benefits exceed costs.
>
> Cannon, T. (1992)[77]

Most of the key issues in medical ethics lack the voluntary involvement of both parties. The classic medical situation involves the *distress-* based involvement of one party. They are obliged through illness or some other factors to engage in the relationship. A similar distinction can be seen in the passive participation of patients and other parties in many of the key cases which shape discussion of medical ethics. The unborn child clearly exemplifies this problem.

The voluntary and active participation of the parties makes the notion of the 'business contract' especially relevant. In this chapter, the derivation and character of this contract is placed in the context of a wider discussion of business ethics and corporate and community responsibility. The contract acknowledges the continuing role of the state.

> Where the public interest . . . is at issue, there is no natural right to be left alone.
>
> Galbraith, J. K. (1973)[78]

It substitutes an opportunity to define a contract based on mutual rights and distinct responsibilities.

QUESTIONS

1 Identify the key features of a meaningful and easy-to-implement code of ethics. How might a firm convert these principles in practice?

2 Describe the corporate social responsibility programmes of a major corporation with which you are familiar. Illustrate how these programmes reflect wider aspirations of the firm.

3 Discuss the proposition that the major determinant of a firm's pattern of corporate philanthropy is the composition of the board.

4 What mechanisms does the community have to shape the attitudes and behaviour of managers and firms? Illustrate with examples of endorsement and censure.

5 Use either the DeLorean Case or the Case of Johnson Matthey to outline the failings of existing systems of internal restraint or external control. Put forward policy proposals which firms or societies might implement to avoid a repetition of the events outlined in the case chosen.

6 Discuss the ethical implications of Friedman's statement[79] that 'capitalism is a necessary condition for political freedom'.

7 'Scientific Management' is fundamentally exploitative and inhumane – outline the arguments for and against this proposition.

8 Using the arguments of a 'school' of philosophy, e.g. Utilitarianism, construct an ethically, sustainable case for a developing country refusing to pay its debts to a British or US bank.

9 Use the information in the 'Vegetable Fats Dilemma' and any directly relevant information gathered elsewhere to advise the European board of the vegetable fats company on an ethically and socially sustainable course of action.

10 Define:

(a) Stakeholders
(b) Social endorsement
(c) Peer group pressure
(d) Utilitarianism
(e) Positivism

(f) Teleological
(g) Kant's notion of 'good will'
(h) Libertarianism
(i) Subjectivism
(j) Golden Rules

CASE STUDY 1

The investment dilemma

In 1972, Platt Oils and Chemicals of Indiana established a large synthetic, organic chemicals plant in Indonesia. For the next ten years the plant prospered. Abundant supplies of local raw materials, low labour rates and very favourable exchange rates made this one of the company's most profitable operations. There were some problems with remission of profits but these had usually been resolved by a mixture of constructive negotiations and export credit transfers. Relations between the company and the government of Indonesia were excellent.

Although the firm had no links with Union Carbide, the disaster at Bhopal had an immediate and direct effect on the firm's operations. The communities in which they operated in the USA demanded that the firm undertake extensive reviews of its operations. At the same time, a Congressional Committee undertook a wide-ranging review of operating practices at US chemical companies at home and overseas. These internal and external reviews prompted the firm to invite a major firm of environmental consultants to examine existing health and safety regulations and propose any changes that they felt were necessary for the firm to 'set and maintain the highest standards for health and safety at work'. The report from the consultants was made available to local community groups and the Congressional Committee.

The firm invited their comments and agreed to involve them in the final decisions about the measures to implement their recommendations. Many of the proposals which emerged from this study were incorporated in the firm's operations over the three years, 1987–90.

Platt Oils and Chemicals of Indiana was soon seen as a bench-mark firm in terms of its approach to health and safety. There were, however, significant costs involved in introducing these changes. These produced price increases in the range 5–7 per cent. Initially this led to a cut in sales in the USA but these soon recovered as other North American processors introduced similar measures. In 1990, George H. Platt Jnr attended a Conference organised by Business in The Community under the auspices of HRH the Prince of Wales in Charleston, South Carolina. At this meeting, he was strongly influenced by debates about the international aspects of environmental and health and safety issues. He came back determined to apply the highest US health and safety regulations to all their plants across the world. Of these, the operations in Indonesia were by far the largest.

He instructed the International Vice President to set this process in motion on his next trip to Indonesia. This took place just over a month later. When the International Vice President reported back, he was forced to indicate the strong objections of the Indonesian government to the proposed changes and the likely price increases. The government of Indonesia wanted the changes postponed indefinitely for three core reasons:

1 Any price increases would cut back exports from the plant and encourage imports.
2 The changes would reduce capacity especially during the time they were being introduced.
3 The government did not believe the changes were necessary and resented the attempt to make plants in its country comply with 'foreign' regulations.

The board of Platt Oils and Chemicals faced a major dilemma. They were strongly of the view that these changes would improve the health and safety of its workers. The government of Indonesia was fiercely hostile. This opposition was strengthened by the value of these exports (the plant was the tenth largest source of foreign exchange from processed or manufactured exports) and the sharp increase in demand which was occurring as the economies of other countries in the region boomed.

QUESTIONS

1 Advise the company on a route forward.

2 Identify a programme of actions designed to implement these proposals.

3 Outline the implications of this type of situation for efforts to set internationally comparable standards of health, safety or environmental protection.

APPENDIX A
THE CO-OPERATIVE BANK MISSION STATEMENT

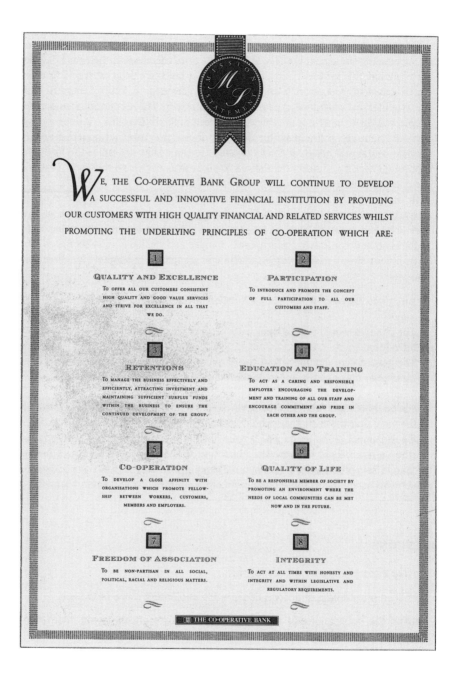

We, the Co-operative Bank Group will continue to develop a successful and innovative financial institution by providing our customers with high quality financial and related services whilst promoting the underlying principles of co-operation which are:

1 QUALITY AND EXCELLENCE

To offer all our customers consistent high quality and good value services and strive for excellence in all that we do.

2 PARTICIPATION

To introduce and promote the concept of full participation to all our customers and staff.

3 RETENTIONS

To manage the business effectively and efficiently, attracting investment and maintaining sufficient surplus funds within the business to ensure the continued development of the group.

4 EDUCATION AND TRAINING

To act as a caring and responsible employer encouraging the development and training of all our staff and encourage commitment and pride in each other and the group.

5 CO-OPERATION

To develop a close affinity with organisations which promote fellowship between workers, customers, members and employers.

6 QUALITY OF LIFE

To be a responsible member of society by promoting an environment where the needs of local communities can be met now and in the future.

7 FREEDOM OF ASSOCIATION

To be non-partisan in all social, political, racial and religious matters.

8 INTEGRITY

To act at all times with honesty and integrity and within legislative and regulatory requirements.

THE CO-OPERATIVE BANK

REFERENCES

1. United Biscuits *Annual Report*, Isleworth, United Biscuits (1991).
2. Soloman, R. and Hanson, K. *It's Good Business*, New York, Atheneum (1985).
3. Clutterbuck, D. *Actions Speak Louder*, London, Kogan Page (1992).
4. Cuilla, J. B. 'Why is Business Talking About Ethics?' *California Management Review*, vol. 34, no. 1, Fall (1991) pp. 101–17.
5. Webley, S. *Company Philiosophies and Codes of Business Ethics*, London, Institute for Business Ethics (1988).
6. Wang, J. and Coffey, B. 'Board Composition and Corporate Philanthropy' *Journal of Business Education*, vol. 11 no. 10 (1992) pp. 771–8.
7. Demb, A. and Neubauer, F. *The Corporate Board*, Oxford, Oxford University Press (1992).
8. Fromm, E. *To Have Or To Be*, London, Abacus (1976).
9. Vogel, D. 'The Ethical Roots of Business Ethics' *Business Ethics Quarterly*, January (1991) pp. 17–26.
10. Gambling, T. and Kavin, R. A. *Business and Accounting Ethics in Islam*, Mansell, London (1991).
11. Benedict, R. *The Chrysanthemum and the Sword*, Boston, Houghton Mifflin (1946).
12. Tomlinson, J. 'This Society of Ours' *Journal of the Royal Society for the Encouragement of Arts, Manufactures and Commerce*, December (1989) pp. 17–24.
13. Posner, B. Z. and Schmidt, W. H. 'Values, Congruence and Differences Between the Interplay of Personal and Organisational Value Systems' *Journal of Business Education*, vol. 12 no. 3 (1993) pp. 341–8.
14. Social Security Committee of the House of Commons, *The Operation of Pension Funds*, London, HMSO (1992).
15. Derry, R. 'Institutionalising Ethical Motivation', In Freeman, R. E. (ed.) *Business Ethics*, Oxford, Oxford University Press (1991).
16. Weaver, P. H. *The Suicidal Corporation*, New York, Simon & Schuster (1988).
17. Saunders, J. *Nightmare: The Ernest Saunders Story*, London, Hutchinson (1989).
18. Fallon, I. and Strodes, J. *DeLorean*, London, Coronet (1983).
19. Comments made to Parliament by the then Chancellor of the Exchequer, Mr Nigel Lawson.
20. Fay, S. *Portrait of an Old Lady*, Harmondsworth, Penguin (1988).
21. Tricker, R. 'Impressive, Inscrutable but not Incorruptible' *Director*, February (1992).
22. Paxman, J. *Friends in High Places*, Harmondsworth, Penguin (1991).
23. Demb, A. and Neubauer, F., ibid.
24. One of the criticisms of the institutions in the Lloyds names case is that they did not keep their clients fully informed – keeping the best opportunities for themselves and 'dumping' the rest on outsiders.
25. Locke, J. *An Essay Concerning Human Understanding*, London, J. M. Dent and Sons (1961).
26. Lillie, W. *An Introduction to Ethics*, London, Methuen (1964).
27. Donaldson, J. *Key Issues in Business Ethics*, London, Academic Press (1989).
28. Friedman, M. *Capitalism and Freedom*, Chicago, University of Chicago Press (1962).
29. Pass, C., Lowes, B. and Davies, L. *Dictionary of Economics*, London, Collins (1988).
30. Pass, C., Lowes, B. and Davies, L., ibid.
31. Hume, D. *A Treatise of Human Nature* (1739).
32. Drucker, P. *Innovation and Entrepreneurship*, London, Heinemann (1985).
33. Adair, J. *Effective Leadership*, London, Pan (1983).
34. Donaldson, J., ibid.
35. Schumpeter, J. *Capitalism, Socialism and Democracy*, London, Geo. Allen and Unwin (1942).
36. Churchill, W. S., London, Hansard, 22 October (1945).
37. Taylor, F. W. *Scientific Management*, London, Harper and Row (1947).
38. Mayo, E. 'Hawthorne and the Western Electric Company', in *The Social Problems of an Industrial Civilisation*, London, Routledge (1949).
39. Woodward, J. *Management and Technology*, London, HMSO (1958).
40. Sloan, A. P. *My Years With General Motors*, Harmondsworth, Penguin (1989).
41. Gay, P. *The Enlightenment: An Interpretation*, New York, W. W. Norton (1966).

42. Raphael, R. *British Moralists 1650–1800*, Oxford, Oxford University Press (1969).
43. Mackie, J. L. *Ethics: Inventing Right and Wrong*, Harmondsworth, Penguin (1990).
44. Lillie, W., ibid.
45. Smart, J. J. C. and Williams, B. *Utilitarianism: For and Against*, Cambridge, Cambridge University Press (1973).
46. Kant, I. *The Critique of Practical Reason*, (1779).
47. Mill, J. S. *Utilitarianism*, (1861).
48. Seldon, A. *Capitalism*.
49. Moore, G. E. *Principlia Ethica*, Cambridge, Cambridge University Press (1903).
50. Warnock, M. *Ethics Since 1900*, Oxford, Oxford University Press (1960).
51. Ayer, A. J. *Language, Truth and Logic*, London, Gollancz (1937).
52. Hare, R. M. *Moral Thinking*, Oxford, Clarendon Press (1981).
53. Flew, R. M. *Dictionary of Philosophy*, London (1982).
54. Geach, P. 'Good and Evil', in Foot, P. *Theories in Ethics*, Oxford, Oxford University Press (1967).
55. Brown, A. *Modern Political Philosophy*, Harmondsworth, Penguin (1986).
56. Nozick, *Anarchy, State and Utopia*, Oxford, Blackwell (1990).
57. Brown, A., ibid.
58. Rawls, A. *A Theory of Justice*, Oxford, Oxford University Press (1971).
59. Rawls, A., ibid.
60. Le Grand, J. 'Equity as an Economic Objective', in Almond, B. and Hill, D. (ed.) *Applied Philosophy: Morals and Metaphysics in Contemporary Debate*, London, Routledge (1991).
61. Brittan, S. *The Role and Limits of Government: Essays in Political Economy*, London, Temple Smith (1993).
62. Mackie, J., ibid.
63. Dawkins, R. *The Selfish Gene*, Oxford, Oxford University Press (1976).
64. Maynard Smith, J. and Parker, G. A. 'The Logic of Asymmetric Contests' in *Animal Behaviour*, 24, (1976), pp. 159–75.
65. Maynard Smith, J. and Price, G. A. 'The Logic of Animal Conflicts' *Nature* 246 (1973) pp. 15–18.
66. Dawkins, R., ibid.
67. Kahn, W. A. 'Towards an Agenda for Business Ethics Research' *Academy of Management Review*, vol. 15, no. 2 (1990) pp. 311–28.
68. De George, R. 'The Status of Business Ethics: Past, Present and Future' *Journal of Business Ethics*, vol. 6, no. 3.
69. Watson, C. 'Managing with Integrity: Social Responsibilities of Business as seen by America's CEOs' *Business Horizons*, vol. 34, no. 4, July/August (1991) pp. 99–109.
70. Clutterbuck, D., ibid.
71. Task Force on Corporate Social Performance *Business and Society: Strategies for the 1980s*, Washington, US Department of Commerce (1980).
72. Murphy, P. E. 'Creating Ethical Corporate Structures' *Sloan Management Review*, vol. 30, no. 2 (1989) pp. 81–7.
73. Dunn, C. P. 'Are Corporations Inherently Wicked?' *Business Horizons*, vol. 34, no. 4, July/August (1990) pp. 3–8.
74. Friedman, F. 'Does Business have a Social Responsibility' *Bank Administration*, April (1971).
75. Mann, R. D., Brahams, D., Lamont, L. and Saunders, P. 'Aspects of Medical Ethics' *Journal of the Royal Society of Arts*, vol. cxl, no. 5433, October (1992) pp. 669–82.
76. Cannon, T. *Basic Marketing*, London, Cassell (1992).
77. Cannon, T., ibid.
78. Galbraith, J. K. 'On the Economic Image of Corporate Enterprise' in Nader, R. and Gree, M. *Corporate Power in America*, New York, Grossman Publishers (1973).
79. Friedman, M., ibid.

PART 2

Governance and compliance

CHAPTER 7

The nature and evolution of governance

> The great modern corporations are so similar to independent or semi-independent states of the past that they can only be fully understood in terms of political and constitutional history, and management can only be properly studied as a branch of government.
>
> Jay, A. (1967)[1]

The issues addressed in Part 1 touch on the debate on the evolving nature of corporate governance. Changes in industrial structures, shifts in economic relationships and the interaction between business and the community are forcing society and firms to review the ways in which organisations are governed. Some of these pressures are long established. Chandler's work[2] describes how the structures and systems of administration and governance evolved to meet the needs of changing environments and new ideas.[3] He indicates how the forms of administration have changed in response to four broad pressures:

1 The firm's 'previous organisation . . . (and) administrative history';
2 The ways in which the enterprise had expanded;
3 The economy 'particularly those affecting the market or demand for the enterprise's products';
4 The 'state of the administrative art'.

Later researchers[4] have broadly endorsed this view which indicates that other factors notably:

5 The legal environment;[5]
6 The strategies of the firm;[6]
7 The character of the industry or community in which it operates;[7,8]
8 Expectations about the firm and its governance.[9]

can have a marked effect on the form of governance and the way it is managed.

The conventional views of governance are being challenged by the demands of different groups. Stockholders 'will become more knowledgeable about how a company is managed and will flex their muscles'.[10] Banks will get 'more freedom'[11] to intervene and will demand higher standards. Employees will seek greater involvement and strive to act as partners in wealth creation not wage earners. Governments make less demands but have higher expectations. The community and other stakeholders will be more expert at presenting their arguments and demanding results. It would be surprising if CEOs 'ever recapture the kind of security enjoyed ten years ago'.[12]

Only a few years ago Galbraith[13] could argue that 'professional management is so entrenched in the very large companies that they cannot be challenged or overthrown'.[14] Today, the leaders of the largest firms are being successfully challenged.

> Seldom can company chairmen and chief executives have been more nervous than they are this spring. Not only are the bosses on both sides of the Atlantic facing the threat of corporate take-over, but they are suffering a much more personal fear – of being knifed by their own board colleagues.
>
> General Motors set the trend when its outside directors took action after years of intense frustration at the leviathon's poor performance. They demoted the company's chairman by ousting him from his post as head of GM's top strategic forum. This sent tremors throughout corporate America: if it could happen at GM it could happen anywhere.
>
> Lorenz, C. (1992)[15]

The high watermark of entrenched corporate power in the post World War II era probably occurred in the late 1980s. The success of corporate raiders like T-Boone Pickens in the USA and Lord Hanson in Britain prompted 'corporate management to do whatever was necessary to protect their capacity to direct their enterprises, and they found that protecting themselves from raiders meant protecting themselves from shareholders and squeezing any remaining semblance of accountability out of the system'.[16] Firms like CBS invented new techniques like 'poisoned pills' to protect themselves from 'greenmail' and other hostile approaches. Poisoned pills are rights issues given to shareholders which have no value unless triggered by a hostile bid. At this point they have a value far out of line with any fair price the acquirer would pay. This new debt would destroy the economic base of the firm. Greenmail is a technique used by raiders who buy a significant holding in a firm. They then offer to hold back from a full bid if the firm or directors pays an inflated price for their shares. The era of 'poisoned pills' and other 'shark repellents' and matching approaches by potential acquirers stimulated levels of creativity that some argued would be better applied to business development.[17]

The apparent pre-occupation of firms in the USA with this type of issue contrasted sharply with the priorities of firms in Germany, Japan and other more successful economies and firms. Public disquiet about local and national economic decline and shareholder disappointment at poor returns and declining asset values provoked newspaper headlines and demands by politicians for reform with the threat of legislative action if change was delayed. In the USA, the Business Roundtable made a series of recommendations for reform.[18] In Britain, the

Cadbury Committee was set up and produced specific proposals for change in the pattern of corporate governance.[19]

The change in the climate of opinion was vividly illustrated by the actions taken by the boards of some of the largest firms in the world to force the resignation of their top managers. These companies included such giants as General Motors in the USA and BP in the UK.

> Behind all the shuffling lies the rising power of boards. Shareholders have been prodding boards to kick out more CEOs. Boards of companies such as Westinghouse, IBM and American Express eased out CEOs earlier this year after losing confidence in them.
>
> *Source: USA Today*, April 19, 1993

These actions mark a major shift in opinion. This is away from the notion that the public company can be viewed as the private enterprise or fiefdom of the proprietor. This is especially true in the concerns about the loyalties, duties and responsibilities of the directors. The directors found that all their needs were now attended to in detail. Bill Anderson of NCR slid into Sticht's chairmanship of the International Advisory Board and was slipped an $80,000 contract for his services. Johnson disbanded RJR Nabisco's shareholder services department and contracted its work out to John Medlin's Wachovia Bank. Juanita Kreps was given $2 million to endow two chairs at Duke, one of them named after herself. For another $2 million, Duke's business school named a wing of a new building 'Horrigan Hall'. (Johnson was named a Duke trustee.) Ron Grierson was also being fussed over lovingly; on his visits to Atlanta, Grierson spent so much time on the phone Johnson took an alcove and marked it 'Ronnie Grierson's office'.

Holdovers from Johnson's Nabisco board did especially well. Bob Schaeberle was given a six-year, $180,000-a-year consulting contract for ill-defined duties. Andy Sage received $250,000 a year for his efforts with financial R&D. In an unusual move, Charlie Hugel took Sticht's post as the ceremonial 'nonexecutive' chairman of RJR Nabisco, for which he received a $150,000 contract. By naming him chairman, Johnson hoped Hugel would cement his increasingly close ties with the board. At the same time, the number of board meetings was slashed, and directors' fees were boosted to $50,000. Burrough, B. and Helyar, J. (1990)

Many analysts in Britain and the USA see the relationship between the independant directors and the executives as too close. These worries can be illustrated by examples from both sides of the Atlantic.

> I decided it was time I exercised **my** option to appoint a further director. I chose Peter Thornycroft. He had been Chancellor of the Exchequer during the late 1950s in the Macmillan government, and had acquired a number of City directorships before becoming a life peer in 1967. I had known him for many years . . . I had strengthened my position.
>
> Forte, C. (1986)[20]

Both the *New York Times* and *Wall Street Journal* . . . accused Henry Ford II of boasting that he had all the outside directors of the Ford Motor Company 'in his pocket', and he bought their loyalty and obedience 'with large pay . . . and with Dom Perignon champagne'.

Lacey, R. (1986)[21]

Among the factors provoking this shift in opinion three are especially important. The first, is the change in relationship between the state and the firm. External regulation of behaviour is viewed as a poor substitute for proper governance. Second, current thinking among business and economic researchers acknowledges and asserts the rights of the owners and shareholders over the paid managers.[22, 23] Both, probably, reflect a third, wider concern that the interests of the managerial groups in large firms are not in tune with current market needs. Their preoccupations do not emphasise the requirements to change, grow and innovate.[24] They prefer to emphasise evolution and security (Table 7.1).

The rapid rate of change seen over the last decade has emphasised the importance of the entrepreneurial approach to business development. This emphasises the search for new opportunities and rapid response to events. Freedom, flexibility and the minimum of overheads are priorities with the entrepreneur.[25] Studies of success during the type of changes seen in recent years suggest that this type of approach is more effective than the risk avoidance, security seeking and bureaucratic style of management characteristic of traditional large firms.[26]

This desire by *the owners* to have a say is reinforced by the publicity given to

Table 7.1 Managerial styles

	Promoter ◄——————— ———————► Trustee Entrepreneur ◄————— —————► Administrator	
Characteristic	*Form (P/E)*	*Form (T/A)*
Strategic orientation	Opportunity driven	Resource driven
Commitment to opportunity	Revolutionary – short duration	Evolutionary – long duration
Commitment of resources	Multistage – minimal at each stage	Single stage – complete commitment on decision
Control of resources	Episodic use or rental	Ownership or full employment of required resources
Management structure	Flat, informal, hub-based	Formal, hierarchical, bureaucratic
Reward philosophy	Value, driven, performance-based, teams	Security driven, resource-based, promotion, careerism
Governance	Personal	Institutional
Priorities	Performance	Security

Source: based on Chell, E. *et al.*[27] and Stephenson, *et al.*[28]

Table 7.2 Matters of governance

The benefits issue	Questions of supervision
Average earnings of the highest paid executives rose by 10 per cent in 1991 despite 'probably the worst financial returns in living memory'[29]	'His [Professor Gower] findings were that no overall system of regulation of the investment media and securities industry existed and such unrelated elements of regulation which did exist consisted of a hotch potch of undetermined controls . . .'[30]
Average increases for senior management of 18 per cent compared with inflation at 8 per cent, middle management increases of 8.5 per cent and average wage increases of 6 per cent	'When big white collar crime comes along, the country does not know what to do and the legal enforcement machinery appears to freeze'[31]

actions which suggest that top management are running the firm for their own benefit; poorly supervised and making major errors of judgement. Events like the rapid increase in top management salaries and the failure of current structures to identify or address major failures and disappointing performance have re-inforced these demands for change.[32]

During the late 1980s and early 1990s these pressures have prompted a large-scale revision of practice, supervision and regulation in Britain, North America and other countries (Table 7.2).

THE CHALLENGE TO CURRENT PRACTICE

The governance of an enterprise is the sum of those activities which make up the internal regulation of the business in compliance with the obligations placed on the firm by legislation, ownership and control. It incorporates the trusteeship of assets, their management and their deployment. The responsibilities of the trustee centre on the disinterested care of assets belonging to another party. The executor is an agent entrusted with the deployment of resources on behalf of another. A manager is expected to marshal assets to get the best returns for his employers. Each of these components are included in the notion of effective governance. The separation of ownership from control in most large firms shaped a view of the the senior management of the firm as the 'elected' government of the firm. They are elected by, and as such are responsible to, their electors, i.e. the voters or shareholders in the enterprise.

This notion of a *government* and an *electorate* grew up initially in the USA.[33] The disappointing performance of many firms in the late 1980s and early 1990s, their seeming lack of competitiveness, prompted investors to look for ways to exert more direct pressure on the enterprise and its top management. The pressure for greater responsiveness was increased by a mixture of *grass roots* radicalism – the most vivid example being Ross Perot's demands for improved performance at General Motors – and the impatience of institutional investors. The latter have often seen the forceful demands of radicals like Ross Perot, T. Bone Pickens and others as powerful endorsements of their demands for greater say in the affairs of the giant corporations. This interventionism by some institutional investors stands in marked contrast to their traditions of non-involvement, especially in Britain. Their impatience is increased by the poor fit which often seems to exist between executive remuneration and corporate performance and the apparently cosy relationship between executive directors and non-executive or independant directors. The self-appointed and re-appointed managerial oligarchy is anathema to many spokespeople for the investor or ownership groups.

This assertion of investor rights is, in part, a reaction to events during the 1970s and 1980s which tended to emphasise the rights of other stakeholder

---

(Gekko is invited forward by the Chairman and CEO)
I appreciate the opportunity you are giving me – as the largest shareholder in Teldar Papers – to speak.

We are not here to deal in fantasies but in political and economic reality. America has become a second-rate power, its trade deficits and its fiscal deficits are at nightmarish proportions.

Now, in the days of the free market when our country was a top industrial power there was accountability. The Carnegies, the Mellons, the men that built this great industrial empire made sure it was – because it was their money at stake.

Today, management has no stake in the company. All together these men sitting up here own less that three per cent of the company. And where does Mr Cromwell put his $million salary? Not in Teldar Stock. He owns less than one per cent.

You own the company, that's right, you, the stockholders and you are all being royally screwed over by these bureaucrats with their stock lunches, their hunting and fishing trips, their corporate jets and the golden parachutes.

Teldar Papers has 33 Vice Presidents each earning over $200,000 per year. I have spent the last two months analysing what these guys do and I still can't figure it out. One thing I do know is that our paper company lost $110 million last year and I'll bet that half of that was spent on the paperwork going between all these Vice Presidents.

The new law of corporate America seems to be survival of the unfittest. Well in my book, you either do it right or you get eliminated. In the last seven deals that I was involved in there were 2.5 million stockholders who made a pre-tax profit if $12 billion.

I am not a destroyer of companies. I am a liberator of them.

Fig. 7.1 Revolt on Wall Street: extracts from Gordon Gekko's speech to the shareholders' meeting
Source: Wall Street, director Oliver Stone, Twentieth Century Fox, 1987

Table 7.3 Stakeholder: an indicative list

Primary	Secondary
Shareholders	Communities and community groups in areas near factories, offices, etc.
Employees	Environmental agencies or groups
Customers	Ethics or standards groups
Suppliers	Monitoring agencies, e.g. professions
Collaborators	Media
Government	Other commentators, e.g. academics
Extra government bodies, e.g. EC	Law

groups.[34] A comprehensive list of other stakeholders would range from investors to environmental pressure groups (Table 7.3). There is an identifiable feeling that the needs of the employee and government stakeholders were gaining precedence over the owners and risk takers.

A CORPORATE PERSPECTIVE

The assertion of investor rights has not gone wholly unchallenged. Sir James Ball is 'a strong advocate of separating the direction and executive management of the business'.[35] The more time executives spend presenting and justifying their actions to stockholders the less time they have for business development through improvements in operations, innovation or marketing. Lord Haslam[36] points out that balance between reporting and doing is the key difference in the work of top management in the public and private sector. In the private sector, 80 per cent of a senior manager's time is spend 'doing one's job' and only 20 per cent reporting on it. In the public sector, 20 per cent of time is spent doing the job and 80 per cent reporting. The concern is that closer scrutiny by investors will mean far more time reporting and far less time doing. Operationally, the concerns about investor demands centre on two basic issues: management discretion and short-termism.

Research into business success consistently highlights the importance of confidence, risk-taking and management discretion. Peters and Waterman's research[37] highlighted the importance of a customer orientation, employee development and management values in determining the success of a business (Table 7.4). Subsequent research in Europe[38] has given broad support for these findings and highlighted the support for these principles among top management.[39] Parallel studies from different perspectives have highlighted other management characteristics which are linked with business success but show the same limited link with greater investor power. These include the work of Kantor[40] on innovation and Porter[41] on competitiveness. Investor intervention

Table 7.4 The characteristics of business excellence

Feature	Characteristics	Fit with investor power
Bias for action	Act – avoid paralysis through analysis	Low
Keep close to customers	Concentrate on meeting customer needs	Medium
Autonomy and entrepreneurship	Be willing to take risks and act like entrepreneurs	Low
Productivity through people	Recognise the importance of the firm's employees	Low
Hands-on, value driven	Promote corporate values	Medium
Stick to knitting	Concentrate on what the firm does well	High
Simple form, lean staff	Avoid bureaucracy and overheads	High
Simultaneous tight, loose management	Allow employees to follow initiative within well-defined strategy	Medium

Source: Peters, T. and Waterman, R. (1982)[42]

which reduced the overall competitiveness of the venture defeats its purpose. There is some evidence[43] from Germany and Japan that secure long-term, partnership-based collaboration between executive management and investors can meet both sets of needs. There is, however, greater suspicion in Britain and the USA that executives will feather their own nests and investors will concentrate on short-term profit taking.

> The standard of achievement has been set too low. Only a low standard is desired and one still lower is acceptable . . . a higher standard of competence is not desired, for an efficient organisation would be beyond the chief's power to control . . . its chief symptom [is] smugness. The aims have been set low and have therefore been largely achieved . . . Their smugness reveals itself in remarks such as this: 'The chief is a sound man and very clever when you get to know him. He never says very much – that is not his way – but he seldom makes a mistake' [or] 'clever people can be a dreadful nuisance'.
>
> Parkinson, C. Northcote (1986)[44]

This last comment can be especially galling to the very clever people who manage investment companies.

Innovation is central to the long-term success of companies in times of rapid change such as exist today. Often, a firm that builds a secure long-term base for success needs to plan for the long term. It invests in building a science base, seeking out new ideas, research and development and sustained support for novel products and services. This means forgoing immediate returns in dividends in return for long-term growth in asset values.[45] This can be inconsistent with the demands of shareholders for immediate returns. There is some evidence that the structure of institutional investment in Britain[46] and the USA[47] reinforces this emphasis on short-term returns.

The chairman of Sony asserts that a company which re-invests in itself instead of concentration on profits alone will in the long run be returning more to the shareholders. It cannot be coincidental that the UK and the USA (two countries with the most free market and highest levels of predatory activity) have the lowest levels of re-investment as a percentage of total output over the last 20 years – at 12 per cent and 13 per cent respectively.

Japan, not surprisingly, has the highest investment rate at 22 per cent . . . The main justification for the capitalist system, is that it provides the best climate for innovation and risk taking. If the managers of a firm are discouraged from taking risks, by the attitudes of the owners, the shareholders, discouraged from undertaking research, from investment in innovation and increasing market share – then capitalism itself is called into question.

Lord Laing (1990)[48]

Effective stewardship and good returns for investors are not inconsistent with business building, risk taking and adding value.[49]

The successful integration of corporate social responsibility and business performance turns on two integrating attributes of good executive management and investor behaviour: *trust* and *confidence*. When executive management does not trust its investor groups to back its judgement and let it manage, it will lose confidence in its ability to succeed. Often this will prompt conspicuous consumption, overhead growth – to cover every option – and risk avoidance. When shareholders do not trust executive managers to act with proper diligence they will lose confidence in their ability to prosper. This produces increasing demands for more information, power and action. Together they create a vicious circle of decline. Due respect for the rights and responsibilities of both parties provides the only effective way to break this and build a virtuous circle of development.

The small number of systematic, empirical investigations into the relationship between corporate responsibility have been relatively inconclusive. McGuire[50] found that 'prior performance is generally a better predictor of social performance than subsequent performance'. Aupperle[51] found 'no statistically significant relation'. All studies in the area have acknowledged the serious difficulties of producing adequate measures of corporate social responsibility and generalising from results.

RIGHTS AND RESPONSIBILITIES

The rights and responsibilities of shareholders and directors of firms are spelt out in substantive bodies of legislation which reflect the legal structures, policies and economic and social values of nations. In Britain and North America, the twin notions of *unity* and *distinction* have characterised the prevailing pattern of governance. In effect, this means that there is a single, unitary board with executive and non-executive directors working together but with the same legal responsibilities. Alongside this, is the proposition that investors keep a largely hands-off approach to the firm. They vote with their feet, investing in firms that perform well, withdrawing from poor performers. In Europe[52] and Japan,[53] there are important differences. A two-tier board is quite common. In Germany, this is the dominant system. The *supervisory* board is kept separate from *executive* board and the management of the firm. Inevitably, local patterns of corporate ownership affect this. In France, less than 10 per cent of companies have *conseils de supervision* (supervisory boards) but over half the largest firms remain in private or family ownership and the state controls almost 20 per cent of stock by value. It is, however, in the separation of powers that the greatest differences exist. In Germany, the main lenders and investors expect to have a direct involvement and say in the development of the firm.

> The banks have the informal power . . . They sit on the board, they give loans to the company, they know the condition of the company.
>
> Quotes in Business International (1992)[54]

In Japan, large financial institutions hold the bulk of shares. A mixture of bottom-up consultation and reciprocity dominates ownership and control. This is under increasing attack from a mixture of external pressure and internal demands for reform.

In Britain a mixture of legislation, centring on the Companies Acts; regulation, enforced by agencies like the Securities and Investments Board and voluntarism, such as the City Code on Take-Overs and Mergers provides the framework for defining rights and responsibilities. Shareholders have shares in the nominal capital of the company. This entitles them to a proportion of the distributed profits of the enterprise. They have a right to a proportion of the residual value if the enterprise goes into liquidation. In effect, this means that they are the last to be paid after all loans and debtors are repaid. Holders of ordinary or voting shares have a right to vote on policies placed before them. They have the power to control the firm if they can mobilise 50 per cent plus one of the shares of the enterprise. Some policies require the support of a larger majority, e.g. a change in the articles of association might require the support of 75 per cent of the shareholder votes. These powers are exercised through the directors appointed by the shareholders.

Directors are responsible for the good governance of the firm.[55] This has both a legal and an operational meaning. Legally, the obligations of directors are spelt out in legislation or defined by precedent. They can extend beyond the liabilities of the firm. A firm, for example, can have limited liability under UK law. A director's liabilities for damages are unlimited. The trends in UK law are strongly towards extending the personal liability exposure of executive and non-executive directors of the firm. The directors act in concert through the board of directors.

> Externally, the Board is concerned with safeguarding the Company's assets in the long-term interest of shareholders. The non-executive directors are particularly con-

cerned with the protection of shareholders' interests . . . the Board also has the responsibility to position the Company's strategy in regard to business development – earnings growth, planning of acquisitions and disinvestments.

Smith, Sir R. (1991)[56]

It is this blend of trusteeship and executive leadership which poses the most complex dilemmas for shareholders and directors seeking to achieve a proper balance of rights and responsibilities.

The traditional assumptions that a combination of informal pressure, information and the power to withdraw support could provide sufficient *control* against excesses or failure are severely threatened by the scale of operations, imperfect information and risks of withdrawal. Investor power – expressed in its current form – could not prevent the decline of major corporations in the USA or Britain such as GM, RJR Nabisco, IBM, Westinghouse, Dunlop, British Leyland, Burma Oil, Chloride, Distillers, etc. By the time shareholders acted against Saunders (Guinness), Davis (Next), Berry (Arrow), Marguiles (Berisford), Halpern (Burton), White (Bunzle) and many others in Britain, it was too late to avoid major losses. Even in these cases, investors could seldom prevent large pay-offs in the form of golden parachutes (Table 7.5). These ran into the millions in cases like Sir Ralph Halpern and Sir Roland Smith. The regulatory system seems unable to fill the gap. Reports by Gower,[57] Roskill[58] and others[59] in Britain highlight the weaknesses of the current system and the inadequacies of the judicial process in tackling the problems. Individual shareholders and shareholder groups are seeking new ways to ensure prompt and effective action.

Table 7.5 Wish me luck as you wave me goodbye

Individual	Company	Reported settlement
Tony Berry	Blue Arrow	£ 1 million
Sir Nigel Broakes	Trafalgar House	£ 1.9 million
Sir Eric Parker	Trafalgar House	£ 1.9 million
Lawrence Cooklin	Burton Group	£ 0.75 million
Sir Antony Tennant	Guinness	£ 2 million
Ed Horrigan	RJR Nabisco	$30 million
Vaughn Bryson	Eli Lilly	$ 7 million

DIRECTORS

Statutory responsibilities regulate the activities of UK companies and their directors. The Stock Exchange has codes which define the behaviour of directors of firms with listing on its markets. These statutes and codes cover such issues as:

- shareholdings and dealings;
- responsibility for public documents;
- mergers and acquisitions;
- loyalty and good faith;
- skill and care.

The obligations of directors in the UK are covered in legislation like the *Company Securities (Insider Dealing) Act 1985, S.325 Companies Act 1985* and codes such as the *Model Code for Securities Transactions by Directors of listed Companies* and the *City Code on Takeovers and Mergers*.

The Company Securities (Insider Dealing) Act 1985 makes it a criminal offence for any insider with unpublished, price-sensitive information to deal in the securities affected by this information. Directors are assumed to be insiders. This constraint is based on the assumption of fair dealing and stewardship. Simply dealing while in possession of the information is deemed to be an offence regardless of whether the information is used or not. There are limitations on the workings of the act which are covered by the Stock Exchange's Model Code. The Code contains three principle rules. These are:

1 Directors must not deal prior to the announcement of unpublished, price-sensitive information. This covers regular events such as yearly or half-yearly results – these are covered by the two-month rule – beside other, one-off events.
2 Directors must inform the Board or Chair of the company of any proposed securities transactions.
3 Directors have a responsibility to ensure that any other employees, who may be in possession of unpublished, price-sensitive information, do not deal except in accordance with the code.

All these provisions are covered by the notion that as trustees, directors must not abuse their position of trust without debarring themselves from positions of trust in the future and be subject to action.

The Companies Act 1985 requires full, complete and early disclosure by directors of any information on dealings in options, shares or debentures. The notion of interest is central to the provisions of the Act. It requires that directors disclose all their interests plus those of the spouse or infant children. The Act gives the Department of Trade and Industry considerable powers to ensure that all the provisions of the Act are complied with. This authority includes the power to conduct investigations and inspect all books and papers. Inevitably, take-over and merger imposes some of the most difficult conditions on directors. The City Code is designed to ensure that all shareholders receive equal treatment in the disclosure of information. Directors who abuse the privileged access to information distort the market and undermine the credibility of the city. The Code covers disclosure of information, dealings in equities or securities and 'interest'. The takeover panel is responsible for implementing policy in this system. Failure to comply with 'statutory Code and Stock Exchange, Yellow Book 2 requirements may have serious consequences for the success of any offer and also involve a criminal offence'.[60]

In all of these duties, no distinction is drawn between the role of the executive and non-executive or independent director. It is in the interest of both to ensure that the basic principles and practices of good governance are fully complied with. This requires recognition of responsibilities, not only those defined in law, but any covered by the firm's Articles of Association or principles of sound and loyal management. The notion of *due diligence* recurs in a discussion of directors' responsibilities.

Due Diligence: The standard of conduct displayed by an ordinary, reasonable, prudent individual.

The Prudent Man Rule: A trustee may invest in a security if it is one that would be bought by a prudent person of discretion and intelligence, who is seeking a reasonable income and preservation of capital.

Rosenberg, J. M. (1978)[61]

The responsibility for ensuring *compliance* is personal not institutional. Directors can delegate activities but not responsibilities. Failure 'to ensure that a company's obligations are met . . . can result in directors being fined, disqualified or, in extreme cases, being imprisoned for contempt of court'.[62]

Risk has been inseparable from speculation throughout history. The chance to employ the assets of others to reduce one's own risk is probably as old. The creation of stocks and shares changed the nature of commercial relationships but did not eliminate investor risk.

> *Subscribers here by thousands float,*
> *And jostle one another down;*
> *Each paddling in his leaky boat,*
> *And here they fish for gold and drown.*

Swift, J. (1720)

Law, regulation, codes of practice and supervision can go some way towards protection against abuse of power but cannot effectively deal with the use of authority and opportunity. This can only be achieved by better communication; improved understanding of each other's needs and goals and a stronger sense of involvement. The revival of the Institutional Shareholders Committee and its expanded membership means that almost all British institutional investors are represented.

They have concentrated their attentions on:

- better information, communication and advice;[63]
- support for a stronger policing role for non-executive directors;

- separation of the roles of Chairman and Chief executive;
- advocating transparency in internal dealings, e.g. directors' pay.

The last is seen to be an especially important feature of their proposals given their recognition of the difficulties of securing shareholders' rights in large corporations. Berle and Means[64] were among the first to point out that 'the entrepreneurial function'[65] in the corporation was split between managers who controlled the shareholding and shareholders who supplied the capital. Institutional investors, in particular, are striving to redress the balance in this relationship through information and involvement. Current forms of capitalism make withdrawal of support a less attractive option.

> Shareholder interests are much more efficiently protected by market forces than by millions of small and unsophisticated shareholders trying to understand the subtleties and complexities of financial reporting.
>
> Manne, H. G. (1966)[66]

At the same time, the lack of expertise and counter-argument[67] is hard to sustain in the light of weakening industrial performance and the extent and scale of shareholder interests.

INDEPENDENT DIRECTORS

There is no distinction in English law between the duties and liabilities of executive and independent (non-executive) directors. In practice, it is assumed that executive directors are responsible for the operations of the enterprise, while independent directors stand back to provide an independent view of the firm. Inevitably, there is some overlap. A good executive director should be able to stand back and critically appraise proposals and ideas. An independent director, with particular expertise or knowledge, will often be expected to contribute this to the firm's operations.[68] A good board acts as a team. A skilled chair will try to separate board deliberations from operations. There is, however, an emerging consensus in Britain that beyond this independent directors have a special, fiduciary responsibility to those owners who cannot be represented on the Board.[69]

> The government, the Bank of England and the different types of investor . . . look to non-executive directors to guarantee boardroom efficiency and proberty
>
> Business International[70]

The Code of Recommended Practice published by PRO-NED (**PRO**motion of **N**on **E**xecutive **D**irectors) identifies four primary responsibilities for independent directors. These are:

1 Giving an independent view on the company and the Board's deliberations.

2   Helping their executive colleagues to provide leadership.
3   Monitoring the effectiveness of executive management and helping to strengthen management.
4   Ensuring high standards of financial proberty.

These place substantial demands on independent directors. They require to be fully informed and willing to develop and if necessary assert their role. Too often in the past, independent directors have been ill-informed or have compromised their position by their relationship with the executive board. There is considerable debate on how to achieve the mixture of knowledge, independence and authority called for by most descriptions of the independent director's role. PRO-NED has argued that these are best found in the ranks of the top management of other British firms. This approach runs a risk of reciprocity and collusion. Some firms look more widely for the balance of experience, expertise and independence. They include in their search researchers, academics, politicians, commentators, civil servants, etc. There remains a powerful prejudice in Britain towards independent directors with a strong financial bias. This may go some way to explain the skew in priorities away from operations and marketing and to finance.[71]

Multiple independent directorships raise other issues. Some argue that a large number of directorships guarantees independence while ensuring a range and depth of experience. There is a shift from this view. The counter-argument is that it precludes proper involvement and care. The gun-fighter role with notches on the boardroom chair seems hard to wed with proper stewardship. The number of directors holding 20–30 board positions has shrunk in recent years.[72] This coincides with a steady increase in the number of non-executives on the boards of Britain's leading firms (Figure 7.2).

Two of the tasks attributed to independent directors are especially important in the current climate. The first is independent stewardship.[73] The second is prudence and supervision to ensure proberty.[74] The growing importance of independent director-based audit and remuneration committees reflects this trend.

AUDIT AND APPRAISAL

There are few aspects of governance which are more ill understood in the wider community than the audit. In part, this reflects misunderstanding about the task set before the auditors, their duties and to whom they are responsible.

> Auditors are the troops who watch a battle from the safety of a hillside and when the battle is over come down to bury the dead and count the wounded.
>
> Anonymous

It also illustrates a conflict between the common parlance meaning of an audit

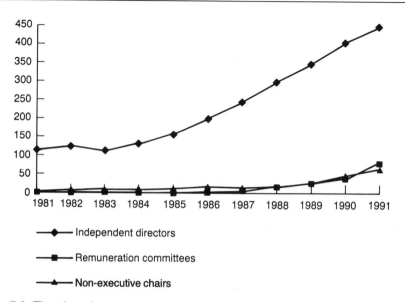

Fig. 7.2 The changing pattern of governance (the top 100 UK firms)

and the precise nature of the financial audit of a firm under prevailing legislation and professional practice. The audit is a report, not a certificate or guarantee: the auditors report their opinion, they do not certify or guarantee anything. . . . No reference is made to the discovery of mistakes or fraud.[75] The audit of a company is the *consolidated statement* of accounts including the balance sheet, trading and profit and loss account *examined by a qualified auditor* and assessed as to whether these financial statements provide *a true and fair account and comply with legal requirements*. Each element of this definition has a precise meaning and affects the view taken to the audit and the responsibilities of those responsible for its preparation and presentation. The consolidated statement or report is exactly what it states. It is not a certificate of worthiness or a guarantee. It must be carried out by a qualified auditor to ensure that the books, records and internal controls have been satisfactorily maintained during the year. Auditors are *not* investigators seeking out wrong doing. They are expected to indicate whether this is a true and fair account. This does not mean that it should be *the* true and fair account only that reasonable judgements have been made about the accounts. The audits are expected to explain any points requiring clarification and bring to the shareholders' attention any qualifications they wish to raise. The auditors are not responsible for the preparation and presentation of accounts. This duty lies with the directors. The auditors are appointed by the shareholders to 'serve as a "watchdog" for the shareholders'.[76]

An auditor is not bound to be a detective . . . He is a watchdog, but not a bloodhound.

Lord Justice Lopes re. Kingston Cotton Mill Co., (1896)

The Caparo decision of the House of Lords made it clear that the auditor owed a statutory duty only to the shareholders.

In the USA, the situation is broadly similar;

> Auditors annually certify the numbers given to them by management and in their opinion unqualifiedly state that these figures 'present fairly' the financial position of their clients. The auditors use this reassuring language even though they know from long and painful experience that the numbers so certified are likely to differ dramatically from the true earnings for the period.
>
> Berkshire Hathaway Inc 'Annual Report to the Shareholders (1985), quoted in Monks, R. A. and Minow, N. (1991)[77]

It is the three Rs of auditing, roles, relationships and reporting procedures, that have caused concern in recent years. The first centres on the *role* attributed to the directors in preparing the accounts. It is sometimes felt that in some circumstances they will have an interest in presenting the accounts in ways which do not match the interests and needs of the investors. This might involve a wish to avoid disclosure of certain information or something more sinister.[78] The *relationship* between the directors and the auditors poses further problems.[79] Although, the shareholders elect the auditors they are usually selected and nominated by the board. Most acknowledge the importance of their working relationship with company management. This might lead to problems of loyalties. The *reporting* responsibility placed upon the auditors is not to root out problems, investigate or perform any other more imaginative tasks sometimes assumed by shareholders or commentators. Their sole responsibility is to arrive at a judgement on whether the accounts are true and fair. They can indicate whether this is an unqualified assessment because they have *no reservations* or they can qualify their judgement.[80]

Detachment

High	Low	
Executives Former executives of company Major shareholders	Institutional investors Bankers and other associated enterprises NEDs chosen for technical expertise	Narrow
Professionally recruited NEDs	Long-term NEDs Personal nominees of CEO	Wide

Perspective

Fig. 7.3 The framework for analysis

The Cadbury committee was established in the wake of recent UK frauds to reassess the three Rs and 'the auditor's role in governance'.[81] At the centre of their deliberations lies the attempt to strengthen the role of the audit committee, developing the contribution of independent directors on the committee and, through this means, strengthening their hand in the firm. It is the responsibility of the audit committee to discuss the audit with the auditor and approve the accounts for issue. Figure 7.3 highlights the different context in which directors operate when performing their role. Recent years have seen a shift from the narrow perspective and low detachment non-executive directors (NED) to the more broadly based, high detachment NED especially in very large, public firms.

The shift to audit committees composed largely, even entirely, of independent directors is an important step in reinforcing the link between the shareholders and the auditors besides reinforcing the role of the independent directors in the firm. There are some investor groups who disagree with the policy adopted in some plcs of including former executive directors among the independent directors on the audit committee. 'A director who is a retired employee is an insider in terms of his business experience and of his position as a company pensioner.'[82]

CASE STUDY 7.1

Terms of reference of the audit committee

The audit committee shall:

1 Review the draft annual accounts prior to their approval by the board focusing in particular on:
  (a) significant changes in accounting policies and practices;
  (b) major judgemental areas;
  (c) significant audit adjustments;
  (d) departures from accounting standards.
2 Review the compliance with statutory and International Stock Exchange requirements for financial reporting.
3 Discuss the scope of the audit with the external auditors.
4 Discuss the matters arising from the audit with the external auditors.
5 Review the preliminary announcement of results prior to publication.
6 Review the annual report taken as a whole.
7 Ensure that the board receives reliable and timely management information.
8 Review the effectiveness of the financial control and systems environment established by management.
9 Review significant transactions outside the company's normal business.
10 Make recommendations on the appointment and remuneration of external auditors.
11 Monitor the ethical behaviour of the company and the senior management.
12 Review prior to publication the press announcements, including advertisements, relating to financial matters.

13 Review circulars issued in connection with a proposed merger or take-over or other major transactions of a non-routine nature.

14 Initiate special projects or investigations on any matter within its terms of reference.

Source: Published with permission of Coopers Deloittes Accountants (1992)

The discussions of the Cadbury committee and the Conference Board have already highlighted the strong view among some shareholders and shareholder groups that the composition of audit committees should be subject to shareholder approval and that shareholders should have the right to put forward their own nominees for audit committees. There is, however, continuing reluctance to develop a stronger role for government and regulation.

The community must not . . . look on the Department of Trade and Industry as an all purpose fire brigade to be called in whenever things go wrong. Still less is it realistic to expect that my department will install automatically triggered sprinkler systems in companies up and down the land. The primary responsibility for exercising surveillance over companies in which they have an interest lies with its members themselves.

Lord Limerick: Address to BIM Conference[83]

There is, however, growing pressure for some form of government action especially in the light of major failures of the present system such as the Maxwell case. Bose[84] comments that 'if Maxwell makes us realise that a system that provides for statutory and comprehensive disclosure and legal protection to those who seek to know the truth is better than one based on trust, some good may come of it'.

REMUNERATION

Much of the emotion surrounding disclosure and transparency centres on the issue of executive remunerations. This, partly, reflects a much wider debate on the character and purpose of business. Ownership groups are striving to wrestle control of industry from management.[85] Managerial capitalism[86] is seen to benefit executives at the expense of owners even if the firm is performing poorly. This can be seen on a fairly crude and personal level when top management are seen to be living lavishly when the firm is struggling. 'That summer RJR Nabisco announced an early retirement programme to trim 2,800 people from the payroll [while] RJR Nabisco [built] the TAJ Mahal of Corporate Hangers [with] an adjacent three-story building of glass, surrounded by $250,000 in landscaping

... more than $600,000 in new furniture was spent throughout, topped off by $100,000 in *objets d'art*.'[87] In Britain apocryphal stories of Chairmen in the 1970s arriving at factories to announce massive lay-offs in a new Rolls Royce and joined by tales of Chairmen in the 1990s reducing dividends, increasing prices, while giving themselves massive wage increases. Examples to reinforce the stereotypes occur too often to reassure investors. James White of Bunzle saw a 75 per cent drop in Bunzle's share price and a drop in profits of £30 million as no excuse for foregoing a wage increase of £20,000. Robert Evans of British Gas took a 23 per cent wage increase although company earnings dropped. A slump in earnings per share of 60 cent at Lasmo did not deter Chris Greentree from accepting a wage hike of 28 per cent. In 15 of the last 20 years boardroom remuneration has run ahead of shareholder value (Figure 7.4). For the last 10 years it has consistently outperformed average earnings.

The response in Britain centres on the attempt to introduce a mixture of a greater sense of personal restraint and improved internal supervision and control. The Prime Minister, John Major was among those calling for top management to show greater restraint, especially during times of economic difficulty. PRO-NED has used its authority and links with its sponsoring organisations to encourage firms to create proper, remuneration committees composed largely of independent directors to set directors' salaries. These committees have two major purposes:

- ensuring a fair system of reward for senior management;
- demonstrating the fairness of this remuneration to shareholders.

This latter is achieved by clear evidence of impartiality and a commitment to transparency on its deliberations and decisions (see Appendix C at the end of this chapter for full details of the PRO-NED recommendations on the composition, remit and reporting arrangements on remuneration committees).

It is unlikely that concern about top management remuneration will disappear even when all public companies have independent director-based remuneration committees. The nature of remuneration packages alone can produce problems. These are well illustrated in the arrangements some firms entered into to level out performance-based payments. Typically these try to avoid massive swings in earnings. This is achieved by lagging or averaging bonuses. A three-year running average of the type illustrated in Figure 7.5 illustrates the problem.

The salary package outlined in Figure 7.5 is based on a percentage of the three-year rolling average of profits increases. In six of the seven years, the chief executive has forgone the higher bonuses that a crude link to current year performance produces. Can she be accused of greed in 1991?

In the USA, Congress raised similar concerns while the Institutional Investor Committee and the Business Roundtable have tried to put teeth into attempts to regulate behaviour.

Fig. 7.4 Money, money, money
Source: The Guardian

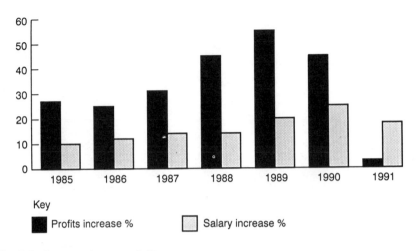

Key

■ Profits increase %   ☐ Salary increase %

Fig. 7.5 A cause for scandal?

NOT SO QUIET MONOPOLIES

Some of the most vigorous criticism of executive remuneration in the UK centres on the remuneration packages offered in the newly privatised monopolies or semi-monopolies. The 1980s in Britain saw a major shift in ownership of large public utilities from the state to the private sector. Many, however, remain virtual

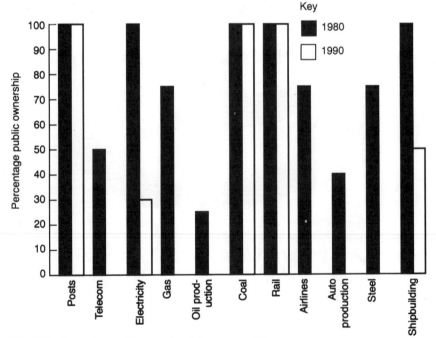

Fig. 7.6 Changing patterns of public ownership

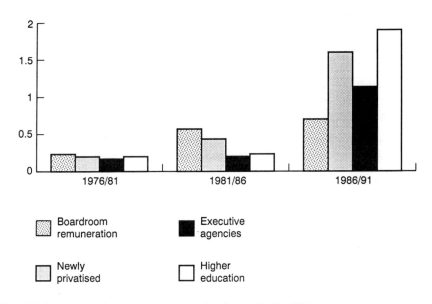

Fig. 7.7 Increases in top management salaries in the UK

monopolies with a few of the competitive pressures seen elsewhere in commerce (Figure 7.6).

The conventional controls of the marketplace do not exist in these massive enterprises. At the same time, government controls on top management wage increases were relaxed without any effective substitute introduced. This loosening of control is hard to separate from the combination of pent-up demand and fear of *rocking the boat* as an explanation for the rapid increases in top management salaries. This had a knock-on effect across the public sector in executive agencies and newly incorporated bodies. This provoked a storm of controversy about the mechanisms for establishing top management salaries in the private sector (Figure 7.7).

Figure 7.7 was compiled using a mixture of secondary sources of information, e.g. the Hay Survey,[88] interviews and other primary sources. It indicates that some parts of the former public sector or newly incorporated sector have seen their salaries increase faster than average boardroom remuneration. Figures for higher education and executive agencies should be treated with some caution as the requirement to report remuneration has not, for example, been extended to all universities. Salaries of vice chancellors, for example, are not included. A survey of top management salaries[89] in the north-west found that virtually all chief executives of public companies declared their salaries but no partners in professional practices, CEOs of public agencies,[90] vice chancellors were willing to declare their income. The rapid increases in salaries across these sectors has prompted calls for greater public scrutiny of the salaries in the *public* corporations.

QUESTIONS

1 Discuss the proposition that the expansion of shareholder rights is incompatible with improved business performance.

2 'The real *barbarians at the gate* are financial institutions trying to exploit the real economy for short term gains.' Use material from several sources to explore and evaluate this proposition.

3 What were the dominant characteristics of the 'Managerial Revolution' described by Chandler – how did it change the relationship between owners and managers?

4 Andrew Large, Chair of Britain's Securities and Investment Board argues that the four main aims of a regulatory system for corporations are:

   1 It should act in the public interest;
   2 It should catch and deal with fraudsters;
   3 It should deal with sharp practice;
   4 It should provide effective investor protection (*Financial Times*, May 1993).

   Do you believe that these constitute an adequate set of goals? Justify your position with reference to specific illustrations.

5 'Either you do it right or you get eliminated.' Is this an effective prescription for successful corporate governance?

6 'Occasional imprisonments, fines and reprimands do not prove that regulators are doing their job. More often than not they are merely ways to flatter the regulators' performance.' How far are these comments justified in the light of the treatment of Boesky in the USA, Saunders in Britain or Zambellitti in Italy? (You can use other illustrations if you wish.)

7 Do the recommendations of the Cadbury Committee go far enough in providing a framework for effective corporate governance?

8 Withdrawal of support by shareholders – through share disposal – remains the only effective form of shareholder sanction – discuss.

9 Describe the role and precise meaning of the phrase 'true and fair' in audited company accounts.

10 Define:

   (a) Governance
   (b) Poison pills
   (c) Greenmail
   (d) Innovation
   (e) Compensation committees

   (f) Investor rights
   (g) Stewardship
   (h) Conspicuous consumption
   (i) Due diligence
   (j) Insider dealing

APPENDIX B
THE FINANCIAL ASPECTS OF CORPORATE GOVERNANCE

The Code of Best Practice

1   The Board of Directors

1.1 The board should meet regularly, retain full and effective control over the company and monitor the executive management.

1.2 There should be a clearly accepted division of responsibilities at the head of a company, which will ensure a balance of power and authority, such that no one individual has unfettered powers of decision. Where the chairman is also the chief executive, it is essential that there should be a strong and independent element on the board, with a recognised senior member.

1.3 The board should include non-executive directors of sufficient calibre and number for their views to carry significant weight in the board's decisions. (Note 1)

1.4 The board should have a formal schedule of matters specifically reserved to it for decision to ensure that the direction and control of the company is firmly in its hands. (Note 2)

1.5 There should be an agreed procedure for directors in the furtherance of their duties to take independent professional advice if necessary, at the company's expense. (Note 3)

1.6 All directors should have access to the advice and services of the company secretary, who is responsible to the board for ensuring that board procedures are followed and that applicable rules and regulations are complied with. Any question of the removal of the company secretary should be a matter for the board as a whole.

2   Non-Executive Directors

2.1 Non-executive directors should bring an independent judgement to bear on issues of strategy, performance, resources, including key appointments, and standards of conduct.

2.2. The majority should be independent of management and free from any business or other relationship which could materially interfere with the exercise of their independent judgement, apart from their fees and shareholding. Their fees should reflect the time which they commit to the company. (Notes 4 and 5)

2.3 Non-executive directors should be appointed for specified terms and reappointment should not be automatic. (Note 6)

2.4 Non-executive directors should be selected through a formal process and both this process and their appointment should be a matter for the board as a whole. (Note 7)

3   Executive Directors

3.1 Directors' service contracts should not exceed three years without shareholders' approval. (Note 8)

3.2 There should be full and clear disclosure of directors' total emoluments and those of the chairman and highest-paid UK director, including pension contributions and stock options. Separate figures should be given for salary and performance-related elements and the basis on which performance is measured should be explained.

3.3 Executive directors' pay should be subject to the recommendations of a remuneration committee made up wholly or mainly of non-executive directors. (Note 9)

4   Reporting and Controls

4.1 It is the board's duty to present a balanced and understandable assessment of the company's position. (Note 10)

4.2 The board should ensure that an objective and professional relationship is maintained with the auditors.

4.3 The board should establish an audit committee of at least 3 non-executive directors with written terms of reference which deal clearly with its authority and duties. (Note 11)

4.4 The directors should explain their responsibility for preparing the accounts next to a statement by the auditors about their reporting responsibilities. (Note 12)

4.5 The directors should report on the effectiveness of the company's system of internal control. (Note 13)

4.6 The directors should report that the business is a going concern, with supporting assumptions or qualifications as necessary. (Note 13)

Notes

These notes include further recommendations on good practice. They do not form part of the Code.

1   To meet the Committee's recommendations on the composition of sub-committees of the board, boards will require a minimum of three non-executive directors, one of whom may be the chairman of the company provided he or she is not also its executive head. Additionally,

two of the three non-executive directors should be independent in the terms set out in paragraph 2.2 of the Code.

2   A schedule of matters specifically reserved for decision by the full board should be given to directors on appointment and should be kept up to date. The Committee envisages that the schedule would at least include:

(a) acquisition and disposal of assets of the company or its subsidiaries that are material to the company;
(b) investments, capital projects, authority levels, treasury policies and risk management policies.

The board should lay down rules to determine materiality for any transaction, and should establish clearly which transactions require multiple board signatures. The board should also agree the procedures to be followed when, exceptionally, decisions are required between board meetings.

3   The agreed procedure should be laid down formally, for example in a Board Resolution, in the Articles, or in the Letter of Appointment.

4   It is for the board to decide in particular cases whether this definition of independence is met. Information about the relevant interests of directors should be disclosed in the Directors' Report.

5   The Committee regards it as good practice for non-executive directors not to participate in share option schemes and for their service as non-executive directors not to be pensionable by the company, in order to safeguard their independent position.

6   The Letter of Appointment for non-executive directors should set out their duties, term of office, remuneration, and its review.

7   The Committee regards it as good practice for a nomination committee to carry out the selection process and to make proposals to the board. A nomination committee should have a majority of non-executive directors on it and be chaired either by the chairman or a non-executive director.

8   The Committee does not intend that this provision should apply to existing contracts before they become due for renewal.

9   Membership of the remuneration committee should be set out in the Directors' Report and its chairman should be available to answer questions on remuneration principles and practice at the Annual General Meeting. Best practice is set out in PRO-NED's Remuneration Committee guidelines, *see* Appendix C.

10   The report and accounts should contain a coherent narrative, supported by the figures, of the company's performance and prospects. Balance requires that setbacks should be dealt with as well as successes. The need for the report to be readily understood emphasises that words are as important as figures.

11   The Committee's recommendations on audit committees are as follows:

(a) They should be formally constituted as sub-committees of the main board to whom they are answerable and to whom they should report regularly; they should be given written terms of reference which deal adequately with their membership, authority and duties; and they should normally meet at least twice a year.

(b) There should be a minimum of three members. Membership should be confined to the non-executive directors of the company and a majority of the non-executives serving on the committee should be independent of the company, as defined in paragraph 2.2 of the Code.

(c) The external auditor and, where an internal audit function exists, the head of internal audit should normally attend committee meetings, as should the finance director. Other board members should also have the right to attend.

(d) The audit committee should have a discussion with the auditors at least once a year, without executive board members present, to ensure that there are no unresolved issues of concern.

(e) The audit committee should have explicit authority to investigate any matters within its terms of reference, the resources which it needs to do so, and full access to information. The committee should be able to obtain outside professional advice and if necessary to invite outsiders with relevant experience to attend meetings.

(f) Membership of the committee should be disclosed in the annual report and the chairman of the committee should be available to answer questions about its work at the Annual General Meeting.

Specimen terms of reference for an audit committee, including a list of the most commonly performed duties, are set out in the Committee's full report.

12 The statement of directors' responsibilities should cover the following points:

- the legal requirement for directors to prepare financial statements for each financial year which give a true and fair view of the state of affairs of the company (or group) as at the end of the financial year and of the profit and loss for that period;
- the responsibility of the directors for maintaining adequate accounting records, for safeguarding the assets of the company (or group), and for preventing and detecting fraud and other irregularities;
- confirmation that suitable accounting policies, consistently applied and supported by reasonable and prudent judgements and estimates, have been used in the preparation of the financial statements;
- confirmation that applicable accounting standards have been followed, subject to any material departures disclosed and explained in the notes to the accounts. (This does not obviate the need for a

formal statement in the notes to the accounts disclosing whether the accounts have been prepared in accordance with applicable accounting standards.)

The statement should be placed immediately before the auditors' report which in future will include a separate statement (currently being developed by the Auditing Practices Board) on the responsibility of the auditors for expressing an opinion on the accounts.

13   The Committee notes that companies will not be able to comply with paragraphs 4.5 and 4.6 of the Code until the necessary guidance for companies has been developed as recommended in the Committee's report.

14   The company's statement of compliance should be reviewed by the auditors in so far as it relates to paragraphs 1.4, 1.5, 2.3, 2.4, 3.1 to 3.3 and 4.3 to 4.6 of the Code.

APPENDIX C
PRO-NED

The composition of the Committee

It is recommended that the members of the Remuneration Committee should be independent, non-executive directors and that the chairperson of the Committee should be a non-executive director, particularly if the chairperson of the company is a full-time chairperson.

Decisions on remuneration should be made by those who do not benefit personally from their recommendations. It is preferable that non-executive directors who, although valuable board members, also receive fees as professional advisors to the company should not be involved in determining the remuneration of executives. Non-executive directors, for whom the fee for that particular appointment represents only a part of their total income, should form the Committee.

It is a matter of choice how many of those contributing to an assessment should attend the relevant meetings of the Committee. The chief executive is a key witness here, but no director should be present when his or her own salary is being discussed.

The recommendation on the salary of the chairperson of the board, whether a full-time or a part-time chairperson should be made only by the non-executive directors.

The remit of the Committee

PRO-NED recommends that the Remuneration Committee should have an official remit, recognising its authority as a Committee of the board and stating the scope of its activities, and that it should have written terms of reference.

Some companies make provision for a Remuneration Committee as a standing committee of the board in their Articles of Association, others by detailing the membership and responsibilities of the Committee in a board minute.

All members of the board should be clear as to who the members of the Committee are and what they are there to do. The agreement of the composition and terms of reference of the Committee presents an opportunity for the board as a whole to decide on its policy with regard to remuneration and to consider such questions as

(a) Where, in terms of executive remuneration, does the company aim to stand in relation to similar companies in their industry sector?
(b) What relationship does the company wish to see between the remuneration of its directors and that of other employees?
(c) In the case of companies operating internationally, what adjustments would they make for directors and senior executives based overseas to reflect local conditions and living costs?
(d) How should they remunerate those senior executives whose skills and scarcity value make them internationally transferable?

The board must also consider the range of executives whose remuneration should be considered and approved by the Committee and what other considerations, if any, should come within the Committee's remit.

The remuneration package

The Committee should be responsible for all elements of directors' remuneration.
The package can consist of a combination of the following elements

(a) Base salary;
(b) A performance-related element, including profit-sharing schemes;
(c) Share options;
(d) Other benefits.

The structuring of these elements, including the pension entitlement, into a suitable package is largely determined by the size, financial circumstances and market position of the company concerned.

Disclosure

It is therefore recommended that the annual report should include

(a) The separation of reported total emoluments into salary and performance-related elements;

(b) An explanation of the broad criteria on which these performance-related elements are based and a clear indication of the trading period to which they apply;

(c) In the case of long-term incentive plans, an early indication of the key factors including

(i)   the number of executives to whom the plan relates

(ii) when the payments or share options begin to fall due under the plan

(iii) what financial provision the company has made for present and future payments under the plan.

There is no requirement to disclose the benefit gained under share option schemes. The value of a share option is only notional until it is exercised, the timing of which is the personal choice of each individual recipient. However, they are an important, respected and widely used form of incentive, and companies in the cause of openness may choose to disclose in their annual report and accounts details of share options exercised by executive directors during the year.

REFERENCES

1. Jay, A. *Management and Machiavelli*, London, Pan (1967).
2. Chandler, A. D. Jnr. *Strategies and Structure: Chapters in the History of the American Enterprise*, Cambridge, Mass., MIT Press (1976).
3. Chandler, A. D. Jnr. *The Visible Hand: The Managerial Revolution in American Business*, Cambridge, Mass., Harvard University Press (1977).
4. Porter, M. *Competitive Strategy: Techniques for Analysing Industries and Competitors*, New York, Free Press (1980).
5. Sheridan, T. and Kendall, N. *Corporate Governance*. London, Pitman (1992).
6. Peters, T. J. and Waterman, R. J. *In Search Of Excellence*, New York, Harper and Row (1982).
7. Drucker, P. *Management: Tasks, Responsibilities and Practices*, New York, Harper and Row (1974).
8. Lessem, R. *The Global Business*, London, Prentice Hall International (1987).
9. Demb, A. and Neubauer, F. *The Corporate Board*, Oxford, Oxford University Press (1992).
10. Rapport, A., quoted in 'Ideas for the 1990s' *Fortune*, 26 March (1990).
11. Winters, R. C., quoted in 'Ideas for the 1990s', ibid.
12. Jensen, M. C., quoted in 'Ideas for the 1990s', ibid.
13. Galbraith, J. K. *The New Industrial State*, Harmondsworth, Penguin (1969).
14. Kempner, T., MacMillan, K. and Hawks, K. *Business and Society*, Harmondsworth, Penguin (1976).
15. Lorenz, C. 'Knives are out in the Boardroom', *Financial Times*, 1 May (1992).
16. Monks, R. and Minow, N. *Power and Accountability*, Glasgow, Harper Collins (1991).
17. Securities and Exchange Commission *The Economics of Poison Pills*, Office of the Chief Economist, Securities and Exchange Commission, October (1986).
18. The Business Roundtable *The Role and Composition of the Board of Directors of the Large Publicly Owned Corporation*, The Business Roundtable, 200 Park Avenue, New York (1990).
19. Cadbury, Sir A. *Report of the Committee on the Financial Aspects of Corporate Governance*, London, Gee (a division of Professional Publishing Ltd), London (1992).
20. Forte, C, *Forte*, London, Sidgwick & Jackson (1986).

21. Lacey, R. *Ford*, London, Pan (1986).
22. Epstein, E. J. *Who Owns the Corporation? Management vs Stakeholders*, New York, Priority Press (1986).
23. Stein, J. L. *Monetarist, Keynesian and New Classical Economics*, Oxford, Basil Blackwell (1983).
24. Kanter, R. M. *The Change Masters*, London, George Allen & Unwin (1983).
25. Peter, T. *Thriving on Chaos*, London, Macmillan (1987).
26. Laurence, A. and Lorsch, J. *Organisation and Environment*, Cambridge, Harvard University Press (1967).
27. Chell, E., Haworth, J. and Brearley, S. *The Entrepreneurial Personality*, London, Routledge (1992).
28. Stephenson, H. H., Sahlman, W. A. and Grousbeck, H. I. *New Business Ventures and the Entrepreneur*, Homewood, Ill., R. D. Irwin (1989).
29. *Guardian*, 3 May (1992).
30. Bosworth-Davies, R. *Fraud in the City: Too good to be True*, Harmondsworth, Penguin (1988).
31. Bose, M. 'White Lies and the British Criminal' *Director*, January (1992).
32. Freudberg, D. *The Corporate Conscience: Money, Power and Responsible Business*, New York, American Management Association (1986).
33. Council of Institutional Investors *Our Money, Our Future*, Washington, January (1990).
34. Freedman, R. E. and Reed, D. L. 'Stockholders and Stakeholders: A New Perspective on Corporate Governance' *California Management Review*, Spring (1983) pp. 36–42.
35. Ball, J. Sir *Short Termism in the UK: Myth or Reality*, Stocton Lecture, London Business School, February (1991).
36. Haslam, Lord 'A Chairman's Perspective' *Vital Topics*, Manchester Business School (1991).
37. Peters, T. and Waterman, R., ibid.
38. Saunders, J. and Wong, V. 'In Search of Excellence in the UK' *Journal of Marketing Management*, vol. 1, no. 2, Winter (1985) pp. 119–38.
39. Eccles, T., Hunt, J. and Chambers, D. *Excellence in Search of Excellence*, London Business School Journal, vol. 9, no. 1 (1984).
40. Kantor, R. B. *The Change Masters*, London, Harper and Row (1987).
41. Porter, M. E. *Competitive Strategy*, New York, Free Press (1980).
42. Peters, T. and Waterman, R., ibid.
43. Ohmae, K. *The Mind of the Strategist*, Harmondsworth, Penguin (1983).
44. Parkinson, C. Northcote *Parkinson's Law*, Harmondsworth, Penguin (1986).
45. Cannon, T. *Innovation and Marketing*, London, National Economic Development Office (1991).
46. Wilson, Lord *Committee to Review the Functioning of the Financial Institutions*, London, HMSO (1978).
47. Mansfield, E. 'Social and Private Rates of Return for Industrial Innovations' *Quarterly Journal of Economics*, vol. 91, no. 2, May (1977).
48. Laing, Lord 'Teamwork to Invest in People and Technology' *Quarterly Enterprise Digest*, November (1990).
49. Alexander, G. and Bucholtz, R. 'Corporate Social Responsibility and Stock Market Performance' *Academy of Management Journal*, 21 (1978) pp. 479–82.
50. McGuire, J. and Garder, M. 'Corporate Social Responsibility and Firm Financial Performance' *Academy of Management Journal*, December (1988) pp. 854–72.
51. Aupperle, K., Cavrolle, A. and Hatfield, J. 'An Empirical Examination of the Relationship Between Corporate Social Responsibility and Profitability' *Academy of Management Journal*, 18, pp. 446–63.
52. Franks, J. and Mayer, C. *Capital Markets and Corporate Control: A Study of France, Germany and the UK*, London, City University Business School (1990).
53. Australian Graduate School of Management *Corporate Governance in Japan*, Sydney, AGSM (1990).
54. Business International Limited *New Directions in Corporate Governance*, London, Business International Limited (1992).
55. Any discussion of this area must recognise the changes occurring and the requirement for sound up-to-date information and advice. The descriptions here are based on material gathered from such sources as Institutional Shareholders Committee, PRO-NED and reports such as the Norton Rose Group's *Directors at Risk*, Manchester, Norton Rose Group (1991).

56. Smith, Sir, R. *Non-Executive or Independent Directors on UK Boards*, Howgate Sable Lecture, Manchester Business School (1991).

57. Gower, L. C. B. *Review of Investor Protection*, London, HMSO, cmnd 9125 (1984).

58. Roskill, Lord *Fraud Trials*, London, HMSO (1988).

59. Levi, M. *The Incidence, Reporting and Prevention of Commercial Fraud*, Cardiff, Cardiff University (1986).

60. Berwin Leighton *Memorandum on Take-Over Rules*, London, Berwin Leighton (1991).

61. Rosenberg, J. M. *Dictionary of Business and Management*, New York, Wiley (1978).

62. Norton Rose Group *Directors at Risk*, Manchester, Norton Rose Group (1991).

63. Institutional Shareholders' Committee *The Role and Duties of Directors – A Statement of Best Practice*, London, Institutional Shareholders' Committee (1991).

64. Berle, M. and Means, G. *The Modern Corporation and Private Property*, New York, Harcourt, Brace and World (1968).

65. Kempner, T. et al. ibid.

66. Manne, H. G. *Truth and Myth in Modern Corporate Theory*, Industrial Education and Research Foundation, Occasional Paper no. 9 (1966).

67. Manne, H. G. 'Mergers and the Market for Corporate Control' *Journal of Political Economy*, vol. Lxxxii (1965).

68. Johnson, E. W. 'An Insider's Call for Outside Direction' *Harvard Business Review*, 68 (1990) pp. 46–55.

69. Artis, S. *Non-Executive Directors: Their Changing Role in UK Boards*, Economist Intelligence Unit, Report 244, London (1986).

70. Business International Limited, ibid.

71. Baysinger, B. D. and Butler, H. N. 'Corporate Governance and the Board of Directors: Performance Effects of Changes in Board Composition' *Journal of Law, Economics and Organisations*, 17 (1985) pp. 46–57.

72. Baysinger, B. D. and Butler, H. N., ibid.

73. Mintzberg, H. 'Who Should Control the Corporation' *California Management Review*, Fall (1984) pp. 36–43.

74. Kesner, I. F. B. and Lamont, B. T. 'Board Composition and the Commission of Illegal Acts: an Investigation of Fortune 500 Companies' *Academy of Management Journal*, 29, pp. 789–99.

75. Parker, R. H. *Understanding Company Financial Statements*, Harmondsworth, Penguin (1988).

76. Parker, R. H. ibid.

77. Berkshire Hathaway Inc 'Annual Report to the Shareholders (1985)' quoted in Monks R. A. and Minow, N. *Power and Accountability* London, Harper Collins (1991).

78. Bacon, J. *Corporate Directorship Practices: The Audit Committee*, New York, The Conference Board (1982).

79. Vinten, G. 'Internal Audit After Maxwell and BCCI: Public Responsibility vs Loyalty to the Organisation' *Management Auditing Journal* 7 (1992) pp. 3–5.

80. Linden D. W. 'Lies of the Bottom Line' *Forbes* 12 November (1990) p. 106.

81. Business International Limited, ibid.

82. Cadbury, Sir A. *The Company Chairman*, Cambridge, Fitzwilliam (1990).

83. British Institute of Management 'The British Public Company: Its Role, Responsibilities and Accountability' Occasional Paper no. 12 (1974), quoted in Smith, N. C. *Morality and the Market*, London, Routledge (1990).

84. Bose, M. 'The Burglar Always Comes Twice' *The Director*, vol. 45, no. 10 (1992).

85. Charkham, J. *Corporate Governance*, Discussion Document no. 25, Bank of England, March (1989).

86. Winkler, J. 'The Coming Corporatism', in Skidelsky, (ed.) *The End of the Keynesian Era*, London, Macmillan (1977).

87. Burrough, B. and Helyar, J. *Barbarians at the Gate*, London, Cape (1990).

88. Hay Management Consultants *Boardroom Remuneration Review*, Hay Group, Spring (1992).

89. North West Business Insider *The North West Corporate Elite*, Insider Publications, Manchester (1991).

90. Chairs of Development Corporations are an exception to this.

CHAPTER 8

Corporate governance: an international perspective

The pressures for disclosure and greater responsibility seen in Britain have their echos across the world. This is fuelled by the speed with which information is communicated and the differences which sometimes emerge between performance and reward. President Bush's *fat cats* visit to Japan provoked anger in Japan and the USA while prompting worldwide discussion of business ethics. Sharp contrasts between the relatively frugal lifestyle and low wages of Japan's corporate elite and the rewards of those on President Bush's party were noted in Japan and the USA. It dulled the effect of the President's attempt to force the Japanese to open up their market and restrict their competitive incursions into the USA. Local media were quick to point out that some restraint at the top in

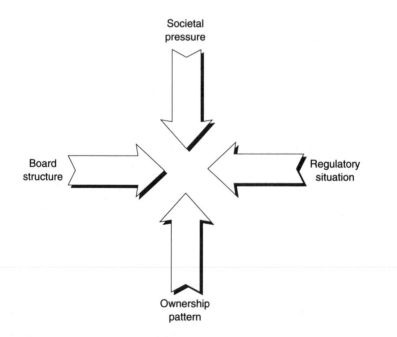

Fig. 8.1 Elements of a national governance system
Source: reprinted by permission from Demb, A. (1990).[1]

US corporations might encourage others to worker harder, demand less and improve their competitiveness. In the USA, the media[2,3] and Congress expressed anger at the lack of leadership while the economy was in the doldrums and workers across America were facing a bleak future. In Western Europe, the same theme has been taken up as competitive pressures increase and politicians, investors and the media demand better performance and higher standards from corporate leaders. In Asia, features of the same debate can be seen in Hong Kong, Bombay, Kuala Lumpur, Jakarta and elsewhere. Few countries with a mixture of private ownership, managerial control and public scrutiny are immune from the debate.

The pattern and nature of corporate governance in specific nations or societies derives from the interaction of the four broad forces described in Figure 8.1, elements of corporate governance.

The concerns, priorities and relative influence of these elements varies over time. Ownership pressure is especially powerful in the USA at present while social pressures are unusually strong in Germany. In Britain much of the debate on governance today centres on board structure but Italian concerns seem to concentrate on the regulatory situation following recent scandals.

THE USA

Andrew Shonfield[4] points out that the USA is one of the few countries in the world where the word *capitalism* has no negative social connotations. The notion that achievement justifies its reward has an important part in the US psyche. The images of *Dallas, Knots Landing* and *Dynasty* provoked relatively little criticism in a society in which the notion that *whats good for General Motors is good for the United States* was relatively largely unchallenged. Corporate capitalism produced the most prosperous and secure society in the world – why should its leaders be criticised if they did especially well. The view was shaped by powerful images such as those of Henry Ford, Thomas Watson jnr, Thomas Edison and Andrew Carnegie. Even if they were ruthless in building their fortunes, they built corporations which dominated the world, gave their shareholders and workers unrivalled prosperity and eventually created major charities which returned their wealth to the public domain.

> There is but one right mode of using enormous fortunes – namely, that the possessors from time to time during their lives should so administer these as to promote the permanent good of the communities from which they were gathered

Carnegie, A. (1862)[5]

This notion was reinforced by the tangible successes of their enterprise. It was claimed that $10,000 invested in IBM in the early 1950s was worth $13 million in the early 1980s. At its peak General Motors employed about 700,000 people

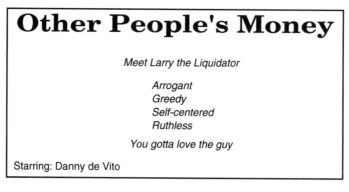

Fig. 8.2 Images of today

with over half in the USA. They were, at the time, some of the best paid workers in the world.

Few challenged Mises's[6] claim in the late 1940s that 'the average American worker enjoys amenities for which Croesus, Crassus, the Medici and Louis XIV would have envied him'. Popular images reinforced this view; Cary Grant and Katherine Hepburn in the *Philadelphia Story* provided one picture of success. It was little changed when Bing Crosby and Grace Kelly returned to the theme almost 20 years later in *High Society*. Charlie Chaplin might introduce a discordant note in *Modern Times* but the enduring image is probably of James Stewart in *It's a Wonderful Life*. Even the bank examiner ends by making his contribution to bailing out the Savings and Loan. The picture has changed over the last decade. In *Wall Street*, incompetent management has left the firm to be fought over by speculators and foreign investors with the union leader's son acting as the whistle blower to bring in the government. Danny de Vito, Richard Dreyfuss, Robin Williams and Michael Douglas as salesmen and speculators give a different picture of corporate America (Figure 8.2).

Books like *In Search of Excess*[7] deliberately play on past images. Even if Microsoft can turn its investors into millionaires, concern about the performance of US industry has raised questions about its governance.

> Well supported by a bevy of consultants, lawyers and research services the governance movement in the US is vocal and very pro-active. Campaigns are often conducted in the full glare of the media and the leaders have become very skillful in making their voices heard.
>
> Business International (1992)[8]

In *Barbarians at the Gate*[9] the picture of declining performance, exploitation, indifference and poorly motivated management is savagely drawn. Faced with these contrasts the demand for reform occurred at both ends of the political economic spectrum. Some argued for a return to the older values of investor/entrepreneurial capitalism. The powerlessness of investors should be replaced by well organised investor groups and responsive management. Others[10] demanded a clearer and more directive industrial policy. The Council of Institutional Investors has proposed a Shareholder Bill of Rights as described below.

The Shareholder Bill of Rights

Preamble

American corporations are the cornerstones of the free enterprise system, and as such must be governed by the principles of accountability and fairness inherent in our democratic system. The shareholders of American corporations are the owners of such corporations, and the directors elected by the shareholders are accountable to the shareholders. Furthermore, the shareholders of American corporations are entitled to participate in the fundamental financial decisions which could affect corporate performance and growth and the long-range viability and competitiveness of corporations. This Shareholder Bill of Rights insures such participation and provides protection against any disenfranchisement of American shareholders.

I One share, one vote

Each share of common stock, regardless of its class, shall be entitled to vote in proportion to its relative share in the total common stock equity of the corporation. The right to vote is inviolate and may not be abridged by any circumstance or by any action of any person.

II Equal and fair treatment for all shareholders

Each share of common stock, regardless of its class, shall be treated equally in proportion to its relative share in the total common stock equity of the corporation, with respect to any dividend, distribution, redemption, tender or exchange offer. In matters reserved for shareholder action, procedural fairness and full disclosure is required.

III Shareholder approval of certain corporate decisions

A vote of the holders of a majority of the outstanding shares of common stock, regardless of class, shall be required to approve any corporate decision related to the finances of a company which will have a material effect upon the financial position of the company and the position of the company's shareholders; specifically, decisions which would:

A Result in the acquisition of five per cent or more of the shares of common stock by the corporation at a price in excess of the prevailing market price of such stock, other than pursuant to a tender offer made to all shareholders;

B Result in, or is contingent upon, an acquisition other than by the corporation of shares of stock of the corporation having, on a proforma basis, 20 per cent or more of the combined voting power of the outstanding common shares or a change in the ownership of 20 percent or more of the assets of the corporation;

C Abridge or limit the rights of the holders of common shares to:

1 Consider and vote on the election or removal of directors or the timing or length of their term of office or;

2 Make nominations for directors or propose other action to be voted upon by shareholders or;

3 Call special meetings of shareholders to take action by written consent or;

D Permit any executive officer or employee of the corporation to receive, upon termination of employment, any amount in excess of two times that person's average annual compensation for the previous three years, if such payment is contingent upon an acquisition of shares of stock of the corporation or a change in the ownership of the assets of the corporation;

E Permit the sale or pledge of corporate assets which would have a material effect on shareholder values;

F Result in the issuance of debt to a degree which would leverage a company and imperil the long-term viability of the corporation.

IV Independent approval of executive compensation and auditors

The approval of at least a majority of independent directors (or if there are fewer than three such directors, the unanimous approval of all such outside directors) shall be required to approve, on an annual basis:

A The compensation to be provided to each executive officer of the corporation, including the right to receive any bonus, severance or other extraordinary payment to be received by such executive officer; and

B The selection of independent auditors.

The pressure for the defence of shareholder rights was reinforced when corporate management in firms like Time, CBS, Champion International adopted strategies like poison pills to protect themselves from hostile take-overs and greenmail without full discussion with shareholders. At Honeywell, Lockheed and General Motors the power of investors, notably institutional shareholders, was asserted in different ways. These efforts to influence policy are an explicit recognition that the scale of the holdings of the large investors is so great that they cannot play the market in the traditional way. A move by a major trust to dump its shares on the market – the Wall Street Walk – because it has lost faith in corporate management would be counter-productive; precipitating a crisis when reform not collapse is the aim. In the USA access to the board achieved voluntarily or forced by legal action has emerged as a key shareholder issue especially given the board's role in guiding top management. In the USA, four broad duties are placed upon directors. These are:

The Duty of Honour: in their dealing with others, and show extraordinary conscientiousness, scrupulousness and diligence in dealing with others involved in the enterprise.[11]

The Duty of Care: for the assets of others and to always act in a manner believed reasonably to be in the best interest of the corporation.

A Duty of Loyalty: to the interests of shareholders (and perhaps other stakeholders), avoiding or declaring all possible conflicts of interest.

A Duty of Responsibility: to ensure that the enterprise meets its legal and ethical duties to other groups affected by corporate actions.[12]

Both the American Law Institute[13] and the Business Roundtable[14] make elect/select, evaluate and replace/dismiss the CEO as important as reviewing corporate performance and compliance in the duties of the board. Intervention through either federal agencies like the Securities and Exchange Commission or state agencies is being influenced by these internal pressures and growing demands from congress and the public for action on issues as diverse as executive remuneration and environmental protection.

A EUROPEAN COMMUNITY VIEW

Within Europe two distinct strands can be discerned in the debate on corporate governance. There are the attempts by the European Community as a whole to shape a framework for action which is common across Europe. There are, also, distinct national patterns some of which operate in the same way, others look the same and operate differently while many features of governance are peculiar to a particular state. There is evidence that shareholders share some of the concerns of their Anglo-Saxon colleagues but the balance of interests are dissimilar. The banks are far more important in Germany, Austria and Switzerland[15] while private or family ownership has greater significance especially in France, Greece, Spain and Portugal. Pension Funds and other institutional groups are less significant.[16] In some countries, shareholder rights are less important in law than employees and other stakeholders. The more obvious causes of shareholder dissent: poor performance allied to financial scandals and generous top management wages (Figure 8.3) have not reached the public agenda to the same extent.[17]

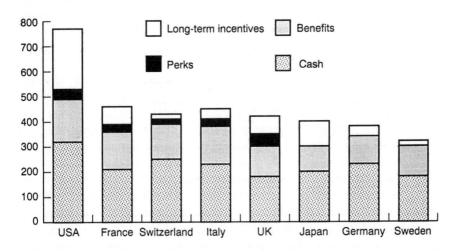

Fig. 8.3 Top management remuneration in large firms ($000, 1991)

The main aim of EC policy in corporate governance is to create a level playing field. This has prompted a series of Directives on company law. The most immediately relevant to governance is the Fifth Company Directive. It incorporates a series of provisions on the duties of directors, rights of shareholders and the conduct of meetings. This should be viewed in the context of a much larger programme of statutes and directives. The demands for transparency, for example, are influenced by the community requirements for the disclosure of information. They require firms to file company statutes and articles of association besides annual accounts, details of ownership and any changes in the company's status, e.g. liquidation.

Current EC proposals include:

- Reducing the barriers to transfer of ownership and control;
- The introduction of two-tier boards;
- Compulsory employee participation in decision making.

The controversy surrounding these makes it unlikely that significant progress will be made in the immediate future. Governance issues in the Community look likely to involve a mixture of broad international concerns, e.g. the balance of power between management, institution and individuals, and debates between members, notably on merger and acquisition and local concerns.

Three distinct features help shape the governance system in Germany within its social market system. These are the two-tier boards, the informal power of the banks and the representational system. These elements are closely interrelated and provide the distinctive character of corporate governance in Germany. The two tiers to the board are the supervisory and the executive. The supervisory board brings together the different interest groups, notably employees, shareholders, professional advisors and bankers. Although there is no overlap the executive board will use the supervisory board as a sounding board while the supervisory board will highlight issues and concerns to executive management. This interlinking of ownership, operations, influence and control plays an important role in securing the stability of industry and specific companies especially during times of difficulty and turbulence.[18]

Much of the same effect is achieved in France through the mixture of private ownership and state involvement which is a distinct feature of French commercial life and corporate governance. Almost 70 per cent of the 'shares' in France's 200 largest firm are controlled by these two parties. Other shareholdings tend to be widely distributed with institutions having little strength or authority. Take-over activity is slowly changing the face of French industry but predatory activity is limited and localised. In the Netherlands, some of the forces at play in Britain and the USA can be seen. The weak performance of leading firms, notably Philips, provoked shareholder action through the Vereniging van Effectenbezitters – the shareholder interest group. In Italy, family ownership of even the largest firms has tended to mute the debate of governance until recently. In recent years fiercely contested mergers and the slump in the performance of specific firms provoked widespread criticisms of the power of the most public CEOs. Shareholder action is gathering momentum. Changes like the 1990 Amato Law and the reorganisation of the financial markets in the same year are providing an environment in which shareholders are making new demands on corporate leaders. These are likely to grow in importance since the SIMs (Societa di Intermediazione Mobiliare; Securities Trading Firms) became legal. Elsewhere in the community, notably Greece, Spain and Portugal, the process of adjustment to Community regulation influenced by the new capital inflows – especially in Spain – is widening ownership and control of public companies.

JAPAN

In the USA and Britain much of the soul searching and debate about corporate governance has been prompted by their apparent failure to compete successfully with foreign rivals. The most notable of these is Japan. Their success, however, has not protected Japanese firms from scandal or criticism. In the years 1988 to 1991, Japan was rocked by a series of corporate scandals which raised serious doubts about the integrity and capability of Japanese corporate leadership. Cronyism, collusion, corruption and criminal links are among the catalogue of complaints. These have forced the resignation of at least one Prime Minister, several Finance Ministers and the heads of Nippon Telegraph & Cable, Recruit, Sumitomo Bank, Itoman Properties, Nomura among others. These have helped turn the stock market into a roller coaster which has seen it halve in value in two years. These events are prompting the worry that 'too much speculation and funny money games could undermine Japan's competitiveness in Manufacturing'.[19]

The overall pattern of corporate control seems designed to achieve maximum stability and keep the risks from speculators and predators to a minimum.[20] A small number of major institutions control the majority of shares. The *keiretsu* are company groups with wide and strong cross-ownership interests. They concentrate control in a relatively small number of hands. These institutions keep close to the firms in which they have invested. The unity of purpose is reinforced by joint membership of sector-based trade associations and the Federation of Economic Organisations (Keidanren) and the guiding contribution of the Ministry of International Trade and Industry. There are seldom, if ever, independent or outside directors on the boards of Japanese companies. The dominant pattern is of a relatively large board with more than 30 members. These are seen to represent the various interest groups *within* the company. Its primary aim is to review, but seldom change, executive recommendations or policies. Extensive consultation is the key feature of this structure. It is underpinned with wide-ranging external consultation with shareholders, banks, employees, government and other interested parties.

The large and relatively unwieldy board relies heavily on its sub-committees. Issues like audit and remuneration will seldom be dealt with directly but will usually be placed in the hands of outside advisors. There has been substantial upwards pressure on top management salaries in recent years. This has led to far greater attention to the nature of the tasks involved and the bundle of benefits especially in senior executives with experience overseas. The overseas challenge to the status quo has taken other forms recently. The most striking is the debate over acquisition and foreign shareholder rights. This has led to a whittling down of the legal barriers to entry and ownership but so far little change of the technical barriers to entry.

CONCLUSION

The forms and character of corporate governance are being reviewed across the world. In some countries, the study is prompted by changes in organisational structures, markets and technologies. These are processes which Chandler[21] and other observers would recognise. Internationalism prompts investors like T. Boone Pickens to seek new opportunities in Japan and respond energetically when frustrated. The convergence of markets like those in Europe prompts close appraisal of the system of governance in the efforts to create a 'level playing field'. Technology affects all these processes. It permits the almost instant transfer of information and creates new opportunities for transparency and collusion.

Some changes are provoked by specific events. Rows over top management salaries can start a debate which goes much deeper into the aims, objectives and control of the firm. It is not surprising to find shareholders questioning a system which allows CEOs like Antony O'Reilly and Stephen Wolf in the USA or Iain Vallence and Robert Horton in the UK to take large increases in remuneration while profits slip and shares slump. This inevitably raises other questions about in whose interest the firm is being operated. The components of reform are relatively common. They include separation of key functions, e.g. chairman and chief executive and establishing external reviews, e.g. remuneration and audit committees made up largely of independent directors. The old adage, make sure that *not only is it fair but it is seen to be fair*, holds good. The risks of cronyism have been vividly illustrated in Japan. Merely, exchanging an old friend for a current friend, e.g. allowing former directors to become non-executives or sitting on each other's boards, will not fit the bill. Transparency is a central plank of reform across the world. It is the best defence for the high-quality, capable and responsible management that exists in the vast majority of firms and the finest reassurance for shareholders against those who do not meet these standards.

This is especially true given the new demands and expectations which will shape the governance agenda in the 1990s. The threat to the environment has prompted governments to impose new requirements on firms and their directors. The Environmental Protection Agency in Britain has made it an offence to carry on certain types of production processes without authorisation or to fail to keep HM Inspectorate of Pollution informed beside introducing regulations on waste disposal and treatment. These demands and the requirement of companies to comply are being matched in many countries. Responsible firms are taking this further. Some have given directors specific responsibility for environment issues. Others are looking to independent directors to undertake this monitoring role. There are, however, limits to the tasks independent directors can be called upon to perform without changing the nature of their role in the firm. The German two-tier board might provide a vehicle for accommodating these different interests. Much of the pressure for change has come from shareholder groups. Their increased expertise, growing confidence and access to the knowledge and technology which was once confined to full-time management might presage a new twist in the pattern of governance.

Managerial capitalism was the result of the coincidence of a specific array of factors: increased scale of operations; dilution of ownership; importance of specialist expertise and the belief that managers knew best. Each of these is under threat. The real size of corporations is changing. This is not only because of deliberate policies of downsizing. It results in part from much wider access to knowledge and information which makes access to the parts of the enterprise much easier. Some ownership groups can match the size of the corporations themselves. This is especially true of institutional groups. Smaller shareholders have become expert at organising themselves to reduce or eliminate the problems of dilution. Expert knowledge continues to be important but boards no longer have monopoly access to expertise. Underscoring each of these elements is a deterioration in shareholder and public confidence in the unique capability of management – especially in the USA and Britain – to manage successfully employing current practices. The apparent combination of eroding competitiveness and questionable standards poses a major challenge to a business leadership striving to demonstrate its right and capacity to lead.

QUESTIONS

1 Describe, with illustrations, how the systems of ownership and control shape the nature of corporate governance in three specific countries.

2 'Some Genius invented the Oreo. We're just living off the inheritance.' (F. Ross Johnson, President RJR Nabisco 1985–91). How far does this comment explain the increasing concern about standards of governance in the USA?

3 Discuss the contribution that a shareholder 'Bill of Rights' can make to effective corporate governance.

4 Outline the duties of a director using material from one of the following:

    (a) The RJR Nabisco LBO
    (b) Time Warner
    (c) International Rent-a-Car.

Show how directors behaved in relation to these duties.

5 Compare the role that disclosure plays in corporate governance in the USA, Germany and Japan.

6 Detail the provisions of the EC's Fifth Company Directive on Company Law. How are these provisions likely to affect company behaviour?

7 It is sometimes argued that supervisory boards work very well during periods of growth and prosperity but are major barriers to change especially during times of economic difficulty. In the light of recent German experience, how far do you accept this criticism?

8 Outline the arguments for and against the separation of the roles of chairperson and chief executive of a large plc. How would your views change when dealing with a medium-sized firm?

9 Analyse the proposition that the key difference between US and UK systems of corporate governance and those prevalent in most of Northern Europe is that in the latter ownership 'is a necessary but insufficient definition of accountability [while] . . . those who give their lives to the company are as important as those who put their money in'. Demb, A. and Neubauer, F. F. (1992)[22]

10 Define

(a) Paternalism

(b) Entrepreneurial capitalism

(c) The Wall St Walk

(d) The duty of loyalty

(e) Supervisory boards

(f) Disclosure

(g) Keiretsu

(h) *Cronyism*

(i) LBO

(j) Co-determination

REFERENCES

1. Crystal, G. 'The Great CEO Pay Sweepstakes' *Fortune*, 18 June (1990) p. 98.
2. Demb, A. 'East Europe's Companies: The Buck Stops Where?' *European Affairs*, vol. 4, no. 22 (1990).
3. Eaton, L. 'Corporate Couch Potatoes: The Awful Truth About Boards of Directors' *Barron's*, December (1990).
4. Shonfield, A. *Modern Capitalism: The Changing Balance of Public and Private Power*, Oxford, Oxford University Press (1969).
5. Carnegie, A. *The Gospel of Wealth and Other Timely Essays* (1862).
6. von Mises, L. *Human Action: A Treatise on Economics*, London, William Hodge (1949).
7. Crystall, G. S. *In Search of Excess*, New York, Random House (1992).
8. Business International Limited *New Directions In Corporate Governance*, London, Business International Limited (1992).
9. Burrough, B. and Helyar J. *Barbarians at the Gate*, London, Arrow (1990).
10. Magaziner, I. C. and Reich, R. B. *Minding America's Business*, New York, Random House (1983).
11. Monks, R. A. and Munn, N. *Power and Accountability*, London, Harper Collins (1991).
12. The Business Roundtable *The Role and Composition of the Boards of Directors of Large Publicly Owned Corporations*, New York, The Business Roundtable (1978).
13. American Law Institute *Principles of Corporate Governance*, New York, American Law Institute (1984).
14. The Business Roundtable *Corporate Governance and American Competitiveness*, Washington, The Business Roundtable (1990).

15. Harm, C. *The Financing of German Industry by German Banks; An Institutional Analysis*, Washington, World Bank (1990).
16. Whitman, D. *The Role of the Board of Directors: To Whom is the Board Responsible?*, Geneva, IMI (1989).
17. Lujkin, J. C. and Gallaher, D. *International Corporate Governance*, London, Euromoney (1990).
18. Demb, A. and Neubauer, F. F. *The Corporate Board*, Oxford, Oxford University Press (1992).
19. Business Week International 'Japan Cleans House – Again' *Business Week*, 8 July (1991).
20. Sheard, P. 'The Main Bank System and Corporate Monitoring and Control in Japan, *Journal of Economic Behaviour and Organisation*, 11 (1989) pp. 399–422.
21. Chandler, jun., A. D., ibid.
22. Demb, A. and Neubauer, F. F., ibid.

CHAPTER 9

Standards, safety and security: issues and obligations

Few issues raise more debate or pose more uncomfortable questions for corporate leaders than standards of health, safety and security.[1] Bhopal, Piper Alpha, *Exxon Valdez*, *Herald of Free Enterprise*, Three Mile Island, Chernobyl are still fresh in the minds of business leaders. They force responsible executives to ask which standards they apply in their factories, plants and offices. Are there absolute standards which the firm establishes even if they are higher than legislators require.[2] Are there those which can be locally enforced or are there standards which are imposed in the richest, most powerful and most health and safety aware locations.[3] Once a set of standards is established who is responsible for enforcement?[4] It can be the external legislator. It can be the employees or their representatives. It can be the company itself. At an international conference on Corporate Responsibility,[5] sponsored by the HRH the Prince of Wales, these issues were at the centre of attention. The problems highlighted at the conference included:

- How can firms wed enterprise and risk taking in business to care and responsibility to the community and the environment?
- In what ways should industry respond to demands for security, greater safety, improved literacy, job and wealth creation in communities that differ widely in their cultures, expectation and capabilities?
- What can firms do to establish systems that work locally, through local staff, to set and maintain standards?

The problems are not new.[6] Economic and industrial growth involves change and risk. The character of the change involved has worried commentators since the start of the industrial age.

> There were trim cheerful villages too, with a neat or handsome parsonage set in the midst; there was the pleasant tinkle of the blacksmith's anvil, the patient cart horses waiting at his door; the basket maker peeling his willow wands in the sunshine; the wheelwright putting the last touch to a blue cart with red wheel; here and there a cottage with bright transparent windows showing pots of blooming balsams or geraniums, and little gardens in front all double daisies or dark wallflowers; at the well clean and comely women carrying yoked buckets, and towards the free school small Britons

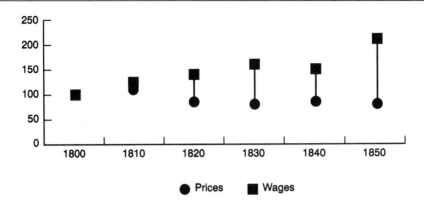

Fig. 9.1 Wages and prices 1800 to 1850 (index of wage and price changes 1800 at 100)

dawdling on . . . The land around was rich and marley, great corn stacks stood in the rick yards . . . this was the district of protuberant optimists, sure that old England was the best of all possible countries . . . But as the day wore on the scene would change: the scene would begin to be blackened with coal pits, the rattle of hand looms to be heard in hamlets and villages. Here were powerful men walking queerly with knees bent outward from squatting in the mine, going home to throw themselves down in their blackened flannel . . . here were handloom-weavers, men and women, haggard from sitting up late at night to finish the week's work, hardly begun till the Wednesday. Everywhere the cottages and the small children were dirty, for the languid mothers gave their strength to the loom.

Eliot, G.: Felix Holt[7]

The accumulated evidence[8] that industrialisation in the early part of the last century was linked with higher wages, better housing and general improvements in the standards of living for the vast bulk of the population does little to change the image shaped by writers like Eliot, Dickens and Disraeli. In the first half of the last century real wages increased rapidly while prices dropped sharply after the end of the Napoleonic War (Figure 9.1).

Although there is an element of romantic nostalgia in the views of the past, other factors came together to blind writers to the material gains from industrialisation. Three go to the heart of the challenge facing those who seek to highlight the gains and bring out the ways industry can respond responsibly to critics. First, industrialisation has, in the past, been associated with far greater aggregations of people in cities and industrial centres. Rural deprivation was dispersed while urban squalor is concentrated. Writers who could remain unaware of the problems of the countryside were forced to acknowledge the problems of the cities in which they lived.

Concentration introduced a second feature. In rural or pre-industrial communities, it was only natural disasters which affected large numbers of workers or users. Farm accidents occurred very frequently but seldom affected more than a

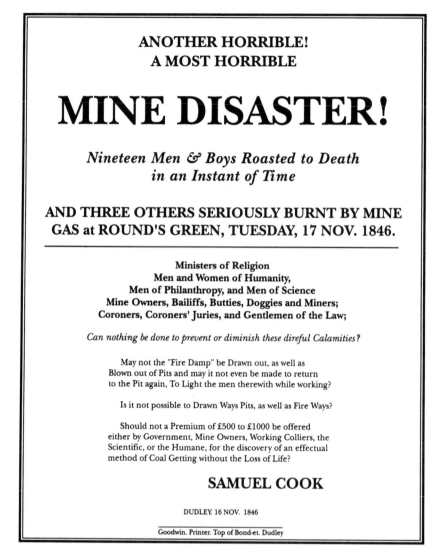

Fig. 9.2 A mining disaster

few workers. The famines, floods or earthquakes which affected large numbers could be explained as God's work or providence in some other form. The advent of mining and industry changed this. An explosion, fire or collapse might involve hundreds of workers and their families. Whole communities were affected. Society saw a 'man made' disaster and wanted an explanation. In its simplest form, technology had created the problem so technology should be able to solve it (Figure 9.2).

Reforms illustrated the potential to improve standards through human intervention.[9] At the same time, the temptation to avoid compliance and its associated costs added the third feature to the challenge to industry. The state could legislate but implementation was the responsibility of the individual or the enterprise. Responsible corporate leaders acknowledge that there is no benefit from ignoring the challenges faced by change, innovation and risk taking.

> I don't want to know about it; I don't choose to discuss it; I don't admit it. The subject is a very difficult one

> Mr Podsnap in Charles Dickens: *Our Mutual Friend*[10]

The word *Podsnappery* has disappeared from use but the risks of ignoring the dangers associated with industry and change are widely recognised.

Legislation has never been a good substitute for prior planning and executive action. The Offshore Safety Act 1992 set in place the most comprehensive offshore safety system in the world but could do nothing for those most affected by the Piper Alpha disaster. A fine of £20,000 can be imposed for certain key health and safety offences but responsible corporate executives give a much higher priority to avoiding the internal failures of compliance. This requires a combination of leadership, endorsement, control and guidance which persists over time.

EVOLVING AGENDAS

The agenda for response and care is shaped by a series of factors. These include:

- new technologies
- new environments
- new markets
- cultural diversity
- managerial ownership and discretion.

Technology places enormous strains on the ability of human systems to cope with change.[11] This can be seen in some of the most difficult areas of compliance with standards in industry and commerce.[12,13]

Risk analysis and management has emerged as a crucial aspect of strategy.[14] Much of the current thinking about risk derives from either the insurance/ assurance sector[15] or the nuclear industry.[16] Both have developed approaches to risk which have valuable lessons for management. There has, however, been relative neglect of other aspects of risk management, notably the influence of psychological factors such as *group think*.[17] Risk assessment is a vital field of insurance and re-insurance. It has grown more complex and demanding as the character and scale of technological risk evolves and grows. Until fairly recently, industrial activity largely dealt with mechanical or electro-mechanical processes. Risks could be seen and understood – even if Podsnappery was widespread. The early reports of the factory commissioners highlight the tangible and visible risks which surrounded workers.

At John Brown & Company's Steel and Iron Works:

Masses of red hot metal, too heavy to be carried about, are wheeled about, sometimes by boys [but, one of the managers observed] we do not think that the work hurts the boys' health. It is hot, but they can often rest, and have plenty to eat and drink . . . the worst is, say, the loss of a finger.

In Northampton, where Wellington Boots were made and stabbing of holes was required:

[Mr Bostock pointed out to the Commissioner that] the stabbing was laborious, requiring great attention, and was even dangerous, for they often sat so close that in drawing the thread with both hands, the awl, which was always held point outwards, in the right hand, not infrequently struck the next child [which prompted the Commissioner to note] I have noticed, before seeing Mr Bostock, that several persons of both sexes, whom I met in the town, had lost an eye, but thinking it merely an odd coincidence, had not inquired about it, till Mr Bostock made the above remark.

Quoted in Martin, I. (1971)[18]

The tangible and immediate nature of these risks made it relatively easy for a combination of legislation, action by insurers and changes in management to overcome the problems at least in the richer, developed countries. The refusal to insure certain types of process or a plant operating in a particular way can be enough to force change or close it down. It is relatively easy to legislate or intervene in areas of high visibility and high impact. The mixture of community awareness and recognised impact reinforces the demands for action. In many areas the impact is high but the visibility is low. This was true of environmental hazards like CFCs and many workplace risks, e.g. carcinogens in the workplace atmosphere. This might mean that problems grow unnoticed until it is too late for effective action. High visibility, low impact hazards are often the easiest to act against. With low visibility, low impact problems the challenge is to persuade people to take action before they have a greater impact. (Figure 9.3) The new technology problems facing firms, legislators and insurers lie in greater awareness of the intangible and long-term nature of risk.[19] This is not a wholly new issue. Pneumoconiosis – black lung – killed more coal miners than mine disasters. The hidden risks to workers in seemingly safe industries like computing and white goods production adds a new dimension to risk management. In chemicals, biotechnology and electronics the risks are harder to identify and tackle.[20] This problem is compounded by the scale of risk, its extension to new groups and changing attitudes to legal intervention.[21]

The combination of these events allied to natural disasters like the San Francisco earthquake, has made insurers acutely aware of the risks involved in new technologies and human error. Sir Bryan Corby of the Prudential admitted that 'the substantial difficulties' facing the company in 1990 stemmed partly from 'a failure properly to assess the exposure and get reinsurance levels right'. Pressure from the insurance companies on firms to improve their risk manage-ment policies is increasing. In the UK, questions are being asked about the notion of *negligence* which has shaped the way the law has dealt with claims. The Times[22]

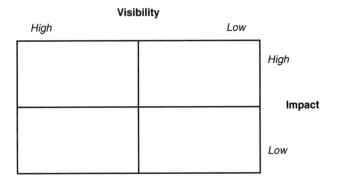

Fig. 9.3 Issues affecting the pressure to intervene

contrasted the British view that 'the public shaming of those adjudged responsible for a catastrophe has been regarded as both punishment and deterrent' with the US view that deterrence 'is enforced through huge claims for damages and consequently swingeing insurance premiums'. It suggested that notions of neglect in the law were due for revision while business must take a more responsible attitude to risk and hazard management.[23]

The appraisal of risk and the successful management of hazards requires a clear understanding of their nature. In Figure 9.4 the various ways in which risk is viewed within the firm and the community are categorised. In some cases both the firm and the community recognise the risks involved in a process. The employers and workers on Piper Alpha knew they were involved in an high risk industry. On one level, the employees knew that they were taking risks working in the off-shore oil industry. This does not, however, reduce the responsibilities placed on management. It creates an opportunity fully to inform and involve

Table 9.1 The monetary cost of ten disasters

The event	The year	The exposure ($million)
The Pinto	1970s	250
Thalidomide	1980s	1,000
IUDs	1980s	1,000
Piper Alpha	1988	1,400
Exxon Valdez	1988	1,500
Herald of Free Enterprise	1988	300
Kings Cross	1989	400
Bradford Stadium	1989	150
Clapham	1989	200
Hillsboro	1989	250
Total		6,450

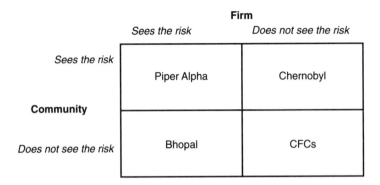

Fig. 9.4 Perception of risk

their workers in reducing and tackling risk. Full partnership is the key to success in reducing risk where both parties understand that *they are at risk*. There are some situations where neither party appreciates the risk. CFCs were introduced before either the companies involved or the wider community recognised the threat to the environment. Constant vigilance is the only way to keep the costs of these risks to a minimum. The type of environmental monitoring employed to highlight new opportunities can play an equally important role in spotting new risks. This may involve efforts to involve others in auditing and appraising risk. The organisation has special responsibilities where it sees the risk but the community is either unaware of the risk or unable to defend its interests. These obligations include early warning, internal openness and hazard reduction. There are occasions where the community identifies a risk that the firm cannot see or acknowledge. This might result from internal blindness, e.g. where the venture is too closely identified with a technology or process, or self-interest, e.g. where groups within the firm are exploiting poor financial safeguards. Openness is essential if these latter problems are to be avoided.

Group think is perhaps the biggest barrier to positive change in attitudes to risk and hazard management.[24] It poses general difficulties to the firm attempting to develop an affirmative approach in these areas beside creating severe difficulties in tackling specific issues and events. Analysis of managerial behaviour before, during and after some of the worst problems shows that the features of group think recur.[25] The problems surrounding the Ford Pinto are a vivid illustration of the consequences of this syndrome.

The Pinto was an important but not vital element in Ford's efforts during the early 1970s to reposition its operations in the face of growing competition especially from overseas. It was, however, closely identified with the egos of several key executives at Ford notably Henry Ford II and Lee Iacocca. The latter was battling to become the leader of the company when Henry Ford II eventually retired. Iacocca had promised to produce the 2,000:2,000 quickly and under budget. This was achieved. The car weighed just over 2,030 lb and sold for $2,000. It took less than six months to develop and was well under budget. *Ego identification* became linked to a sense of *invulnerability*, the first reports of problems added to this sense of invulnerability. Henry Ford II rejected Nader's criticisms arguing that people wanted 'good cars, good looking cars, fast cars, cars with power and styling'.[26] Reading the accounts of the principals, there is a powerful sense of *collective rationalisation* – people were getting the cars they wanted. Critics were *stereotyped* as ignorant or hostile. This reinforced the sense of *inherent morality* which prompted the firm to ask the National Highway Traffic Safety Administration to put a price on Auto Safety. The figure produced was $200,725. This was then used to calculate the cost per vehicle of improvements needed to solve the problem. The internal report virtually concluded that it was cheaper to pay the accident claims. This symbolised the *pressure* on group members to rationalise decisions, repress doubts and keep members in line. Even in his autobiography, a decade later, Lee Iacocca[27] gives a clear impression of self-justification. Although he admits 'we resisted making any changes and that hurt us badly', he argues that 'the Pinto was not the only car with this problem' of fire breaking out if hit from the rear. At no point does he comment on the deaths or injuries caused by the problem. His argument seemed to centre on the notion that no one 'deliberately [tried] to make this car unsafe'. No critics had made this accusation but had argued that no one put enough effort into making it SAFE.

Group think was identified by Janis[28] as a characteristic of the ways groups respond to external threat or challenge. It has eight key characteristics:

1   *Invulnerability* – members are overoptimistic. This lead them to take excessive risks with little serious consideration of alternatives.
2   *Collective rationalisation* – contrary evidence is dismissed through explanations which avoid serious reappraisal of assumptions.
3   *Inherent morality* – the group is so confident of the rightness of its actions that doubts are rejected.
4   *Stereotyping* – critics and opponents are allocated a stereotype which eliminates the need seriously to consider their position or response.
5   *Pressure* – demands for loyalty are used to repress doubts and keep members in line.
6   *Self-censorship* – members suppress their questions to retain group esteem.
7   *Illusion of unanimity* – this is maintained vigorously. Silence is treated as agreement.
8   *Mindguards* – specific individuals take on the task of controlling information flows and restricting those ideas which threaten the consensus.

Achieving high standards and managing systems of safety and security demand that group think is avoided and risks and hazards are properly managed. This is as important in new environments or markets as in new technologies.

Special challenges exist when firms address different cultures where knowledge, values and assumptions place the onus on the firm to identify issues and potential hazards even if this is not expected or required within the culture.[29]

MANAGERIAL RESPONSIBILITIES IN PRACTICE

The complex nature of modern technologies and the varied nature of the environments in which firms operate call for risk, hazard or crisis contingency planning of a high order. There are three fundamental stages of this. First, there is preplanning, especially risk identification or analysis. This is inseparable from the second element – hazard or crisis management. Third, firms require post-event learning, feedback and adjustment. An example of the structured approach can be seen at Du Pont. Edgar Woolar, Du Pont's CEO describes the approach in the following terms:

> First we said that we were going to make commitments and measure our progress (pre planning) . . . we would be cutting toxic air emissions 60%, carcinogens 90%, hazardous waste 3% and so on . . . The second thing we did was to take some of our top leaders and form a group called the Environmental Leadership group (management) . . . Another very important change was making this (safety or environmental improvement) one of the primary measures of people's success . . . he or she gets a bonus or salary credit (feedback).

Birchard, B. (1993)[30]

The responsible firm knows that it has no guarantee of immunity from risk or threat. This can range from extreme forms of life or survival threats to limited threats to the firm's operations. Identification of these risks and their key characteristics is an important feature of contingency planning.[31] In many cases, these risks can be analysed in terms of technology or people. In Figure 9.5 the extent of dependency on people or technology is used to classify risks.

The most taxing risk management situations exist where security is highly dependent on both people and technology. On Piper Alpha, security depended on both highly skilled staff and advanced safety systems interlocking successfully. Failure of either system to work placed everyone at risk. Total system security and integrity was essential for safety. There was, however, limited scope to substitute technology for people or vice versa. The *Herald of Free Enterprise*, employed relatively simple technology to identify hazards but was totally dependent on human intervention to recognise the problems and act. Improvements in security require either better people management, i.e. make the current system work better, or substitution of technology for people. At Seveso, there was relatively little people could do to arrest the problems once they started. Investment in better monitoring and containment technologies was critical to minimising risk and controlling the aftermath. Some hazards exist outside the

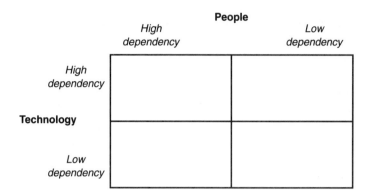

Fig. 9.5 The dependency matrix

immediate control of people or technology. Natural disasters provide the clearest examples of these hazards. It is, however, management's responsibility to recognise these risks and minimise the opportunity for nature and process to interact to create a crisis.[32]

Experience in the nuclear, chemicals and transport sectors highlights the importance of creating a culture of risk awareness and minimisation.[33] This is underpinned by clear lines of responsibility and authority for the installation and monitoring of safety and security systems. In most projects, these are required from the start. The Challenger disaster vividly illustrated the need to allocate proper responsibility for overruling commercial demands in favour of safety requirements when construction started. Design errors and procedural violations lay at the heart of the problems with Chernobyl. There is a strong case for distancing the safety audit from line management while providing good lines of communication. In many operations, there is a call for regular reviews of existing or historic practice based on formal procedures. The Kings Cross underground railway fire in London was put down to an almost complete absence of formal procedures.[34] A mixture of *it couldn't happen here* and *we've never needed these procedures* is potentially fatal. Enforcement is crucial.[35] Systems which are not tested or procedures which can be ignored soon become discredited. Over elaboration which contributed to neglect is as dangerous as insufficient attention. The systems introduced into the London Underground immediately after the Kings Cross fire produced 'knee jerk reactions . . . every time anyone smells smoke'[36] which soon undermined the quality of response. AID is the key to successful preplanning. This is **A**nalysis, **I**nitiative and **D**evelopment.

Once problems occur, executives find themselves facing challenges which they may face only once in their life. Openness, use of well established routines, refusal to panic and a willingness to admit ignorance are integral elements in successful hazard or crisis management. British Airways plans for 84 different contingencies. Hazard management practice has shifted in recent years from a preoccupation with equipment and system failure to a recognition that people still lie at the centre of effective response to crisis. Properly organised management teams with procedures for working together are more effective than the heroic individuals portrayed in films and books. Information management is increasingly part of an effective response to problems. Judith Cooke comments that 'very rarely . . . does it emerge that just one single thing went wrong. It is usually a combination of things – equipment failure, management failure, human error, all too often compounded by lack of judgement and failure to heed advice or warnings.'[37] The standards needed by the firm are those which can cope with multiple failure not just single issue problems.[38]

Post crisis management involves responsibilities to the individuals involved, the enterprise and the community.[39] After the Piper Alpha, the Health and Safety Commission identified over a hundred issues which needed to be addressed if the lessons learned were not to be lost. Among the most important were:

- The creation of an effective safety management system.
- Regular audits of operations to ensure that hazards were identified, risks assessed and adequate controls in place.
- Adequate emergency arrangements.
- Use of properly trained support staff.

The company's responsibilities extend beyond the firm to the community especially the victims. Poor-quality victim support has emerged as a common criticism of firms involved in problems. In part, this reflects a form of group think – acknowledging the victims means acknowledging the failures. Effective feedback within the firm and to the community requires a degree of candour that is alien to some firms.[40] It can, however, be a crucial factor in avoiding a blame culture which prevents lessons being learned.

LEGISLATION

The legislative environment surrounding standards management, safety and security is changing rapidly.[41,42] The United Nations has highlighted six basic principles which should be built into local legislation or company practices. These are:

Industrial disclosure of risk information on proposed or current construction and resources utilisation projects – in effect this places the onus on the firm to disclose *in advance* any risks.

Industrial disclosure of risk information on facility operations – the firm is responsible for ensuring that all those likely to be involved either directly in production or dealing with problems are given full information on hazards.

Industrial disclosure of risk information on products – the firm must secure prior approval of potentially harmful products and is responsible for avoiding uses which place members of the local community at risk.

Industrial disclosure of risk information on the workplace – full information on the health and safety hazards of production or service should be given in advance to workers, their representatives and other authorities.

Other disclosures – freedom of information laws, disclosure requirements should be honoured.

These policies reflect and develop the requirements which already exist in many countries. The common strands are that responsibility for disclosure lies with the firm; prior notification is needed and full information is essential. The US National Environmental Policy Act, the EC's Environmental Impact Assessment Directive, beside policy recommendations made by the International Labour Office and the Organisation for Economic Co-operation and Development support this broad pattern of policy. There is some evidence[43] that 'formal and explicit requirement, such as those of the US agencies and the Netherlands, work better than the informal procedures of the UK and most Scandinavian countries'.[44] A major contrast between US and European practice is the public right-to-know principles incorporated in US Laws and the resistance to this within the EC. There has been a shift within the Community to the notion of active transfer of material on risk.

> Member States shall ensure that information on safety measures and on correct behaviour to adopt in the case of an accident is supplied in an appropriate manner and without their having to request it.
>
> European Commission[45]

Responsible corporations have reacted favourably to these developments. Manville Corporation label their products 'regardless of whether the country requires it'.

EMPLOYEES

Individual or group action by employees lies at the heart of any system for introducing and maintaining standards in areas like safety and security. They have responsibilities to the firm just as the firm has responsibilities to its employees. These are:

Avoidance – shunning practices which are counter to the standards set in the firm, are contrary to law or expose others to risk.

Prevention – taking steps to prevent breaches of the firm's standards or the law. There is an imperative to prevent actions which could harm others.

Exposure – exposing wrong doing.

Exposure poses some of the most complex problems for firms and their employees. Corporate fraud has often been dealt with internally despite breaking national laws. Banks, for example, have been accused of covering up fraud among their employees in order to avoid questions about their internal security. In the public sector, damage limitation can mean wrong-doers escaping proper punishment.

CASE STUDY 9.1

The journal

The newly appointed head of the Economics Department at Brummage University faced a problem. The department had been the home for 20 years of the prestigious *World Journal of Economic Studies*. Before joining Brummage, she had assumed that the University or the Department owned the journal. She had, now, found that this was not the case. This discovery was largely accidental. A colleague had complained that a course outline he needed had not been distributed because his secretary had been working on a mailing for the journal. He shared the secretary with a colleague who was its reviews editor. In the subsequent argument in the head's office it had emerged that the journal was owned by a firm set up years ago by one of her predecessors.

There was little doubt that the journal gave added prestige to the department but it paid very little for the services provided. Once, however, the chairman of the company owning the journal heard of this row and the subsequent questions he moved all the records and the business address off-campus. He was helped in this by the finance officer who was also paid to be company secretary. This prompted the head to enquire at company's house about just what assets were involved. She was surprised to discover that the cash reserves were almost £200,000 despite payments of about £30,000 to the editors and for overseas travel. The dilemma she faced was whether to ignore these events or express her concerns.

Whistle blowing poses major problems for employees.[46] They place their jobs and future at risk to highlight concerns they hold about company practices.[47] Some firms are introducing hotlines to enable worried employees to identify their worries so that immediate action is taken without unnecessary public exposure.

ESTABLISHING CORPORATE STANDARDS

Organisations seeking to establish standards which can be implemented effectively are building these around a series of common elements. These include an understanding of the firm and its environment, an appreciation of the needs of those stakeholders involved in implementation and control and endorsement by corporate leaders. The decision to prepare or revise the company's code of standards for tackling dilemma, risks and responsibilities is best seen as public endorsement of responsible behaviour.[48] It acknowledges the challenges facing managers, workers and the community in the face of new capabilities, demands and expectations.

> Not only are the simple rates of change unnerving, but so are their pervasiveness and the effects on both the larger environment and individual organisations. For example, jet transportation permits the development of global markets, but it also has a direct environmental impact on the areas surrounding airports and is indirectly linked to the oil spills that have ruined thousands of acres of pristine Alaskan wilderness. The latest office technology permits vast improvements in clerical productivity, but it also engenders new, often frustrating relationships between workers and supervisors . . . Rapid technological development also adds layers of ethical complexity to the decisions made by individuals and leaders of governments and corporations.
>
> Commission Report (1990)[49]

The statement of standards acknowledges these challenges and attempts to address them within the firm. This requires that the statement is put in writing. Ownership matters, which means that extensive consultation with stakeholders during preparation builds a sense of involvement beside giving valuable insight into issues and implementation. In some firms, independent assessment is essential. Union Carbide – right after the Bhopal tragedy – appointed the former head of the US Environmental Protection Agency as its vice president in charge of safety, health and the environment. Others employ external 'standards' auditors to give this type of guidance and support. Extensive dissemination of the standards is the first step in effect implementation. This starts a process of education and training which highlights the individual's roles and responsibilities. The key to success lies in making it clear to all stakeholders what the statement means to them and their associated rights and responsibilities.

Some firms attempt to make their ethics statements as brief and accessible as possible. This approach is seen in the statement adopted by Forte Plc.

CASE STUDY 9.2

Forte plc

The company philosophy

- To increase profitability and earnings per share each year in order to encourage investment and to improve and expand the business
- To give complete customer satisfaction by efficient and courteous service and value for money
- To support managers and their staff in using personal initiative to improve the profit and quality of their operations while observing company policies
- To provide good working conditions and to maintain effective communications at all levels to develop better understanding and assist decision-making
- To ensure no discrimination against sex, race, colour or creed and to train, develop and encourage promotion within the company based on merit and ability
- To act with integrity at all times and to maintain a proper sense of responsibility towards the public
- To recognise the importance of each and every employee who contributes towards these aims.

This approach defines a broad philosophy to guide all actions. Other firms strive to identify key areas of action and draw out more detailed guides to action, as at Shell.

CASE STUDY 9.3

Royal Dutch/Shell Group of Companies

Statement of general business principles

1. Objectives
The objectives of Shell companies are to engage efficiently, responsibly and profitably in the oil, gas, chemicals, coal, metals and selected other businesses, and to play an active role in the search for and development of other sources of energy. Shell companies seek high standards of performance and aim to maintain a long-term position in their respective competitive environments.

2. Responsibilities
Four areas of responsibility are recognised:
a. To shareholders
   To protect shareholders' investment and provide an acceptable return.
b. To employees

To provide all employees with good and safe conditions of work, good and competitive conditions of service; to promote the development and best use of human talent and equal opportunity development; and to encourage the involvement of employees in the planning and direction of their work, recognising that success depends on the full contribution of all employees.

c. To customers

To develop and provide products and services which offer value in terms of price and quality, supported by the requisite technological, and commercial expertise. There is no guaranteed future: Shell companies depend on winning and maintaining customers' support.

d. To society

To conduct business as responsible corporate members of society, observing applicable laws of countries in which they operate, giving due regard to safety and environmental standards and societal aspirations.

These four areas of responsibility can be seen as an inseparable whole.

3. Economic principles

Profitability is essential to discharging these responsibilities and staying in business. It is a measure both of efficiency and of the ultimate value that people place on Shell products and services.

It is essential to the proper allocation of corporate resources and necessary to support the continuing investment required to develop and produce future energy supplies to meet consumer needs. Without profits and a strong financial foundation it would not be possible to fulfil the responsibilities outlined above.

Shell companies work in a wide variety of social, political and economic environments over the nature of which they have little influence, but in general they believe that the interests of the community can be served most efficiently by a market economy.

Criteria for investment decisions are essentially economic but also take into account social and environmental considerations and an appraisal of the security of the investment.

4. Voluntary codes of conduct

Policies of Shell companies are consistent with the two internationally agreed voluntary codes of conduct for multinational enterprises, the OECD Declaration and Guidelines for International Investment and Multinational Enterprises and the II O Tripartite Declaration of Principles.

5. Business integrity

Shell companies insist on honesty and integrity in all aspects of their business. All employees are required to avoid conflicts of interest between their private financial activities and their part in the conduct of company business. The offer, payment, soliciting and acceptance of bribes in any form are unacceptable practices. All transactions on behalf of a Shell company must be appropriately described in the accounts of the company in accordance with established procedures and subject to audit.

6. Political activities

a. Shell companies endeavour always to act commercially, operating within existing national laws in a socially responsible manner, abstaining from participation in party politics. It is, however, the legitimate right and responsibility to speak out on matters that affect the interests of employees, customers and shareholders, and on matters of general interest, where they have a contribution to make that is based on particular knowledge.

b. Political payments

As a policy, Shell companies do not make payments to political parties, organisations or their representatives.

c. Employees

Where employees, in their capacity as citizens, wish to engage in activities in the community, including standing for election to public office, favourable consideration is given to their being enabled to do so, where this is appropriate in the light of local circumstances.

7. Environment

It is the policy of Shell companies to conduct their activities in such a way as to take foremost account of the health and safety of their employees and of other persons, and to give proper regard to the conservation of the environment. In implementing this policy Shell companies not only comply with the requirements of the relevant legislation but promote in an appropriate manner measures for the protection of health, safety and the environment for all who may be affected directly or indirectly by their activities. Such measures pertain to safety of operations carried out by employees and contractors; product safety; prevention of air, water and soil pollution; and precautions to minimise damage from such accidents as may nevertheless occur.

8. Grants and general community projects

The most important contribution that companies can make to the social and material progress of the countries in which they operate is in performing their basic activities as efficiently as possible. In addition, the need is recognised to take a constructive interest in societal matters which may not be directly related to the business. Opportunities for involvement, for example, through community, educational or donations programmes, will vary depending upon the size of the company concerned, the nature of the local society and the scope for useful private initiatives.

9. Information

The importance of the activities in which Shell companies are engaged and their impact on national economies and individuals are well recognised. Full relevant information about these activities is therefore provided to legitimately interested parties, both national and international, subject to any overriding consideration of confidentiality proper to the protection of the business and the interests of third parties and the need to avoid wasteful information exercises.

Increasingly, the behaviour of large companies is subject to rigorous external scrutiny. The reputation of the Royal Dutch/Shell Group of Companies depends on the existence and acknowledgement of clearly understood principles and responsibilities and their observance in day-to-day practice in widely differing environments.

Although individual operating companies may elaborate their own statements to meet their national situations, this statement of general business principles serves as a basis on which companies of the Royal Dutch/Shell Group, in their operations, pursue the highest standards of business behaviour. Shell companies also promote the application of these principles in joint ventures in which they participate.

Many corporations incorporate a statement on corporate ethics or governance in their annual report or statement of accounts.

Ultimately commitment and trust will determine how successfully these programmes are in practice. Top management has a special responsibility in this. Robert Kennedy of Union Carbide acknowledges that 'responsibility for convincing the workforce falls on senior management, and particularly on the CEO. We know what signals to send the troops: "This is for real. We are not spending half a billion a year on superficial programs. We're doing it to stay in business." '[50] The standards work where top management commit the resources to ensure systems can be maintained. These, in turn, need to be fully integrated into the wider systems of reward and control in the firm.

BHOPAL

Few events illustrate more clearly the challenges facing communities and companies than the cyanide gas leak at the Union Carbide plant in Bhopal, India. The disaster itself vividly illustrated the reasons why corporations are under pressure to establish effective standards especially in health and safety. It contains all the elements which place the primary onus on the firm to act responsibly in advance, tackle problems quickly and effectively when they occur and build the lessons from the event into the firm's operations. The episode itself contained elements which guaranteed that society would demand an effective answer from industry. It brought together a US multinational and India's poor. The media inevitably made much of the contrasts between the standards which applied in and around Union Carbide's US operations and those which prevailed at Bhopal. The images of silent and hidden death striking the people of the shanties provoked a powerful reaction across the world. The eventual discovery that the gas involved – cyanide – was a gas being stockpiled around the world for military purposes merely strengthened feeling. The immediate reactions of the firm increased local and international suspicion of its motives and values.

The sequence of events which took place was frighteningly simple. Union Carbide, the US Chemicals giant had owned and administered their plant at Bhopal for a number of years. It was managed almost entirely by local staff. This was in compliance with Indian legislation on the ownership and control of foreign operations. Around the factory a large shanty town had grown up. This type of development is common in India. The poorest members of the community live as close as possible to a potential source of work, money, materials and any other scraps which might improve their lot. In the early days, the company had tried to keep the shanty at a distance. Over time, their efforts in this direction seem to have diminished. They faced a difficulty encountered by other multinationals. It is hard for the rich, US corporation to be seen acting against the most deprived members of the local community – even if it is for their own good.[51] The picture of bulldozers owned by Union Carbide destroying a shanty town, to keep it away from the factory, was not an image the firm wished to cultivate. There is some evidence that Union Carbide was viewed very favourably in the local community until December 1984.

It now seems that water leaked into one of the processing tanks in the plant. At the high temperatures which existed this produced a chemical reaction which led to a gas leak into the surrounding area. The gas was heavier than air and spread through the local area causing 2,500 deaths and many injuries. Critics of the firm identified four basic failings:

1   Inadequate information about the risks in advance.
2   Poor contingency planning and staff training.
3   Failures in information during and immediately after the crisis.
4   Reluctance to tackle the problems of those affected and the local community in the immediate aftermath.

Perhaps most damning criticisms came from those doctors who 'say that many lives could have been saved if they had known that cyanide gas was present'.[52] These comments provoked widespread criticism that the firm's priorities were limiting the damage to the company rather than tackling the problems in the community.

There was a strong sense of, at least, three sets of cultural, social and economic imperatives at work. Inevitably, the corporation's response was affected by the background of the US leadership. Responsibility and liability are close together in the thinking of North American business leaders. The Indian government seemed to seek a mixture of retribution and economic response. Those immediately affected were hurt, confused and in need of immediate assistance. All were affected by shock. The knock-on effects hurt virtually every aspect of the firm's operations. Communities around every plant owned by the firm demanded information on its operations. New safety demands were imposed. Recruitment plummeted while the credibility of the existing leadership dropped. The share price slumped and profits dropped. This had a knock-on effect across the entire US chemicals industry. It is hard to estimate the total cash cost of the disaster (Figure 9.6). The $470 million settlement by Union Carbide to the victims may not be the largest single element in these costs.

The failures before and during Bhopal highlight the need for prior planning and effective and open management during a crisis based on company-wide standards.

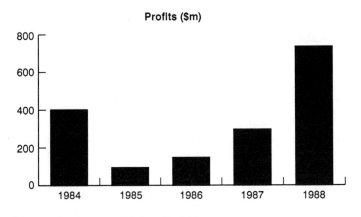

Fig. 9.6 The performance of Union Carbide

There is evidence that Union Carbide have learned these lessons. The firm has introduced a Business Charter for Responsible Care which addresses most of the issues highlighted as major concerns. Robert Kennedy, the CEO, identifies 10 key elements in the firm's current approach to shaping and implementing the Responsible Care programme.[53] These are:

1 *The personal commitment of top management* – 'when the CEO says that the environment and safety comes before profit and production', when people are held accountable, the message gets across.
2 *A vision for the future* – firms need a 'simple and straightforward' commitment which is disseminated and implemented throughout the firm.
3 *A strategic plan* – a plan is needed which has clear performance standards and proper budgets.
4 *Independent assessment* – at Union Carbide the 'environmental audit unit' has a budget of 'more than $6million' and is appraised externally.
5 *Industry-wide effort* – the firm has advocated higher standards throughout the industry. Adherence to the Responsible Care programme is a condition for membership of the US Chemical Manufacturers Association.
6 *Dialogue with the public* – this willingness to inform and communicate lies at the heart of a successful standards strategy. It includes breaking down the barriers to communication – the temptation to stonewall, education and training followed by an active community awareness and dialogue programme.
7 *Realism* – acknowledging limitations and making effective implementation the cornerstone of action.
8 *Internal dialogue* – reshaping attitudes and making it clear that performance and high standards are compatible.
9 *Co-operation* – this extends to all agencies with a genuine interest in the issue.
10 *Total quality management* – the integration of all systems for establishing and maintaining standards.

These actions converted the response of the firm from a damage limitation exercise to a strategy for the future.

PIPER ALPHA

The explosion on the rig Piper Alpha highlighted a series of problems associated with projects which operate at the frontiers of technology in hostile environments. The fire on the Occidental Oil rig in July 1988 cost 167 workers their lives, hit Britain's balance of trade, shook the insurance market and provoked a major reappraisal of standards and security throughout the offshore oil industry. The Cullen Report on the disaster highlighted a series of weaknesses in company, industry and national policies. Although the firm denied the most severe criticisms of its actions it immediately committed itself to changes (in practice) arising from the Cullen Report. The events leading up to the fire on Piper Alpha are well documented in the Cullen report. Some were specific to the Occidental rig, others were part of more general industry practice.

There can be little doubt that the success with which North Sea operations had developed was largely due to the research and investment of firms like Occidental. They had developed techniques which allowed oil to be extracted in a harsh and dangerous environment. There are claims that this very success produced a sense of complacency at least in government and the public mind.[54] The oil flows had made the pound petrocurrency and secured the UK's balance of payments. High wages were earned by workers but some of the elements which led to the disaster might be discerned in attitudes to union or worker representation on safety matters. The partnership which is so important to successful implementation of standards when both parties recognise the risks had been eroded. The reluctance to have the Safety Representatives and Safety Committees Regulations 1977 extended offshore weakened the confidence of some in the good intentions of the firm and government.

> For a decade the government has ignored voices in the industry calling for this change . . . So it cannot be claimed that the dogs did not bark, only that those particular dogs had barked too often without good cause for the government to pay attention. It is an unconvincing case.
>
> The Times (1990)[55]

There were suggestions in the Cullen Report that the safety regulations were not implemented with all the rigour that the hazards facing workers demanded. The company denied these accusations but the extent of loss of life makes it clear that weaknesses existed. Only through an active prior partnership *in advance* can these be eliminated.

The firm's immediate response had much to commend it. The chief executive took a leading role in ensuring that rapid response teams were in place while onshore relatives obtained help. There were suggestions that support during the post-crisis period was less effective. This highlights a major issue which has been identified in a series of comparable events including Hillsboro, the Bradford Football Stadium fire and numerous smaller events. Those affected need counselling, care and other support for far longer than used to be assumed. Responsible organisations are extending their help for much longer periods than in the past. Inevitably, this will require close collaboration with public agencies.

The toll of lives from work in the dangerous conditions of the North Sea is high. This highlights the need for firms to learn the lessons of hazard management and build into their operations. The Cullen Report highlighted changes in practice that have implications far beyond its immediate remit. The first – independent assessment – repeats a theme raised in Union Carbide's response to Bhopal. The specific recommendation that responsibility for supervision of standards should be transferred from the UK Department of Energy to the Department of Employment reflects the wider concern about balancing different interests in managing standards. The penalties for failure to comply and implicitly the rewards for compliance were clarified and strengthened. This brings out the wider need for management to introduce specific and implementable standards. The detailed analysis in the Report was welcomed throughout the oil industry as a model of objectivity and appraisal. Rebuilding management's credibility is a key feature in post-crisis management. This, in turn, depends on a determined effort to reconstruct relationships between management, workers and the community on the basis of trust and partnership. Worker and community representatives can play a vital part in this process. A restrictive or selective approach to partnering can undermine the effort to establish and renew standards.

PERRIER

The problems affecting Perrier in the late 1980s and early 1990s are very different to those in the tragedies at Bhopal and Piper Alpha. They do, however, raise issues of standards, hazards and crisis management which touch on key aspects of management's responsibilities to its stakeholders. The firm's difficulties went to the heart of its customer relationships and threatened the viability of the enterprise. The firm's problems emerged when its products failed to satisfy the US Food and Drug Administration's standard of purity in a routine test of benzene which took place in a state laboratory in North Carolina. The resulting publicity forced the firm to withdraw all its products for sale, cease production and relaunch the product across the world. The company's share price dropped by almost one-third in just two months while lost sales and reduced market share cost the firm about $100million. The founder of the company M. Gustav Leven retired from the firm within months of the disaster.

The nature of the product especially its image of healthiness made its problems seem all the more unlikely. This seems to explain partly the initial difficulties

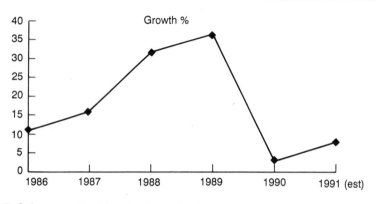

Fig. 9.7 Sales growth of Perrier (by value)

faced by the firm. It seemed so unlikely that problems could occur that internal standards of safety and security allowed a careless employee to splash the wrong cleaning fluid on to a bottling plant. There is no evidence that existing controls within the firm were sufficiently stringent to pick up the problem before it reached the market. The firm had few contingency plans for problems of this scale. The maxim that no one is immune was well illustrated. Once the firm was informed of the difficulty the gap in planning was further exposed. The firm's reputation for being 'secretive and tight lipped'[56] made the media suspicious and increased its difficulties with regulatory bodies around the world. Confusing and somewhat contradictory signals from the firm added to the confusion. At one point it seemed that the firm was going to withdraw only the US product, later all output was withdrawn. Confusion in the market made the recovery package harder to develop and implement. Sales by volume were down by over 20 per cent a year after the product was withdrawn temporarily (Figure 9.7).

The underlying strength of the market plus the diverse nature of the firm's operations provided a platform for survival and recovery but better management of the crisis might have reduced the need for remedial action.

The crisis highlighted a lack of effective contingency planning. The company changed its explanation several times. Worldwide production and distribution was first stopped then restarted then stopped again. This sense of confusion pervaded its operations. Reaction in the US market hardened at reports of an anti-American view being expressed in Vergeze the centre of Perrier production. There was a delay of four days between the first benzene reports from the US and Perrier issuing the results of its own test. The crisis management team which was already in place failed to manage the key components of crisis management. These were keeping calm, combining a clear sense of urgency with clarity in communication, avoiding recriminations and remaining consistent to the firm's core values.

There is evidence that the company management team has learned many of the lessons of its difficulties. Crisis management programmes have been development and contingency plans are in place. There remain some worries about the firm's overall approach. Key customers continue to complain about their lines of communication with the firm. Sainsburys refused to stock Perrier long after its reintroduction because it insisted that the word 'naturally' should be removed from labels. The decision to reduce the size of the large bottle from 1 litre to 0.75 litres caused further problems in the year after the crisis. The combination of these factors undermined trade relations. They indicate the impact a problem in one aspect of the firm's business can have across its operations.

CONCLUSION

The difficulties faced by Union Carbide, Occidental and Source Perrier forced their leadership groups and those directing firms across the world to re-examine the standards they set and the ways they were implemented. There is greater awareness of the internal responsibility for standards and a recognition that externally imposed standards are no substitute for responsible management. Corporate leaders recognise that they must address issues of health, safety and security if their firms are to prosper in a healthy community. At the Conference organised under the authority of the Prince of Wales in Charleston, industrial leaders accepted these responsibilities. The answers given were not the same.

One debate centred on the problems facing a steel firm operating two identical plants. One was in the US, the other in the fictional country Volvic. The Environmental Protection Agency in the USA undertook a survey of the US operations which prompted it to instruct the operator to introduce environmental safeguards costing $350 million. The dilemma facing the executives on the panel was – should they introduce the same changes in Volvic? The local government did not require it. There was even the suggestion that the national leaders will discourage it if it increased prices and reduced exports. For some the answer was simple. Allan Shephard of Grand Metropolitan argued that the firm should spend the money on its Volvic plant. He argued that 'you should not start shipping your sulphur dioxide round the world'. Lord Laing of United Biscuits and Sir Simon Hornby of W. H. Smith agreed. Sir Simon addressed the issue of standards: 'If I've gone ahead and done it at home – yes – I've got to protect standards'. Lee Raymond of Exxon was less certain. He did not feel the firm 'should volunteer' the investment and changes immediately. John Elliott of Elders suggested that the issue centred on the competitive position in the local market. Unless, other producers were meeting the same standards they could undercut prices and even drive the firm out of production. Lodwrick Cook of Atlantic Richfield developed the same point by saying that shareholders would expect to 'see the numbers' to justify the decision. The vigour of the debate highlights the importance that corporate leaders now give to questions of standards, their introduction, maintenance and development.

The emerging consensus is that companies:

- Can wed enterprise and risk taking in business to care and responsibility to the community and the environment by developing strategies which improve standards overall, win endorsement by their stakeholders and build competitive advantage by doing things right.
- Respond to demands for security, greater safety, improved literacy, job and wealth creation in communities that differ widely in their cultures, expectations and capabilities by recognising diversity but wedding standards to systems of control and ownership that can be replicated internationally. The sense of 'ownership' that the best firms get from their employees can mean that relevant adaptations can be introduced which match diversity of input with consistency of output.
- Establish systems that work locally, through local staff, to set and maintain standards by wedding ownership to effective preplanning, comprehensive contingency planning and quality feedback.

For the last 200 years and beyond, successful firms have coped with change, diversity and difficulty by creating internal standards and systems that work. Inevitably, these reflect the needs of their different stakeholders, the demands of their markets and the capacity of the technology they employ. Success in the future will call for the same blend of creativity, insight, quality and commitment to standards. These standards can only work if they are underpinned within the company.

> Everyday we read about the folks who get caught. Citicorp fires a vice president and senior executive of a credit card processing division for allegedly overstating revenues. American Express cans several executives for failing to write off accounts of customers who had filed for bankruptcy, as required by company policy. Alamo Rent a Car agrees to refund $3 million who were overcharged for repairs to damaged vehicles. There is clearly a moral iceberg down there.
>
> Labich, K. (1992)[57]

These problems exist in the public as well as the private sector. Resources are misused in public works departments. Expenses are fiddled in health boards. University academics neglect their students or fail to publish. Management is aware but does nothing. They are, in effect, breaking an important part of their contract with their employer. The emergence of a crisis merely exposes the weakness of the prevailing standards. They have lost the authority their contract gave them along with the legitimacy this endowed. The actions and their neglect undermine the ability of management to manage with authority and credibility in any area. This undermines the legitimacy of the firm and weakens or breaks its contract with the community.

QUESTIONS

1 In establishing standards for health and safety in the workplace, what should come

first, local custom and tradition or absolute company wide criteria? Justify your choice and identify three significant problems with the stance adopted.

2 What should be given priority, enterprise and opportunity or care and responsibility, in setting company goals?

3 Using secondary sources of information describe the events and circumstances that led up to, one of:

   (a) The Piper Alpha fire
   (b) The *Exxon Valdez* oil spill;
   (c) The sinking of the *Herald of Free Enterprise*;
   (d) Another safety crisis with which you are familiar.

   Describe how an effective programme of corporate responsibility management could either have prevented the problem or minimised the tragedy.

4 What factors have contributed most to awareness and attention to workplace standards and safety in post-industrial society.

5 Judith Cooke has pointed out that 'a combination of things – equipment failure, management failure, human error' are usually responsible for safety problems and hazards. How can firms design systems to cope with these rare, even unique, combinations of events?

6 Discuss the notion that 'whistle blowers are traitors to their colleagues and employers'.

7 Compare the codes of ethics of Forte plc, Shell and Marks and Spencer. Draw out the distinct approaches of each firm, indicating how they might reflect the distinct nature of the firm and the environments in which they operate.

8 You are the international Vice President of a US multinational, on your recent visit to India you were alarmed to see a shanty town growing up around your largest chemical plant. The local Indian managers have told you that they have done everything – short of bulldozing the shanties – to persuade those living in the shanties to move. Propose a set of measures which will keep the plant operating but eliminate the risk while not alienating the Indian government or the media. You are aware that your contract with the Indian government precludes closure of the operations.

9 Using the information provided on the issues facing the manufacturer with a factory in Volvic, analyse the dilemma faced by the firm and recommend an internally and externally sustainable course of action.

10 Define:

   (a) Compliance   (f) Inherent morality
   (b) Podsnappery   (g) Avoidance
   (c) Group think   (h) A company code of ethics
   (d) Collective rationalisation   (i) Partnership
   (e) Environmental impact assessment   (j) Whistle blowing

CASE STUDY 2

The Maxwell affair

The death of Robert Maxwell in 1991 exposed levels of dishonesty, greed, collusion and failures by supervisory and regulatory agencies that are, only now, coming to light. At the end of 1992 *The Times* commented, 'A year after his death, the regulatory rulebook is being rewritten'. Just weeks before his death and the collapse of the system of subterfuge he created, the Investment Management Regulatory Organisation (IMRO) had reviewed the records of Maxwell's Bishopgate Investment Management – one of his primary instruments for this actions – and given it a clean bill of health. It seemed that Maxwell had found a system of regulation and supervision capable of being exploited with ease.

When Maxwell took over Mirror Group Newspapers, he found its pension fund fully funded, 'in fact with a sizeable and growing surplus'. The previous managers of part of the fund, Reed Organisation, had sought to protect some of the pensioners through a formal agreement with Maxwell. Despite his failure, as the employer, to make any contribution to the fund since buying MGN, the law gave Mr Maxwell the power to do what he wished with the pension fund surplus without even consulting the beneficiaries. The scheme's beneficiaries could be ignored 'not merely on how the proceeds of the pension funds surplus might be distributed, but in determining the investment strategy, of calling trustees to account, of being notified of proposals to reduce the surplus or to be notified of changes in trustees or fund managers'.[58]

Trustees were incapable of coping with a management style which involved Maxwell whirling in 'in his shirt sleeves and conducting two hours of business in five or six minutes. You just could not raise matters, they were steam rollered through . . . we could protest, but . . . Mr Maxwell had the casting vote'.

Captain Peter Jackson, Mirror Group Pension Fund Trustee until his resignation

QUESTIONS

1 Use this and other information about the Maxwell Affair to describe how Maxwell exploited the opportunities available to him.

2 Could the trustees have done more?

3 Do you believe the lessons of the Maxwell affair have been learned?

REFERENCES

1. MacLagan, P. W. 'The Concept of Responsibility: Some Implications for Organisational Behaviour and Responsibility' *Journal of Manufacturing Studies*, vol. 20 (1983) pp. 411–23.
2. Cook, L. M. and Welch, J. F. 'What CSR Means to Me' *Business and Society Review*, no. 18 (1992) pp. 87–9.
3. Bassiry, G. R. 'Business Ethics and the UN: A Code of Conduct' *Advanced Manufacturing Journal*, vol. 55, no. 4, Autumn (1990) pp. 38–41.

4. Roberts, R. W. 'Determinants of CSR Disclosure' *Accounting Organisations of Society*, vol. 17, no. 6, August (1992) pp. 595–612.
5. The Prince of Wales, Business Leaders' Forum *Stakeholders: The Challenge in a Global Market*, Charleston, South Carolina (1990).
6. Heald, M. *The Social Responsibilities of Business: The Company and Community*, Cleveland, Case Western Reserve University Press (1970).
7. Eliot, G. *Felix Holt*, Harmondsworth, Penguin Edition (1986), first published 1866.
8. Mitchell, B. R. and Deane, P. *Abstract of British Historical Statistics*, Cambridge, Cambridge University Press (1962).
9. Vogel, D. 'Business Ethics: New Perspectives on Old Problems' *California Management Review*, vol. 23, no. 1, Summer (1991) pp. 101–17.
10. Dickens, C. *Our Mutual Friend*, Harmondsworth, Penguin (1986).
11. Zuboff, S. *In the Age of the Smart Machine*, London, Heinemann (1988).
12. Rion, M. *The Responsible Manager*, London, Harper and Row (1990).
13. Cook, J. *An Accident Waiting to Happen*, London, Unwin Hyman (1989).
14. Comfort, L. (ed.) *Managing Disasters*, Durham, Duke University Press (1988).
15. Jones-Lee, M. W. *The Economics of Safety and Physical Risk*, Oxford, Blackwell (1989).
16. Health and Safety Executive *The Tolerability of Risks from Nuclear Power Stations*, London, HMSO (1988).
17. May, E. and Neustadt, I. (eds) *Thinking in Time: The Uses of History for Decision Makers*, New York, Free Press (1986).
18. Martin, I. *From Workhouse to Welfare*, Harmondsworth, Penguin (1971).
19. Boehmer-Christiansen, S. A. and Skea, J. F. *Acid Politics: Environmental and Energy Policies in Britain and Germany*, London, Belhaven Press (1991).
20. Perrow, C. *Normal Accidents: Living with High Risk Technologies*, New York, Basic Books (1984).
21. Hood, C. and Jackson, M. W. *The New Public Management: A Recipe for Disaster*, London, London School of Economics (1992).
22. *The Times*, editorial, 12 September (1990).
23. Shearing, C. D. and Stenning, P. C. *Private Policing*, Newbury Park, Sage (1987).
24. May, E. and Neustadt, I., ibid.
25. Douglas, M. *How Institutions Think*, London, Routledge (1987).
26. Lacey, R. *Ford*, London, Pan (1986).
27. Iacocca, L. *Iacocca*, New York, Bantam (1984).
28. Janis, I. I. *Victims of Group Think: A Psychological Study of Foreign Policy Decisions and Fiascos*, Boston, Houghton-Mifflin (1972).
29. Wimes, W. A. and Napier, N. K. 'Toward an Understanding of Cross Cultural Ethics: a Tentative Model' *Journal of Business Ethics*, vol. 11, no. 11, November (1992) pp. 831–42.
30. Birchard, B. 'Corporate Environmentalism and Du Pont' *Greener Management International*, Issue 2, April (1993) pp. 64–71.
31. Turner, B. A. *How Can We Design A Safe Organisation?*, Second International Conference on Industrial and Organisational Crisis Management, Leonard N. Stevin School of Business, New York University, November (1989).
32. London Emergency Planning Centre *Acts of God? An Investigation into Disasters*, London, Association of London Authorities (1990).
33. Brackley, P. *World Guide to Environmental Issues and Operations*, London, Longmans (1990).
34. Pendrous, R. 'Risk Management' *The Engineer*, December (1991).
35. Priest, G. L. 'The New Legal Structure of Risk Control' *Daedalus*, 119 (1990) pp. 207–27.
36. Comments by Jack Rose, Head of London Underground's Risk Assessment Unit.
37. Cook, J. *An Accident Waiting to Happen*, London, Pan (1990).
38. Rose, N. *Governing the Soul: Technologies and Human Subjectivity*, London, Routledge and Kegan Paul (1989).
39. Gow, H. B. and Kay, R. W. (eds) *Emergency Planning for Industrial Hazards*, London, Elsevier (1988).
40. Legal considerations will inevitably shape company actions.
41. Priest, G. L., ibid.

42. Horton, T. R. and Reid, P. C. *Beyond the Trust Gap*, Business One Irwin, Homewood, Illinois (1991).
43. Kennedy, T. 'Environmental Impact Assessment in North America and Western Europe: What Has Worked Where, How and Why' *International Environment Reporter*, vol. 11 (1988).
44. United Nations *Transnational Corporations and Industrial Hazards Disclosure*, Washington, United Nations (1991).
45. European Commission, Eighth Directive, 88/610/EEC (1988).
46. Ewin, R. E. 'Corporate Loyalty: Its Objects and Its Grounds' *Journal of Business Ethics*, vol. 12, no. 5, May (1993) pp. 387–96.
47. Larimer, R. A. 'Whistleblowing and Employee Loyalty' *Journal of Business Ethics*, vol. 11, no. 2, February (1992) pp. 125–8.
48. Webley, S. *Company Philosophies and Codes of Business Ethics*, London, Institute for Business Ethics (1988).
49. Commission on Admission to Graduate Management Education,*Leadership for a Changing World*, Los Angeles, Graduate Management Admission Council (1990).
50. Kennedy, R. 'Achieving Environmental Excellence: Ten Tools for CEOs'. *Prism*, third quarter (1991).
51. Donaldson, T. 'Can Multinationals Stage a Universal Morality Play?' *Business and Society Review*, no. 18, Spring (1992) pp. 51–5.
52. *Observer*, 10 November (1985).
53. Kennedy, R., ibid.
54. Parker, D. and Handmer, J. (eds) *Integrated Disaster and Emergency Management*, London, James and James (1992).
55. *The Times*, editorial, 13 November (1990).
56. Dawkins, W. 'Perrier Counts the Cost of Contamination' *Financial Times*, 13 February (1990).
57. Labich, K. 'The New Crisis in Business Ethics' *Fortune*, April (1992).
58. Social Security Committee *The Operation of Pension Funds*, London, HMSO (1992).

PART 3

The environment

CHAPTER 10

The slowly dawning green revolution

In the early 1960s Rachel Carson's book *Silent Spring*[1] triggered a public debate which has gathered force over the last 30 years until it is seen as, perhaps, the most powerful challenge facing mankind. In this debate the role of industry and commerce remains at the centre of the storm of discussion, claim and counter-claim. Carson placed industry, commercial farming and careless innovation at the centre of her argument. Chemical insecticides, fertilisers, concentrated single crop production were among the 'elixirs of death' that were wreaking havoc with 'Earth's green mantle' so that 'rivers of death' flowed under skies where 'no birds sing'. The strength of the imagery, the clarity of the prose and the message itself set an agenda which has forced an increasingly determined response from industry.

> Today, the message of the scientists is being heard: the earth has finite assimilative capacity. Pollution – if unchecked – will cause deforestation and desertification, loss of species, increased incidence of cancer and other destructive consequences. The challenge is for business and government to find ways of managing growth for sustainable development, without stressing the Earth's resources to a point from which they cannot recover.
>
> Robinson, N. (1991)[2]

The prose has deteriorated with the environment but the central message of concern is the same. Industry has a pivotal role to play in tackling the issues, developing and delivering the response. In part, this business input is important because of the pervasive nature of industrial processes. The contribution gains added moment from the challenge which notions of sustainable development pose to established notions of economic, industrial and business development.

> Living sustainably depends on accepting a duty to seek harmony with other people and with nature. The guiding rules are that people must share with each other and care for the earth. Humanity must take no more from nature than nature can replenish. This in turn means adopting life styles and development paths that respect and work within nature's limits.
>
> IUCN (1991)[3]

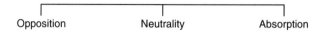

| Opposition | Neutrality | Absorption |

Fig. 10.1 The spectrum of response

Each element in this proposition poses challenges to an industrial economy based on competitiveness rather than harmony, rivalry not sharing and investing to increase yields and adding rather than merely replenishing. This notion of changed values is accepted by those who acknowledge that 'development for a sustainable future is as much about shifting values as it is about shifting practices'.[4] There is no consensus on the view of business development and environmental protection. It is possible to place the proposed responses to the environmental challenge along a spectrum which extends from corporations resisting proposals to change until forced by legislation and enforcement and firms building their futures around internalising environmental concerns (Figure 10.1). There is, however, evidence emerging that no long-term solutions can be produced without industry's involvement. There is widespread consensus that business must play a part in resolving the challenges it has helped to create

The old dichotomy which insisted that people had to be in favour of either economic progress or environmental protection hurt the environment movement by keeping out

Table 10.1 Organisational implications of environmentalism

Organisational System	Environmentalist Concerns
Inputs	
Raw materials........	Depletion of forests
	Harm caused by toxic materials like pesticides, solvents
Fuels......................	Depletion of oil, coal, natural gas
	Pollution created by fossil fuel, hazards of using nuclear energy
Throughputs	
Plant	Plant safety and accidents
	Risks to surrounding neighbourhoods
Workers	Occupational diseases/hazards
	Work related injuries/ill-health
Wastes...................	Hazardous waste disposal
	Emissions of pollutants
	Emission of environmentally destructive chemicals like CFCs
Transportation	Risk of spills and losses in transporting hazardous materials
Outputs	
Products	Product safety
	Health consequences of products such as tobacco, liquor, fats, beef, etc.
Packaging..............	Garbage created by packaging
Servicing................	Reliability, hazards of failure

of it exactly those people needed to solve the 'environmental problems': economists, the business community, the majority of government officials and hundreds of millions of poor people.

Holmberg, J. et al. (1991)[5]

Many of the worries raised by those concerned about the negative effects of environmental degradation are shared by industry. This concern extends beyond the simple 'we share the planet as well' type proposition. Production managers want factories located in healthy and diverse environments because output is higher and workers are healthier. Office staff consistently opt for facilities in tune with the local environment rather than at war with its context. Marketing executives learned long ago that balance, health and prosperity were far more secure contexts for business development than distorted, unhealthy growth. Finance staff are discovering that hidden costs do not stay hidden for ever. Shrivastava[6] summarised some of these in terms of their impact on the input, processes and output of the firm. (Table 10.1).

The challenge exists at every stage in the evolution of the corporation from its formation or the acquisition of new business to the internationalisation of the firm.

One of the highest risk areas is the acquisition of new businesses, which may carry unknown environmental skeletons. No due diligence would now be complete without considering potential environmental problems, especially when the target owns land. Cleaning up contaminated land is one of the biggest causes of multi-million pound environmental liabilities.

Chovril, R. and Shortis, A.[7]

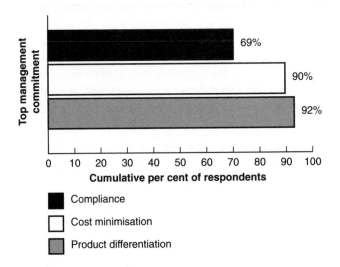

Fig. 10.2 Competitive product differentiation
Source: Hochman, S. D. et al. (1993)[8]

This growing awareness of the costs and benefits of positive environmental programmes is endorsed by corporate leaders across the world. A major survey of the top management of large US corporations showed that they are increasingly seeing adaptation to the needs of the environment as a major source of a competitive product differentiation (Figure 10.2). It provides a potential bridge between Gaia[9] and those others involved in deep ecology,[10] the environmental reformers[11] and communities aspiring to capitalise on the results of industrial development.

A SILENT SPRING OR FALSE DAWN?

The picture presented by Carson was vivid and clear. Technologies were being employed to excess, in areas in which they were not needed, crudely and without sufficient thought. Even where alternatives existed, commercial pressures prompted farmers, businesses and countries to use the *quick fix* of a new chemical spray or pesticide rather than resist the temptation to act until the consequences were known. The images presented of the 'town in America . . . [robbed of its] dawn chorus . . . [where no] bees droned and streams were lifeless' became part of the imagery of the era.[12] Her reforms had a similar appeal. Restraint, allied to a use of natural processes could be the key to a 'reasonable accommodation' between the needs of the environment and man. There were early successes from this approach. Some are identified in her book. Natural predators can do the job of chemical predators. There can be few gardeners today who do not see the ladybird as a powerful ally against aphids. Farmers in Europe and North America look increasingly to natural means to combat natural enemies. The use of DDT, the major villain of the Carson text, is banned in many countries and its use heavily restricted. There are however new guilty parties. They range from acid rain produced by power stations to the litter from fast food outlets and excess packaging. However, it is possible to identify clear and easily accessible successes against a deteriorating overall picture. It is sometimes surprising to see how quickly and easily successes in waste reduction can be achieved, especially in

Table 10.2 Reduction in packaging volume at Digital Equipment Corporation

Computer product	Product volume (cm³)	Packaging volume (cm³) Before	Product volume (cm³) After	Reduction (%)
Mouse	216.96	8.62	0.94	89.1
Module	791.98	2.79	0.72	74.3
Software	181.90	15.17	1.79	88.2
Cabinet	900,472	0.36	0.25	31.0

Source: Nielsen, L. J. (1991)[13]

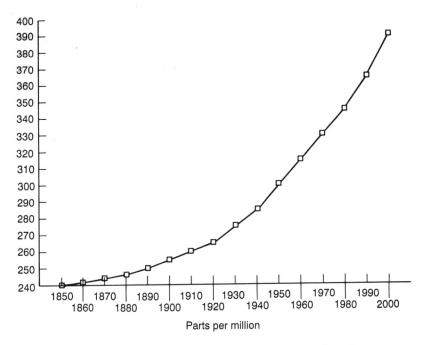

Fig. 10.3 Increasing levels of carbon dioxide in the atmosphere (parts per million)

areas like packaging. A programme to reduce packaging volume at Digital Equipment achieved the dramatic results shown in Table 10.2.

Atmospheric pollution has increased rapidly while worries about global warming raise questions about the ability of the planet to sustain itself. The sharp increase in levels of carbon dioxide in the atmosphere is closely linked with the spread of industry and the use of the car (Figure 10.3). Corporate leaders are learning to accept their responsibilities even if it affects their immediate business interests.[14] Charles Luce, Chair of the Board of Consolidated Edison Company acknowledged this[15] when he commented that 'if we are to preserve a habitable earth we are going to have to accept fewer foods and services, including less electricity'. In effect, industry has accepted that the full care and maintenance clause that exists with most leases or property contracts *applies to the planet*. There are a variety of ways to enforce this contract. They include:

● Internal reform of business practices;
● Long-term adjustments made to damaging social and economic activities;
● Restrictions placed on certain activities or products;
● Polluter pays programmes by governments;
● Income from taxes employed to 'clean up';
● Economic growth and industrialisation limited to the amount that the area, community or planet can absorb;

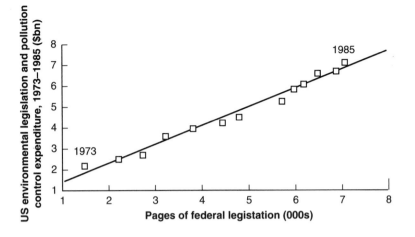

Fig. 10.4 Pollution control spending has risen with environmental regulation in the US
Source: US Office of Technology Assessment

● New technologies developed to correct harmful effects.

Each of these has played a part in shaping responses to threats to the environment. The growth in public concern, partly reflected in increased government legislation as illustrated in Figure 10.4 has played its part.

Companies have adjusted their behaviour to reduce the impact of their activities on the environment while developing systematic strategies using approaches such as those outlined in Figure 10.5. Some have introduced 'green imperatives' into their mission statements. In effect, this places an embargo on activities likely to have a negative impact on the environment. New products will not be introduced which cannot be recycled and the environmental impact of all activities is assessed. Sometimes these programmes are internally managed or monitored. Elsewhere, firms collaborate with government departments or pressure groups to undertake environmental (green) audits or environmental impact analysis.

Environmental Audits examine every aspect of the firm's operations including production, delivery, office and development to appraise in an objective and replicable way their impact on the environment, progress since previous audits and ways to minimise any negative effects. *BS 7750* is Britain's new environment management standard. *Environmental Impact Analysis* takes a strategic view of the firm's relationship with the environment. It aims to provide overall direction to the firm as it attempts to adjust its operations to achieve competitive advantage while achieving a better fit between its operations and the needs of the environment.

There can be immediate and long-term benefits from this approach. Companies like The Body Shop employ their positive attitudes to the environment as a key element in their market strategy. This enabled the firm to build up a distinctive

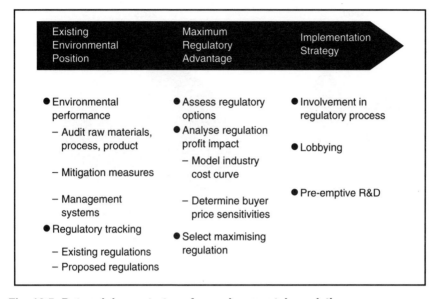

Fig. 10.5 Determining a strategy for environmental regulation
Source: Clark, J. (1993)[16]

and loyal franchise. Other companies have found that waste reduction and recycling programmes reduce costs and adds value to their business.

This has increased enthusiasm for longer-term adjustments in business, economic and social practices. Welford[17] suggests that Total Quality Management and Total Environmental Management can be seen as part of the same system of discipline and restraint. He argues that 'total quality and as such zero defects also means zero negative impact on the environment'. Some firms have used the notion of environmental auditing to shift their company policies from resource exploitation to resource development. There are, however, some key aspects of social behaviour that cannot be addressed solely by firms. Perhaps, the most important global, environmental issue is population growth. The world's population is expected to virtually double in the next 50 years with growth in the poorest parts of the world increasing even faster (Figure 10.6).

The 1990s will see two whole Europes, East and West, added in just ten years. An extra United States every two and a half years. Two United Kingdoms every fourteen months. A Sweden or two New Zealands every month. A Birmingham every four days. Every twenty-four hours a town the size of Walsall or Wolverhampton. A school class of thirty every ten seconds.

Such figures are apt to induce panic.

But is the panic justified? Do we need to worry? Is population growth a problem? Is it something we can handle? Or is it, as some would make out, a positive benefit?[18]

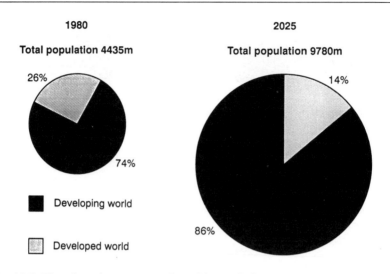

Fig. 10.6 The changing pattern of world population

There are suggestions that firms should become actively involved in birth control programmes. It is more likely that industry will participate in schemes to reduce the impact of population growth on certain types of ecosystem especially rain forests and fragile areas like arid semi-desert areas. At the same time there is evidence that part of the cause of population growth is poverty[19] which can only be tackled through a combination of economic development, industrial success and distribution of the benefits which follow on a more equitable basis.

Most proposals for social or economic change are closely linked with suggestions that certain types of products or activities are banned or their use restricted. Carson pointed out the dangers of excess use of pesticides especially DDT. This and a range of other products including mercury compounds, non-degradable detergents, lead-based paints are now restricted or prohibited. Voluntary restrictions of non-banned products have cut the use of a host of products from certain polymers, through CFCs to specific gauges of nets for fishing. Major firms like Heinz, MacDonald's, IBM, ICI have been at the forefront in this voluntary abstinence.[20] Research into products which use up less scarce resources or which are alternative to harmful products dominate the R&D budgets of progressive companies around the world. In some areas, there has been dramatic progress in reducing raw materials usage.[21] This can be seen in examples as basic as the aluminium in cans and the humble yoghurt pot (Figures 10.7 and 10.8). Governments are recognising that a virtuous circle can be created in encouraging firms to keep to the forefront of environmental protection.

Without a clear indication that central government meant business the paint industry would not have had the necessary incentive to develop, to solve separate problems, new decorative paints free of added lead, or anti-foulings free of the organotins which were polluting our waters. If we succeed in our attempts to persuade the EEC to ban altogether

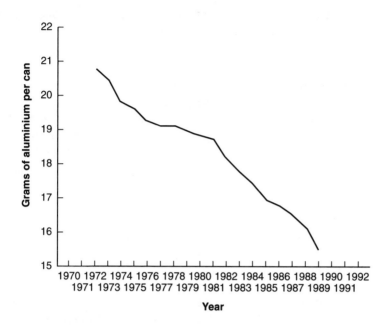

Fig. 10.7 Grams of aluminium per can
Source: Fortune, 3 June 1991 (modified)

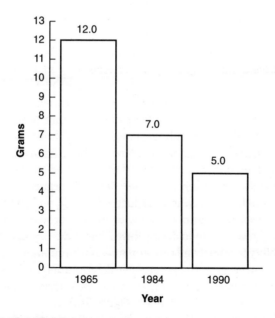

Fig. 10.8 Weight of yoghurt pot
Source: The Economist, 13 April 1991

the use of added lead in decorative paints or organotin-based anti-foulings, our own industry will have a useful head start in providing alternatives.

Waldegrave, W. (1987)[22]

Peters[23] has argued that the effective integration of affirmative environmental strategies into business development will give firms a powerful competitive edge.

For many governments positive action to support industry is matched by determined efforts to ensure that polluters pay.[24] This line of development takes several forms. Solow[25] was among the first to suggest that waste and environmental harm was a result of the 'free good' view of natural resources. A solution is to increase the price which will create a market in which some members will have an interest in maintaining the quality and integrity of the resource. Polluter pays programmes can be linked to *green taxes* such as the differential tax rates on leaded, unleaded and diesel fuels in Britain. Elsewhere, punitive penalties are advocated. These transfer the entire cost on to the polluter. The simplest expression of polluter pays is the use of government funds raised through taxes to clean-up the environment. This was the strategy adopted in the last century when municipalities built sewage systems and government underpinned restraint with legislation. It seems inevitable that some element of cleaning up will be necessary for the long term. Few observers expect that the problem of environmental degradation will disappear. Even if pollution stopped there is a massive residue of damage and pollution to be tackled.

Information on these residues is vital if the problems are to be addressed. Many countries have very poor records of the types of materials used in earlier stages of industrial development. Data on waste disposal is often even harder to obtain. Many governments now require a proper register of material use and disposal. This may be linked with efforts to build an historic picture of land use. These registers are slowly being constructed. There are, however, many barriers to the construction of these registers; not least the reluctance of some land owners to disclose information that could have a negative effect on property values.

The scale of these residual effects allied to the unknowable results of many forms of technology has prompted many groups to advocate a slow-down even a halt to growth. The Club of Rome Report[26] argued that the only way significantly to reduce risk was to reduce economic and industrial growth. In essence, finite resources cannot cope with infinite growth. The authors of this Report now suggest that industrial growth has gone beyond the limits[27] of the planet's capability to adjust and restraint may not be enough. These writers argue that extent of land erosion, the progressive deterioration in the sea allied to other changes in the ecostructure may impose their own catastrophic limits to growth if some action is not taken in advance (Figure 10.9).

Critics of this view argue that technology itself holds the key to tackling these problems. The US Office of Technology Assessment has suggested that advanced technologies could 'slash hazardous industrial waste in the US by 75 per cent'.[28] Technologies have emerged to clear pollutants from power station emission to

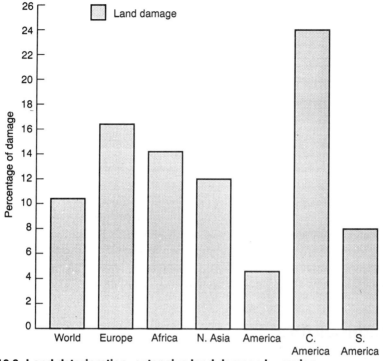

Fig. 10.9 Land deterioration: extensive land damage by region

reduce acid rain, reduce emission from car exhausts, remove metals and other pollutants from factory discharges and tackle a host of hazards. Technology may hold the key to new products which can be substituted for environmentally damaging items. Large-scale recycling requires technologies which are either novel or unknown. Alternative energy sources will call for innovative products and processes. Biotechnology might provide the key to land reclamation and crop management.

The Earth Summit in Rio, 1992, was called to address these and the host of related questions. A strategy for sustainable development which combines internal reform of business practice, restrictions, investment and innovation was seen by the participants as the key to genuine progress. Those who previously doubted the willingness of industry to reform their practices, acknowledge the progress to date and the ability of firms to integrate environmental protection into their corporate development. There are limits to this element of the approach. Small and medium-sized firms have been slow to emulate the policies followed by larger firms. In parts of central and eastern Europe, some developing countries and in specific industrial sectors the notion of restraint does not sit easily with imperatives to build industry especially given the attitudes adopted by some of the richest countries. Long-term adjustments vie with short-term imperatives. The notion that population growth should be limited is hard to get over to peasant families without any security apart from the labour of other family members.

Trees before people, restricted economic growth, blocks on the use of certain natural resources are easier policies to advocate from the vantage point of a rich developed country than a poor, emerging nation. The emergence of the G77 group of Third World countries has positive and negative implications. Its strength will force richer countries to negotiate more equitable development agreements. It is, however, worrying that much of its strength was deployed to tone down proposals on rain forest development.

EUROPE

Perhaps the clearest outcome of the Rio Summit was acceptance that any efforts to tackle the problems of the environment must be international. Within the European Community the Eco-Management and Audit Regulations are part of a wider process of harmonising regulations while improving standards. The adoption of these Europe-wide regulations is likely to be linked with rapid progress in setting up systems of national regulation and accreditation (Table 10.3).

RESPONSIBILITIES

Many of the worst problems cross the boundaries of control of individual countries.[29] The reluctance of the countries bordering on the North Sea to abandon dumping in rivers, sewage emissions into the sea or burning toxic waste at sea illustrates the difficulty of action in the seas linking one of the richest parts of the world. International action may be the only means to tackle problems which cross national boundaries. The Montreal Protocol, various EC directives and sector-specific agreements like the bans on whaling provide some clues to the opportunities and constraints on this type of activity. The risk exists that the demands for internationally effective regulation and the call for national economic competitiveness will provoke new tensions between rich and poor countries. Jacobs argues that the notion of absolute restrictions on growth must be replaced with a recognition that 'current patterns of economic growth are causing major ecological problems'.[30] The optimum solution lies in finding safer alternatives. These would provide rich and poor with politically realistic options. The Bruntland Report[31] develops this theme by integrating the three themes of protection of the environment, sustainable growth and active partnerships. Future generations have a right to expect access to environmental resources at least as good as exist today. Growth strategies that do not deliver this are mortgaging tomorrow for today and industry must be an active partner in building this relationship not just a controlled and regulated agent.[32]

The evidence presented to the Rio Summit gave some scope for cautious optimism that the technological innovation, regulation and industrial partnering can work in this complex area. Clean technologies, properly enforced laws and

Table 10.3 Links between the EC Eco-Management and Audit Scheme and BS 7750 (a cell containing an x represents a connection between the requirements of the EC Scheme and of the BS 7750 EMS specification)

Requirement of EMAS	Requirement of BS 7750 Subclause 4										
	1	2	3	4	5	6	7	8	9	10	11
Environment protection systems	x	x			x	x	x		x	x	x
Environmental policy		x									
Environmental objectives					x						
Environmental programmes						x					
Data generation for performance evaluation				x				x			
Assessment of impacts on the environment				x							
Control and prevention of impacts on the environment					x	x		x			
Minimisation and saving of energy, materials and waste					x	x		x			
Selection and planning of product and production processes					x	x	x				
Prevention and limitation of accidents					x		x	x			
Employee training and awareness			x								
External information and response to public concern		x		x	x						
Assess performance against BAT (British American Tobacco)				x							
Regular management review of policy, objective and programme		x			x						x
Encourage responsibility amongst employees at all levels			x								
Prior assessment of new activities, products and processes					x		x				
Assess and monitor current effects on environment					x				x	x	
Minimise environmental effects		x			x			x			
Reduce waste and conserve resources		x			x			x			
Prevent accidental releases					x		x	x			
Verify and record compliance with policy									x	x	
Plan corrective action in case of non-compliance								x			
Prepare contingency procedures for accidents						x	x				
Provide information to public and respond positively to concern		x		x	x						
Advise customers on products		x		x				x			
Contractors to operate to company standards								x			
Environmental Audit										x	x

Source: British Standards Institute (1992)[33]

better management can break the link between industrialisation and pollution.[34] Since the early 1970s industrial output in Europe, for example, rose rapidly but lead emissions dropped and air quality improved (Figure 10.10).

The OECD research[35] suggests that too little growth can prompt some communities to adopt exploitative methods of economic development while sustained growth provides the resources to adopt cleaner technologies. Polluter

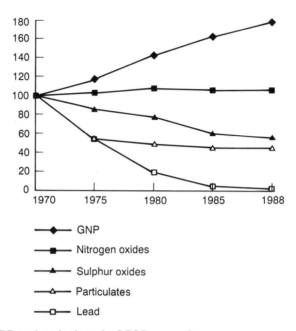

Fig. 10.10　GDP and emissions in OECD countries
Source: OECD (1991)

pays programmes work best if distortions which shift the balance away from environmental protection are eliminated. The World Bank notes that in a number of areas the costs of replacement are far less than the costs of exploitation. Deforestation is encouraged when the logging firm is charged fees which do not cover the cost of replanting.[36] Sustained, integrated strategies based on partnerships between industry and the community provide the best hope for real progress in linking economic growth and environmental protection.

CONCLUSION

The threat posed to the natural environment by industrial development is not new. The Romans saw people crippled and the environment polluted by mining. Overproduction, inefficient management saw the North African 'bread basket' of the Roman Empire turn into a desert in a few hundred years. In China during the seventh century, T'ang canal networks linked the Yangtze valley and the Yellow River and irrigation systems opened up new lands for development. The population expanded rapidly and the character of Chinese development was set for the next 500 years. Deforestation in the Western Isles during the eighth and ninth centuries altered the character of the islands and their economic base. New techniques of irrigation allowed the Chola Kingdom of southern India to exploit 'waste land' but the increases in population led to extensive forest clearing.

The expansion of the central African state of Ghana in the eighth century was based on its exploitation of iron. Its collapse seems to be linked to overexploitation of its reserves. The introduction of sheep into the north of England and Scotland during the late Middle Ages to meet the needs of the expanding textile industry changed the landscape and reshaped communities. The exploitation of the native peoples of South America and the destruction of the environment started almost as soon as Europeans arrived on the continent in the fifteenth century. The dust-bowl effect in the mid-west of the United States earlier this century was caused by the same combination of exploitation and inefficiency. The annihilation of the herring shoals in the North Sea; the massacre of whales in the Pacific and the Atlantic; the destruction of the rain forests vividly illustrate the increasing power of man to destroy key parts of the natural environment.

Until recently, this impact was limited, localised and poorly reported. Rachel Carson's book vividly illustrated how this had changed. She documented the extensive and pervasive impact of these changes. Since then a series of reports have highlighted the extent of destruction and its cumulative effects. Despite the initial shock on publication, these warnings like others have been ignored not least because of the failure to develop coherent, industry-based policies for change. More recently, changes have occurred. First, the rapidly increasing scale of damage is recognised.[37] Second, the political will to tackle these issues is being mobilised.[38] Third, the role of industry and management as part of the answer and the problem is acknowledged.[39] The following chapters link these developments into a framework for effective action.

QUESTIONS

1 Shrivastava[40] claims that 'we are now witnessing the first round of the greening of corporations'. What form does this first round take and how are subsequent rounds likely to evolve?

2 Using data from locally available sources, e.g. your college or university, identify readily available ways to reduce waste. Indicate the barriers to reducing this waste.

3 In the light of the success of Total Quality Improvement programmes, including those linked to national systems of recognition such as the Baldridge Awards in the USA and BS5750 in Britain, describe the potential contribution of similar schemes addressing environmental concerns. Link your analysis to BS7750.

4 Describe the 'polluters pay' approaches adopted in at least one country with which you are familiar. Draw out the strengths of this approach and identify any weaknesses.

5 Does technology hold the key to tackling the problems of environmental degrad-ation? Analyse this argument and draw conclusions based on the evidence collected.

6 Outline the opportunities and limitation on EC policies and programmes for improving environmental standards in industry.

7 Paul Harrison[41] argues that 'the 1980s were our best chance to act [to stop undermining the future of the planet]'; indicate any reasons why this was the case. Has anything changed to increase the chance of remedial action? If your answer is yes, please specify the changes. If your answer is no, please indicate the actions needed to introduce this change.

8 Describe some of the limits to the growth of 'green consumerism' locally, nationally and internationally. Illustrate with examples of successes and failures.

9 Packaging remains the 'dark continent' of environmentalism. Spell out reasons why occasional successes have not produced a major change in attitudes to packaging and its use by industry.

10 Define:

(a) Environmental Audit

(b) Strategic Environmental Assessment

(c) Gaia

(d) Sustainable development

(e) Biohazards

(f) Industrial partnering

(g) Clean technologies

(h) Eco-labelling

(i) Renewable energy sources

(j) Green consumerism

REFERENCES

1. Carson, R. *Silent Spring*, Harmondsworth, Penguin (1962).
2. Robinson, S. N. 'Safeguarding the Environment: Critical Issues for Today and Tomorrow' *Prism*, third quarter (1991).
3. International Union for the Conservation of Nature and Natural Resources (IUCN), United Nations Environment Programme (UNEP) and the World Wildlife Fund (WWF) *Caring for the Earth: A Strategy for Sustainable Living*, Gland, Switzerland, IUCN, UNEP and WWF (1991).
4. Palmer, J. 'Towards a Sustainable Future', in Cooper, D. and Palmer J. (eds) *The Environment in Question*, London, Routledge (1990).
5. Holmberg, J., Bass, S. and Timberlake, L. *Defending the Future: A Guide to Sustainable Development*, London, IIED, Earthscan (1991).
6. Shrivastava, P. 'Corporate Self Renewal: Strategic Responses to Environmentalism' *Business Strategy and the Environment*, vol. 1, no. 3, Autumn (1992) pp. 9–21.
7. Chovril, R. and Shortis, A. *Green Issues*
8. Hochman, S. D., Wells, R. P., O'Connell, P. A. and Hochman, M. N. 'Total Quality Management: A Tool to Move from Compliance to Strategy' *Greener Management International*, Issue 1, January (1993) pp. 59–70.
9. Lovelock, J. *Gaia: A New Look at Life on Earth*, Oxford, Oxford University Press (1979).
10. Sessions, G. and Devall, B. *Deep Ecology: Living as if Nature Mattered*, Layton, Peregrine Smith (1985).
11. Ashby, E. *Reconciling Man with the Environment*, Oxford, Oxford University Press (1978).
12. Carson, R., ibid.
13. Nielsen, L. J. *Measurement Techniques in Packaging Waste Management*, Proceedings of Corporate Quality/Environmental Management, Washington DC, 9–10 January (1991).
14. Davis, J. *Greening Business*, Oxford, Blackwell (1991).
15. Quoted in Galbraith, G. K. *Economics and the Public Purpose*, Harmondsworth, Penguin (1973).
16. Clark, J. 'Green Regulation as a Source of Competitive Advantage' *Greener Management International*, vol. 1, January (1993) pp. 51–8.
17. Welford, R. 'Linking Quality and the Environment: Strategy for the Implementation of Environmental Management Systems' *Business Strategy and the Environment*, vol. 1, part 1, Spring (1992).

18. Harrison, P. *The Third Revolution: Population, Environment and a Sustainable World*, Harmondsworth, Penguin (1992).
19. Harrison, P., ibid.
20. Williams, J. O. and Goluke, V. *Business and Sustainable Development*, London, International Chamber of Commerce (1992).
21. Waller, D. L. 'Environmental Issues: Technology Challenges for Industry' *Greener Management International*, vol. 2, April (1993) pp. 35–52.
22. Waldegrave, W. 'Environment and Industry: Progress through Co-operation' *Journal of the Royal Society for the Encouragement of Arts, Manufactures and Commerce*, December (1987).
23. Peters, T. *Lean, Green and Clean: The Profitable Company of the Year 2000*, Munich, The Greening of European Business Conference, October (1990).
24. Department of Trade and Industry/Department of The Environment *Report of the Financial Sector Working Group Advisory Committee on Business and the Environment*, London, HMSO (1993).
25. Solow, R. M. 'An Economist's Approach to Pollution Control' *Science*, August (1971).
26. Meadows, D. H., Meadows, D. L., Randers, J. and Behrens III, W. W. *The Limits to Growth*, London, Earth Iseland (1972).
27. Meadows, D. H., Meadows, D. L. *Beyond the Limits*, New York, Chelsea Green Publishing (1992).
28. 'Growth vs Environment' *Business Week*, 11 May (1992).
29. Hawkins, K. *Environment and Enforcement: Regulation and the Social Definition of Pollution*, Oxford, Oxford University Press (1984).
30. Jacobs, M. *The Green Economy: Environment, Sustainable Development and the Politics of the Future*, London, Pluto (1991).
31. Bruntland Commission *Our Common Future*, Oxford, Oxford University Press (1987).
32. Schmidheiney, S. *Changing Course: A Global Business Perspective in Development and the Environment*, Cambridge, Mass., MIT Press (1992).
33. Adapted from British Standards Institute *Specification for Environmental Management Systems (1992)*, published in Hunt, D. and Johnson, C. 'The Systems Approach to Corporate Environmental Management and Environmental Auditing' *Business Strategy and the Environment*, Spring (1993) pp. 37–43.
34. Chandler, W. U. *Carbon Emissions Control Strategies: Case Studies in International Cooperation*, Worldwide Fund for Nature and The Conservation Foundation, Washington DC (1990).
35. Prowse, M. 'Clean Environment "compatible with growth" ' *Financial Times*, 18 May (1992).
36. The World Bank *Development and the Environment*, Washington, The World Bank (1992).
37. Bennett, R. and Estall, R. (eds) *Global Change and Challenge*, London, Routledge (1991).
38. IUCN *Caring for the Earth – A Strategy for Sustainable Living*, London, Earthscan (1991).
39. Smith, D. *Business and the Environment: Implications of the New Environmentalism*, London, Paul Chapman (1992).
40. Shrivastava, P., ibid.
41. Harrison, P. *The Third Revolution*, Harmondsworth, Penguin (1992) p. 297.

CHAPTER 11

The natural environment: development compliance and activism

The last 50 years have created few more powerful images than those forged by the impact of industry on the natural environment. Among them are the scars left on the landscape by opencast mining in Britain and the wastelands created by logging in Tasmania or Brazil. The sight of former miners, ex-building workers or textile operatives unable to breathe because of lung damage echoes the pictures of children from the Japanese fishing village of Minamata maimed and blinded by mercury dumped in the sea by chemical plants. The images include surreal landscapes wrought by acid rain on forests in Canada, Germany, Scotland and Scandinavia, blackened countryside in the newly liberated workers' paradises of Rumania, Bulgaria, Poland, East Germany and the brutal simplicity of multi-coloured effluents pouring from waste pipes into rivers and seas.

Individually and together these pictures and the concerns they create are shaping the environment in which firms operate. The United Nations Conference on the Environment and Development – the Rio Summit – took as one of its dominant themes the responsibility of corporations to the natural environment. Many leading companies have already acknowledged their role in protecting the environment so that future generations can benefit and enjoy its bounty.[1] Sometimes this awareness has emerged gradually as leaders have recognised that their long-term survival and prosperity depends on a healthy environment.[2] Occasionally a dramatic event like the *Exxon Valdez* oil disaster has forced companies, industries and communities to recognise the cost of inaction.[3] There is, however, widespread recognition that the implicit contract between society and industry contains powerful injunctions of protection and maintenance.[4] This implicit contract will become more explicit if firms fail to respond to the mounting pressures for responsible action and improved performance. Changes in corporate approaches to such sensitive areas as hazard reduction, resource use, waste, pollution, etc., will require coherent change strategies backed by top management if they are to work.[5]

AN EMERGING CRISIS

The pressures on the natural environment have grown with increasing technology, wider use of potentially damaging processes and expanding populations (Figure 11.1). Finite resources in all parts of the world are struggling to cope with increasing rates of change.

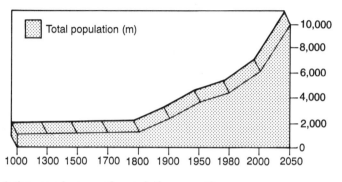

Fig. 11.1 A thousand years of population growth

A number of issues have emerged[6] as critical to the efforts to match environmental protection and business development. Each highlights a mixture of general and specific features of the relationship between business and the environment. These include:

- *Ozone depletion* – The ozone layer protects the planet from harmful ultraviolet rays. 'Holes' in the ozone layer or its erosion increases risks of cancers and other dangers to people, animals and plants.
- *Global warming* – The ecological balance on the planet is foundered on specific – if variable – climatic conditions. A major shift caused by the build-up of carbon in the atmosphere might create a greenhouse effect which can affect the crops on which millions of people depend.
- *Acid rain* – This poisons the forests, rivers, lakes and seas on which locals depend for their livelihood and the planet needs for equilibrium.
- *Toxic air emissions* – These can place communities at risk from the immediate effects of a Bhopal or gradually threaten the landscape or nearby groups such as those near brickworks.
- *Waste* – People, factories, farms produce waste products which can overwhelm the ability of man-made or natural systems to cope.

Ozone depletion highlighted a range of issues that were either new or neglected for business. Perhaps the two most significant lessons for industry from the growing awareness of the threat from ozone depletion were the range of industrial activities that could affect the environment and the insidious nature of these threats. Companies who were perceived as environmentally neutral found that their technologies have a massive but hidden effect. The build-up of ozone was slow and largely unobserved. This meant that firms, industries and technologies were highly dependent on the products which produced the damage. Remedial action has only a lagged effect. The effects are worldwide and raised questions about the value of local action.

> The potential impacts were drastic. If CFC use had continued to grow, by the year 2075 there could have been an additional 43 million cases of cataract, plus 96 million cases of skin cancer, including 2 million extra cancer deaths.
>
> Enhanced ultraviolet radiation also cuts the yields from plants – from 5 per cent for wheat up to 90 per cent for squash. It reduces plant height and leaf area, and reduces flowering and germination. It damages cyanobacteria which fix nitrogen in paddy fields and could slash rice yields. It could speed global warming by damaging trees and phytoplankton, which absorb large amounts of carbon dioxide.
>
> The overall costs of uncontrolled ozone depletion to the USA alone would have reached $150 billion by AD 2075, including lost crop harvests of $42 billion and fish catches worth $7 billion. Indeed, if skin cancer deaths are accounted at typical compensation rates, the total costs rose to $3,517 billion.
>
> Harrison, P. (1992)[7]

Roome[8] has suggested that analysis of corporate vulnerability to environmental demands can be analysed in terms of scientific significance and public perception (Figure 11.2).

Industries like chemicals, oil and defence are at the centre of the debate on environmental protection. The public sees them as providing clearly identifiable threats through their factories, processes and products. Highly publicised events like the *Exxon Valdez* oil spill, the spills in the river Mersey, the pollution of the Danube and Bhopal have influenced the public image of these firms. This is probably inevitable as the potential impact of their products on the environment is immense. Firms in these industries wishing to overcome their problems manage

		Public perception of environmental impact	
		High	*Low*
Scientific significance of environmental impact	*High*	**Posture:** Reactive **Pressure:** Law **Case:** Chemicals companies like Union Carbide and the processes employed	**Posture:** Reactive **Pressure:** High **Case:** Computer companies like IBM using CFCs in production
	Low	**Posture:** Reactive **Pressure:** Communications **Case:** Steel producers like British Steel with easily recycled output	**Posture:** Discretionary **Pressure:** Management **Case:** Telecommunications firms like BT with satellite communications

Fig. 11.2 Assessing corporate vulnerability

a portfolio of strategies based on the four Ps; **P**re-emption, **P**articipation, **P**roduct development and **P**ositioning.

Pre-emption means introducing changes in practices which pose a threat to the environment *before* they are required by law. A number of companies operating in the North Sea banned flaring off waste gases before legislation forced them to. This produces a number of benefits for the firms. The most basic is that the approach is compatible with existing company practice not forced by legislators who will inevitably look for more general solutions. Pre-emption can build greater trust between the firm and the community. The firm increases its standing by acting before it is forced to act. This may persuade politicians to allow firms to solve a wider array of problems in the future. The enormous capital costs involved in change in these process or extractive industries can be reduced if the firm introduces modification in a planned and internally controlled way instead of through government fiat. There is some evidence that positive prior action has a neutral effect on share values. The decision by Conoco to adopt a nine-point plan to reduce toxic emissions and prevent oil spills at a cost of over $50 million had a neutral effect on share prices.[9]

> It is clear that DuPont matched or outperformed the market at the time of the announcement of their environmental spending performance.
>
> Plesse, J. (1992)[10]

This contrasts with the sharp drop in the share price of Exxon following the *Exxon Valdez* disaster (Figure 11.3). This drop in price occurred long before the extent of the fines and penalties became known. The growing public hostility to firms responsible for damage to the environment seems likely to increase the penalties

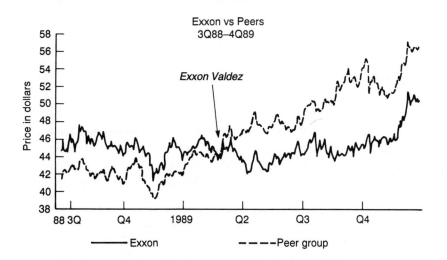

Fig. 11.3 Exxon share price compared with the basket of peer group companies
Source: Plesse, J. (1992)[11]

Table 11.1 The bill for meeting environmental protection, health and safety requirements

Country	Annual bill ($billion)
USA	46
Japan	17
Germany	12
France	9
UK	8
Italy	6
Other EC	9
Total	107

for failure and increase the gains from early action. There is accumulating evidence that the affirmative actions adopted by the nuclear industry has gone some way to allay public fears and convince legislators that it is seeking environmentally friendly solutions to the challenges it faces.

> Last year (1989), Three Mile Island, the would be icon for everything that is wrong with the nuclear power industry, was ranked by respected international Trade magazine *Nucleonics Week* as the most efficient nuclear power plant in the world.
>
> Meeks, F. and Drummond, J. (1990)[12]

Some legislative, regulatory and supervisory action is inevitable in a complex and sensitive area like environmental protection. It is estimated that firms in the major developed countries are spending around $100 billion on compliance to meet the needs of environmental protection, health and safety requirements (Table 11.1).

The scale of these cost, plus the near certainty that they will increase, demands that industry plays an active role in shaping legislation and supervision. All companies have a vested interest in producing policies that recognise the constraints under which firms operate. Responsible companies have a similar concern for ensuring that legislation does not leave gaps that the unscrupulous can exploit. In each area of government action industry can help shape policies to ensure that the environmental protection programmes emerge which meet their declared aims with minimum costs to responsible firms. A specific view of this approach was expressed by the UK's Minister of the Environment in 1987.

> It is Government's role to set standards and priorities. It is industry's role by developing the technologies to meet and improve these standards. The dialogue should be continuous. The environment does not benefit from calls for all pollution everywhere to be stopped immediately 'just in case'. But nor is it in industry's interests to cry wolf too loud or too often.
>
> Waldegrave, W. (1987)[13]

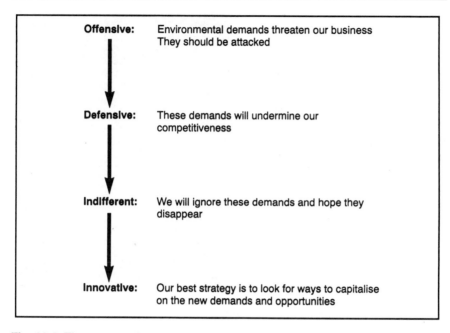

Offensive: Environmental demands threaten our business
They should be attacked

Defensive: These demands will undermine our
competitiveness

Indifferent: We will ignore these demands and hope they
disappear

Innovative: Our best strategy is to look for ways to capitalise
on the new demands and opportunities

Fig. 11.4 The stages of corporate response

Companies appreciate that they are not bystanders. Organisations like Business and the Environment in Britain and the Business Council for Sustainable Development in North America strive to encourage their colleagues to adopt more responsible attitudes and behaviour while persuading the state to listen to their views. Steger[14] argues that firms adopt four basic strategies to environmental issues: offensive, defensive, indifference and innovative. Organisations like Business in the Environment adopt a progress view of this model – striving to help firms move from offence to innovation (Figure 11.4).

The immediate reaction of most organisations to accusations that they are harming the environment is to counter-attack. Farmers assert that chemical fertilisers do far more good than harm. Plastics companies allege that critics are backed by producers of rival products. Physical attacks on investigators are not unknown. The public and government may interpret these reactions as the natural response of an enterprise *with something to hide*. A defensive approach to environmental concerns is widespread. This can be seen in firms that see themselves as victims of new, social expectations. They are trading in good faith but someone with no knowledge of their company or industry identifies a problem. These companies typically retreat into secrecy and a refusal to explore effective responses and corrective action. Chemical companies build higher fences round their plants. Timber companies emphasise the lack of alternatives. Indifference is perhaps the dominant response especially in small and medium-sized firms. The paint producer will ignore demands for alternatives until legislation

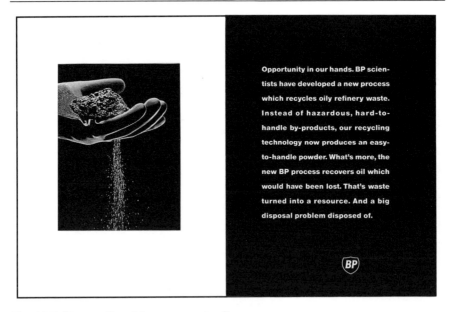

Opportunity in our hands. BP scientists have developed a new process which recycles oily refinery waste. Instead of hazardous, hard-to-handle by-products, our recycling technology now produces an easy-to-handle powder. What's more, the new BP process recovers oil which would have been lost. That's waste turned into a resource. And a big disposal problem disposed of.

Fig. 11.5 From a threat to an opportunity

or market pressures forces a change in approach. There is, however, a shift towards a more positive approach. Innovation is used to eliminate harmful products or processes and substitute safer alternatives. Some firms use this approach as a platform to penetrate new markets. At each stage, companies work with government to mesh their efforts into the wider programme of government action.[15]

Product development programmes of companies are linked increasingly to the demands for greener products and the opportunities these create for firms capable of matching capacity to need (Figure 11.5).[16]

Every aspect of the marketing system provides opportunities for innovations based on a better fit with the needs of the environment. Government programmes create opportunities in services, processes and products. The Environmental Council's 'Issues and Impacts Analysis' is a new service designed to help fit in with government requirements. Blue Circle's LINKman process control technology was introduced to reduce emissions of oxides of nitrogen from Cement Kilns so that new government standards can be met. The successful development of catalytic converters to reduce fumes from car exhausts was prompted by new regulations in the USA and Europe. These new products have grown in importance as customers have shown a determination to seek out and buy *green* products. Ten years ago, it was rare to see a new product or process to meet the needs of the *green* market. Now, it is rare to see innovations that ignore this dimension.

New detergents are launched which boast that they are 'less harmful to the environment with significant reductions in everything, except performance'.

Catalytic convertors are included on cars ranging from family saloons to four wheel drives. New ranges of chilled and fresh food products are introduced which 'use rainwater for irrigation and not one single pesticide'. New washing machines boast that they use '34 per cent less detergent and 55 per cent less water'. Supermarkets now offer bottle banks, box bins and paper or plastic bins as new services to their customers.

> *One green bottle*
> *Drop it in the bank,*
> *Ten green bottles,*
> *What a lot we drank.*
> *Heaps of bottles*
> *And yesterday's a blank*
> *But we'll save the planet,*
> *Tinkle, tinkle, clank.*
>
> Wendy Cope *A Green Song*

A mixture of customer or competitive pressure and opportunism has provided opportunities through the marketing chain (Table 11.2). The sharp increase in penetration of unleaded petrol shows how quickly a market can expand when government, industry and consumers share a common sense of opportunity and interest (Figure 11.6).

In key sectors like car and food production innovative activity is dominated by environmental concerns. Some car firms promote the speed with which their new model can be recycled with the same enthusiasm with which they once promoted its speed from 0 to 60 miles per hour. New food products highlight their green attributes. Heinz recently repositioned their canned tomato soup. It was promoted with the strap line – *the only artificial preservative we use is the one you have to open.* The increased market share of energy saving or environmentally safe products is prompting increasing numbers of firms to develop new offerings

Table 11.2 Opportunities and demands in the marketing chain

Stage	Event	Response
Raw materials	User action	Heinz refuse to use tuna caught in certain ways
Processing	Buyer resistance	Customer reluctance to accept products with certain E numbers
Supplies	Embargoes	Unilever refuse to use non-biodegradable chemicals in detergents
Packaging	Customer interdict	MacDonald's instruct packaging suppliers to stop using CFCs
Manufacturing	Voluntary restraint	Habitat stop using hardwoods in furniture
Distribution	Community demands	British Gas use underground pipes
Retailing	Affirmative action	Bottle banks
Consumption	Consumer boycotts	Buyers refuse to use certain kinds of aerosols

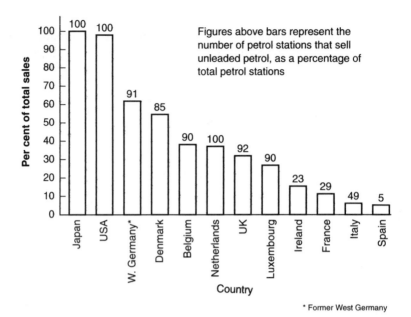

* Former West Germany

Fig. 11.6 Unleaded petrol sales
Source: The Economist, 2 March 1991

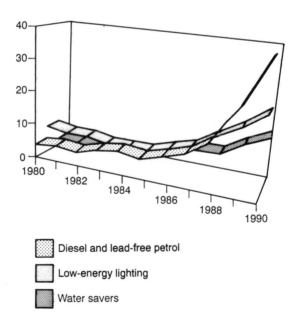

Fig. 11.7 The growing importance of green innovation (% total market UK)

(Figure 11.7). There is evidence that the fastest shifts occur when environmental gain and financial benefit coincide.[17] This has strengthened the arguments for taxation policies which reinforce the link between these gains and benefits.

> Carbon taxes act as a continuous incentive to adopt ever cleaner technology and energy conservation. Standards tend to be 'technology based' and therefore encourage technology switches up to the point judged by the regulator to be the 'best available'.
>
> Pearce, D. (1991)[18]

The repositioning of the whole enterprise to a positive environmental stance is still rare in Britain although increasing numbers of US, German, Dutch and Scandinavian concerns are adopting this position. It calls for internal adjustment to strengthen corporate commitment to affirmative action, systematic scanning of the environment and co-ordinated product and process innovation. Roome[19] links these changes with a search for 'environmental excellence' (see Table 11.3).

Table 11.3 The search for environmental excellence

Position	Policy
Corporate values and ethos	Openness is encouraged with links to concerned groups and the science community – environment gatekeepers flag issues and spot opportunities. Top management adopt a clear stance
Responsibilities and accountability	Emphasis on individual and local responsibility, management reward and control systems reinforce green policies, worker-based environment circles and linked rewards
People policies	Recruitment, selection, management, motivation and control linked to environment protection
Organisational structure	Lean and flexible with emphasis on need-based structures not bureaucracies
Senior management	Visible, committed, close to customers and aware of wider responsibilities
Operations	Developmental, emphasis on effectiveness, waste elimination – lean production
Marketing	Developmental, continuous but responsible innovation
Finance	Emphasis on added value and needs of multiple stakeholder responsibilities – ethics matter
Resourcing	Partnership and supplier development-based with emphasis on integrated development and innovation – JIT works
Corporate strategy	Anticipates needs, emphasises long-term value added, awareness-based with clear visions

Source: Roome, N. (1992)[20]

INFORMATION AND INFORMATION SYSTEMS

Information is the lifeblood of the modern corporation. New technologies allied to a need for control systems which allow resources to be deployed effectively in complex and changing environments have made information and information systems central to every aspect of corporate policy.

Information technology is affecting everyday life across a broad spectrum of the workforce.[21]

Environmental management information systems pose special problems for corporations. These include:

- The qualitative nature of much of the data;
- The length of the time scales involved;
- The interdependencies between effects.

Unless systems are designed which can overcome these problems, environmental information will remain on the periphery of the main corporate information and intelligence systems. This, in turn, will reduce the effectiveness of policies and

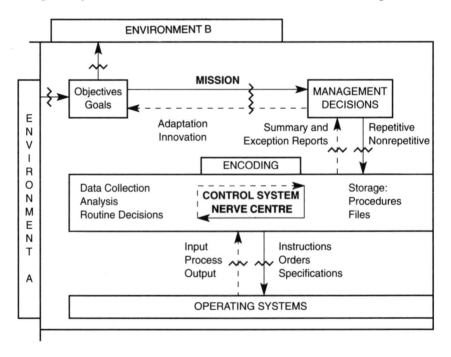

Fig. 11.8 Environmental management information system

controls. Early attempts to tackle these issues became so discredited that respected companies like Florida Power and Light 'banned' the term 'Environmental Information Management System'.[22]

The lynch-pin of any effective Environmental Management Information System (EMIS – see Figure 11.8) is the specification by decision makers – inside and outside the organisation – of the key areas for action, implementation, control and allocation. A combination of openness and transparency is an integral feature of this stage in the design of EMIS. Openness ensures that all key groups have access to the process of decision information specification. Transparency is important to enable all stakeholders to observe the choice and decision process and endorse its outcomes.

Once the key decision areas are identified, the basic system design becomes a priority. Typically, this will consist of four key components:

1   The information nerve centre; the hub of the system where data is stored, tested, integrated (where possible) and organised.
2   The need identification structure; the nerve ends of the system which identify users or decision makers and their needs and external concerns.
3   The integrators; these feed information into the nerve centre and out to managers who need it, in a form that they can use – in time for them to take effective action.
4   System integrity checks; these ensure the internal and external integrity of information systems while minimising noise and distortion. This is especially important for an EMIS as noise and distortion can undermine the quality of the data and the ability of managers to use the information.

In an EMIS clear specification of operational and strategic responsibilities must be linked with an understanding of:

1   The level at which decisions and actions must be made. These can then be linked with monitoring, feedback and reward systems.
2   The types and sources of data.
3   The characteristics, nature and limitations of the data.

Table 11.4 shows a hierarchy of environmental management information requirements. Despite some pioneering work, especially by environmental consultants, EMIS development remains in its infancy. Many of the information systems which exist rely on informal sources or data gathered for other purposes and managed through the environmental advisory committee, advisory panels or directors with specific responsibilities for the area (Figure 11.9).

Environmental advisory boards are often chaired by a non-executive director of the firm. The executive director responsible for the issue may be a member of the board. The advisory board will gather information and advice from sources ranging from consultants recruited to examine specific issues to employee

Table 11.4 A hierarchy of environmental management information requirements

Responsibility	Task level	Typical data sources	Data characteristics
Environmental performance	Corporate environmental policy and programmes	Auditing Permit management	Highest integration Summary and exception
Compliance/Risk management	Internal compliance External compliance	Facility reports Surveys Impact studies	Relatively lower volume
Materials management	Plant-level processes	Chemical inventory Waste tracking Material and emissions balances	High integration High volume
Source monitoring	Engineering task Market assessment R&D	Air and water reporting Tank testing Exposure monitoring Groundwater and soils	Low integration High volume

Source: Adapted from Fitzgerald, C. (1993)[23]

'hot-lines' set up to permit staff to identify issues in confidence.[24] The integration of these information and advisory systems into the firm's strategic stance is an integral part of a process of repositioning the enterprise.

ACCIDENTS, LIABILITIES AND CHALLENGES

Some of the most important developments in corporate environmental policies have followed specific events. The *Exxon Valdez* oil spill illustrates key features of the process of crisis, response, adjustment, reaction and compliance. These characterise the ways in which the firms involved, the wider community and the business system generally manage the corporate contract with the community and the environment. The specific events surrounding the oil spill were well documented at the time. The supertanker *Exxon Valdez* ruptured its tanks in a collision off the coast of Alaska. The spill polluted the coast and endangered vast numbers of wildlife. There were several elements which made this event an especially powerful symbol for those concerned about the impact of commercial activity on the natural environment.

The first and perhaps the dominant factor was it location. Alaska's remoteness allied to its climate made it 'the last frontier' to many Americans. It was seen as a remote wilderness scarcely touched by the pressures which affected the industrial world. The discovery of oil had prompted many observers to warn that this fragile ecosystem was at risk. There was, however, a counterview at least in the USA that industry and society had learned the lessons of Oklahoma, Texas

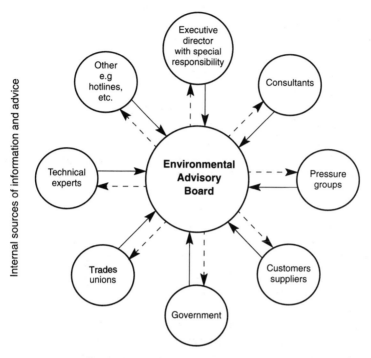

Fig. 11.9 Hub-based environmental advisory structure

and California. Destruction was a thing of the past. In effect, the oil industry could be trusted. At the same time, there was a more pervasive view that the USA was rich enough to pay the price needed to protect the environment while exploiting natural resources. Thoughtless exploitation might occur in poor or badly regulated economies but the USA was rich and had an impressive system of supervision and control. In effect, it could not happen here.

The spillage shattered these illusions. It was alleged that the captain of the ship was not even on the deck when the accident occurred. Stories are confused about the reasons for his absence but the most basic system of management control had failed. The systems installed on the ship and locally failed to stop or contain the spillage. Most were wholly inadequate to the needs which existed when a major crisis blew up. Technology existed to control and minimise the effects but the necessary investments had not been made. Key security and defence elements in the 'contract' between the enterprise and the community were neither endorsed nor implemented. It seemed that industry could not be trusted to either protect the environment or to establish the information and control systems to ensure that corporate environmental commitments made centrally were implemented locally. Inevitably, the media's attention strayed beyond the shoreline to the catalogue of previous failures. Earlier, minor spills had given prior warning. Parts of 'the last frontier' had been turned into minor industrial slums by neglect and poor supervision. State and national systems of regulation had failed to address the problems. Even the richest country in the world could not trust its industries or those it paid to regulate commerce.

The response of Exxon, the rest of the industry and the support agencies did little to reassure the community.[25] The slow response, the arguments about liabilities seemed more akin to a row about the fine print of a contract than an attempt to implement the spirit of the agreement or solve the problem. This reaction highlights a special dimension to environmental issues. They carry on getting worse until something effective is done. There is no standstill clause. The status quo 'ante' cannot be rebuilt merely because all the parties agree to go back to where they started. Something has to be done. The inexorable spread of the oil, the helplessness of the wildlife and the apparent impotence of corporate and political leaders was a powerful juxtaposition of interests and image. Nowhere has the value of environmental contingency planning been more vividly illustrated than by its apparent absence in Alaska. Environmental contingency plans are the arrangements drawn up by a company, usually in collaboration with local or expert partners to cope with serious environmental problems. Even the basic notion built into most insurance contracts – solve the problem first and worry about liabilities later – seemed lacking. The eventual efficiency of the clean up and containment operation raised questions about why this was not in place earlier.

A large-scale adjustment in attitudes took place later. Oil companies, especially Exxon, saw their share prices drop. Customers switched brands. Employees asked questions about the values of their enterprise. Potential recruits were reluctant to join. Planners, politicians and regulators imposed more stringent requirements. Billion dollar installations such as the Texaco offshore installation in California were regulated, almost out of existence. The trading climate of the industry was changed. The total cost is hard to estimate but figures in the range $5–15 billion for Exxon alone have been estimated (Table 11.5). Losses on this scale affected the attitudes of the business and financial community. It prompted a group of investors to formulate the famous Valdez Principles (Table 11.6). These must be accepted by a public company before members of the group allow their funds to be invested in the corporation's shares.

The immediate reaction to this clear statement of first principles was favourable. Companies saw it as a powerful means to confirm their values while the public acknowledged the seriousness of the intent. Parallel developments saw companies and communities make similar demands of their suppliers and collaborators.

The longer-term response has been less enthusiastic.[26] Some clauses, e.g. the whistle-blower's charter in point 8 poses particular problems to firms with a tradition of confidentiality.[27] Some firms objected to the imposition by investors of broad brush requirements which affected their core business operations.

Table 11.5 Exxon's cost of failure

Item	Cost ($ million)
Clean up	2,250
Fines	2,000
Loss of market share	1,750
Disruptions to supplies	750
Compliance with new regulations	500
TOTAL	7,250
Discount on shares	5,000–15,000*

*The shares were trading at a premium of $2–4 before the disaster and a discount of $2–8 afterwards.

Elsewhere, resistance centred on the failure to acknowledge the marked differences in the constraints under which firms operate. The nadir was reached when Exxon refused to endorse the principles. Since then, recognition that shareholders have a right to impose conditions has restored some of the momentum.[28] There has, also, been an attempt to shape different principles which acknowledge diversity and the different costs of compliance. Management strategies are increasingly shaped by awareness that accidents impose liabilities that affect all aspects of the firm's operations.[29] The challenge lies in reshaping the firm to blend responsibility and robustness in the business system. This will require a new formulation of the business contract with new duties made explicit through initiatives like the Valdez declaration or implicit through changes in operations.

A GREEN BUSINESS ECOSYSTEM

Companies are faced by a range of pressures which affect every aspect of their business system. The internal ecosystem of the enterprise is adapting to these pressures (Figure 11.10). The firm's operations are shaped by a combination of general environmental pressures. These include technologies, climate and population and the economy. The series of dry summers and winters in Britain imposed massive strains on the insurance industry as the ground dried and claims for house repairs soared. The shifts in the population structure of Europe and North America creates new opportunities for firms able to exploit the large, relatively rich ageing population but produced shortages of new recruits. Often, the effects of these forces are interpreted by intermediaries. Financial institutions will cut off funds for firms under suspicion but back companies who seem able to exploit new opportunities. Criticism in the media can persuade customers to boycott or back certain products and services. The state can act directly through its massive purchasing power or indirectly through fiscal and monetary measures. The marketplace itself is shaped by the rivalries of firms seeking to capitalise on

Table 11.6 The Valdez Principles

1 Protection of the Biosphere: We will minimise and strive to eliminate the release of any pollutant that may cause environmental damage to the air, water, or earth or its inhabitants. We will safeguard habitats in rivers, lakes, wetlands, coastal zones, and oceans and will minimise contributing to the ozone layer, acid rain or smog.

2 Sustainable use of Natural Resources: We will make sustainable use of renewable natural resources, such as water, soils and forests. We will conserve non-renewable natural resources through efficient use and careful planning. We will protect wildlife habitat, open spaces and wilderness, while preserving biodiversity.

3 Reduction and Disposal of Waste: We will minimise the creation of waste, especially hazardous waste, and wherever possible recycle materials. We will dispose of all wastes through safe and responsible methods.

4 Wise use of Energy: We will make every effort to use environmentally safe and sustainable energy sources to meet our needs. We will invest in improved energy efficiency and conservation in our operations. We will maximise the energy efficiency of products we produce or sell.

5 Risk Reduction: We will minimise the environmental, health and safety risks to our employees and the communities in which we operate by employing safe technologies and operating procedures, and by being constantly prepared for emergencies.

6 Marketing Safe Products and Services: We will sell products or services that minimise adverse environmental impacts and that are safe as consumers commonly use them. We will inform customers of the environmental impacts of our products or services.

7 Damage Compensation: We will take responsibility for any harm we cause to the environment by making every effort to restore the environment fully and to compensate those persons who are adversely affected.

8 Disclosure: We will disclose to our employees and to the public incidents relating to our operations that cause environmental or pose health or safety hazards. We will disclose potential environmental, health or safety hazards posed by our operations, and we will not take any action against employees who report any condition that creates a danger to the environment or poses health or safety hazards.

9 Environmental Directors and Managers: At least one member of the board of directors will be a person qualified to represent environmental interests. We will commit management resources to implement these principles, including the funding of an office of vice president for environmental affairs or an equivalent executive position, reporting directly to the CEO, to monitor and report upon our implementation efforts.

10 Assessment and Annual Audit: We will conduct and make public an annual self-evaluation of our progress in implementing these principles and in complying with all applicable laws and regulations throughout our worldwide operations. We will work towards the timely creation of independant environmental audit procedures which we will complete annually and make available to the public.

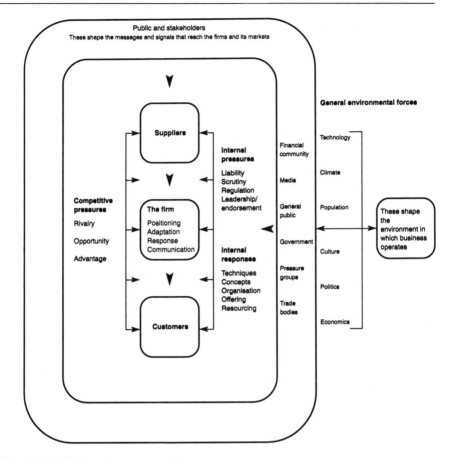

Fig. 11.10 The business ecosystem

opportunities or avoid problems. The success with which a firm operates in this environment is determined by a mixture of internal pressures and responses.

The leadership groups in the enterprise can supply specific guidance or endorse certain policies. These groups act under pressure from a mixture of perceived and actual liabilities, threats and opportunities. The notion that today's success is won through eternal vigilance is probably more true today than ever before. The concept of environmental scanning has developed a twin meaning in modern markets. Its strands are spotting threats and identifying opportunities. The techniques the company employs and the capacity of the organisation to respond lie at the core of the firm's ability to win competitive advantage. Most research into business development and competitive success indicates that virtually all the firms in a market are aware of the threats and opportunities but only a minority are able to adapt and respond.[30] These are the ones that succeed. It is seldom ignorance that causes failure. Even when businesses spot opportunities some provide sufficient resources to succeed while others cannot or do not employ them effectively.[31] Long-term effectiveness in building a business which will wed commercial success to environmental responsibility turns on the integration of the firm's positioning, adaptation, response and communication.[32] These determine the marketing, people, operations, networking and finance policies of the firm, its suppliers, collaborators and rivals.[33]

> Today there is a fast-spreading recognition around the world that progress can no longer be measured in terms of technology or material standard of living alone – that a society that is morally, aesthetically, politically, or environmentally degraded is not an advanced society, no matter how rich or technically sophisticated it may be. In short, we are moving towards a far more comprehensive notion of progress – progress no longer automatically achieved and no longer defined by material criteria alone.[34]

The organisation and structure of the enterprise evolves to reflect the nature and the expectations of the wider social and economic community. The most successful firms are those that have strategies and policies which can be delivered through its organisation while meeting the needs of the environment – in all its forms.[35]

> The magnitude of the problem forces more than fine-tuning, more than incremental change. It requires a serious rethinking of the way the company organises to do business.
>
> Wider horizons mean wanting to do more. A smaller – that is, more crowded – world means having less to do it with. Success thus requires finding new ways of managing, in our businesses and our lives, that address this central contradiction of our times. Succeeding in the corporate Olympics means operating under a new, apparently contradictory strategic imperative: to 'do more with less'.[36]

Every aspect of the firm's current and future operations is affected by its fit with the environment.

MARKETING

The marketing policies of firms are perhaps the most public aspect of its work. New product development programmes of firms are increasingly influenced by efforts to reduce the negative effects of innovations while strengthening their positive features.[37] Industries like food, personal hygiene, travel, energy and transport are at the fore of these developments.[38] The personal hygiene market, for example has been reshaped over the last decade by the success of firms like The Body Shop and the launch of products which avoid cruelty, minimise waste and have a generally neutral or positive effect on the environment.

> Beauty without cruelty has grown by an astonishing 1,100 per cent during the past decade, increasing its retail turnover from £430,000 to £5,5 million (although pre-tax profits halved from £500,000 to £250,000 in 1991 mainly due to the recession). And while other great success stories of the eighties, such as Body Shop and Next, have spent the last few years licking their wounds, The Body Shop, set up in 1976, has gone from

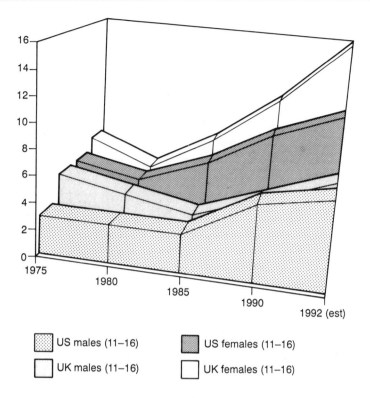

Fig. 11.11 The growing vegetarian market among the young

strength to strength increasing pre-tax profits by 38 per cent to £20 million in the year to February 1991. Now capitalised at £500 million on the stock market, it has over 700 shops – most of them franchises – trading in 39 countries.

O'Kelly, L. (1992)[39]

This approach has been translated to the advertising and promotional policies of companies. In some sectors notably food, this trend is reinforced by specific events such as food scares[40] and general trends notably the shift to *healthier* eating. During the 1970s and 1980s consumption of fats, sugars and certain types of red meats declined in many advanced economies while fruit, fish, certain white meats and grains have increased.[41] The growth in vegetarianism especially among the younger, female age groups in the USA and Britain reflects broadly speaking the same pattern of change (Figure 11.11).

Green imagery dominates much advertising copy in print media and on television. This has prompted some authors to suggest that this had gone too far and was producing a proliferation of spurious and sometimes false claims which added to customer confusion in key sectors like food.[42] Packaging is an especially controversial aspect of the presentation of products and services. Many firms are

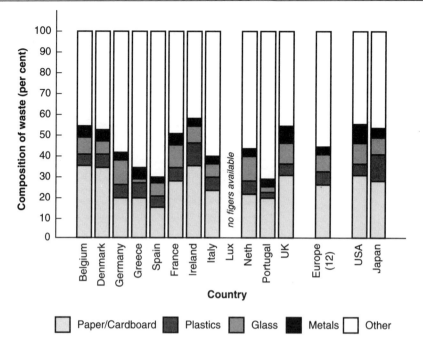

Fig. 11.12 The percentage of waste from packaging in municipal waste (1980)

now engaged on sustained initiatives to reduce the amount of packaging used, use recycled material or employ safer or biodegradable materials. This requires a change in relations with material suppliers. Procter and Gamble is one of many companies engaged in a sustained joint research initiative with their packaging companies to substitute recycled material wherever possible. End users are being actively involved through schemes to re-use packs or collaborate in returning materials (Figure 11.12).

OPERATIONS

Sourcing and purchasing, production, logistics and distribution play a vital part in company attempts to adopt policies which are less harmful to the environment.[43] There is a potential source of conflict in the fit between the traditional imperative on buyers to obtain supplies at the lowest cost and new demands for hazard reduction and fairness. This encourages some companies to engage in long-term sourcing programmes in collaboration with major raw material, component, equipment and service suppliers. 3M's Pollution Prevention + programme is closely integrated into the operations of its major suppliers. Major utilities now require their equipment suppliers to concentrate on minimum energy wastage. Food processors are insisting that capital projects minimise the effect on the environment. The poultry industry in Europe has been working with its suppliers to improve the quality of water intakes and outlets to improve internal standards and reduce pollution.

The manufacturing operations of firms face many new demands from the community, legislators and employees. Responsible firms are looking for ways to minimise their impact on the environment and replace hazardous processes with those which are safer and less noxious.[44] The mobility of industry and the efforts of some poorer communities to encourage inward investment poses a major dilemma to some companies. The internal pressure to withdraw from certain activities while still using the products or components forces firms to choose between costly new developments and cheaper alternatives.

CASE STUDY 11.1

The manager's dilemma

Kurt Vortgern of RB industrial drills was facing a major problem. His CEO had instructed him to stop producing the plastic cladding panels used on the firm's popular industrial drill. The CEO had pointed out that the materials used had been criticised in a recent research report. There was evidence that processing the plastic gave off potentially harmful fumes. The problems centred on the production process not the finished product. *We are under pressure from the government and I want to respond positively.* Kurt faced three alternatives:

- He could invest about $10 million in developing a new range of drills which used different soundproofing systems.
- He believed, however, that the team working on this process might be persuaded to initiate a management buy-out. They would expect some guarantees of orders which might cost about $500,000.
- He had just been approached by a firm based in Rumania who could supply the cladding. They pointed out that they were keen to get the work and the foreign exchange – *we cannot afford to be fussy about pollution.*

He needed to make an early decision. The CEO wanted environmentalism to be the key theme for his annual report to shareholders in two months. He wanted to show how the firm was cutting back on hazardous systems.

There are wide variations in the environmental standards imposed in communities. Metzger[45] identifies four tiers of European Environmental Protection in Europe (Table 11.7).

The refusal to merely ship harmful process out of the firm or locality elsewhere is increasingly seen as part of a wider notion of responsibility. This stretches from a willingness to pay fair prices and accept wider responsibilities to other communities. The introduction of 'Fair Trade' marks is employed to identify products where Third World suppliers are paid a 'fair price for a fair day's work'.

Table 11.7 Tiers of European environmental regulation

Level	Countries
Highly developed	Norway, Denmark, The Netherlands, Germany (W), Sweden, Switzerland
Moderately developed	UK, Finland, France, Belgium, Austria
Relatively undeveloped	Eire, Portugal, Spain, Italy, Greece
Undeveloped	Germany (E), Poland, Czechoslovakia, Hungary, Rumania, Baltic republics, former Yugoslavian republics, Bulgaria, Albania

PEOPLE

The firm's employees determine the effectiveness of all aspects of the company's response to the new expectations. Many of the pressures on the enterprise to respond to environmental pressures come from current or potential employees.[46] It may take the form of potential recruits asking about the firm's attitude to pollution or existing workers raising questions about fumes given off by certain processes. The information, recruitment, training and development programmes of companies are central to their response to demands for information, guidance and reassurance. Hirsch[47] highlights the importance of making people know the contribution they are making to shaping the firm's response. An appreciation of the importance of a responsible attitude to the environment is the first step in winning active co-operation. The integration of education for environmental responsibility into degrees in business education is being support by endowments by business leaders.[48] This approach is permeating the operative training pro-gramme, technician support, supervisory training and management development at all levels.

The redirection of the enterprise to satisfy the new demands placed on the firm is a major exercise in organisational change.[49] It calls for the systematic application of an effective change strategy.[50] The key steps in managing this change are:

- The need to change is recognised;
- The features of the adjustment are diagnosed;
- The implications for those involved are identified and their contributions specified;
- A coherent strategy for managing the change is developed;
- The adaptations needed by groups and individuals are spelled out;
- A consultation process is initiated to allay fears and give those involved a sense of ownership;
- Feedback is encouraged;
- Implementation takes into account the needs for training and development;
- Scope for adjustment based on consultation and feedback is built into the process.
- It is acknowledged *from the start* that anything can go wrong.

Lewin[51] suggests that there are three basic stages in a change process: unfreezing, change, refreezing. Unfreezing means identifying and breaking down the barriers to change. Change is the move from 'an old state to a new one'.[52] Refreezing is the creation of the new status quo.[53] In a complex area like this Force Field Analysis can be a valuable role in identifying the forces driving change and those restraining it (Figure 11.13). This provides the opportunity to move the enterprise forward by strengthening the driving forces or weakening the restraining forces.

Successful adaption occurs where:

● The need for the changes is recognised and accepted throughout the firm;
● Communication and participation is high;
● The adaption or innovation is widely endorsed;
● Progress and success is recognised and disseminated;
● The leadership act together and transmits consistent messages;
● A holistic view of the enterprise is adopted;
● Change is backed by training and development of *at risk* staff.

These changes can be undermined or supported by internal[54] and external[55] forces.

FINANCE

Force Field Analysis highlights a range of areas in which the internal and external finance community plays a vital role in shaping the patterns of adaptation to

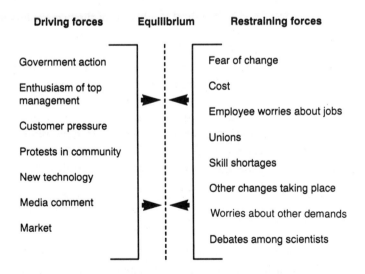

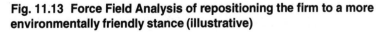

Fig. 11.13 Force Field Analysis of repositioning the firm to a more environmentally friendly stance (illustrative)

environmental demands.[56] Resources are required to finance change inside the firm. New technologies may be needed or alternative products or processes deployed. The willingness to deploy resources is a powerful indicator of seriousness of intent by top management. The Valdez Principles and the relative success of ethical and responsible investment funds highlights the growing support in the financial community for positive action to tackle environmental issues. There are, however, important principles of consultation which are central to any effort to win the backing of financial stakeholders in the venture. In part, the need to understand the nature of the process explains the interest among researchers in agency theory.[57]

Perhaps the most important of these steps in ensuring support are early consultation and transparency. Properly managed financial institutions know the environmental challenges facing the firm. They acknowledge the lack of negative short term costs and the long-term gains from responsible attitudes to pollution control, waste reduction and the elimination of hazards.

Aupperle, K. *et al.*[58] noted that the merits of corporate social responsibility 'simply do not show up on the bottom line'. This measure tends to be a better indicator of short-term performance. McGuire and his colleagues[59] suggest, however, that two measures of performance – Return on Total Assets and Total Asset Values – are positively correlated with corporate social responsibility. These asset-based measures may be better long-term indicators of the firm's performance. It is important to note that the main conclusion of the McGuire study is that 'prior performance is generally a better predictor of corporate social responsibility than subsequent performance'. The specifics of the change process may be outside their normal remit. Early involvement is a key component in winning trust and long-term support. Some bankers suggest that the willingness to address environmental issues is a good indicator of the health of the firm and its ability to plan and position itself for the long term. The extent, cost and process of change is part of the essential briefing of financial partners. This is especially important when clean up operations have an effect on the firm's property portfolio or balance sheet. Other sources of financial support – notably government agencies – can play a vital part in providing the resources, expertise and technology for change. In Europe a mixture of nation government and EC aid is available especially in older industrial areas or those affected by mining, heavy industry production and large-scale processing. The creation of a comprehensive financing package is an increasingly important feature of a positive environmental stance.

CONCLUSION

In 1972 the Stockholm Environment Conference initiated a process of government and institutional debate and adjustment which has shaped much of the recent debate on environmental responsibility. The Rio Summit highlights the complexity of the tasks which exist. The focus has shifted from

Table 11.8 A shifting agenda

Stockholm	Rio
Awareness of the challenge	Recognition of the need for action
National governments the primary agents	International agencies working with national government
Industry to respond	Industry to initiate
Public awareness and interest	Public demands and action

the actions of national government to international and local action (Table 11.8).

The shift in the role of industry from passive responders to demands to active initiators in developments is a result of a mixture of pressures. Three are central to this discussion. First, there is widespread recognition that industry holds the key to successful adaptation.[60] International corporations have resources and expertise that can only be matched by the richest countries. They can deploy them with a flexibility and creativity which few states emulate. Their active participation is essential if an international response is active. The last two decades have highlighted the limitations on government action. The next decade will indicate whether participation offers the key to success. Small and medium-sized enterprises can deliver the enterprise, creativity and innovation which are essential to local resolution of complex problems.

The second key feature of industry's role is central to this chapter. Companies will be among the primary beneficiaries of a healthier and more prosperous environment.[61] There is growing evidence that more prosperous communities invest in a wider portfolio of goods and services than stressed groups. More immediately, firms suffer with their communities when breakdowns occur. Markets are reacting with increasing sharpness to failure by firms to meet their responsibilities. Third, a positive stance can improve the performance and position of companies. Firms that manage their response effectively and reposition themselves are capable of building more secure and more prosperous positions in the marketplace. Successful compliance with the terms of business's contract to sustain the environment will generate profits in the long term and add value to the enterprise as well as the community.

Opportunities for positive action are emerging. Lessons learned from failures and successes in accident prevention or response to accidents, programmes for disposal of waste and recycling products provide clues for future successes. Some easy answers might not work. Industrial composites reduce weight and energy consumption but are very difficult to recycle. The successful firm will be the enterprise which deploys the skills it has learned in the past to capitalise on the opportunities of the future while meeting its obligations to the environment.[62]

QUESTIONS

1 The failure of the Rio Summit to ratify the biodiversity convention places a special responsibility on multinational corporations to include programmes of sustainable diversity in their long-term strategies. How far does this proposition reflect a realistic expectation?

2 Use the corporate vulnerability framework to analyse the challenge facing firms with which you are familiar but excluding the firms mentioned in the discussion surrounding Figure 11.20.

3 Identify the main features of an effective EMIS. Illustrate, where possible.

4 John Elkington, author of *The Green Consumer Guide* argues that 'without a shadow of a doubt, the most impressive environmental success story has starred 3M'. What features would you expect to see in this type of success story? Why do you think 3M, or any other firm you can identify, merits these plaudits? Justify your answer with evidence of specific action or systems.

5 One of the distinctive features of environmental problems is that 'they carry on getting worse until something effective is done to reverse the harm, merely stopping or doing nothing does little good'. Discuss the implications of this statement for corporate environmental policies.

6 Use the 'Business Ecosystem' to describe and analyse the pressures on a European firm in one of the following industries: automobile production, dyestuffs, fast food catering or pharmaceuticals.

7 Waste recycling offers the best and cheapest routes for better environmental management.

		Annual waste	
Product	*Location*	*(kg/person)*	*recycled (%)*
Paper	Western Europe	170–180	40–45
	Japan	170	50
	USA	270	25
Aluminium	Western Europe	18–20	30
	Japan	22	40
	USA	10	32
Glass	Western Europe	25	30
	Japan	7	55
	USA	50	12
Plastic	Western Europe	17	5
	Japan	25	0
	USA	55	1

Source: Euromonitor, 1989

Using data such as that provided above, show how collaboration between industry, government and users can cut waste locally, nationally and internationally.

Use illustrations from your own experience to support this discussion wherever possible.

8 Analyse the environmental and resource management implications of 'The Manager's Dilemma'.

9 Use Force Field Analysis to describe the steps in a change programme designed to introduce a major commitment to environmental protection into the mission strategies and operations of a firm – illustrate where possible.

10 Define:

(a) Biodiversity

(b) Ozone depletion

(c) Greenhouse effect

(d) Pre-emption

(e) Duty of care legislation

(f) EMIS

(g) Environmental contingency planning

(h) The tiers of European environmental legislation

(i) 'Fair trade' marks

(j) Compliance

REFERENCES

1. Post, J. E. 'Managing as if the Earth Mattered' *Business Horizons*, vol. 34, no. 4, July/August (1991) pp. 32–5.
2. Thomas, T. 'Going Green to Stay out of the Red' *European*, 11 May (1990).
3. Sanyal, R. N. and Neves, J. S. 'The Valdez Principles: Implications for Corporate Social Responsibility' *Journal of Business Ethics*, vol. 10, no. 12 December (1991) pp. 883–90.
4. Barker, T. (ed.) *Green Futures for Economic Growth*, Cambridge (UK), Cambridge Econometrics (1991).
5. De Borchgrave, R. 'It's not Easy Being Green? Developing an EC Environmental Strategy' *Journal of European Business*, vol. 14, no. 3 January/February (1993) pp. 48–52.
6. Robinson, S. 'Safeguarding the Environment: Critical Issues for Today and Tomorrow' *Prism*, third quarter (1991).
7. Harrison, P. *The Third Revolution: Population, Environment and a Sustainable World*, Harmondsworth, Penguin (1992).
8. Roome, N. 'Developing Environmental Management Strategies' *Business Strategy and the Environment*, vol. 1, no. 1, Spring (1992).
9. Plesse, J. 'Environmental Spending and Share Price Performance: The Petroleum Industry' *Business Strategy and the Environment*, vol. 1, part 1 Spring (1992).
10. Plesse, J., ibid.
11. Plesse, J., ibid.
12. Meeks, F. and Drummond, J. 'The Greenest Form of Power' *Fortune*, 11 June (1990).
13. Waldegrave, W. 'Environment and Industry: Progress Through Co-operation' *Journal of the Royal Society for the Encouragement of Arts, Manufactures and Commerce*, December (1987).
14. Steger, U. 'The Greening of the Board Room: How European Companies are Dealing With Environmental Issues' *Business and Society Review*, Braintree, Maryland.
15. North, K. *Environmental Business Management: An Introduction*, International Labour Office, Geneva (1992).
16. Peattie, K. *Green Marketing*, London, Pitman (1992).
17. Cairncross, F. *Costing the Earth*, London, Economist Books (1991).
18. Pearce, D. 'Environment and Taxation' *Economic Journal*, October (1991).
19. Roome, N., ibid.
20. Roome, N., ibid.

21. Zuboff, S. *In the Age of the Smart Machine*, London, Heinemann (1988).
22. Fitzgerald, C. 'Selecting Measures for Corporate Environmental Quality' *Greener Management International* vol. 1, January (1993) pp. 25–40.
23. Fitzgerald, C., ibid.
24. Clutterback, D. *Actions Speak Louder*, London, Kogan Page (1992).
25. Barnard, J. W. 'Exxon Collides with the Valdez Principles' *Business and Society Review*, Summer (1990) pp. 32–9.
26. Barnard, J. W., ibid.
27. Brabeck, M. 'Ethical Characteristics of Whistleblowers' *Journal of Research in Personality* vol. 18, pp. 41–53.
28. Sanyal, R., and Neves, J. S. 'The Valdez Principles: Implications for Corporate Social Responsibility' *Journal of Business Ethics*, vol. 10, no. 12 December (1991) pp. 883–90.
29. Shane, P. and Spicer, B. 'Market Response to Environmental Information Produced Outside the Firm' *Accounting Review*, July (1983) pp. 521–38.
30. Porter, M. *Competitive Advantage*, New York, The Free Press (1985).
31. Kantor, R. M. *When the Giants Learn to Dance*, London, Routledge (1989).
32. Hammer, M. and Champy, J. *Re-Engineering the Corporation*, London, Harper Collins (1993).
33. Cannon, T. *Enterprise: Creation, Development and Growth*, London, Heinemann (1991).
34. Toffler, A. *The Third Wave*, New York, Bantam (1980).
35. Hersey, P and Blanchard, K. *Management of Organisational Behaviour*, Englewood Cliffs, New Jersey, Prentice Hall (1982).
36. Kantor, R. M., ibid.
37. Roussel, P. A., Saad, K. N. and Erickson, T. J. *Third Generation R&D*, Boston, Harvard Business School Press (1991).
38. Elkington, J. and Hayes, J. *The Green Consumer Guide*, London, Gollancz (1988).
39. O'Kelly, L. 'Face Value' *Marketing Business*, May (1992).
40. Mitchell, V. W. and Greatorex, M. 'Consumer Perceived Risk in the UK Food Market' *British Food Journal*, vol. 92, no. 2 (1990).
41. Frank, J. and Wheelock, V. 'International Trends in Food Consumption' *British Food Journal*, vol. 90, no. 1 (1988).
42. Cannon, G. *The Politics of Food*, London, Century (1987).
43. Karch, K. M. Getting Organisational Buy-in for Benchmarking: Environmental Management at Weyerhaeuser, *National Productivity Review*, Winter (1992/93) pp. 13–22.
44. Jerry, R. 'Hazardous Waste Management: It's management with a Capital M' *Environment Today*, February (1993) pp. 10–15.
45. Metzger, B. H. 'European Environmental Trends in the 1990's' *Prism*, Third Quarter (1991) pp. 33–45.
46. Caplan, D. W. 'Sylvania's GTE Product Problem Stoppers: No. 1 Employee Involvement Team' *Total Quality Environmental Management*, vol. 2, no. 2 Winter (1992/93) pp. 159–64.
47. Hirsch, F. *Social Limits to Growth*, Cambridge, Mass., Harvard University Press (1979).
48. DeGeorge, R. 'Will Success Spoil Business Ethics', in Freeman, R. T. (ed.) *Business Ethics: The State of the Art*, Oxford, Oxford University Press (1991).
49. Kleiner, A. 'What Does It Mean To Be Green' *Harvard Business Review*, July–August (1991).
50. Tietenberg, T. H. 'Managing the Transition: The Potential Role for Economic Policies' in Mathew, J. T. (ed.) *Preserving the Global Environment: The Challenge of Shared Leadership*, New York, W. W. Norton (1991).
51. Lewin, K. *Field Theory in Social Science*, New York, Harper and Row (1951).
52. Griffin, R. W. and Moorhead, G. *Organisational Behaviour*, Boston, Houghton Mifflin (1986).
53. Cannon, T. *Enterprise: Creation, Development and Growth*, Oxford, Heinemann (1991).
54. 'Green Executives Find that their Mission isn't a Natural Part of Corporate Culture' *Wall Street Journal*, 5 March (1991).
55. Wilkes, A. 'The Business Implications of a Future EC Environmental Policy' *Business Strategy and the Environment*, vol. 1, part 3, Autumn (1992).
56. Miller, P. and O'Leary, T. 'Accounting Expertise and the Politics of the Product: Economic Citizenship and Modes of Corporate Governance' vol. 18 no. 2/3, February/April (1993) pp. 187–206.

57. Eisenhardt, K. 'Agency Theory: An Analysis and Review' *Academy of Management Review*, vol. 14 (1989) pp. 57–74.
58. Aupperle, K., Cerolle, A. and Hadfield, J. D. 'An Empirical Examination of the Relationship Between Corporate Social Responsibility and Profitability' *Academy of Management Journal*, vol. 28 (1985) pp. 446–63.
59. McGuire, J. B., Sundgren, A. and Schneedweis, T. 'Corporate Social Performance and Firm Financial Performance' *Academy of Management Journal*, vol. 31 (1981) pp. 854–72.
60. Royal Commission on Environmental Pollution, London, HMSO (1988).
61. Peters, T. *Lean, Green and Clean: The Profitable Company of the Year 2000*, The Greening of European Business Conference, Munich 4–5 October (1990).
62. Roome, N., ibid., pp. 11–24.

CHAPTER 12

The built environment

Over the last decade much of the debate on the environment has concentrated on the problems of the natural environment. The attention given to the role and contribution of industry in tackling these problems has distracted attention from the built environment. This, broadly speaking, is those parts of our locality, country or the plant which has been built by man. It includes the villages, towns and cities, the road, rail, sea, air and other communications systems beside the factories and offices in which we work and the homes in which we live. This built environment is largely the creation of industry and commerce. Rural or agricultural society lacked the need to develop cities or the resources to maintain them. Prior to the sixteenth century few cities had more than 50,000 inhabitants. Even the 'giants' of the ancient world seldom held populations of more than 500,000.[1] This pattern was transformed first by the growth of the nation state then by industrialisation.

The size and structure of cities is determined by the needs of commerce. Communication systems largely reflect the needs of industry. Most people in the developed world chose where they live largely to satisfy their requirements for access to industry or commerce. The highs and lows of the built environment are primarily a reflection of the patterns shaped by commerce mainly over the last two centuries.[2] The canyons of New York, the Eiffel Tower, Liverpool's St George's Hall and Glasgow's Town Hall, San Francisco's Water Front, The Burse at Shanghai, Hong Kong's Banking Centre, are the confident assertion of the capacity of industry and commerce to stamp their identity on the landscape.[3] Downtown Los Angeles, parts of Brixton, Hulme and Moss Side, the desolated landscapes around most airports, ravaged and empty factories in the Pern region of Russia, the shanties in Bombay, provide another darker side to industrial development.

> In Mexico City total emissions of local air pollutants rose by 45% between 1972 and 1983. Street booths sold puffs of oxygen. Dried and powdered excrement wafted through the air.[4]

It is in these communities that the effects of industry are already the most marked. The same localities will provide a powerful indicator of the willingness of industry to meet its wider responsibilities. In effect the repair and maintenance clause in the contract is clearest – nearest. Business in The Community played an important role in shaping this debate. In part this reflects its wider concerns about the environment. It also mirrors the wider belief that the nature of the immediate communities in which people grow shapes their responses to more general issues.[5] Growing up in a barren or despoiled urban environment is not likely to generate wider feeling of respect, enterprise or development.[6] This was recognised by the business people who shaped projects like the St George's Hall in Liverpool, the Rockefeller Centre in New York and the Hong Kong and Shanghai Bank in Hong Kong. The pragmatic and commercial gains were recognised by Levis when it moved out of its new Tower block to a rambling, *human* development. It is seen in the creative redevelopment of river front area in Boston or the renewal of Dijon. The exodus from Bathgate, Bochum and other 'new towns' and the inner cities is part of the same process. The changing pattern of transport and communications mirrors the same process of re-examination and redevelopment.[7]

In some senses, the problems of the built environment are more intractable than those of the natural environment. Many of the solutions to the latter are clear if painful to some. Logging can be stopped in the rain forests if the political will exists and the economic burdens on the developing countries are eased. Dumping of chemical waste can be ended by firms if accessible technologies are used and the market will pay the price. It is hard not to feel some sympathy for the wildlife threatened by river pollution or the destruction of their habitats. The built environment raises more complex issues. The urban sprawl of Mexico City,

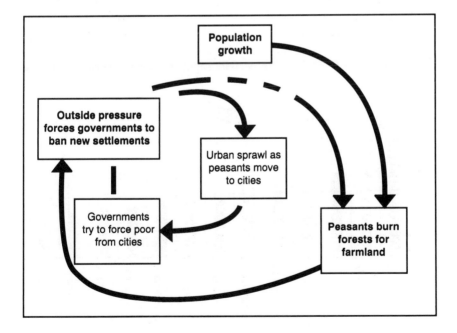

Fig. 12.1 The vicious circle of urban development

Bombay or Manila seems inexorable.[8] There might even be a vicious circle at work. Stop the logging and forest clearance and the families wanting to settle in the new territories will gravitate towards the cities (Figure 12.1).[9] It is harder to feel sympathy for the young, hostile, urban poor than dispossessed Amerindians.

CITIES

The growth of the cities is one of the dominant features of industrialisation.[10] It continues to characterise the development process in newly emerging countries. The great cities of the pre-industrial era: Florence, Madrid, Rome, Kyoto, Boston were soon overtaken in population by Milan, Glasgow, Chicago, Nagasaki and London. The explosive growth in the populations of British cities during the last century is well documented. As recently as the 1950s, London still had the largest population of any city in the world. Only two cities had populations approaching 10 million in 1950: New York and London. Now, they are dwarfed by Tokyo, Mexico City, São Paolo. Each saw growth and continues to grow because of the commercial and industrial developments in their localities. During the 1990s over three-quarters of the world's population increase is expected to take place in cities (Figure 12.2).[11]

By the year 2000 nineteen cities will have a population of over 10 million. Their combined population will exceed 300 million. Population densities in cities like Calcutta, Cairo, Teheran, Delhi and Shanghai already exceed 50,000 people per square mile. By the end of the decade, densities in the region of 100,000 per square mile will be common.[12] The fastest growth is taking place in the developing world. Africa saw an especially rapid shift from a rural to an urban

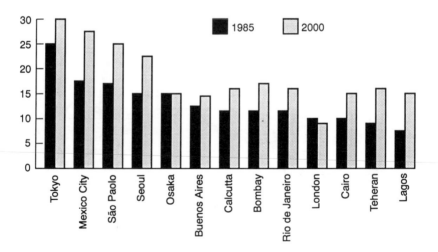

Fig. 12.2 Urban growth (populations in millions)

population with primate cities, i.e. first generation, unplanned urban communities, playing a major role. These contrast with the population densities of 10,000 to 11,000 in cities like New York, Los Angeles, London and Essen. The cities provide the working environment for much of global industry beside providing their primary markets. The health of the cities and the vitality of commerce are closely interrelated.

Within the cities a range of problems can be seen.[13] These range from local impoverishment as communities find it hard to break out from a spiral of decline and deprivation to wholesale erosion of the quality of life.[14] The riots in Los Angeles in early 1992 symbolised the threat to social order posed by a community which sees no hope of jobs, opportunity or improvement. The riot is a well documented form of protest by the urban poor.

> Through this vast throng, sprinkled doubtless here and there with honest zealots, but composed for the most part of the very scum and refuse, whose growth was fostered by bad criminal laws, bad prison regulations, and the worst conceivable police . . . (and later) . . . Beginning with the private houses so occupied, they broke open the doors and windows; and while they destroyed the furniture and left but the bare walls, made a sharp search for tools and engines of destruction, such as hammers, pokers, axes, saws, and such like instruments. Many of the rioters made belts of cord, of kerchiefs, or any material they found at hand, and wore these weapons as openly as pioneers upon a field day . . . In the same manner, they marched to the place of rendezvous agreed upon, made great fires . . . they danced and howled, and roared about these fires till they were tired.
>
> Dickens, C. (1841)[15]

The parallels with the 'shooting and looting . . . the death and destruction in the rich districts as well as the ghettos'[16] are clear. 'The thick smoke that darkened . . . dawn skies'[17] are part of the same imagery. The relationship with industry is even more vivid as many of the television and newspaper pictures now show the impact on the Los Angeles business districts around Vermont and Manchester.

In Britain, the decline of the major cities is well documented. Local progress such as the success of Leeds or the improvements around the Meadowhall and Canal Basin area of Sheffield show what can be achieved, but these pale alongside the continuing problems of Easterhouse, Moss Side and Brent. The potential contribution of industry can be seen in four critical areas: people development, job creation, environmental improvement and infrastructure programmes (Table 12.1). In each area, opportunities exist for firms to use their expertise to add value to communities in ways which better the lot of those affected while improving the business opportunities for the firm.[18]

In each of these key areas immediate business problems can be tackled while communities are assisted.[19] Programmes like *Compacts* give young people in the inner cities a promise of a better future while giving firms access to new, talented employees.[20] Job creation schemes such as Enterprise Agencies have supported

Table 12.1 Reshaping the built environment

Key area	Contribution	Example
People development	Firms can link self-improvement to job opportunities	Inner city compacts
Job creation	Operations can be relocated in inner cities or new small firms encouraged	Enterprise Agencies
Environmental improvements	Physical redevelopments can strive to add value to the community beside achieving immediate functionality	Collaborations like the Albert Dock development
Infrastructure programmes	Transport and communication strategies shaped by community beside commercial needs	Ford's use of rail for car distribution

the formation of new firms. These, in turn, become the suppliers and clients of established companies.[21] Environmental improvements – notably those which improve architectural, design and environmental standards – draw in clients and customers, reduce vandalism and add to the motivation of employees.[22] Infrastructure programmes can reshape the logistics costs curve while winning new collaborators.[23]

Those firms which have followed in this type of programme have built their success on a mixture of visionary commitment, local collaboration, planning and effective operational management.

CASE STUDY 12.1

A development model

Local Community Investment Fora
The key requirement, according to respondents in many organisations, is for an overall 'lead' strategic 'Community Investment Forum' within cities for co-ordination of partnership initiatives. This would ensure that schemes do not proliferate unduly, and would provide a focus for enquiries from, and information provision to, organisations in all sectors. This body needs to include representatives of, or at least have excellent contacts with, the private sector, local authority, urban development corporation (if one exists), voluntary sector representation, and bodies from intermediary agencies. It would become the lead body in localities for various functions in relation to business action in the community. For example:

- Lead role in co-ordinating the flow of information around local networks of companies and public/voluntary sector bodies in relation to business action in communities;
- Forum for discussion and action on community investment issues and on multi-sector partnerships in infrastructural development and social regeneration;
- Close liaison with business leadership teams and equivalent partnership bodies;

- Partnership with BitC in establishing new local per cent clubs;
- Partnership with common purpose in setting up new common purpose initiatives.

Which bodies would join such a forum would depend on the circumstances in each area. It would comprise representatives of the local authority, leading firms and business-led groups such as Business Leadership Teams (where they exist), the Chamber of Commerce, the TEC or LEC, educational institutions, the urban development corporation where one exists, City Action Team and Task Force where these exist, and leading local voluntary agencies and umbrella groups.

Source: Christie, I. *et al.* (1991)[24]

Vision

The vision is important.[25] Programmes in communities which are under pressure will face many setbacks.[26] The immediate 'beneficiaries' have long memories of failure, rejection and alienation. The environments in which they live have been neglected for a long time. Often, there are those who seek to exploit the fears and distrust within the community for their own ends. The corporation or leader working in this area will find major differences in perception and attitude. This was, for example, the experience of The Body Shop in Easterhouse in Glasgow.[27] This community showed all the key indicators of neglect and decay. The quality of housing was poor, unemployment was high, car ownership was low while public transport was inadequate. Simple gestures like the decision by The Body Shop to give the project a high media profile was resented in the community as highlighting their problems. The more distant the community, the harder it is for corporate leaders to appreciate the issues which will motivate or alienate those involved. Targeting or focusing efforts on strategically important areas like education has been an effective way to overcome some of these problems.[28]

Collaboration

Partnerships provide much of the answer to the problems of understanding and insight. The Body Shop overcame many of its initial difficulties because of the backing of the Easterhouse Partnership. This is a consortium of businesses, local authorities and other agencies. Its aim is to mobilise the resources of all those who can help to improve the standards and prospects in the community. The redevelopments in Sheffield were backed by SERC – the Sheffield Economic Regeneration Committee. Its members are drawn from business, national and local government and the local community. In Manchester, the Business Support Group works with community leaders on projects varying from job creation programmes to the development of the NIA Centre. The NIA centre illustrates the gains that can be obtained when business responds positively to local initiative.

CASE STUDY 12.2

The NIA Centre

In April 1992, the NIA Centre completed its first year as a centre for African and Caribbean Culture. The project had been conceived some years earlier by members of the African Caribbean community in the Moss Side and Hulme areas of Manchester. This area suffered from most of the ills of a northern inner city. Poor quality houses had been built during the 1960s. Communities were relocated but failed to get the jobs or the social improvements promised or expected. Decline during the 1970s and 1980s was accompanied by further deterioration in physical conditions. Despite this, the community contained many strengths. One of these was a lively arts and entertainment community. There was however, no natural base for training, rehearsal or performance.

The decision of the proprietors of an old cinema complex to dispose of the site created such an opportunity. A group of community entrepreneurs developed an ambitious scheme to refurbish the facility and develop it as a centre for African and Caribbean culture. They faced major resource constraints. Neither the community nor government had the resources to complete the project. This could only be achieved with the support of industry. A consortium of organisations had come together to form the Business Support Group. It included: 3M, Amec plc, Barclays Bank, BT, Cobbett Leak Almond (Solicitors), Co-Operative bank plc, Gardiner and Theobald (Quantity Surveyors), Kellogg, Laing NW, Manchester Business School, Norweb, Price Waterhouse, Royal Mail, Scottish and Newcastle Breweries, Siemens and Whitbread. They provided a mixture of expertise, resource and endorsement for the project. Central to their approach was the notion that local ownership was critical. The physical redevelopment of the complex was a powerful symbol of the ability of the community to redevelop *itself* with support from outside.

In some communities the natural allies do not exist or are unwilling to play a part. In these cases, industry may need to play a more proactive role. In the UK, central government stepped into the breach in some communities. Elsewhere, voluntary agencies can play a part. There is little doubt that some *local* groups will require a clearer lead from industry before their potential contribution is tapped.

Higher education may be such an agency. It might be said that if you want to find dereliction look no further than the area around the local university. In part this reflects the very limited role that most city centre universities see themselves playing in their immediate environment. The land they own is designated for some future programme. Until this occurs, it can lie fallow. The infamous 'education precinct' scheme in Manchester illustrates this. The original 1960s vision was a campus stretching from the University to UMIST (University of Manchester Institute of Science and Technology). The elevated walkways led to it being dubbed the Broadwater Farm of Higher Education. Most were not completed. They remain as a monuments to the dead ends of much 1960s urban architecture. The area around them remains derelict. It is a sharp contrast to the potential and talent of those working in the universities. A similar picture can

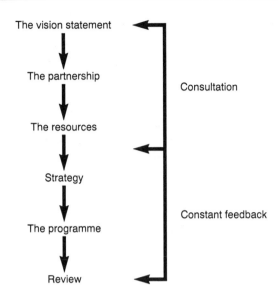

Fig. 12.3 The stages in development

be seen in the areas adjacent to universities in many parts of the world. Industry has the leverage and resource to unlock this potential.

Planning

Large-scale projects of the kind seen in most renewal schemes call for comprehensive planning process. This has a series of key stages (see Figure 12.3).

Partnering, consultation and feedback are the cornerstone of a successful programme. It is not a novel process. Its value was acknowledged by business people and civic leaders who shaped cities like Birmingham, Munich, Turin and Chicago. This is especially important in determining the nature and character of the building projects. The city is a built environment. The buildings; their nature, scale, type and distribution form the environment.[29]

A sense of personal ownership was lost in much urban architecture in the post-war environment. A sense of disposability and lack of personal involvement grew from a mixture of styles that used new materials in inappropriate ways; seemed to assume that context was irrelevant; ignored the link between form and nature and presumed function was an end itself.

> The typical Third World City is an island of concrete, steel and glass surrounded by an ocean of wood, tin and plastic. In 1980, around one in three or four urban dwellers in Asia lived in shanty towns; two out of five in Latin America and the Far East; two out of three in Africa.

> Harrison, P. (1992)[30]

Much of the blame can be laid at the door of institution-based developers in local authorities, public agencies, developers and large corporations. A revival of urban, commercial or industrial architecture depends on the willingness of leaders, from communities like industry, to challenge the assumptions listed above.[31]

Disposability is perhaps the most dangerous assumption. It emerged from an attempt to design buildings that could be changed quickly or contained a floating population of tenants. Low-amenity industrial estates, some city centre office blocks and some of the worst peripheral retail developments show these features. Business leaders can redirect the efforts of those responsible for these schemes by a mixture of boycott and active collaboration. The initiative shown by Sainsburys in supporting retail schemes shows this personal involvement. It contrasts sharply with the dreary red-roofed outlets which show the type of active participation needed to replicate the designs of a minor US fast food franchise. This involvement is returning to some of the most innovative and popular office complexes. Scale seems to be an important feature in creating this sense of involvement. It is harder to achieve in industrial estates. There is growing evidence that high-amenity developments are far more popular with companies. Their employees prefer these environments. These is some evidence of better performance and higher productivity. Voting with their feet is unlikely to produce a short-, even medium-term improvement. More active participation in commercial undertakings allied to a clearer stance on public projects will play a vital part in reshaping the built environment. The public sector remains a major player in industrial developments. Some initiatives have shown a commendable commitment to quality and adding value. The Science Parks in the west of Scotland and Cambridge have indicated what can be achieved while those in Manchester and Warrington indicate how far there is to go.

Management

The management skills of industry and commerce provide the clearest potential for added value in development programmes.[32] This input can take a number of key forms. The most useful can centre on the need for strategic planning in the urban environment. This concentrates on the overall pattern of development rather that the more detailed view which had dominated local authority planning. In Germany, this difference in the planning regime and the participation of industry is well illustrated in retailing developments in Dortmund and Cologne.

Dortmund, with a weak chamber of commerce, allowed many new retail developments in various parts of the city. Cologne, on the other hand, has long had a very powerful chamber of commerce . . . The Dortmund Inner City Area declined by 23.5 per cent in real terms (between 1978 and 1984) . . . (in 1985) it set aside five hectare sites for retail warehouses that could not be integrated with traditional centres. (Cologne avoided these problems and prospered through partnerships.)

Roberts, J. (1990)[33]

The integration of different elements into a coherent unity instead of the rigid zoning is likely to characterise the successful urban environment in the future. New technologies and service industries pose few of the threats to the community of more traditional sectors. Their less intrusive nature makes links with social and domestic development easier. Holistic solutions will require full involvement by key players, notably commerce. Initiatives like the City Challenge provide a comprehensive framework for advancing this type of partnership.

SMALLER COMMUNITIES

New technologies are changing the character of the built environment just as technology determined its nature in the past. The key features of cotton production, steel making, shipbuilding and materials extraction were large concentrations of labour in the workplace and the local area. The factory system grew because processing large amounts of product or material required large numbers of people. Even the layout of the factory was determined by the needs of flow or batch production and the necessities of manual supervision. Factories were located near to sources of energy because the machines drew hungrily on this power. Even the exterior works reflected basic needs like updraughts on chimneys or shop-floor lighting. The familiar factory gate was designed to allow large numbers to enter and leave at predetermined times. Few of these imperatives exist today.

Electronics, plastics, new composite materials and biotechnology operate in smaller, more mobile facilities. Their plants are less intrusive. Even car production deploys far less labour per unit of production than in the past. Telecommunications allows office work to be distributed far from the point of use. An enquiry on the London telephone exchange is likely to be answered from Paisley in Scotland. Hong Kong Telecom's enquiries are dealt with in mainland China. The shift from manufacturing to services has reshaped the dominant features of the cities. The call for massive concentrations of labour to facilitate the production process is declining. London, which once accommodated furniture makers in Bethnal Green, switch gear manufacturers in south London, rubber processors in Islington, is even more a city of civil servants and other office workers. In a modern economy the capacity exists to move an increasing proportion of business activity from the large city into smaller towns and communities. In the UK, this is seen in the relative decline of Liverpool, Glasgow, Birmingham and the relative growth of Chester, Bath and Edinburgh. The shift creates new challenges and opportunities for development in both types of communities. The challenge to the cities lies in adjusting an infrastructure designed to meet the needs of, perhaps, a million largely static, residential inhabitants to the requirements of less than half a million residents but perhaps two million transients. Industry has a crucial role to play in shaping that process.

In smaller communities a different challenge exists. This is the move from small, local communities to hubs where a variety of groups with different needs coexist. These groups may be international. Milton Keynes in Britain, for example, has a number of schools for different nationalities including the Gyosei Japanese school. The onus exists on industry to ensure that developments are sympathetic with the requirements of the local community while avoiding the formation of a series of separate, potentially hostile ghettos. In international firms, the workforce is increasingly transient. A US computer firm in Stirling, Scotland will inevitably bring some workers in from America or another posting. This can introduce strains on the housing market or novel demands on local facilities. Collaboration with other local agencies is especially important in local communities. It is part of the pressure for sympathetic not intrusive development in urban communities.

The urban village

The urban village is an attempt to tackle two of the features of recent developments which have caused special difficulties to the cities of Britain, Northern Europe and the USA. These are:

1   The tendency of urban centres to 'over-expand vertically, resulting in excessive density of buildings and central activities, creating excessive real estate and land values which then drive the economic need for even higher densities and even taller buildings'.[34] These taller buildings and higher densities draw in increasing amounts of related infrastructure. Road and rail systems are required to shift even larger numbers of people. The costs of this infrastructure grows as the land values increase. It draws in resources from other parts of the country. Their relative decline pushes even more people into the urban centres. In Britain, it is estimated that almost half the road and rail infrastructure expenditure during the 1980s was concentrated on London. The cost per passenger (road, rail and air) of moving people into and out of London is twice that of other major urban centres in the UK.

2   The proliferation of suburban peripheries which 'over expand horizontally because of the lower cost of land, resulting in densities of buildings and activities that are too low, which in itself causes and maintains the congestion in historic centres whilst perpetuating a form of development which leads to suburban sprawl over several miles from the centre'.[35] In the USA and Australia ribbon developments cluster around the highways providing a façade of car dealerships and fast food restaurants interspersed with shopping malls. These get bigger and bigger as the volumes needed to meet costs grow. Motorists travel increasing distances for the biggest J. C. Penny or Woolco. In Europe, ribbon development has given way to vast commercial parks which compete with city centres for custom. Motorway networks cut across the countryside to shift larger numbers of people in the quest for an Ikea or a Carrefoure.

The urban village is an attempt to redress this trend by re-creating the holistic communities that existed in towns before the industrial revolution provoked the pressure for growth. They are possible because new industries and technologies created different requirements. Three features characterise the urban village:

1   It is at a human scale. It should be less than 100 acres in area. People should be able to locate themselves, their neighbours, their services even their work within the village. This is a psychological as well as a physical feature of the village.
2   It should follow the natural topography. It should be moulded around its environment. This notion of sympathy with the context reflects the underlying philosophy of the village itself.
3   People should come before private transport.

The village concept confounds the trends of this century in the developed world by emphasising the link between the individual and his or her environment. The notion of disposability is rejected and replaced with a sense of the integral value of the community and its members. The lack of commitment is supplanted by a sense of involvement and participation. It is part of a process of redefining man's relationship with the built environment which takes a tangible form in buildings and cities and intangible form in support for community and developments.

CONCLUSION

Most people and firms operate in an urban or built environment. The factories, offices, schools, government buildings and houses in which people live and work have an immediate effect on their lives and lifestyles. This is as true in Blackburn as it is in Bombay. The built environment is largely the creation of industry. Buildings like the Royal Liver Building in Liverpool (Figure 12.4) went beyond merely accommodating insurance clerks and operatives. It was a statement about the company, the city, and the wider community. The Chrysler Building in New York and others around the globe portray the same assurance and commitment to the role of industry and its contribution to the built environment. The reverse is true of a host of eyesores from Centre Point in London to the Koala Motor Inn in Sydney. The buildings themselves are key components in the built environment. The road, rail, air and other transport systems serve the needs of commerce. These are parts of the environment which the community has placed at the disposal of business so that its primary economic functions can be performed. But, this is not a transfer without responsibility. The quality of the built environment is perhaps the most tangible expression of the contribution that business is making to the health of the society in which it operates.

Fig. 12.4 The Royal Liver Building in Liverpool

QUESTIONS

1 Describe the inter-relationships between communication, industry and urban growth.

2 The Vicious Circle of Urban Development describes a powerful link between urban growth, industrialisation and population growth. Outline some ways in which industry can break this circle of decline.

3 Harrison[36] calls the expansion of 'private' cities 'cancerous'. Why does he use this term? Explain the reasons why the growth of these cities poses special problems to communities.

4 Describe the key areas in which industry can collaborate with local communities to improve the quality of life in urban communities. Illustrate where possible.

5 Projects like the NIA Centre in Manchester indicate the scope for partnership between industry and local communities. Describe the nature of this partnership. How far is it true that their long-term development is seriously limited by the preference of many firms to support large-scale prestige projects, not small local groups.

6 It is often suggested that the partnership between industry and higher education can make a major contribution to regeneration of the inner cities. Outline the potential contribution of this type of project. Illustrate the analysis with examples with which you are familiar.

7 Outline the contribution that seconded managers can make to local economic development projects. Indicate some of the ways the lessons they learn during their secondments can help their firms.

8 Describe the stages in development of a local economy. Discuss and illustrate the role that feedback and consultation can play in the success of a local economic development programme.

9 'The integration of different elements into a coherent unity instead of rigid zoning is likely to characterise the successful urban environment of the future.' Outline the implications of this comment for industrial location and urban planning.

10 Define:

(a) Urbanisation
(b) Primate cities
(c) Compacts
(d) Enterprise Agencies
(e) Partnering

(f) Disposability
(g) Science parks
(h) Zoning
(i) The urban village
(j) Holistic Solutions

CASE STUDY 3
UNION RAILWAYS: THE CHANNEL LINK

Environmental input at the option development stage

Introduction

At the Option Development stage, the design teams were developing options which had been carried forward from the Option Definition stage.

Environmental input to the design process was made through the application of the Simplified Environmental and Planning Appraisal Framework, supplemented by appraisals by the Environmental Assessment Consultants (EACs). The planning elements of the framework were completed by the Union Railways Planning and Development Group (RDG) which carried out an appraisal of the planning implications of the options.

The framework was based on the Comparative Appraisal Framework presented in the *Union Railways Environmental Handbook*. The framework was completed by the engineering design teams and validated by the EACs. The results of the appraisals carried out by the EACs were brought together at a series of environment team meetings held prior to the Option Development stage meeting of the RDG.

The aim of the meetings was threefold:

- to identify route options that were environmentally unacceptable by the standards associated with major infrastructure projects in the UK;
- to establish a ranking on environmental grounds of the route options within each route section; and
- to identify where further work was necessary.

The EACs were asked to identify, based on their professional experience, any subroute options that they believed to be unacceptable for their particular topic by the standards applied to major transport infrastructure projects in the UK. The environment team identified two types of critical concern:

- direct physical disturbance to environmental resources of international importance; and
- the demolition of more than 10 houses at any one location.

Route options which raised such concerns were appraised as being unacceptable in environmental terms. These views were subsequently taken into account in the RDG's deliberations at the second sift meeting.

The methodology for establishing a ranking of route options consisted of three stages:

- categorisation of the significance of the effects of the subroute options on identified receptors or resources;
- comparison of subroute options; and
- derivation of overall conclusions.

Categorisation of effects

Each EAC classified the significance of the effects of the subroute options on identified receptors or resources in two ways:

- by looking at the relative acceptability of the subroute options for that particular topic; and
- by looking at the importance that a hypothetical decision maker might place on the range of effects.

In classifying the relative effect that each subroute option had on identified receptors/resources, the EACs based their classifications on:

- the data contained in the validated Simplified Frameworks for each route section; and
- expert judgement as to the way in which the resources would be affected.

The expert judgement was made using the approach adopted during the Environmental Assessment of the Safeguarded Route in 1991 and also by assessing the degree of compliance with the design aims as published in the *Union Railways Environmental Handbook*. Where a series of resources within a particular environmental topic was identified as being affected by subroute options, the EACs based their appraisal on the combination of the effects.

The results of the classification were captured on a topic by topic basis. The resulting table consisted of a matrix with environmental topics along the vertical axis and subroute options along the horizontal axis. The environmental topics considered fall under two general headings:

Effects on people
community effects (residential demolitions or landtake, number of dwellings within 100 m, commercial premises and public facilities affected); noise;
vibration and reradiated noise;
visual impact; and
contaminated land.

Effects on resources
agriculture;
archaeology;
ecology;
historic features;
landscape; and
water.

Comparison of subroute options

Having established a significance matrix of environmental effects by subroute options, pairwise comparisons were then carried out within the route sections with the aim of deriving an environmental preference ranking. The pairwise comparisons were carried out using data from the Simplified Framework and by expert judgement by the EACs.

For each pairwise comparison, the EACs stated their preferred option and the implications of each option in terms of resources or receptors affected. The EACs indicated whether their preference for a particular option was clear or marginal. After each EAC had reported the preference for its particular topic and the strength of that preference, the environment team then debated the merits of the two subroute options to derive an overall view. In coming to an overall view, the team was mindful of the importance that each EAC had attached to the effects of the subroute options. As with the individual environmental topics, the meeting attempted to express any identified overall preference as clear or marginal.

In some cases, the environment team was able to reach a clear conclusion as to the result of the pairwise comparison. In other cases, the team felt unable to differentiate between the subroute options, either because they had similar effects, or because the effects were so dissimilar as to make the identification of an overall preference potentially misleading.

In deriving the order for carrying out the pairwise comparisons, groups of subroutes that shared common alignments for substantial lengths were identified. This allowed the initial pairwise comparisons to focus on the differences within the different groups of subroutes. Comparisons were carried out to enable preferences within a group to be identified. After exploring the preferences within groups, pairwise comparisons between subroutes from different groups were carried out to enable an overall environmental preference ranking to be derived.

Derivation of overall conclusions

For each route section, cross-checking between the results of the pairwise comparisons was carried out in order to establish the overall validity of the emerging environmental preference ranking. For example, if option 1 was preferred to option 2 and option 2 preferred to option 3, then, although it would be logical to assume that option 1 would be preferred to option 3, this was checked whenever time allowed. Where logical conflicts between the results of pairwise comparisons were revealed, the comparisons were re-evaluated to clarify the situation.

Examination of the resulting environmental preference rankings for the route sections enabled conclusions to be drawn about particular lengths of the subroutes, some of which were common to a number of them. In this way, it was possible in some cases to derive 'hybrid' routes that combined lengths from a number of subroute options that had been appraised. These were fed back into the route development process.

Environmental input at the option definition stage

At the Option Definition stage, the design teams were identifying, modifying and rejecting route options as they defined ways of traversing the respective route sections. The Environmental Design Aims published in the Union Railways Environmental Handbook provided important guidance to the design teams on the avoidance or mitigation of environmental concerns.

Environmental Features Mapping (EFM) provided the baseline information necessary for the engineering design teams to be appraised of environmental features within the route corridor. The features mapped covered the following environmental topics:

- agriculture;
- contaminated land;
- ecology;
- groundwater features;
- historic and cultural features; and
- landscape features.

The features were presented on Ordnance Survey base mapping. This provided the engineering design teams with a practical tool to enable them to take account of environmental concerns during the Option Definition stage.

EFM data were used to complete the environmental elements of an option proforma which was completed for each option considered by the RDG at the Option Definition stage. The proforma presented key environmental information and was supplemented with more detailed information from the EACs where particular issues required further study. The proformas were validated by the Union Railways Environment Department.

QUESTIONS

1 Use this information and other data to review the consultation approach adopted by Union Railways.

2 Outline the role of external consultants in this process.

3 Comment on the lessons learned from the political interference on route planning for this project.

REFERENCES

1. Chandler, T. and Fox, G. *3000 Years of Urban Growth*, New York, Academic Press (1974).
2. Pollard, S. 'Industrialisation and the European Economy' *Economic History Review*, vol. 26 (1973) pp. 636–48.

3. Chandler, T. and Fox, G., ibid.

4. Harrison, P. *The Third Revolution*, Harmondsworth, Penguin (1992).

5. United Nations Centre for Human Settlements *Global Report on Human Settlements 1986*, Oxford, Oxford University Press (1987).

6. Kahnert, F. *Improving Urban Employment and Labour Productivity*, Washington, World Bank (1987).

7. Mitchell, B. R. 'The Coming of the Railways and United Kingdom Economic Growth' *Journal of Economic History*, vol. 24, pp. 315–36.

8. United Nations Population Division *World Urbanisation Prospects, 1990*, New York, United Nations (1991).

9. Bairoch, P. *Urban Unemployment in Developing Countries*, Geneva, ILO (1973).

10. Mumford, L. *The City in History*, Harmondsworth, Penguin (1966).

11. *World Urbanisation Prospects, 1990*, ibid.

12. Some estimates already put the population density in Hong Kong, Dhaka and Shenyang at over 100,000 per square mile.

13. Maclennan, D. and Gibb, K. *Urban Land Markets – Report to the OECD*, Paris, OECD (1991).

14. Martin, C. J. 'Poor Housing, Unemployment and Poverty: The Effects on Child Health' *Radical Statistics*, vol. 44 (1990) pp. 16–22.

15. Dickens, C. *Barnaby Rudge* (1841).

16. *Sunday Times*, 3 May (1992).

17. *Guardian*, 1 May (1992).

18. Maclennan, D. 'Urban Change Through Environmental Investments', in *Urban Challenges: A Report to the Commission on Metropolitan Problems*, Swedish Government Publications, Stockholm (1990).

19. Crowther-Hunt, E. and Billinghurst, L. *Inner Cities, Inner Strengths: Recognising People Potential in Urban Regeneration*, London, Industrial Society Press (1990).

20. Department of the Environment *Getting People into Jobs: Good Practice in Urban Regeneration*, London, HMSO (1990).

21. Confederation of British Industry *Initiatives Beyond Charity: Report of the CBI Task Force on Business and Urban Regeneration*, London, CBI (1988).

22. Forrester, S. *Business and Environmental Groups, A Natural Partnership*, Directory of Social Change (1990).

23. Audit Commission *Urban Regeneration and Economic Development: The Local Government Dimension*, London, HMSO (1989).

24. Christie, I. et al. *Profitable Partnerships*, London, Policy Studies Institute (1991). Reproduced with the permission of the Controller of HMSO.

25. 'Cultural Change' *The Economist*, 7 July (1990).

26. Johns, R. I. *Company Community Involvement in the UK, An Independent Study*, Warwick (1991).

27. MBA Project *The Body Shop: Easterhouse Initiative*, Manchester, Manchester Business School (1991).

28. Doyle, D. P. and Keavus, D. T. *Winning the Brain Race: A Bold Plan to Make our Schools Competitive*, New York, ICS Press (1988).

29. Jacobs, J. *The Economy of Cities*, Harmondsworth, Penguin (1972).

30. Harrison, P., ibid., p. 172.

31. *Global Report on Human Settlement, 1986*, ibid.

32. Fogarty, M. and Christie, I. *Companies and Communities*, London, Policy Studies Institute (1991).

33. Roberts, J. 'Britain in 2010: Future Patterns of Shopping' *Journal of the Royal Society for the Encouragement of Arts, Manufactures and Commerce*, March (1990).

34. Business in The Community *Urban Villages*, London, Business in The Community (1990).

35. Business in The Community, ibid.

36. Harrison, P., ibid.

PART 4

The economically and socially disadvantaged

CHAPTER 13

Local inequalities

The economic downturns of the early 1980s posed a host of problems for the disadvantaged regions of many countries. The Rust Belt of the USA, northern Britain, southern Italy, the mining areas of Australia and north east France were among those regions which faced rapid increases in unemployment. The downturns coincided with a loss of faith in the ability of governments to solve these problems using the conventional tools of direct intervention.[1] Job creation and the reconstruction of these communities was seen as a local priority which could only be solved through partnership between the community and industry.[2] The state established the environment and acted as an enabler.[3] Responsibility for action lay with those having the operational skills and direct needs.[4,5] As the recession of the late 1980s and early 1990s bit, the questions remained but the form of the response was under closer scrutiny. Reservations about the potential for state intervention increased with the collapse of the command economies of Central and Eastern Europe.[6] There is, however, increased debate about the extent to which firms can deploy resources when their core operations are under greater threat.

This has forced a reappraisal of the optimum form and level of corporate involvement in tackling the economics and social problems of communities under pressure. The nature of these communities varies considerably. Even within Britain it is possible to identify five basic types:

1 High stress environments
2 Structurally disadvantaged areas
3 Crisis zones
4 Transitional areas
5 Economic engines

High stress environments are those in which a long period of disadvantage, perhaps allied to a specific crisis or its demography, creates a volatile situation and pernicious disadvantage. There are few indigenous change agents, resources within the community are virtually non-existent. Primary agents for social change, e.g. education have either abandoned the area or the community has lost confidence in their ability to make a difference. Crime and social disorder are common. Areas like Brixton in London or the St Paul's area of Bristol have come to represent this type of community in Britain. The USA Watts areas of downtown Washington or Los Angeles show these characteristics. There are pressured arrondissements in Paris, parts of Marseilles, communities in Amsterdam and similar areas in most countries.

Structurally disadvantaged areas suffer because some key feature of their locality or situation places them at a disadvantage. The peripheral areas of Europe, the rural areas of Australia or Canada and some regions in southern Africa illustrate these features. Areas like the West of Ireland or the Western Isles have been affected by this problem for much of the last two hundred years. The costs of transport increase prices for them and make their products uncompetitive. Migration can worsen the situation especially when younger age groups leave the area for work elsewhere. Some forms of structural disadvantage occur because of economic change. The shift of Britain's trade from transatlantic to the USA to cross channel to Europe undermined the economic base of Liverpool. Mining, iron and steel and shipbuilding communities in Europe and North America have faced comparable difficulties. Many rural areas face these problems. There has, however, been a tendency to ignore the plight of rural communities.

Crisis zones occur where a specific event or sequence of events hits the economic base of a community. The problems of British carmakers in the late 1970s and early 1980s prompted the firm to end its production in Scotland. Towns like Bathgate were largely dependent on this one firm. Company towns such as Deerborne in the US are especially vulnerable to these difficulties. Even where the firm survives, its problems are those of its community. The failure of McDonnell Douglas to win major US airforce contracts can hit St Louis hard. The so-called *peace dividend* is viewed with some trepidation by communities dependent on the defence industry.

Transitional areas are moving from one stage or level of economic activity to another. Sometimes it is an area like the West Midlands in Britain or the Ruhr in Germany. The cornerstones of its economic strength are being weakened by wider changes. They still matter but their contribution to the well being of the community is declining. This decline seems likely to continue. Some transition communities face the opposite problem. New or growing industries are increasing the strains on the fabric of the community or its infrastructure.

Economic engines are the parts of a community that drive it forward. Economic growth and development has never been neat or evenly distributed. There are parts of a community that create wealth faster than others at any point in time. They are not immune from difficulties. A change in the economic climate can make these engines falter. The difficulties of Boston in the late 1980s illustrated how a basically strong, local economy can be buffeted by external pressures. Comparable problems affected southern England and northern Italy in the early 1990s.

A corporation which is striving to develop its stance on corporate responsibility

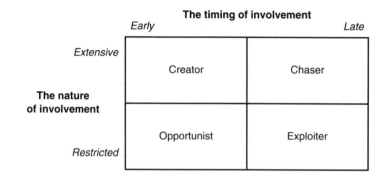

Fig. 13.1 The success matrix

will be influenced by its perception of the needs of these – and other – communities and the contribution it can make.[7] Most will acknowledge that their prosperity turns on the health of the communities it serves.[8] Firms cannot perform their economic functions in a negative or hostile environment. Most mainstream business activity is a blend of collaboration and support.[9] The firm that does not support its suppliers when they face difficulties will soon find itself short of quality suppliers. The notion of integrated marketing[10] grew because it became clear that those firms that looked furthest down the marketing chain and built extensive, collaborative networks performed better than those that concentrated on the immediate transaction and one feature of the relationship – price.

Early and extensive involvement in innovative activity allow the customer and the supplier to work together to create the best solution for both. This approach is identified with some of the most successful German firms as they innovated successfully. Late and limited involvement leave the firm trying to exploit opportunities created elsewhere.[11] Sometimes it works but the odds of this shrink as suppliers and potential partners see that collaboration is a one-way street. Restricted but early involvement is typically based on keeping a watchful eye on programmes of work. There might be some involvement but it is very restricted. Often, it is interpreted by potential allies as exploitation although this is not usually the aim. Late, but extensive involvement characterises the attempt to catch up on developments elsewhere.[12] This is a high-risk policy which – in the strategic analysis of markets – often leads to large numbers of questionable businesses but few stars or cash cows (Figure 13.1).[13] In building the firm's portfolio of corporate affairs activities the same basic principles of support and development have a vital part to play. This is as true in dealing with a community facing a crisis as it is in one in transition.

What is the use of England – and England in this connection means the City, Fleet Street and the West End clubs – congratulating herself upon having pulled through again when there is no plan for Lancashire . . . we have marched so far, not unassisted in the past by Lancashire's money and muck, and we have a long way to go yet, perhaps carrying Lancashire on our backs for a spell . . . It does not matter now whether Manchester does the thinking today and the rest of England thinks it tomorrow, or whether we turn the table on them and think today for Manchester tomorrow.

Priestley, J. B. (1934)[14]

The strategies adopted by firms to local economic development will reflect the needs of the community, the capabilities of the firm and its overall corporate affairs strategy.

A STRATEGY FOR CORPORATE RESPONSIBILITY

Strategies perform a number of related functions within a firm. These strategic decisions are concerned with:

- The scope of an organisation's activities;
- The matching of an organisation's activities to the environment;
- The matching of an organisation's activities to its resource capability;
- The allocation and reallocation of major resources in an organisation;
- The values, expectations and goals of those influencing strategy;
- Implications for change throughout the organisation.

Johnson, G. and Scholes, K. (1988)[15]

A sense of strategic direction is a vital component in an effective approach to corporate responsibility. It allows the firm to deploy its resources effectively while ensuring that expertise is developed within the firm to improve internal value for money and external effectiveness. This underlying mission or vision varies between firms. At Atlantic Richfield the notion of fairness underpins virtually all its corporate affairs activity.[16] Levi Strauss concentrate on participation.[17] Marks and Spencer highlight involvement.[18] United Biscuits return to themes like enterprise.[19] Lilly are committed to notion of welfare.[20] Although none of these notions are exclusive they provide a powerful core around which specific strategies can be developed, decisions made and resources allocated. This can be seen in each of the key operational areas of corporate affairs work.

The scope

The commitment to fairness at Atlantic Richfield has lead the firm to concentrate its resources on programmes which break down the barriers which stand in the way of individuals or communities realising their potential. It has acted 'aggressively to bring minorities, women and the handicapped into job areas where few of them have worked in the past . . . line managers must set and meet annual goals for the hiring and promotion of women and minorities.'[21] Whitbread adopt, broadly speaking, the same approach. It prompted the firm to back the introduction of inner city compacts in high-stress environments. The aim was to break the vicious cycle of deprivation at the roots by helping young people to follow studies with a realistic prospect of a job. Two goals were achieved simultaneously. The role of education as a means of personal improvement was endorsed while job opportunities were provided. Scottish and Newcastle Breweries have adopted fair job opportunities programmes in their plants. In effect, this means people from disadvantaged groups in the local community are given preference over more prosperous groups outside. Top management has an especially important role in determining the scope of the firm's corporate responsibility programmes.

Environmental fit

This plays a crucial role in the programmes developed by Levi Strauss and Co. It concentrates its resources on local schemes built around employee voluntarism. This means that local employees are expected to make a material contribution themselves to problems they identify in their local communities. They avoid some of the more popular employee causes, e.g. expensive medical equipment, by concentrating on social and economic issues. Their programmes have been especially effective in communities suffering from structural difficulties. Their worldwide networks can help these communities overcome the logistics problems which may be the cause of these difficulties. New technologies are producing novel opportunities for peripheral regions. IBM, NatWest Bank and BT have collaborated to create opportunities in software design and development in outlying regions. These can be done just as easily away from the main conurbations and downloaded along telephone lines. This is a variation on the 'electronic village' concept pioneered in Finland. Collaboration with local partners is often the key to a quality fit with the environment. On Merseyside the Business Opportunities On Merseyside (BOOM) initiative has been backed by government agencies and firms like Littlewoods and Unilever. In the Western Isles the Highlands and Islands Development Corporation's Community Co-operatives were linked with firms like Booker plc. Success often depends on line management becoming involved and corporate control systems recognising the value of this work.

Resources

Resources to match the needs identified are central to successful corporate responsibility programmes. Marks and Spencer achieve this by wedding central resources to locally raised finance. The involvement of their workforce is almost an essential prerequisite for action. British Steel achieved a similar result by concentrating its effort in steel closure areas and wedding their investments to public funds. Its offshoot British Steel Industry deployed these resources with particular effect in crisis zones. Often immediacy and symbolism are important to rebuild confidence and stop decline before it becomes congenital. The scale of

Table 13.1 The growth in corporate giving (£million)

	1986/87	1987/88	1988/89	1989/90
NatWest	8.0	9.7	11.0	11.0
Barclays	5.5	7.0	8.0	10.0
BP	4.1	5.7	9.0	9.0
British Gas	0	0.23	6.0	6.0
M&S	1.2	2.26	3.71	4.29
Smithkline Beecham	0.24	0.25	0.3	4.1
ICI	1.4	1.8	2.7	3.6
BAT	1.7	1.9	2	3.2
BT	0.35	0.75	2.33	2.98
Glaxo	0.85	0.72	1.8	1.89
RTZ	0.6	1.2	1.7	1.8
GrandMet	0.58	0.58	1.22	1.74
Hanson	2.6	1.43	1.0	1.56
Shell	1.07	1.06	1.2	1.5
Unilever	1.0	1.0	1.0	1.0
Guinness	0.21	0.3	0.49	0.81
GE	0.24	0.23	0.27	0.5
Cable & Wireless	0.16	0.3	0.41	0.49
Reuters	0.22	0.27	0.09	0.41
BTR	0.1	0.1	0.1	0.15
TOTAL (top 20)	30.12	36.78	54.32	66.02

Source: Philanthropy Database: MBS

corporate giving in the UK has increased as firms have responded to needs by deploying increased resources (Table 13.1).

Crisis zones can make remarkable progress if strategic resources are deployed effectively. The St Helens Partnership demonstrated the progress possible when a firm adopts an affirmative stance in its local community. The crisis was precipitated by the need for Pilkington plc to restructure its operations in the locality and cut its workforce.

The firm eschewed the easy options and decided to look for ways to replace the jobs lost by new firms especially those created by former employees. The company committed people, plant and funds to build the St Helens Trust – one of the first enterprise agencies in the UK. Within a few years, there were as many people working in this enterprise as had, formerly, been employed by Pilkington. This type of programme gets its greatest strength from extensive involvement in the firm. The internal management systems and structures are fully integrated into the corporate affairs work of the firm. Champions are needed to endorse the activities.

Communities, cultures and champions

Another factor in the history of failed initiatives in areas such as Moss Side is the 'cultural gap', as one respondent put it, between the private sector and local community groups which are likely to be hostile to, or at least suspicious of, business and public sector interest after years of being left on the margins of the Manchester economy. There are no short cuts to partnership between private, public and community bodies in such cases, and this is fully recognised by Kellogg and its partners in the Business Support Group in Moss Side. The development of renewal projects in inner city districts will need patience, willingness to experiment and fail, long-term commitment and above all dialogue with the community rather than imposition of 'solutions'.

Although it is too early to judge the success of the BSG in Moss Side and the new Community Development Trust, the experience to date is widely regarded as encouraging and respondents from all sectors said that there is a genuine sense of trust and partnership emerging after initial suspicion from the multiplicity of community groups as to the motives of the private sector partners and the Task Force. The Moss Side area now has a Business Support Group which connects the area to wider company networks; an enterprise agency backed by major firms; and a Community Development Trust to provide a forum for discussion and co-ordination between all partners in the area. This 'triad' seems to be highly promising and an effective model for other 'problem areas'. East Manchester needs a similarly coherent approach by partnership bodies: it has a Community Forum which could develop into a focus for co-ordination and debate as in Moss Side; there is an initiative for economic strategy for the area involving the Chamber of Commerce and the City Council; it now needs to draw in private sector support, and the creation of a Business Support Group for the area deserves to be considered in the light of the Moss Side experience.

Such initiatives involving the community groups fully in partnership would also help to place social regeneration issues higher up the agenda for urban renewal in the city; as in our other cities, the emphasis has been on property-led development to date and there is a lot to do in tackling the social problems which persist in the inner city areas. The establishment of Community Development Trusts as in Moss Side can provide a focus for what is often a highly fragmented set of community groups and voluntary bodies.

Source: Christie, I *et al.* (1991)[22]

Kellogg as the 'Champions' of both Moss Side and the Business Support Group (BSG) provided a mixture of authority, credibility and resources. This helped the community and the BSG gain access to backing that was unavailable before.

The level of professionalism needed has prompted many firms to work with organisations like Business and The Community to improve standards of professionalism. A development spiral is built (Figure 13.2). Internal training programmes highlight the value and contribution of corporate affairs work in local communities. Individuals become involved. They face tasks which test them beyond their normal requirements. Their achievements encourage them to stretch their capabilities within their normal work. This encourages their

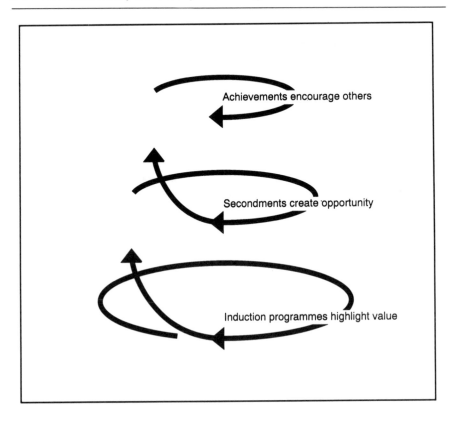

Achievements encourage others

Secondments create opportunity

Induction programmes highlight value

Fig. 13.2 The development spiral

superiors and colleagues to support this work. Eventually, they reach senior positions and encourage others to follow.

VALUES AND EXPECTATIONS

Corporate community affairs programmes bring out the values that underpin the company. At United Biscuits – founder member of the One Per Cent Club – this encourages the firm to give special emphasis to initiatives which re-create the spirit of enterprise in individuals and communities. This takes several forms including support for enterprise agencies, backing for enterprise education and assistance to such initiatives as the Prince's Youth Business Trust. The creative synergy between the integration of enterprise into the firm's commercial activities and the wider support for enterprise is closely linked to the growing importance of value-driven businesses. Peters and Waterman[23] touched on this when they highlighted the success of tight–loose management styles. The tightness lay in the overall direction of the firm. The looseness provided opportunities for individual managers – close to the action – to use their enterprise to win business. Without this enterprise this model cannot work. ⟨

> The . . . quality that will be critical (to corporate success) is the will to project a corporate vision . . . (the) statement of purpose, of aspiration, and of values . . . that has common meaning to its customers, its employees, its suppliers, its shareholders, and the many communities in which it lives.
>
> Riker, H. A. and Roetter, M. F. (1990)[24]

In transitional areas, the combination of firms willing to take a lead and companies with a core capability can be especially effective. The launch of the One Per Cent club in 1988 drew both these themes together. It was a notion endorsed by the then Prime Minister, Margaret Thatcher, when she commented 'the great news is that business is once again giving a lead, not only in your companies but in the life of the community as a whole'.[25]

The work currently taking place in Birmingham (England) highlights many of the features of the integration of values and expectations in a transitional area.[26] The economic problems of the late 1980s hit Birmingham especially hard. It had a recent history of prosperity based on engineering, automobile production and other manufacturing. It suffered from government policies in the 1950s, 1960s and 1970s which seemed to suggest that the area was invulnerable to economic problems. Firms were encouraged (forced?) to relocate to other parts of the country with little thought to the long-term effects on international competitiveness or local enterprise. The economic chickens came home to roost – with a vengeance – in the late 1980s. Individual firms such as Rover or Grand Metropolitan took a leadership role in the mid to late 1980s. Others collaborated with central and local government and community groups to establish a series of initiatives to tackle specific problems, e.g. skills shortages, through the GATE initiative (Group for Action in Training and Employment) or wider problems. The Birmingham Business Action Team, for example, brings together firms like BT, Cadburys, British Gas, Ansells, Glynwed, Foseco, Tarmac, Streetley and British Rail in a co-ordinated effort to support firms with up to 200 employees. This mixture of enterprise, self-help and community involvement provides the key to success in tackling the problems of communities in transition in Britain and elsewhere.[27]

DIRECTION

There are those who argue that the sense of direction provided by a responsible company in a community facing economic difficulties is perhaps its greatest contribution. The funds, even the expertise, is less important than the community leadership role.[28]

> It is impossible to follow the history of corporate giving in the United States without

Total $93 million

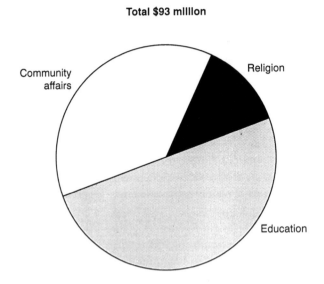

Fig. 13.3 The allocation of funds by Eli Lilly (1989)

realising that the chief way in which it has grown and spread has been through personal and local initiative, influenced by example, consolidated through associations and systematic promotion, but always coming back to person to person contacts and networking, particularly but not always at top management level: between companies, within companies, and between companies and other public or voluntary agencies.

Fogart, M. and Christie, I. (1990)[29]

Eli Lilly achieve this by concentrating the bulk of their corporate community investment in education and community development (Figure 13.3). In recent years this has meant substantial support for educational grants especially research facilities in universities in Indianapolis. This notion of reinvesting in basically strong areas mirrors the way firms maintain their core business while exploring opportunities to make a contribution elsewhere.

The twin themes of welfare and corporate action determine the pattern of Lilly's corporate giving. Great Western Enterprise based in the Swindon area of Britain concentrates its efforts on ensuring the continued, competitive success of this area. The value of preparation was illustrated when Swindon was affected by the economic downturn of the early 1990s. The networks and systems existed already. They could be deployed to the new threats of contraction and slowdown. Allied Dunbar played a lead role in these developments in part because of the vision of the company founder but the firm has consistently gained from the strong sense of involvement – volunteering – among its workforce.

Some trusts, such as the Baring Foundation change the balance of their activities quite significantly over time (Table 13.2). Over the five years covered

Table 13.2 The Baring Foundation: funding allocation over a five-year period

	1989 £1'000	%	1988 £'000	%	1987 £'000	%	1986 £'000	%	1985 £'000	%
Arts	300	6.8	296	7.9	270	10.3	306	17.0	68	5.3
Church/Religion	27	0.6	22	0.6	39	1.5	17	1.0	19	1.5
Conservation	292	6.6	258	6.9	209	8.0	178	9.9	119	9.2
Education	565	12.8	443	11.8	252	9.6	223	12.4	140	10.8
International	335	7.5	393	10.5	252	9.6	124	6.9	166	12.9
Medicine	514	11.6	519	13.8	501	19.1	233	12.9	271	21.0
Social Welfare	2,283	51.5	1,708	45.6	1,043	39.8	650	36.1	422	32.6
Miscellaneous	97	2.2	67	1.8	21	0.8	26	1.4	8	0.6
Youth	16	0.4	43	1.1	34	1.3	43	2.4	80	6.1
Total	4,429	100.0	3,749	100.0	2,621	100.0	1,800	100.0	1,293	100.0

Source: Fitzherbert, L. and Forrester, S. (1992)[30]

by the figures in Table 13.2 support for social welfare and education dropped while expenditure on youth and international work increased.

IMPLICATIONS

Intervention to tackle the economic problems of communities has implications for most aspects of the firm's activities. At the most basic level, it shifts the strategic perspective of the firm from the immediate and self to the long term and others. It produces an emphasis on adding value while it brings out the interdependence between the firm and its community.[31] These affect the overall positioning of the company. Human resource policies are affected directly and indirectly.[32] The direct effects lie in the staff time deployed and the skills they learn.

CASE STUDY 13.1

A suitable case for development

Arthur Young in Glasgow (now part of Ernst and Young) used its link with the Graduate Enterprise at Stirling University programme as a key element in its training programme. Graduate Enterprise was developed to help recent graduates set up their own businesses. It encompassed all institutes of Higher Education in Scotland. It had won considerable support from government. Each year Arthur Young provided the co-ordinator for the course. This task involved liaison with all the universities, identifying potential participants, linking the course to wider business development activity and eventually managing the subsequent PR.

None of these activities were part of the normal activities of a young accountant in the Glasgow office. The links with Higher Education took the co-ordinator into the highest levels of universities and central institutions. Their different traditions and approaches came together into a unified scheme. The major sponsors, such as 3*is*, Ivory and Sime, Bank of Scotland, IBM, had to be kept involved and informed. The participants needed a range of support. Integrating and developing this partnership was an invaluable insight into networking. The government support took many forms. There were Secretaries of State with a personal interest like the Rt Hon. John McGregor and Lord Young and senior civil servants with budgets to manage. As the former co-ordinators moved up the firm the range of the experience and insight stood them in excellent stead.

The sense of individual or community worth built up through this type of work increases employee loyalty even during crises. Perhaps the most vivid recent illustration of this was the involvement of the Pilkington workforce in the battle to fight off the hostile bid from BTR. Many firms use their involvement in local economic activity as a feature in their resourcing and marketing policies. New businesses created in local communities can be suppliers or customers. The evolution of supplier development approaches in Britain and the USA are closely linked with the programmes of community development.[33]

The approach adopted by firms to community development evolves over time. There seems to be a corporate responsibility life cycle (Figure 13.4). In the early stages, companies are largely *reactive*. Problems occur, perhaps around plants or other facilities. Requests for help proliferate. Marketing and public relations concerns often dominate thinking at this stage. As the scale of activity increases, the firm's skill in dealing with specific issues increases. It can filter out those which are inconsistent with its goals or expertise. This is a time of constructive *response*. Logistics and operations play a vital role as company capacity to help is fitted to community needs for help. This skill often leads to a professional phase of development. Internal systems are improved and response turns to *initiation*. The underlying causes of the economic problems become the centre of attention. This

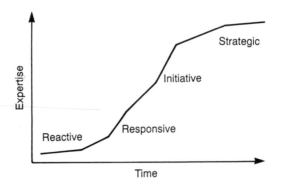

Fig. 13.4 The corporate responsibility life cycle

can lead to an emphasis on the training or education issues inside and outside the firm. At the mature stage, corporate responsibility policies have a powerful internal *strategy* and help shape the strategic positioning of the enterprise.

The UK is relatively underdeveloped in terms of firms with a strategic view of corporate responsibility. The research, training and development systems that convert a passing interest into a coherent and integrated feature of corporate activity are only slowly emerging. Ruth Johns[34] sounds a warning note when she observes: 'my unease at the long term effect of current practice is increased when the private conversation of some senior business people depicts a degree of cynicism about the community which belies much public rhetoric'. There are still relatively few firms in Britain or Europe that have maintained this commitment through several generations of managers.[35] Many of these are the larger *family* type companies where a different culture has been shaped. The continued importance of the Cadburys, Seiffs, Whitbreads, Laings, Pilkingtons is a cause for pleasure when they are surrounded by the new entrepreneurial or managerial groups.

There is nothing wrong with paternalism if it is fair, open and benign.

Seiff, M. (1990)[36]

It is cause for concern when they carry the torch alone through several generations. It poses special problems in local economic development. In part, this is because their traditions incline them to back programmes where the firm or family has a direct involvement – the Cadburys in Birmingham, the Pilkingtons in Lancashire.[37] Analysis of the expenditure of the major trusts[38] indicates the extent to which they are directed (Figure 13.5). Over one in five have a commitment to invest their funds in specific locations, e.g. The Cripplegate Foundation for Social Welfare in Cripplegate in Islington (London), or particular religious groups. In economic development, there is another concern. Many of the communities under pressure have been disappointed before. Deprived regions and inner city communities have seen Macmillan's relocation of industry, Wilson's reconstruction, Benn's co-operatives and now local enterprise. Each

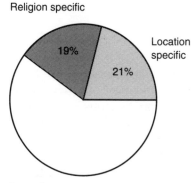

Fig. 13.5 The direction of grants

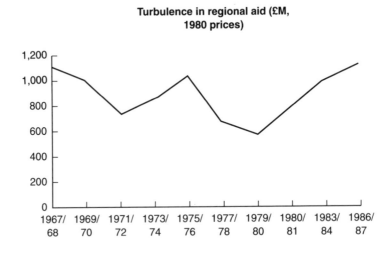

Turbulence in regional aid (£M, 1980 prices)

Fig. 13.6 Changes in regional aid
Sources: Economic Trends, National Income and Expenditure, Inland Revenue, Various Public Expenditure White Papers

failure makes the next external effort harder and internal confidence more difficult to find. Efforts by government to use monetary or fiscal measures to stimulate local or regional economic growth go back to the mid 1930s (Figure 13.6). Development Areas, Grey Areas, Special Development Areas have co-existed with controls through Industrial Development Certificates (IDCs), incentives by Investment Grants, variable schemes like regional employments and others to push, encourage or force growth. Overall, their effect has been unspectacular.[39] The Highlands and Islands of Scotland have an even longer history. A visit to the Western Isles sees monuments to intervention going back further than Lord Lever's efforts in the early part of this century. Sustained effort backed by significant resources targeted on the needs of the community are now required.

TARGETING

Different local communities have needs which are specific to their particular situation and the nature of the challenge they face. It is possible to look at the primary tools of intervention in terms of the classification of communities identified earlier: high stress, structurally disadvantaged, crisis zones, transitional areas and economic engines. The importance of a particular instrument will vary considerably (Table 13.3). Symbols of support are very important to a high stress area. Neglect, alienation and frustration can only be addressed if there is clear, public evidence that the community matters and the support is genuine. These

Table 13.3 The local enterprise checklist

	High stress	Structurally disadvantaged	Crisis zones	Transitional areas	Economic engines
Symbols of support	High	Medium	High	Medium	Low
Concentrated injections of new resources	High	Medium	High	Low	Low
New businesses	Medium	High	High	High	Medium
Technology	Low	High	Medium	High	High
Basic education	High	Low	Low	Medium	Low
Job links	High	High	Medium	High	Medium
Affirmative action	High	Low	Low	Medium	Medium
Training	Medium	High	High	High	Medium
Further education	Medium	High	Medium	High	Medium
Higher education	Low	High	Low	High	High
Research and technology transfer	Low	Medium	Medium	High	High
Partnering	High	High	High	Medium	Medium
Local venture finance	Low	High	High	Medium	Low
Security	High	Medium	High	Medium	Medium

symbols are less important to an economic engine. In contrast, the sustained and high-quality research allied to effective technology transfer is vital to the performance of an economic engine. The capacity exists to respond but knowledge is, increasingly, the main fuel.

REGIONAL DISTORTIONS

Even in a relatively small, concentrated country like Britain there are wide regional distortions in population, wealth and business ownership. London and the South East do relatively well while areas like the North and Scotland perform badly (Table 13.4). This calls for corporate interventions which reflect the diversity of communities and their varied needs. In Scotland a range of initiatives have emerged which reflect this agenda.

One hundred years ago, as the world faced the challenges of the 'Great Recession' of the 1880s few countries appeared more able to cope with the difficulties posed by this downturn than Scotland. The industrial base appeared secure and balanced. The heavy industries of Glasgow were counterbalanced by the powerful financial sector of Edinburgh. Although the textile industry faced growing competition, burgeoning electronics and chemicals industries seemed able to provide a vehicle for future economic prosperity. In contrast to the rest of the UK (and much of Europe).

Table 13.4 The regional distribution of population and wealth

Region	Population 1990 (million)	(%)	GDP 1990 (£billion)	(%)
North	3.1	5.4	22.2	4.7
Yorks and Humberside	5.0	8.6	37.4	8.0
East Midlands	4.0	7.0	32.3	6.9
East Anglia	2.1	3.6	17.3	3.7
London and South East	17.5	30.4	169.3	36.0
South West	4.7	8.1	36.3	7.7
West Midlands	5.2	9.1	39.7	8.4
North West	6.4	11.1	47.4	10.1
Wales	2.9	5.0	20.0	4.3
Scotland	5.1	8.9	38.7	8.2
England	47.8	83.3	402.2	85.4
Northern Ireland	1.6	2.8	9.8	2.1

The Scottish limited companies appear to have been smaller, to have enjoyed a more lengthy existence, to have been less bedevilled by fraud, ignorance and gross mismanagement and to have been controlled by their founders a little longer, than their English counterparts; and they probably produced a marginally higher net return to their shareholders.

Payne, P. (1983)[40]

Despite these apparent strengths a century later, the decline was such that

Consistently poor growth performance has resulted in Scotland slipping gradually into the economic backwater of Europe. It now lags behind the major EC countries to such an extent that it is considered one of the poorest regions of Europe, and as such, is eligible for many forms of EC regional assistance.

Bell, P. (1982)[41]

By the late 1970s traditional industries such as engineering, shipbuilding and textiles had declined while new sectors were increasingly dependent on foreign-based firms. The decline affected virtually every sector of Scottish economic life.

The extent and pace of this is more remarkable given two specific assets which are seen to be critical to modern economic success.

1   A strong, autonomous financial sector.
2   Abundant energy resources.

The financial sector is large, ranking second in the UK. In energy sources, the decline in mining over the last 20 years contrasts with the growth of the North Sea oil industry. Despite the importance of this sector it is clear that the multiplier effect, i.e. the influence on other parts of the economy, has been far less than originally hoped. The failure of either this 'windfall' or the traditionally strong finance sector to arrest the pattern of decline required policy-makers to look at other aspects of Scotland's economic life. This is the challenge faced by the business and other agencies seeking a long-term and self-sustaining solution to decline. Even during periods of relative economic growth, new business formation rates were low. These deteriorated even further during the 1950s, 1960s and 1970s. There has been a burgeoning consensus that significant increases in the levels of self-employment, and growth in the rate of new business formation allied to reductions in the levels of industrial risk are central to revitalising an economy. In endorsing this overall policy, government emphasised their rejection of statist, centralist solutions. Devolved partnership-based mechanisms were required. These used local networks developed with business leaders to create local solutions.

Scottish Enterprise and the Highlands and Islands Enterprise are the primary statutory agencies in Scotland. They perform a diverse array of roles in supporting the development of enterprise. Besides providing an 'umbrella' for other organisations they provide financial and direct support services in a variety of situations and see as a primary goal mobilising business support for wealth creation. Two initiatives provide some insight into the potential contribution of these agencies. The Scottish Enterprise's programme of concentrated initiatives in relatively limited areas called 'Local Area Initiatives' are designed to inject sufficient resources to break the cycle of decline being experienced in these localities. These employ the resources and skills of Local Enterprise Companies (LECs) to widen the levels of participation especially business. Highland Enterprise sponsored Community Co-Operatives seek to bring together local needs. They have shown themselves able to combine the resources of the board with local funds and commitment. This is indicating the value of these mutually supportive relationships.

The early 1980s saw major new factors introduced onto the array of support agencies. Many reflect the determination of private enterprise to work with public agencies in two key areas. Most sought to tackle local problems by mobilising local resources. Scottish Business in The Community (SCOTBIC) seeks to mobilise the resources of the private sector to tackle the problems of the communities in which they operate. SCOTBIC has been instrumental in creating over 40 local enterprise agencies in Scotland. These serve many functions but primarily exist to aid new or small firms by tapping into the resources of larger firms. The extent of their current activities are now remarkable: with over 20,000 client contacts per year; high rates of start up and relatively low rates of failure. In all this the private sector is taking the lead and providing the key resources. The diverse nature of this contribution can be seen in two illustrations.

CASE STUDY 13.2

STirling Enterprise Park (STEP)

In 1982 a major employer in Stirling closed its manufacturing unit. At the time it employed almost 500 workers. It decided to invest resources in the future of the community it was leaving. This involved donating the factory and its lands to the local community, paying for its conversion to small factory units (40 in all), funding a detailed research study of skills and needs as well as paying for the management team to develop the facility. This cost approximately $2 million. Within five years the complex employed almost 600 people.

CASE STUDY 13.3

Glasgow Opportunity (GO)

The second case is drawn from the much larger city of Glasgow. Here an organisation was created by firms as diverse as IBM and the local soccer club – Rangers – to tackle the massive problems of decline in the city. Most of these firms provide secondees to work for periods of up to three years in this Enterprise agency – Glasgow Opportunity.

These agencies and SCOTBIC seek to support the entrepreneurial spirit through a strategic combination of private and public sector resources. The pace of this development illustrates the continuing power of the move to promote enterprise in Scotland.

CONCLUSION

Economic change poses a host of problems to communities. Some have the resources and capabilities to overcome setbacks and develop organically. Others require external support of the more effective mobilisation of internal resources. The opportunity exists under these conditions for industry to perform a leadership role while reinforcing its own commercial position. The more that industry adopts this role, the less likely it is that the state will feel obliged to intervene to deploy resources raised from industry to meet the needs of its disadvantaged communities. During the late 1970s and 1980s the steady withdrawal of the state from the more extensive forms of intervention created a gap for industry to show its capacity to integrate the first part of its economic function – the management of exchanges – with the second part of its economic function – the creation of wealth. The implicit economic contract in any community is that these roles will go together. Smith[42] highlighted the problems of mere mercantilism while Schumpeter[43] drew out the essential contribution of enterprise and innovation to the dynamics which underpin capitalism. The disadvantaged local communities in our society are the proving ground of these propositions.

QUESTIONS

1 Explain why corporate involvement in tackling the problems of local communities grew during the 1980s.

2 The different types of economically challenged communities require different approaches to their problems. Outline the differences between these communities and indicate the ways industry can play a part in tackling the difficulties of two distinct types of community.

3 Use the success matrix to analyse the approach of three different firms of your choice.

4 Strategy is as important for effective corporate responsibility as for any other aspect of a firm's activities. Explain the role of strategy and draw out a comparison between corporate responsibility and any other aspect of business with which you are familiar.

5 Why has 'culture gap' been such an important factor in the history of failed initiatives in areas such as Moss Side, Manchester?

6 Outline the corporate responsibility life cycle, indicate and illustrate how the response of firms changes over time as their position on the life cycle evolves.

7 Do you share the concern expressed by Ruth Johns in her comment 'my unease at the long-term effect of current practice is increased when the private conservation of managers . . . belies much public rhetoric'? Explain the cause of this disquiet and the implication of these concerns. Outline ways in which these worries might be resolved.

8 Examine the contribution of local enterprise agencies in local economic development. Draw out and illustrate their potential contribution and the limitations on the work they can perform.

9 Describe the role of Training and Enterprise Councils, use information gathered from the annual reports of at least three TECs to indicate the extent to which they are true partnerships between the public and private sectors.

10 Define:

(a) Command economy	(f) One Per Cent Club
(b) Crisis zones	(g) Regional aid
(c) Chaser	(h) Multiplier effect
(d) Environmental fit	(i) TECs
(e) Champions	(j) LECs

REFERENCES

1. Eisinger, P. K. *The Rise of the Entrepreneurial State*, Madison, University of Wisconsin Press (1988).
2. Business in the Cities *Leadership in the Community*, London, Coopers & Lybrand (1989).
3. HMSO *Policy for the Inner Cities*, cmnd 6850, London (1977).
4. Berger, R. 'Partnership's in the US' *Action Line*, Winter (1988).
5. Jennings, M. *The Guide to Good Corporate Citizenship*, Cambridge, Director Books (1989).
6. Osborne, D. and Gaebler, T. *Reinventing Government*, Harmondsworth, Penguin (1992).
7. Doyle, D. P. and Keavins, D. T. *Winning the Brain Race: A Bold Plan to Make Our Schools Competitive*, New York, ICS Press (1988).
8. Business in The Community, *Agenda for Action*, London, BITC (1990).
9. Drucker, P. *Managing for Results*, Oxford, Heinemann (1964).
10. Hammarkvist, K. O. *Markets as Networks*, Marketing Education Group, Annual Conference, Cranfield (1983).
11. Cannon, T. *Basic Marketing*, London, Cassell (1992).
12. Rothwell, R. 'Innovation and Re-Innovation: The Role of the User' *Journal of Marketing Management*, vol. 12 (1986) pp. 109–23.
13. Boston Consulting Group *Perspectives on Experience*, Boston (1968).
14. Priestley, J. B. *An English Journey*, London, William Heinemann (1934).
15. Johnson, G. and Scholes, K. *Exploring Corporate Strategy*, London, Prentice Hall (1988).
16. Task Force on Corporate Social Performance *Business and Society*, Washington, US Department of Commerce (1980).
17. Logan, D. *US Corporate Grantmaking in a Global Age*, Washington, Council on Foundations (1989).
18. Johns, R. L. *Company Community Involvement in the UK*, Warwick, Mimeo (1991).
19. Lynn, M. 'Bob Clarke' *Management Today*, April (1992).
20. Chetwood, P. et al. *UK Corporate Giving in the 1990s: An International and Empirical Study*, Manchester, Manchester University Business School (1991).
21. Task Force on Corporate Responsibility, ibid.
22. Christie, I., Carley, M., Fogarty, M. and Legard, R. *Profitable Partnerships*, London, Policy Studies Institute (1991). This extract is reproduced with the permission of the Controller of HMSO.
23. Peters, T. and Waterman, R. *In Search of Excellence*, London, Harper and Row (1982).
24. Riker, H. A. and Roetter, M. F. 'The New Business Topography' *Prism*, December (1990).
25. Thatcher, M. *Companies Committed to the Community*, speech to the One Per Cent Club Annual Meeting, London, RSA (1988).
26. Much of this discussion is based on Christie, I., *et al.*, ibid.
27. Salamon, L. M. (ed.) *Beyond Privatisation: The Tools of Government Action*, Washington D.C., Urban Institute Press (1989).
28. Moore, C. M. (ed.) *The Colourful Quilt*, Indianapolis, NACLO (1988).
29. Fogart, M. and Christie, I. *Companies and Communities: Promoting Business Involvement in the Community*, London, Policy Studies Institute (1990).
30. Fitzherbert, L. and Forrester, S. *A Guide to the Major Trusts* Directory of Social Change, London (1992). A current edition of the Guide is available.
31. Council on the Foundations *The Climate for Giving*, Washington, Council on the Foundations (1988).
32. Rion, M. *The Responsible Manager*, San Francisco, Harper and Row (1990).
33. Rogers, T. G. P. 'Partnership with Society: The Social Responsibility of Business' *Management Decisions*, 25, vol. 2 (1987) pp. 76–80.
34. Johns, R. *Corporate Community Involvement in the UK*, Mimeo, Warwick (1991).
35. Zahra, S. A. 'Boards of Directors and Corporate Social Responsibility' *European Management Journal*, vol. 7, no. 2 (1989) pp. 240–7.
36. Seiff, M. 'Good Human Relations' *Independent*, 23 May (1990).
37. Barker, T. C. *The Glassmakers*, Weidenfeld and Nicholson, London (1977).
38. Fitzherbert, L. and Forrester, S., ibid.
39. Brittan, S. *Steering the Economy*, London, Macmillan (1969).

40. Payne, P. L. *The Early Scottish Limited Companies 1856–1895: An Historical and Analytical Survey*, Scottish Academic Press (1983).
41. Bell, P. 'Trends in Scottish Industry', in Hood, N. and Young, S. *Industry, Policy and the Scottish Economy*, Edinburgh University Press (1982).
42. Smith, A. *The Wealth of Nations* (1736).
43. Schumpeter, J. *Business Cycles: A Theoretical, Historical and Statistical Analysis*, New York, McGraw Hill (1939).

CHAPTER 14

Fairness in the workplace: issues, opportunities, affirmative action and positive discrimination

Some of the most complex problems facing organisations today centre on the nature and composition of the workforce. To be more exact, they revolve around the opportunities provided within industry and commerce for the different members of the community. The debate on these opportunities goes to the heart of the corporation's responsibilities to the community. The licence to perform the economic function is granted by society on the assumption that all its members will have a comparable if not equal chance to benefit from the performance of this function.

> What deregulation has achieved in the US is the creation of vast numbers of low-paid and frequently part-time jobs in the service sector – which have become the preserve of women. Unskilled American men would rather 'work' in the escalating black economy of drugs and street crime, where the rewards are higher and the image more 'manly', than in unskilled, low-paid service-sector employment.
>
> The other side of America's jobs miracle is the way prison incarceration has been concentrated among the uneducated caught in the black economy. In 1986, 26 per cent of black male drop-outs were in prison.
>
> In fact, if the numbers of adult men aged between 25 and 54 who declare themselves economically inactive are added back into the unemployment statistics, the relationship between low social cost and low unemployment beloved of the new right breaks down completely.
>
> The average US unemployment rate over the 1980s of some 5 per cent more than doubles to over 12 per cent, while France and Germany, the targets of new-right opprobrium have comparable rates of 9 per cent and 12 per cent, and the combined rate of the unemployed and non-employed in the deregulated UK is, at just under 15 per cent, second only to regulated Spain.
>
> Source: Hutton, W. (1993)[1]

In the USA this theme recurs in the literature on corporate responsibility. ARCO annually 'reviews the equal employment performance of each of ARCO's ten operating companies'.[2] Levi Strauss have a public commitmen people without regard to race, religion, color, sex, age, national origi or sexual preference'.[3] IBM place equality of opportunity at the core (values.[4] Control Data sought to help the deprived because it 'benefits i enlarging the pool of skilled dependable workers'.[5] In part, this reflects pressures placed on firms by government legislation and affirmative action programmes, community protest and an external climate of opinion that emphasises opportunity.[6]

CASE STUDY 14.1

Affirmative action at Cornell

High school records and standardised tests began to be criticised as insufficient guides to real talent. But the goal was unchanged – to educate black students as any student is educated and to evaluate them according to the same standards. Everyone was still integrationist. The belief was that insufficient energy had been devoted to the recruitment of talented black students. Cornell, where I taught for several years, was one of many institutions that announced great increases in goals for enrolment of blacks. The president, adding a characteristic twist, also announced that not only would it seek blacks, but that it would find them not among privileged blacks but in the inner cities. At the beginning of the 1967 academic year there were many more blacks on campus and, of course, in order to get so many, particularly poor blacks, standards of admission had silently and drastically been altered. Nothing had been done to prepare these students for the great intellectual and social challenges awaiting them in the university. Cornell now had a large number of students who were manifestly unqualified and unprepared, and therefore it faced an inevitable choice: fail most of them or pass them without their having learned. Moralism and press relations made the former intolerable; the latter was only partially possible (it required consenting faculty and employers after college who expected and would accept incompetence) and was unbearably shameful to black students and university alike. It really meant that blacks would be recognisably second-class citizens.

Source: Bloom, A. (1988)[7]

The individual commitment of corporate leaders has played an important role in shaping this agenda in North America. Some features of the same process appear to be emerging in Britain today. There is deep suspicion of the type of affirmative action or positive discrimination programmes seen in the USA but some business leaders have highlighted the problems associated with passive or reactive approaches. Positive discrimination means discriminating in favour of certain groups in order to ensure that they constitute a stated proportion of the workforce. Affirmative action involves introducing measures to make it easier for specified groups to enter a workforce with discriminating in favour of this or against others. A form of positive discrimination is legislation which might require (in the USA) the Federal Contract Compliance Office to check that suppliers have a workforce with a minimum number of blacks, hispanics, etc. An affirmative action programme could include efforts to ensure that job advertisements are placed in media which reach all members of a community – even those who do not read conventional media.

Mr John Moores of Littlewoods is among a growing band of British business leaders who are striving to convert the wish to attack disadvantage into action.

CASE STUDY 14.2

A simple case of prejudice

Mr John Moores of Littlewoods tells a story of his education in social disadvantage. Littlewoods is Britain's largest private company. The Moores family have built it into a leisure and retailing group with a turnover of over £2 billion and profits in 1992 of almost £100 million. It is based in Liverpool with a headquarters building overlooking the Mersey. Their roots are deep in this community. Not surprisingly, the Toxteth riots shocked the company's leadership, especially members of the family. Mr John Moores was among the corporate leaders who visited Toxteth shortly after the riots. He talked to members of the minority communities to try to understand their bitterness and resentment.

He was struck by one comment. This was that the main shopping street in Liverpool was virtually segregated. African Caribbean people never shopped there. In part, it was explained that this merely reflected the total failure of any members of the minority communities to get jobs in the shops. The largest store on the street was owned by Littlewoods. Mr John was not aware that a virtual colour bar was in place. In the great tradition of entrepreneurs he and his father, Sir John Moores, decided to tackle the problem immediately. The next half dozen jobs in the store on Church Street were to be given to members of ethnic minorities. Several weeks later, knowing that these jobs had been filled he visited the store. He was surprised that he could not see any of the new staff. On enquiring, he was told that all had been set to work in the storerooms!!!

Before simply ordering the manager to give them front-of-house jobs, he decided to think the firm's policies through. He and his father realised that a sea change in attitudes could not be achieved through orders from the top. The only way forward lay in fully worked out programmes backed by training and development. Over the succeeding years, the firm has made huge strides. An affirmative action programme is in place. It is owned by the managers and workers who are responsible for implementation.

The Littlewoods story is slowly being replicated across the private sector. The details vary but the basic steps are common:

- Acknowledge the existence of the problem;
- Analyse its nature and causes;
- Break down the barriers;
- Initiate staff development programmes;
- Create opportunities;
- Adopt – where necessary – affirmative action;
- Establish standards and measure performance against these targets;
- Communicate progress.

THE NATURE AND SCALE OF THE ISSUE

Three groups face special problems in realising their true potential in Britain today: women, ethnic minorities and the disabled. This breakdown does not ignore the difficulties faced by other communities, e.g. the Irish, but policies to tackle problems of gender, race and physical disability will hold the key to success for other communities. These groups together constitute a clear majority of the potential labour force in any nation. Conscious or unconscious impediments to them benefiting from the opportunities created by industry are a clear breakdown of the contract between industry and the community.[8]

Women easily make up the largest of these groups. Since the late 1970s the female share of employment has risen in all sectors of the labour market with the exception of operatives and labourers.[9] In 1987, over 9 million women were employed in Britain; 5.1 million in full-time jobs and 4.4 million in part-time jobs. This sharply contrasts with the pattern of male employment. Among men, over 90 per cent of the labour force are in full-time employment. Research[10,11,12] into the nature and character of female employment has highlighted other sharp differences in the nature and quality of their work experience. Women work overwhelmingly within a narrow range of industrial sectors and within specific occupational groupings. Their working lives differ substantially from their male counterparts.[13] They are likely to spend far more time in involuntary unemployment. They have more enforced job changes. Women find it hard to win jobs after a break in work. Their chances of finding work deteriorate far more sharply than those of men in late middle age. Their job security is less. Average pay rates are roughly 70 per cent of those for men working in the same job groups. Women are concentrated in the secondary labour market.[14] This 'is characterised by low-paid, insecure occupations, offering poor working conditions'.[15] A broadly similar pattern can be seen across Europe.[16] Women now account for the majority of the labour force but only 52 per cent are in full-time employment which compares with 83 per cent for men. Although higher educated women do better than their less well educated peers, education does little to close the gap on the male colleagues. Some groups are especially disadvantaged, notably single parents. Some estimates put the rate of unemployment among female single parents two or three times higher than male single parents.

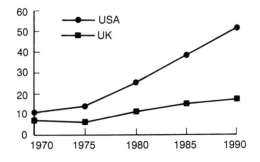

Fig. 14.1 MBA participation rates in Britain and the USA

The pattern has not changed significantly over the recent past. Women now spend more of their potential working lives in paid employment and the trend is towards even greater participation. But their employment profile has not changed.[17] Women still tend to hold low-paid, unskilled or semi-skilled positions.[18] Employment is largely part-time and concentrated in the service sector.[19] In the 20 years between the mid 1960s and the mid 1980s the bulk of female employment stayed concentrated in the junior, non-manual grades. The proportion of women in managerial positions remained stuck at roughly 5 per cent. Even here, the glass ceiling effect – they could see but not touch the top[20] – dominated their career aspirations. Training opportunities are restricted. Participation of women managers in executive training is low. The numbers on MBA and equivalent programmes is far lower than in the USA (Figure 14.1). There is some recent evidence of greater convergence[21] but women are still more likely to attend part-time courses and pay their own fees.

The difficulties facing ethnic minorities are made more complex by wide regional and local variations and significant differences between ethnic groups. The concentration of many members of the minority communities in inner city areas allied to the low skill base makes them extremely vulnerable to changes in the economic climate. There are myths which distort attempts to tackle some of the problems. Among the more pernicious is the belief that the problems are concentrated in the African Caribbean community. Although this group faces the most severe difficulties, the levels of employment, types of work and wage rates in the Asian community are broadly similar. The labour force survey found that in the mid 1980s 'the weekly gross earnings for white men was £129 compared with £109.2 for those of West Indian origin and £110.7 for those of Asian origin. This difference in earnings has hardly changed during the last fifteen years'.[22] Among certain groups, the disparities are even greater. Young, black people are four times more likely to be unemployed than their white compatriots.[23]

Education, training and development opportunities are similarly restricted. Average terminal education ages are lower. Participation in external and internal training programmes is poor. There is some evidence that employers are less likely to nominate members of ethnic minorities to external training courses than members of the majority community. Higher education participation rates are low with even smaller proportions taking part in MBA or comparable programmes. The numbers reaching senior or middle management programmes is dismal. The public commitment of government expressed in its backing for the Commission for Racial Equality and Race Relations legislation defines the contract with industry. There is some way to go before it is fully implemented.[24]

Information on career opportunities for the disabled is poor. The available material indicates a picture of poor employment prospects, inadequate training and serious problems of access and support. The notion that disability should not equal disadvantage has entered the lexicon of US usage but has made little progress in Europe. Government schemes are characterised by low wage rates which seem to be repeated in the commercial environment. Estimates of rates of unemployment vary between 40 and 60 per cent. Few enter management. Many workplaces have inadequate facilities while ramps and other basic provisions are poor in most industrial and commercial environments.

The type of broad brush commitment to equality of opportunity *without regard to race, religion, colour, sex, age, national origin, handicap or sexual preference* is emerging in Britain. The promise raises important issues of implementation and delivery in the responsible corporation. The type of scenario described by John Moores indicates that it is not enough, simply, to not knowingly discriminate. There was no formal colour bar at Littlewoods. Top management were shocked to be told of the situation in their stores. The challenge they face is to take action to implement their beliefs.[25] Many British firms have now formally endorsed the UK government's Ten Point Plan on equal opportunities (Table 14.1).

RECOGNITION

Awareness is the essential prerequisite of managerial action. Many executives or recruits do not see the patterns of discrimination that emerge from the series of specific transactions which make up their working life. In the USA and among those firms which have made significant progress, information is the vital first step to action. Sawyers[26] found that an unrelated decision can have profound effects on employment prospects. The introduction of electronic point-of-sale equipment in food retailing eliminated the need for a level of supervisory management in larger outlets. This provided a key element in the savings and improvements in operations which justified the investment in the new technology. It was, however, the first step on the promotional ladder for women operatives. For many, it provided the transition from part- to full-time employment. The vital, first step on the ladder to career progress was eliminated with no alternative introduced. Information and monitoring of results is a key element in tackling inequalities in the workplace.

Table 14.1   The UK government's ten point plan for equal opportunity

1	Develop an equal opportunities policy, embracing recruitment, promotion and training.
2	Set an action plan including targets, so that staff have a clear idea of what can be achieved and by when.
3	Provide training for all staff to help people including management, throughout the organisation, to understand the importance of equal opportunities, with additional training for staff who recruit, select and train employees.
4	Monitor the present position to establish the starting point and monitor progress towards objectives to identify successes and shortfalls.
5	Review recruitment, selection, promotion and training procedures regularly, to ensure good intentions are put into practice.
6	Draw up clear and justifiable job criteria and ensure they are objective and job-related.
7	Offer pre-employment training, where appropriate, to prepare potential job applicants for selection tests and interviews and positive action training to help underrepresented groups.
8	Consider the company's image within the community to see whether it encourages applications from underrepresented groups, and feature women, ethnic minority staff and people with disabilities in recruitment literature to ensure the company is not seen as an employer that marginalises these groups.
9	Consider flexible working, career breaks, provision of childcare facilities and so on to help women in particular meet domestic responsibilities and pursue their occupations; and the provision of special equipment and assistance to help people with disabilities.
10	Develop links with local community groups, organisations and schools to reach a wider pool of potential recruits.

Source: Clutterback, D. (1992)[27]

Analysis of existing practices is equally important. The consequences of some employment and recruitment traditions are prejudicial to notions of fairness and equity. In public agencies this is best seen in the *grapevine* recruitment approach adopted to fill key posts.

CASE STUDY 14.3

Irony or hypocrisy on the campus

The Charters and Statutes of most British universities contain an implicit or explicit statement of commitment to equal opportunities. The guardian of these standards in most cases is the vice chancellor. The appointments of these officers in many – if not most cases – run counter to most basic principles of equality of opportunity. The post of vice chancellor is usually advertised in the conventional academic media. Some will appear in more widely read sources. In practice, this formal process is largely symbolic. The conventional assumption was spelled out by the professor at one university who commented: 'we advertise to find out who we do not want'. Even the formal closing date is not used in any structured or formal way. It might be used to schedule a meeting of the appointment's committee at which the respondents to the advertisement are examined 'to set a bench-mark' for the serious candidates.

At that point, the search starts in earnest. It concentrates on two sources; the external nominations from community leaders and the networks or contacts of committee members. Inevitably, these reflect the white, male, traditional communities from which the existing leadership groups are drawn and which dominate the appointment boards. The controls which exist in the private sector or other parts of the public sector – transparency, structure or external, e.g. shareholder control – are absent. It means that – at the time of writing – every vice chancellor but one fits into the white, male stereotype.[28]

The sources of bias in the recruitment or development process can be diagnosed on this basis.[29] Often they are associated with the pool of applicants. In the case of the vice chancellors in the case study, a white male pool of potential candidates will produce white male candidates. Similar biases can be discerned in the formal media. Readership profiles will indicate the likely pattern of respondents. Women suffer from the bias in newspapers towards a male readership. Magazines are used less often by recruiters because of time lags and costs. Ethnic minorities and other disadvantaged groups are even worse served by the media. In the USA, some organisations have adopted a pool of candidates approach to appointments. In effect, this means they continue advertising until a shortlist is constructed which reflects the balance sort. This avoids some of the problems of attempts to impose a balance of appointments from unbalanced shortlists. This reflects the first stage in a process of tackling unfairness which has evolved along several routes over the last 30 years.[30]

STRATEGIES FOR IMPROVEMENT

Perhaps the key lesson from those communities which have initiated major programmes to address unfairness is that passive measures are largely ineffective. The decision to be unprejudiced only works when a delivery system is employed to back this up. A legal framework exists across Europe and in the USA which creates a backcloth for corporate action.

In Europe the Social Charter provides important provisions on the rights of women, minorities and the disabled (Table 14.2). In North America efforts to tackle problems of discrimination have taken more directive forms. Two features of this have been subject to widespread debate; positive discrimination and

Table 14.2 European Community Directives on equal opportunities for women

Council Directive of 10 Feb 1975	Established the principle of equal pay for men and women
Council Directive of 9 February 1976	Established principle of equal treatment for men and women as regards to access to employment, vocational training and promotion and working conditions
Council Directive of 19 December 1978	Confirms principle of equal treatment for men and women on matters of social security
Council Directive of 24 July 1986	Establishes principle of equal treatment for men and women on matters of occupational pension schemes
Council Directive of 11 December 1988	Established principle of equal treatment for men and women who are self-employed

contract compliance. Along with affirmative action these are the main strands of corporate action to deliver fairness in the workplace.

Affirmative action

Affirmative action programmes are designed to endorse the company's support for a fair workplace. They take many forms from simple endorsement of a principle with little or no follow up, to actions which reinforce the company's commitment. In the former, there are bland statements of the '**** is an equal opportunity employer' to schemes which set managers targets for recruitment and promotion. The latter might involve advertising for recruits in media which give a balance of candidates. Some employers introduce clear signals to disadvantaged groups of the type 'we are especially keen to hear from women returners' or 'crèche facilities are provided to assist female workers' or 'disabled facilities are available'. The prominence given to these gives a clear indication of the values of the firm. In some communities groups of companies collaborate to provide opportunities for members of disadvantaged communities. In Manchester a consortium of firms have collaborated to provide job opportunities for people from certain communities.

Affirmative action programmes can play an even more important part in the daily operations of the firm. Nominations to training schemes, executive development programmes and promotion panels can play a central role in the attempt by the firm to establish a fairness agenda. The image the company projects is part of this. Corporate literature which fits into stereotypes reinforces images (Table 14.3).

Affirmative action programmes rely on a sustained effort to change the image and character of the firm by persuasion and development.

Table 14.3 Images of reality

Medium	Number of people	Ethnic minorities
Company annual report	64	8
Corporate magazine	16	0
Research Council annual report	25	10
Public authority annual report	27	8
Business magazine	53	3
University annual report	98	6*

*Including the equal opportunities officer and the participants at an international society function.

Contract compliance

Contract compliance seeks to tackle unfairness by discriminating in favour of enterprises which achieve specific targets in terms of employment and recruitment. In the USA, many government contracts are only given to firms which satisfy specified equal opportunities requirements. Other contracts require that suppliers must be, or use, firms owned by women, minorities, disabled, veterans, etc. Contract compliance is seen by many as 'a very important factor, both in terms of sending a strong signal to the employer community and by enabling government to set the pace for change'.[31] The early resistance to contract compliance in the USA has declined.

> The overall reaction of US employers is currently deemed to be positive and supportive of contract compliance procedures.
>
> McEwan, W. (1986)[32]

The move towards compliance requirements in the UK has gathered strength partly as a result of US experience and the apparent success of the small initiatives in contract compliance that have taken place in the UK.

Positive discrimination

Positive discrimination provokes far more controversy. The core argument in favour is that certain groups face such immense difficulties that discrimination in their favour is the only effective means to redress the balance. *Set asides* and *quotas* are used to ensure that minimum numbers of members of the disadvantaged communities are given specific types of jobs. It has been condemned for forcing employers to introduce new features of unfairness into their business practice.[33]

After reviewing several applicants, you are left with the two engineers you consider the

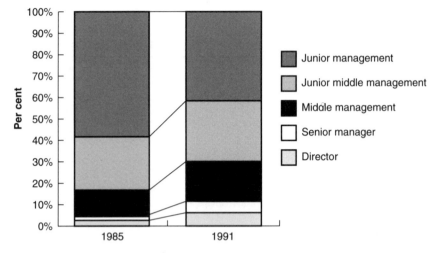

Fig. 14.2 Littlewoods: Women in management

best qualified, and you must make choice between them. One applicant is black, and the other is white. The only real distinguishing characteristic is their colour. Following the preferring hiring and promotion spirit that is implicit in law, you veer toward the black engineer. But is this fair to the equally well-qualified white applicant? Isn't this a case of compounding rather than correcting a social evil?

Tuleja, T. (1985)[34]

The scale of discrimination in Europe is increasing the pressure for a stronger line on positive discrimination. It is argued that the best way to avoid social enforcement is to pre-empt the need for action.

Littlewoods has made considerable progress in increasing the number of women in senior management positions (Figure 14.2). This progress reflects the commitment of top management to:

meet our legal and moral obligations; to utilise people's abilities to the full by removing artificial and irrelevant barriers to their recruitment and promotion; to draw from the widest possible pool of talent; to implement good management practice.

John Moores, Director and son of founder, quoted in Clutterbuck, D. (1992)[35]

THE WAY FORWARD

Badarocco[36] suggests that firms face five basic options in response to these types of pressures. These are: do nothing, exit, modify existing policies, try to dominate the political process or develop a politically negotiated outcome. Others like Yoffie[37] and Mahon[38] have developed a broadly similar analysis. There is no doubt that some firms prefer to do nothing until obliged by law. This makes them

Table 14.4 External support and internal need

	Age	Disability	Gender	Race	Sexual preference	Other
Consultancy						
Crisis Management						
Organisational Development						
Planning						
Training						
Troubleshooting						

Source: Directory of Equal Opportunity Consultants (1992)[39]

vulnerable to imposed laws which are worse than might occur with their participation. Exit is not a realistic option for large firm trading in major markets. The risks of attempts to dominate the political process are high. It is likely that the costs of dominance can be as high if not higher than the costs of compliance. For most firms the route forward is one of modification of existing policies, working towards a political outcome or some combination of both.

Once the nature of the problems faced by the firm are identified and a commitment to act is chosen, a change programme can be initiated. Breaking down barriers calls for a mixture of detailed staff work, external support and alliances (Table 14.4). The publication of *The Directory of Equal Opportunities Consultants*[40] identifies a range of organisations capable of providing this external support and staff work. These agencies have expertise in a range of areas.

External allies are especially important in developing effective programmes of actions. The Equal Opportunities Commission and The Commission for Racial Equality have built up a portfolio of case material and expertise to assist firms. There is an expanding network of firms in the UK like Littlewoods, Grand Metropolitan and NatWest Bank who have shaped programmes of development and support within their own organisations which provide valuable insights for others.[41]

Top management support is a critical element in the success of these schemes. They determine the credibility of the initiative besides ensuring that adequate resources are available. Clear line and staff responsibilities and ownership have played important roles in successful schemes elsewhere. In the USA, the external contract with the community is converted to an internal contract with employees. Managers are set targets and their performance measured and evaluated. Ownership of the outcomes by those involved ensures that local adaptations are introduced and initiative is used to tackle immediate difficulties. Communication of success is part of the ongoing process of endorsement and development of efforts to ensure a healthy and fair business community. This means avoiding the ghettoising of these programmes. Integration of this work into the main-stream of the company's business, human resource, sourcing, marketing, etc., policies is an integral part in the strategic redirection of firms.

CONCLUSION

Inequalities with communities have been addressed in many ways. The barriers and disadvantages facing women, minorities, the physically disabled and others are seen as unjust and a waste of scarce talent. The agenda of the ways in which firms can tackle these issues are part of the wider social and economic agenda today.

The contribution of top management is central to any attempt to shift attitudes in the firm on issues like discrimination and disadvantage. Robert Townsend[42] acknowledges that 'the vast majority of firms are still operating with dice loaded against Jews, Black people and women of all creeds . . . it is time to unload the dice. This has to start with a conviction in the chief executive officer'.

This is increasingly an integral part of the value change strategies introduced by firms that are determined to adapt the actions of their companies to new environments. Re-engineering is the catch-all phrase used to describe the process by which companies toss 'aside old systems and start over. It involves going back to the beginning and inventing a better way of doing work.'[43]

Rosabeth Moss Kanter[44] highlights an irony which is emerging as firms combine efforts to open up career opportunities with attempts to restructure their businesses.

Entrepreneurial opportunities for some coupled with longer professional service for others means that the bureaucratic career pattern applies to fewer and fewer people.

Of course, the bureaucratic career logic never applied to all corporate jobs; the career logic associated with jobs varies even within the same corporation. Companies provide career ladders for some jobs, but not for others; the length of ladders and the salary 'height' they reach can vary greatly. For example, product managers with MBAs may have a long progression of promotions ahead of them in some companies, but internal human resource consultants in those same firms may find that their entry and terminal positions are roughly the same, meaning few if any promotions. One of the major thrusts of equal employment opportunity programs for women and minorities is to eliminate this difference in bureaucratic opportunity – to generate career ladders for people at lower levels who were denied access to promotions because their jobs were not viewed as leading to other, 'higher' jobs. In large corporations as well as in the federal bureaucracy, upward mobility programs begun in the 1960s have indeed opened entry-level administrative positions to people. But there is an irony here. The proportion of lower-level managerial jobs filled internally began to increase at just the same time that many companies, like Kodak, started looking outside for top talent previously found only from within. Thus, there are more competitors for middle management jobs while the jobs themselves are scarcer and less likely to automatically lead to top management.

At the same time that traditional career ladders are being built at the bottom, the higher rungs are being lopped off. More people at lower levels have *theoretical* access to promotion while the *actual* number of slots 'above' is declining.

In local communities, pressures for change or bitterness at the lack of progress can make the mainstream activities of the firm harder to perform. Nationally, the lack of progress is forcing the state and agencies to review their *contract* with employers in this crucial area. Some progress has been made. Leading firms have illustrated the potential for action. Some of the worst abuses exist in the public sector – even in the agents for social progress themselves. The European Community is set to take a more active role especially through the Social Charter. Fairness may lie at the centre of the business agenda for most of the next decade. The responsible corporation is developing its strategies to tackle these future demands today.

QUESTIONS

1 How far does Bloom's criticism of affirmative action at Cornell University extend to all forms of affirmative action. In the face of this criticism put forward proposals to prevent a community such as the African American community in the USA being and remaining 'second class citizens'.

2 Analyse the Littlewoods' case study 'A simple case of prejudice'. Bring out the key lessons for this and other firms.

3 How far is it true that 'policies to tackle the problems of gender, race and physical disability will hold the key to success for other (disadvantaged) communities'. Illustrate your answer with reference to one of the following groups:

(a) Homosexuals
(b) The Irish in Britain
(c) The aged
(d) Another group

4 Outline the barriers to entry to a higher education institution of your choice faced by one of

(a) Women
(b) Members of ethnic minorities
(c) The physically challenged

Examine this in terms of recruitment, selection, attendance, participation, assessment and graduation.

5 Describe the potential contribution of the UK government's Ten Point Plan for Equal Opportunities.

6 Is the criticism of the appointment processes for vice chancellors outlined in the case study 'Irony or hypocrisy on the campus' justified? If so, what steps can be taken to overcome these problems?

7 Using readership profile information on the main national newspapers and magazines, draw up a media schedule to recruit a middle manager for a large, national retailer. The profile should reach an audience in which there is no inherent bias towards white, male candidates.

8 Robert Townsend, in *Up The Organisation*[45] observes that 'stamping out racism is a process not an action'. What are the implications of this statement for the internal development of companies?

9 Outline the likely contribution of the Maastrict Treaty and its Social Chapter to fairer working conditions in Europe.

10 Define:

(a) Positive discrimination	(f) Re-engineering
(b) Affirmative action	(g) The Social Chapter of the Maastrict Treaty
(c) The 'glass ceiling' effect	(h) Career ladders
(d) Contract compliance	(i) Corporate social reporting
(e) Set asides	(j) Equal opportunities

CASE STUDY 4

Knoxbridge: A suitable case for treatment?

Introduction

The closure by British Rail of the Knoxbridge Engineering Works brought the problems of this once-prosperous town in the Central Belt of Scotland to national attention. The loss of 500 jobs was a severe blow to a community which had seen its major industries and leading firms steadily decline for a number of years but with increasing speed during the recent recession.

Knoxbridge has an industrial history dating back as far as that of Scotland itself. Although links with the railways have always been strong, the industrial base was much wider. Coal and fireclay were mined for much of the last century. The last pit closed as recently as 1962. Although there was a steady rundown in the mining industry, jobs emerged in new industries such as papermaking, refactory brick making, iron castings, general engineering and more recently plastics processing and some chemicals. As recently as the late 1960s Knoxbridge was sufficiently prosperous to offer most of the youngsters leaving its schools a good chance of an apprenticeship or a job.

Besides its manufacturing base, Knoxbridge has been an important commercial centre for the nearby rural community. The shopping centre is large and contains a number of retail outlets, such as Marks & Spencer and House of Fraser. However, business has been lost to nearby Silvertown. The new indoor shopping centre in that town has drawn trade from Knoxbridge.

Although Knoxbridge is within 30 miles of both Edinburgh and Glasgow, access to the motorway network could be improved. Rail links are good but the closure of the engineering works has raised some questions about this.

Recent decline

There are now about 46,000 people living in the Knoxbridge area. The conurbation is bounded by the motorway to the west; with the exception of some more recent housing development, the town is skirted by good 'A' roads to the east and south. The newer developments mentioned were primarily developed to accommodate overspill from Glasgow. Almost 90 per cent of these houses are local-authority owned. An industrial and commercial estate was developed near this. Unfortunately, this has been especially hard hit by the recession. Unemployment in this area is very high.

The rest of the township is less well defined and concentrated. Home ownership is low, with 77 per cent of all houses Council owned. There are a number of relatively isolated communities in outlying areas such as the old mining community of Kintry. Here there are major social problems, especially with the ageing population.

These particular problems have to be seen in the context of the area's progressive decline. Unemployment has grown rapidly. At the same time there is low demand for existing skills. The College of Technology has recently opened an Information Technology Centre. The College of Commerce has a well established programme of work. There has been a dramatic increase in youth unemployment. These have to be seen in the national context of long-term decline in industrial output and rising unemployment of surviving firms and a number of major closures such as that experienced in Knoxbridge recently.

Figures from the Knoxbridge Employment Office show that it is proportionately one of the worst affected areas in Scotland. It is now estimated that the workforce has contracted to just over 7,500 in 1982 from just under 14,000 in 1971.

The general picture is dismal with:

- a number of recent closures;
- negligible growth in existing firms;
- low rate of new company formation;
- poor prospects of inward investment.

Between 1974 and 1980 there was a 35 per cent decline in total employment in the area. At least 34 companies have closed and job losses of at least 1,400 people have occurred between the beginning of 1978 and March 1983: 25 of these were in manufacturing and construction, accounting for over 1,000 of the jobs lost.

Overall employment changes

Knoxbridge Employment Office statistics show the following employment changes:

Sector	1983	%	1988	%	Change
Primary	386	2.7	222	2.0	−164
Manufacturing	7,226	51.5	5,424	54.0	−1,802
Construction	1,484	10.6	1,404	14.0	−80
Services	4,946	35.2	3;084	30.0	−1,842
Total	14,042	100.0	10,134	100.0	−3,908

Although the last few years have seen some new developments, especially a new hypermarket and a major DIY superstore, these have done little to arrest the overall decline.

Community action

The announcement of the closure of the Knoxbridge Railway Engineering Works prompted a number of people from different parts of the community to come together to explore ways of tackling their problems. The Regional and District Councils, along with the Chamber of Commerce and a number of employers, met with the Scottish Development Agency. The latter strongly advised them to *set up* an Enterprise Trust. This has now been done with the Region, the District providing pump-priming financial support and ABL Distilleries providing a secondee as director.

The challenge: *Where do you go from here and how do you get there?*

Develop an action plan for the town. This should highlight the main challenges facing the community. Ways to tackle the social and economic problems should be outlined. A clear indication of priorities and the mechanisms for gaining and allocating resources is necessary.

REFERENCES

1. Hutton, W. 'The Delegators Labour under an Illusion' *Guardian*, 13 September (1993).
2. Task Force on Corporate Social Responsibility *Business and Society*, Washington, Department of Commerce (1980).
3. Levi Strauss & Co. *Corporate Mission Statement*, Levi Strauss, London (1989).
4. Watson, T. *A Business and Its Beliefs*, New York, McGraw Hill (1963).
5. Tuleja, T. *Beyond the Bottom Line*, New York, Fact on File (1985).
6. Reimers, C. 'Labour Market Discrimination Against Hispanic and Black Men' *Review of Economics and Statistics*, vol. 45 (1983) pp. 570–9.
7. Bloom, A. *The Closing of the American Mind*, Harmondsworth, Penguin (1988).
8. Casson, M. *Economics of Business Culture*, Oxford, OUP (1991).
9. Equal opportunities Commission *Women and Men in Britain 1989*, London, HMSO (1989).
10. Hakim, C. *Occupational Segregation*, London, Department of Employment Research Paper no. 9 (1979).
11. West, J. *Work, Women and the Labour Market*, London, Routledge, Kegan and Paul (1982).
12. Dex, S. *Women's Occupational Mobility*, London, Macmillan (1987).
13. Jensen, J., Hagen, E. and Reddy, C. (eds) *Feminisation of the Labour Force: Paradoxes and Promises*, Cambridge, Polity Press (1988).
14. Martin, J. and Roberts, C. *Women and Employment: A Lifetime Perspective*, London, HMSO (1984).
15. Carter, S. and Cannon, T. *Women as Entrepreneurs*, London, Academic Press (1991).
16. Directorate General, Employment, Industrial Relations and Social Affairs *Employment in Europe*, Bruxelles, Commission of the European Communities (1991).
17. Barron, K. D. and Norris, G. M. 'Sexual Divisions and the Dual Labour Market' in Barker, D. and Allen, S. (ed.) *Dependence and Exploitation in Work and Marriage*, London, Longman (1976).
18. Amsden, A. H. *The Economics of Women at Work*, Harmondsworth, Penguin (1980).
19. Bruegel, I. 'Women as a Reserve Army of Labour: A note on recent British Experience', in Evens, M. (ed.) *The Women Question*, London, Fontana (1982).
20. Hymounts, C. 'The Corporate Women – the glass ceiling' *Wall Street Journal*, 11 November (1986).
21. Green, K. 'Stalking the MBA Class of 1999' *Selections*, Autumn (1991).

22. Spencer, L. 'Bridging the Unemployment Gap between Black and White People in Britain' *Journal, Royal Society for the Encouragement of Arts, Manufactures and Commerce*.
23. Hayes, A. *The State of Being Black*, London, Commission for Racial Equality (1983).
24. Balls, E. *Full Employment*, London, Prudential, Mimeo (1993).
25. Ashenfelter, O. and Layard, R. *Handbook of Labour Economics*, vol. 1, North Holland, Amsterdam (1986).
26. Sawyers, L. *The Impact of New Technology on Female Employment in Retailing*, unpublished Ph.D. thesis, Stirling University (1987).
27. Clutterbuck, D. *Actions Speak Louder*, London, Kogan Page (1992).
28. Some heads of colleges in universities are female, e.g. Baroness Blackstone at Birkbeck.
29. Cockburn, C. *Machinery of Dominance*, London, Pluto Press (1985).
30. Collinson, D., Knight, D. and Collinson, M. *Managing to Discriminate*, London, Routledge (1990).
31. Spencer, L., ibid.
32. McEwan, W. *Speech to Delegates*, London, British and American National Symposium (1986).
33. Sethi, S. P. and Falbe, C. *Business and Society: Dimensions of Conflict and Co-operation*, Lexington, MA; DC Heath (1980).
34. Tuleja, T., ibid.
35. Clutterbuck, D., ibid.
36. Badaracco, J. L. *Note on Corporate Strategy and Politics*, Harvard Case Clearing House, Cambridge, MA; Harvard University (1982).
37. Yoffie, D. B. 'Corporate Strategies for Political Action: A Rational Model' in Marcus, A. M. (ed.) *Business Strategy and Public Policy*, New York, Quorum (1987).
38. Mahon, J. F. *Corporate Political Strategy*, vol. 2, no. 1 (1989).
39. *Directory of Equal Opportunities Consultants*, London, Linbert Spencer Consultancy (1992).
40. *Directory of Equal Opportunities Consultants*, ibid.
41. Gray, R., Owen, D. and Maunders, K. *Corporate Social Reporting: Accounting and Accountability*, Englewood Cliffs., New Jersey, Prentice-Hall (1987).
42. Townsend, R. *Up the Organisation*, New York, A. A. Knopf (1970).
43. Hammer, M. and Champy, J. *Re-Engineering the Corporation*, Harper Collins, New York (1993).
44. Kanter, R. M. *When Giants Learn to Dance*, London, Routledge (1992).
45. Townsend, R., ibid.

PART 5

Issues and conclusions

CHAPTER 15

The evolving agenda: issues, actions and conclusions

No single text on a topic as complex, wide-ranging and dynamic as corporate responsibility can cover all issues or satisfy all needs. This book is an attempt to give form to the developing area while putting forward three basic propositions. The most basic is that the subject has a unity which encompasses such issues as business ethics, respect for the natural and built environments and affirmative action by business to play its part in tackling the problems of disadvantage. This view is shaped by the related proposition that industry has an economic contract with society. This contract shapes the relations between commerce and other groups. Its primary aim is to enable industry to perform its economic function in the most effective manner. This economic function stands alongside, but is not separate from, the other functions performed by society. The defence and maintenance function allows business to execute its affairs against a background of security and reassurance. The education and development function develops the skills and sustains the values which industry requires to build and prosper. The governance function establishes the legitimacy of certain behaviour and defines the rules under which commerce pursues its trade. This contract is explicit in some areas, implicit elsewhere and open to negotiation, but it underpins all commercial activity.

The renowned market economist develops this theme in his criticism of the notion of selfish rationality in modern economics[1].

> This is not just immoral – it is grossly inefficient, too. Honesty is not always the best policy for a selfish individual, but mutual honesty is better than mutual cheating for society as a whole. The cheapest way to stamp out cheating is to make people want to be honest: to recognise their ethical sense and reinforce it.

He goes on to argue that

> Mathematics can model markets in Newtonian style – as a balance of forces achieved by an equilibrium price. This 'general equilibrium theory' triumphantly formalises the idea of the 'invisible hand'. The formal calculation of equilibrium is dramatically simplified if selfishness is assumed.
>
> The fallacy then emerges that markets work only if people are selfish. In fact, the opposite is true! In general equilibrium theory, price adjustment is handled by an

auctioneer who has a monopoly of intermediation but never takes a penny for himself. Ultimately it is the altruism of this monopolistic auctioneer, and not competition between selfish traders, that makes the theory work. In the real world, it is the visible hand of the entrepreneur that sets the price and not the mystical presence of an invisible auctioneer.

. . .

'Ethical man' . . . derives emotional well-being from honouring obligations to others. Ethical man can trade with his friends by a handshake, but economic man must hire lawyers to draw up a contract and employ accountants to check that he has been paid.

While economic man considers selfishness as natural, ethical man considers reciprocity natural instead. Reciprocity allows ethical man to transact informally, undertaking small transactions for which it is not worth negotiating the price or recording the obligation to pay. This sustains informal markets of great diversity, and strengthens institutions such as the family and the firm whose 'internal markets' typically work along these lines.

The form of contract varies over time. The different players have varied beliefs and expectations. In the 1980s and early 1990s an apparent consensus emerged which prompted the state to withdraw from some activities. Private enterprise won a greater freedom to develop its responses to challenges and issues. This reflected the aspirations of many business leaders who believed 'that the vast majority of economic and social needs of society are best met by private sector institutions rather than government programmes'.[2] The *rolling back of the state* was not based on the proposition that tasks of social development and maintenance were unnecessary. The core proposition is that industry operating within a business contract employing a variety of market-based mechanisms could deliver these more effectively than the state or that the state could deliver them more effectively in collaboration with the private sector. The terms of the contract were, in effect, redefined to meet contemporary needs and circumstances. This notion of the contract is not new. It is articulated in writings at least as far back as Rousseau. Contracts are, however, about deliverables.

There is little point in preparing a contract if the parties to it cannot deliver against it, do not wish to deliver against it or do not believe they should deliver against it. High-quality governance and delivery lie at the heart of the effective corporate responsibility management. The third proposition around which this book is built is the notion that management can deliver. The skills, knowledge and competence exists to take action to address issues. This action can produce gains to the enterprise and benefits to the wider community. Many of the actions will rely on the core competencies that mark out quality management from other forms. The construction of a meaningful link between analysis, diagnosis and action marks out the entrepreneur from the bureaucrat. Strategic visions distinguish the corporate leader from the follower. The ability to plan for the long term while faced with pressing immediate problems is the basis on which outstanding firms have been built for the last two centuries. These are the skills which will help business to shape 'the future of our children and our communities'.[3]

Faced with this situation Toffler[4] argues that new types of corporate structures are needed and will emerge.

> The multipurpose corporation that is emerging demands, among other things, smarter executives. It implies a management capable of specifying multiple goals, weighting them, interrelating them, and finding synergic policies that accomplish more than a single goal at a time. It requires policies that optimize not for one, but for several variables simultaneously. . . .
>
> Moreover, once the need for multiple goals is accepted we are compelled to invent new measures of performance. Instead of the single 'bottom line' on which most executives have been taught to fixate, the corporation requires attention to multiple bottom lines – social, environmental, informational, political, and ethical bottom lines – all of them interconnected.

MANAGING THE CORPORATE RESPONSIBILITY FUNCTION

New responsibilities call for a mixture of new and old skills. Education, training and management development lie at the heart of effective management. The contribution of leaders like the Carnegies, Fords, Lillys, Cadburys and Laings needs to be matched by improved competence among current specialist managers, ownership by line managers and new awareness by entrants to management. The long-term impact of courses in business ethics, environmental awareness and corporate governance highlight their strengths and shortcomings.[5] There is an active debate on the nature of the material and its relevance to managers.[6,7] The proliferation of these programmes in recent years is a tribute to the successful advocacy of business leaders. Their novelty raises questions about the values of the educational institutions which are now hurrying into the field.[8] Their diversity poses deeper issues about the nature of the discipline and the character of the intellectual paradigm that is emerging.[9] The professionalism of the area relies heavily on industry lead bodies like Business in The Community; specific, creative individuals like Professor Jack Mahoney and a burgeoning network of practitioners. Greater form to these developments and an increased sense of cohesion are the essential prerequisites of a move beyond anecdote and experience to a coherent body of knowledge.[10]

Specialist staff require the support of top management. This is essential for two key aspects of their work. There is the internal management of the corporate responsibility function. It has evolved to deal with the preparation of mission statements, ethic policies, responses to requests for support and tackling crises. This portfolio has grown rapidly over the last few years as good business practice has become a measure of corporate quality. Contributions from outside have highlighted the link between corporate or personal performance and corporate or personal pride.[11] It is evident that endorsement plays a much larger longer-term role. Effective programmes are owned and implemented by and through line managers. They need access to expert staff but the systems of reward and control

Table 15.1 The main Cadbury recommendations

1 Boards should have separate audit and remuneration committees made up entirely of independent directors.

2 Audit committees should meet with the external auditors at least once a year and without executive directors.

3 The full remuneration package of all directors – including performance-related elements – should be disclosed in annual reports.

4 Directors' terms of office should run for no more than three years without shareholders' approval.

5 Companies must make funds available to non-executive directors who wish to get independent professional advice.

6 The board must meet regularly.

7 It ought to have a formal schedule of matters for decision.

8 Independent directors should be appointed for specified terms.

9 Independent directors should be appointed through a formal process.

10 Independent directors should have a standing outside the company which ensures that their views carry weight.

11 Independent directors should be fully independent and free from links with the company other than fees and shareholdings.

12 Fees for independent directors should reflect the time they spend on company business.

13 There should be an 'accepted division at the head of the company, which will ensure a balance of power and authority such that no one individual has unfettered powers of decision. Where the chairman is also chief executive, there should be a strong independent element on the board with an independent leader'.[12]

which shape their wider management behaviour will need to mesh in with those which determine their response to issues of corporate responsibility.

Many of the basic principles are spelt out in the text. Some have become watchwords for the standards by which industry regulates its behaviour. Transparency is one of these. Put bluntly, secrecy breeds suspicion while openness is the most public symbol of a clear conscience. In many ways the private sector has made progress over the last decade that is scarcely matched in the public sector. The recommendations of the Cadbury committee go some way to tackle the more obvious problems (Table 15.1). A first, clear step toward transparency is achieved in the key recommendations. There is, however, insufficient progress on the issue of shareholder rights. The vexed issues of sources and numbers of independent directors, the disciplines imposed on directors, presentation of findings and other key features of corporate governance are only touched on.

There was some irony that the date of publication of the Cadbury report

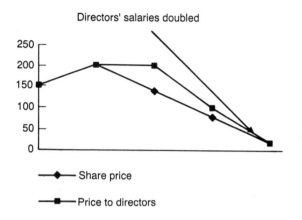

Fig. 15.1 Mountleigh – a snack for Cadbury

coincided with the arrival of receivers at the Mountleigh Group. The extent to which Cadbury's recommendations resolves serious issues of governance can be tested against the behaviour of Mountleigh's directors (Figure 15.1). The responsibility now lies with corporations in Britain to ensure that the report is implemented. Preliminary evidence suggests that many corporations are implementing the recommendations despite initial media reservations (Table 15.2).

Managerial integrity and independent directors with the courage to tackle colleagues are essential to a reform of behaviour.

> Maxwell exploited and exposed a uniquely British condition. He could not have prospered without the aid and comfort of many. His accomplices should now be identified and asked to account for their deeds.
>
> Bower, T.[14]

Cronyism is anathema. The public sector faces a similar challenge to reform its behaviour to achieve transparency, eliminate cronyism and achieve a more fair system. Staff development, training and external scrutiny are integral features of this. A strategic overview is seen as the best way to create the virtuous circle between doing the right thing and have right done to you. Strategies are underpinned by programmes that allow decisions to be made and resources

Table 15.2 Cadbury: a cautious welcome[13]

The Times	The Cadbury reforms, only barely sufficient, will take a superhuman effort of commercial consensus to introduce
Independent	A timid step in the right direction
Financial Times	More to offer than might be expected . . . But, it will not, inevitably, be the last word
Guardian	Properly implemented it could prove a lifeline for self-regulation

allocated. These, in turn, provide a basis for evaluation and development. These programmes need to be delivered locally, nationally and internationally.

AN INTERNATIONAL DIMENSION

Many of the issues raised in the text require industrialists to look beyond their immediate environment. Outside events have forced this. The collapse of totalitarianism in Central and Eastern Europe symbolised the synergy that can exist between corporate responsibility and corporate gain. The newly liberated markets are unlikely to produce short-term gains. They are even less likely to produce long-term gains if businesses in the West fail to play an active role in redeveloping their economies. Part of the wider contract with the international community is ensuring a profitable and successful future. This poses many problems for commerce. Some of the most committed supporters of corporate giving programmes concentrate their expenditure near to home. The evidence from the USA suggests that there is a poor link between the sources of the earnings of firms and the distribution of their corporate giving (Table 15.3). The superior quality of US data should not disguise the anecdotal evidence that the US pattern is replicated elsewhere.

This notion of transfer of earnings, sometimes from poorer countries to the rich, is increasingly hard to sustain while governments everywhere are looking for greater corporate involvement. The type of internationalist perspective adopted by firms to their business development is increasingly important in approaches to corporate responsibility.

Internationalism is moving to the centre of the corporate responsibility agenda. In part this reflects the global nature of some of the problems industry is asked to address. A successful Rio Summit is likely to be viewed as the start of an effort by governments, international agencies, industry and the wider community to tackle global problems from a global perspective. Carlo Ripa di Meana, the EC environment commissioner points out that after Rio 'we must now open

Table 15.3 Internationalism in corporate giving

Firm	Foreign Revenues(%)	Foreign Giving (%)
Hewlett-Packard	50	16
Eli Lilly	36	6
Levi Strauss	30	18
HB Fuller	46	32
Chevron	29	4.5
Alcoa	32	5

Source: Logan D. (1991)[15]

new talks to arrive at additional protocols which will put flesh onto the bare bones of the climate convention. These protocols will thus result in concrete decisions with binding obligations to achieve precise targets'.[16] The mixture of power and responsibility that characterises the well-managed company gives industrial leaders a special role in shaping this agenda for development.

THE FUTURE

The challenge to respond to the needs of the environment is part of the wider issue of corporate responsibility. Executives, corporations and policy-makers work in a world which is increasingly accessible by people, money, products and services. Access and understanding do not necessarily go together. Values, attitudes and acceptable behaviour shift over time and between cultures. The need to adopt a stance based on a generalisable moral code does not change. Part of the contract between the manager, the corporation and the community is an acceptance that neither office nor position give immunity from responsibility. Increasing numbers of corporate leaders recognise that a secure moral position, respect for the needs of others, business performance and enterprise quality go together. There is an emerging awareness in the public sector that high moral statements cut little ice with a private sector striving to improve its standards while the public officials look on complacently.

Policies need to be backed by actions inside the firm to ensure fairness across the firm and integrity in individual behaviour. It has a role in the local community to ensure that talent, commitment and need are the keys to resources, power and privilege. The motor of economic growth for most of the last 200 years has depended on members of out groups having access to opportunity so that communities can be built, businesses develop and enterprise prosper through innovation and development. The global nature of the business environment means that these responsibilities exist in those regions where businesses operate or seek to operate. This is a global responsibility which lies at the heart of the business contract. The economic function of business and its wider responsibilities are integral features of this contract.

APPENDIX D
MANAGING AN INFORMATION-BASED PROJECT

The research-based thesis, project report or dissertation provides a most complex, information 'hungry' environment. Those involved in enterprise will find the underlying disciplines invaluable in virtually all investigative project work. The entrepreneur starting a new commercial enterprise requires a business plan based on a coherent structure. A research paper without a clear framework will ramble and confuse readers. The initiators of a charitable venture need a clear understanding of the role and purpose of their work. A project report needs to be clear and relevant to the brief. A theatre group blends a sense of direction with personal insights. A dissertation gets its direction from knowledge of the literature and insights from the evidence gathered. Underlying each of these aspects of enterprise is a use of networks and information.

Defining the task

At the core of any project is a definition of the task or work to be done. The researcher and the entrepreneur share several common problems. Both have a body of knowledge to draw on but it is inadequate. Established wisdom provides the hypothesis, the questions, an insight into the opportunity, even a view of the most promising way forward. Enterprising investigators will generally make the initial mistake of trying to do too much in the time available. Fascination with the issue blinds enthusiasts to the limitations of resources. The final-year student seeking to understand the implications for technology of high-temperature superconductivity has much in common with the entrepreneur striving to launch a new business based on teleshopping. Unless they are uniquely skilled or backed by the equivalent of Huber Corporation's superconductivity experts or Tesco's retail specialists they will fail. Successful enterprise depends on an appreciation of the challenge faced and the resources needed. In research, this means a summary statement of the issue and the hypothesis to be tested. In a commercial enterprise, the equivalent is a description of the business and an answer to the question: *why will I succeed?*

Project search and initial development

In the research situation, the investigator often faces the same need to seek out ideas and projects as the potential entrepreneur. The primary, initial assignment lies in defining an achievable project and programme of work that can be undertaken. It is useful to ask:

- why is the project interesting?
- what is known about the issue?

- is success dependent on forces outside my control?
- how much help is needed?
- is the help easily and readily available?

The preparation of a time-based plan of action, with contingencies built in, often provides useful insights. The time plan (below) from the fictitious University of Inverness Enterprise Project indicates just some of the constraints based on a 'final-term' project:

4 June	Hand in project
30 May	Give proofread version to typist
25 May	Receive proofs from typist
11 May	Provide final draft for typist
7 May	Revise and edit final draft (rl)
23 April	Start final write-up
17 April	Collate information (rl)
6 April	Send out reminders to respondents
23 March	Mail survey
19 March	Type up final questionnaires
12 March	Review pilot survey
7 March	Start pilot survey
1 March	Draft questionnaires (r2)
26 February	Complete initial literature review

Some of the basic planning ground rules are outlined above. The most basic is 'plan from the end-date'. It is easy to look forward and believe time stretches out indefinitely. This is dangerous in itself and can be fatal when absolute and practical restrictions exist. A typist might not drop existing plans to squeeze this report in. The print room will not be able to reschedule other work. The last minute rush can destroy the value of earlier painstaking work. The reviewers' irritation at poor English, recurrent spelling mistakes and bad presentation will soon blind them to intrinsic merit.

At most stages of a project some scope for recycling work is necessary. The (r) identifies the more common areas. The draft is unlikely to be 'right first time'. The initial sort through responses will not bring out all the main issues. Questionnaires take several efforts to get things right. In this illustration a project based on a mail survey is proposed. The scope for delays and difficulties is as great in personal questionnaires and experiments. Some problems are shared. Equipment failure with an experiment is akin to the respondent refusing to answer. Sitting in front of a person who clearly has no knowledge of the issue is as wasteful as finding that the computer is 'down' or the equipment is broken.

In research projects Murphey's Third, Fourth and Fifth laws are a sure guide to planning:

- Murphy's Third Law
  In any field of scientific endeavour, anything that can go wrong, will go wrong.

- Murphy's Fourth Law
  If there is a possibility of several things going wrong, the one that will cause the most damage will be the one to go wrong.
- Murphy's Fifth Law
  If anything just cannot go wrong, it will anyway.

It is, however, unlikely that the researcher will be able to use Maier's Laws to win past the astute client or supervisor. These are:

- If facts do not conform to the theory, they must be disposed of.
- Knowledge advances more by what it has learned to ignore than what it takes into account.

REFERENCES

1. Casson, M. 'Ethics Mark East-West Divide' *Guardian*, 13 September (1993).
2. Lilly Foundation *Corporate Contributions Policy and Guidelines*, Indianapolis, Lilly Industries (undated).
3. HRH the Prince of Wales 'The Future of Business in Britain' *Financial Times*, 20 November (1989).
4. Toffler, A. *The Third Wave*, New York, Bantam (1980).
5. Weber, J. 'Measuring the Impact of Teaching Ethics to Future Managers: A review, assessment and recommendations' *Journal of Business Ethics*, vol. 9 (1990).
6. MacLagan, P. 'Learning from an Ethics Workshop on an MBA Programme' *Management Education and Development*, vol. 22, part 2 (1991).
7. Jackson, N. 'Case Material in an Ethics Workshop: A reply to Patrick MacLagan' *Management Education and Development*, vol. 22, part 2 (1991).
8. David, F. R., McTier-Anderson, L. and Lawrimore, K. W. 'Perspectives on Business Ethics in Management Education' *Advanced Management Journal*, vol. 55, no. 4, Autumn (1990) pp. 26–32.
9. Kahn, W. A. 'Toward an Agenda for Business Ethics Research' *Academy of Management Review*, vol. 15, issue 2, April (1990) pp. 311–28.
10. Dolenga, H. E. 'An Iconoclast Looks at Business Ethics' *Advanced Management Journal*, vol. 55, no. 4 (1990) p. 13–18.
11. Carmichael, S. and Drummond, J. *Good Business: A Guide to corporate responsibility and business ethics*, London, Business Books (1989).
12. Cadbury, Sir, A. 'Calling Firms to Account without Stifling the Spirit of Enterprise' *The Times*, 18 May (1992).
13. Editorial comments on 28 May 1992.
14. Bower, T. 'Maxwell: The Real Culprits exposed' *The Times*, 26 May.
15. Logan, D. *International Giving by US Multinationals*, Washington, Council of the Foundations (1991).
16. Ripa di Meana, C. 'Why Rio Must Deliver' *Financial Times*, 24 May (1991).

INDEX

Note: page references in *italics* refer to illustrations.